Also by Virginia Spencer Carr

The Lonely Hunter:
A Biography of Carson McCullers

Dos Passos: A Life

Understanding Carson McCullers

Katherine Anne Porter's "Flowering Judas":
Text, Essays, and Criticism (editor)

Paul Bowles in his island home of Taprobane, Sri Lanka, 1955.

Paul Bowles

A LIFE

Virginia Spencer Carr

SCRIBNER
New York London Toronto Sydney

SCRIBNER
1230 Avenue of the Americas
New York, NY 10020

For information about special discounts for bulk purchases, please contact Simon & Schuster Special Sales:
1-800-456-6798 or business@simonandschuster.com

DESIGNED BY ERICH HOBBING

Text set in Berthold Garamond

Manufactured in the United States of America

1 3 5 7 9 10 8 6 4 2

Library of Congress Cataloging-in-Publication Data
Carr, Virginia Spencer.
Paul Bowles : a life / Virginia Spencer Carr.
p. cm.
Include bibliographical references (p.) and index.
1. Bowles, Paul, 1910– 2. Authors, American–20th century–Biography.
3. Morocco–Intellectual life–20th century. 4. Composers–United States–Biography.
5. Morocco–Social life and customs. 6. Americans–Morocco–Biography.
I. Title.
PS3552.O874Z625 2004
813'.54–dc22
[B] 2004054748

ISBN 0-684-19657-3

Frontispiece: Photo by Ahmed Yacoubi, courtesy of Touria Haji Temsamani

Paul Bowles

A LIFE

Virginia Spencer Carr

SCRIBNER
New York London Toronto Sydney

SCRIBNER
1230 Avenue of the Americas
New York, NY 10020

For information about special discounts for bulk purchases,
please contact Simon & Schuster Special Sales:
1-800-456-6798 or business@simonandschuster.com

DESIGNED BY ERICH HOBBING

Text set in Berthold Garamond

Manufactured in the United States of America

1 3 5 7 9 10 8 6 4 2

Library of Congress Cataloging-in-Publication Data
Carr, Virginia Spencer.
Paul Bowles : a life / Virginia Spencer Carr.
p. cm.
Include bibliographical references (p.) and index.
1. Bowles, Paul, 1910– 2. Authors, American–20th century–Biography.
3. Morocco–Intellectual life–20th century. 4. Composers–United States–Biography.
5. Morocco–Social life and customs. 6. Americans–Morocco–Biography.
I. Title.
PS3552.O874Z625 2004
813'.54–dc22
[B] 2004054748

ISBN 0-684-19657-3

Frontispiece: Photo by Ahmed Yacoubi, courtesy of Touria Haji Temsamani

FOR

Mary Elizabeth Robbins

CONTENTS

A FEW WORDS BEFORE

I am grateful to Paul Frederic Bowles for his cooperation and spirit of generosity while I worked on his biography, most of which was completed before his death on November 18, 1999, at the age of eighty-eight, in Tangier, Morocco. Ultimately he gave me carte blanche to present his life as I saw it, and I have done just that. Unfortunately, Bowles's literary executor, Rodrigo Rey Rosa, declined to authorize the biography, despite Bowles himself having written to me on October 24, 1996: "While I assume that the legal right to allow the reprinting of published texts rests with the copyright holders, I give you my personal permission to quote from my letters, manuscripts, books and any other materials pertaining to my life and work. This permission also includes the writings of Jane Bowles, both published and unpublished."

When I wrote Bowles in the spring of 1991 that it was his biography I wished to write next, rather than a biography of Tennessee Williams, about whom we had talked during my first visit to his bedside in September 1989, he replied that he would be very pleased if I should decide to write about him, and that he was confident there would be "no malevolence" in it. By return mail, I assured him that I was a straight arrow when it came to truth, and that I had not a malevolent bone in my body.

Whereas both Carson McCullers and John Dos Passos were deceased when I commenced their biographies, I was delighted that I now had an extraordinary and willing subject who, over the years, proved to be generous-spirited, cooperative, and forthright. From the onset, Bowles concluded his letters with the phrase "Until soon, I hope." Neither of us imagined that my biography would be some ten years in the making or that I would make thirteen trips to Morocco from my home in Atlanta, Georgia. Even more surprising was his coming twice to Atlanta in 1994 for three different surgeries at Emory University Hospital. While recuperating, he was my houseguest for over three months. "The expertise of Emory's surgeons who excised a rapidly growing cancer in my nose, cheek, and mouth during my return visit and performed delicate repair surgery later–all made my trips to Atlanta exceedingly worthwhile," remarked Bowles with characteristic understatement.

He was astonished that many of his friends, some from abroad who had never imagined seeing him again in the country of his birth, came to Atlanta to attend a party in his honor before his first surgery. "One friend from afar even brought me kif in the hospital, and that was a shocker," said Bowles. "Of course I couldn't smoke it there, and shouldn't have been smoking it at all, not to mention that even possessing it in the United States was illegal and could have gotten my hostess in trouble, too. Yet it seemed such a waste when she confirmed that I must throw it out."

His friends were surprised, too, when he donated $100,000 to establish a Paul Bowles Fellowship in Fiction Writing at Georgia State University during my tenure as chair of the Department of English. When I told him that I intended to work very hard to raise the necessary funds for such a fellowship, he replied, "But wouldn't it be better if I wrote a check now for the entire amount?" And he did! Although some of Bowles's intimates in Tangier thought of him as "the cheapest man in town," I can vouch for his generosity in ways that many who knew him could not imagine. I am sure that few were aware that less than six months before his death, Bowles sent $1,000 to help establish a privately endowed graduate fellowship in medicinal chemistry at my university. He apologized for not being able to send more, but said that "too many Moroccan families are now dependent on me for sustenance."

During our many weeks together in Tangier and in an exchange of more than a hundred letters, Bowles sometimes asked, with disarming innocence, "And now what would you like to know?" At the onset, of course, I wanted to know far more than he had allowed in his veiled autobiography, *Without Stopping*, which Ned Rorem and William Burroughs described as "without telling"; yet, eventually, Bowles did tell me everything I wanted to know. To my knowledge, his only request regarding what I might, or might not, be shown related to the financial records maintained by his New York accountant, who was very cordial when we did meet, and I did not probe.

I am indebted to many people besides Bowles himself in the making of this book. A key person who unlocked a number of doors for me was New York composer Phillip Ramey, a close friend of Bowles who routinely spends four or five months each year in Tangier and lives in the same flat that had been Bowles's wife's until her death in 1973. It was Ramey who arranged for Bowles to return to New York in 1995 for two concerts of his music at Lincoln Center and a program at the New School for Social Research in which Bowles was an active participant; more than anyone else, it was Ramey who "talked music" with Bowles and fanned the flames of his composing in his late years. Generous with his time and recollections, Ramey granted me numerous interviews in Tangier and New York and provided me with important new material for inclusion in the final draft of this book. Exceedingly helpful, too, was Kenneth Lisenbee, who recently established the official Paul Bowles website, www.paulbowles.org.

I am grateful to Irene Herrmann, Bowles's friend, heir, and music executor, who located and brought much of his music back into print and edited with her colleague, Timothy Mangan, the music reviews that appeared regularly during the 1940s in the *New York Herald Tribune* and elsewhere. Others who have been exceedingly helpful are Polly Marks Smith, who read several drafts of the manuscript with a fine-toothed comb and who knows more about Bowles than any other resident of the Glenora/Dundee area of New York, in which he and his family spent countless summer holidays during his boyhood, and where his ashes are interred; Robert J. Burns, Allen Hibbard, Hugh T. Keenan, and Robert Luttrell McBath, Jr., who read the manuscript in its myriad forms and offered helpful suggestions; and a number of others who knew Bowles well and shared generously their reminiscences, photographs, and permission to quote from their letters and books, including Andreas Brown, Gena Dagel Caponi, Harold Wesley Danser III, Millicent Dillon, Daniel Halpern, Cathy Henderson, John Hopkins, Joseph A. McPhillips III, Cherie Nutting, Ned Rorem, Emilio Sanz de Soto, Claude-Nathalie Thomas, and Gore Vidal.

Especially valuable to my research, and to that of other Bowles scholars, were Jeffrey Miller's scrupulously researched *Paul Bowles: A Descriptive Bibliography* and *In Touch: The Letters of Paul Bowles*, and I thank him immensely for his dedication and achievement.

In addition, without the cooperation of Ahmed T. Abdelal, dean of the College of Arts and Sciences at Georgia State University, and Robert D. Sattelmeyer, my successor as chair of the Department of English, this biography would have been far more difficult than my previous books to research and write. To them, I am exceedingly grateful.

Especially important during the early stages of my research were the resources and staff of the Harry Ransom Humanities Research Center of the University of Texas, Austin, which awarded me an Andrew W. Mellon Foundation Fellowship; most notable were Jake Baxter, Charles Bell, Ken Craven, Elizabeth Dunn, Cliff Farrington, Patricia Fox, Willard Goodwin, Cathy Henderson, Dell Hollingsworth, John Kirkpatrick, Sally Leach, Peter Mears, Sue Murphy, Linda Briscoe Myers, Richard Oram, Ann N. Paterra, Barbara Smith-LaBorde, and director Thomas F. Staley.

I am indebted, also, to the Hugh M. Morris Special Collections Library of the University of Delaware, where Susan Brynteson, Judy Hamm, Rebecca Johnson Melvin, Timothy D. Murray, Francis Poole, and Craig Wilson shared their rich repository of manuscripts and letters comprising the Paul Bowles Collection, which includes more than forty boxes of newly catalogued manuscripts and letters from Bowles's personal archives acquired a few months before his death.

I am similarly grateful to Richard Wendorf and Rodney Dennis at the Houghton Library of Harvard University for awarding me the Frederick J. Kahrl Visiting Fellowship in Theatre History, an appointment that enabled me to work in the Theatre Collection of the Nathan Marsh Pusey Library, the University Archives, the Loeb Music Library, the Widener Library, the Hilles Library, and the Lamont Library. All proved vital to my mission.

I thank my editor, Nan Graham, for her encouragement, patience, and wise counsel during the winnowing and creative process that enabled me to convert what was originally a 1,308-page manuscript to what it is today. I am similarly indebted to Alexis Gargagliano for her superb guidance, editing, and the care with which she has responded to my text and the documentation it entailed; to Peter Karanjia, who combed the manuscript for legal issues and advised me accordingly; to John McGhee, production editor; to George Wen, copy editor; and to Lucy Kenyon, Kathleen Nolan, Dena Rosenberg, Ileene Sobel, and others who made important contributions to the publication of this book.

In addition, if it were not for my gifted literary agents, Georges, Anne, and Veronica Borchardt, and DeAnna Heidel, this biography would not be in your hands today. To each of you I am grateful, indeed.

Finally, I acknowledge the extraordinary assistance of my colleague and friend, Mary Elizabeth Robbins, who accompanied me on most of my research trips to Morocco, took careful notes during my interviews with Bowles and other intimates, and read and discussed with me my presentation of his life and work. It is she to whom this book is dedicated.

Virginia Spencer Carr
Atlanta, Georgia
May 1, 2004

Paul Bowles

A LIFE

CHAPTER ONE

The Early Childhood of Paul Bowles

(1910–1918)

"At birth I was an exceptionally ugly infant. I think my ugliness caused the dislike which my father immediately formed for me."

—Paul Bowles to Bruce Morrissette,
Jamaica, New York, January 14, 1930

Paul Bowles hated his father. There was never a time that he could remember not hating him. When Bowles was six, his grandmother Henrietta Winnewisser told him that his father had tried to kill him when he was an infant. Henrietta could not abide her son-in-law and hoped that he would simply disappear before the child was irreparably injured. Bowles never doubted for a moment that his grandmother spoke the truth.[1]

Claude Dietz Bowles, Paul Bowles's father, was a dentist who spent far more time with his patients than he did with his family, whom he sometimes found asleep when he climbed the steep steps of the old brownstone at 317 Fulton Street in Jamaica, New York, where he lived with his bride of fourteen months and a son whose presence he resented. If Claude did not appear promptly at 6:00 p.m. for dinner—when he insisted that it be ready and on the table—his wife, Rena, ate alone, then left the dining room to breast-feed her infant in the nursery. On such nights Claude found his dinner in the oven, and he picked at it grudgingly as though he resented each bite. Claude saw his interloping son as the real culprit. A fresh-air enthusiast, he hated finding the infant swaddled in blankets in a stuffy nursery. One evening when his son was scarcely three weeks old, Claude stripped him naked and placed him in a wicker basket beneath the window, which he threw open to its full height. Had Henrietta not been awakened by her grandson's persistent cries and discovered him lying under a dusting of snow, she was certain he would not have survived the night. To Claude she had overstayed her welcome, and he was impatient for her to leave. He even offered to hire a maid, temporarily, to help with the chores, but his wife would not hear of it and insisted that her mother could stay as long as she wished.

Paul Frederick Bowles was not a pretty sight upon his breach birth on December 30, 1910. An ugly gash creased the side of his head, and on both temples a doctor's forceps had left deep imprints. His mother's two sisters noted that their nephew's brow and crown were stretched grotesquely out of shape, but said nothing for fear of offending Rena herself. As a child, upon poring over early photographs, Bowles concluded that he resembled the pinheads at whom people gawked and snickered in the circus midway to which his mother's two brothers had taken him. He, too, had gawked at his baby pictures and demanded an explanation. Rena admitted that for a time she had concealed his misshapen head under flounced bonnets, but onlookers were quick to assume that something terrible had occurred in the birth process.[2] "The scar over my eye today is a reminiscence of those natal difficulties," said Bowles, whose father begrudged the precious time he had taken from his dental practice to accompany his wife to the hospital. Scarcely an hour after their son's birth, two nuns marched ceremoniously to her bedside and wrenched the infant from her arms.

"Your baby must be baptized into the Roman faith at once," the nuns whispered ominously. Rena threatened to scream and thwarted their mission. She and her husband were atheists, and the state of their son's soul was a moot point should he fail to survive the night.[3]

Rena's parents had traveled by train from their home in Bellows

Falls, Vermont, to see their newborn grandson, and Henrietta stayed on for several weeks to help with the chores. She could tell that Claude was inordinately jealous of the baby and warned her daughter that his ill will would mount if she were not vigilant. When Rena announced that she wanted to name their son after her brothers, Frederick and Paul, Claude did not object. Any name suited him so long as the child was not a junior.

Despite his inauspicious appearance as an infant, Bowles developed into a handsome boy with full lips, a well-shaped nose, a hint of a dimple in each cheek, a broad high forehead, blue eyes, and a crop of reddish-blonde curls that his mother refused to cut until he entered first grade. Bowles was twenty months old when Rena sent his picture to her sister Emma. "Paul has changed some since you saw him, hasn't he?" she wrote on the back of the snapshot.[4]

Even Claude was startled when at the age of two his son was reading aloud from cereal boxes and the labels on various household objects. Some of Bowles's earliest recollections were of a circle of adults around him while he answered orthographical questions. Claude, already displaying his lifelong skepticism of his son's talents, concluded that his wife had tutored him so that he would appear far brighter than he was.[5] At three, Bowles wrote his first short story, an animal tale of two pages. "I wrote many short stories at that age, all of them about animals. I wrote every day, but seldom showed them to anyone, even my mother. Sometimes I read them to my Aunt Emma when she stayed with us, and she seemed impressed."

Among Bowles's fondest memories as a child was the half hour he was allowed to spend with his mother after dinner in the privacy of his bedroom. "Here I could count on having her all to myself. I could carry on a conversation with my mother, who treated me as an adult. When I was very young, she called me 'Honeybunch.' I could sit on her lap and put my arms around her and hug her, but such behavior was strictly forbidden by my father once he witnessed it. I hated him for coming between us and spent much time thinking how I might retaliate."[6]

Bowles was four when his mother read to him the stories of Edgar Allan Poe, which both terrified and intrigued him. "Looking back now, I am sure I would have discovered Poe eventually on my own, for we had five volumes of his books in that sad little first apartment. I was six when I read, from cover to cover, every Poe volume in the house, and before the year was out I read them all again." Yet nothing by Poe was more horrifying to Bowles than his mother's account of her brothers' noses being smashed with a hammer by their father. She said that her grandfather's nose had also been smashed, as were the noses of his brothers, a tale her father confirmed.[7] "I was astonished when he told me that if the blow were performed well, there would be no permanent discoloration. Although I thoroughly disliked my father, I was relieved that I was not a Winnewisser. My nose was bad enough as it was," he concluded.[8]

Bowles's mother told him that she herself had devoted many hours to the improvement of his nose by gently squeezing and pressing the tender cartilage at its bridge. "Young bones and cartilage were malleable, she told me, and you had to be very careful what shape they took. I wondered privately if I were slated to be the next victim of the hammer," said Bowles, who made no connection at first between his mother's massaging of his nose and a conversation he overheard regarding a cousin's allegation that the family was Jewish. Both before and during World War I, Marjorie Winnewisser spent several years in Berlin studying voice and performing in opera, and after the war she returned home to announce her engagement to an officer in the Royal Dutch Naval Reserve. "Why didn't you tell me we were Jewish?" she demanded upon confronting her father. She told him that in Germany the name *Winnewisser* was originally spelled *Vennevitz*, and that her friends in Berlin feared for her safety. The name is "definitely Jewish," they insisted and urged her to go home before she was persecuted.[9]

"Tell me the truth, Mother, are *we* Jewish?" asked Bowles.

Rena replied that if it were so, she had no knowledge of it. "Your great-grandfather was a firebrand when he came to this country. He didn't think much of religion and wanted nothing to do with it." Bowles concluded that his mother was skirting the question. A few months later he observed her looking at a photograph of herself in profile and heard her exclaim with obvious disdain: "'Jewy, Jewy, Jewy!' I am sure my mother thought she looked Jewish, but I had no idea what characterized 'a Jewish look,' and still don't," he added.[10]

Composer Leonard Bernstein, who knew Bowles well over the years, whispered upon meeting his mother: "Oh, Paul, she's such a nice Jewish lady, and so very pretty." Bowles was taken aback by his friend's glib assumption and assured Bernstein that his mother was by no means Jewish.

"Get off it! Are you pretending, don't you know she is or what?" Bernstein retorted.[11]

Bowles never knew for certain if the Winnewissers actually were Jewish, but declared that if they were, it would serve his father right since he was "rigidly anti-Semitic" and never got over his marrying Jane Stajer Auer, a Jew.[12]

Bowles's great-grandparents Frederick George Winnewisser and Caroline Christiana Landshultz left Germany in 1848, as did thousands of other emigrants of all ethnicities and national origins. Whether Frederick and Caroline knew each other before leaving their homeland is unclear, but both families came from the region of Essen, in Westphalia. Whereas Winnewisser came alone as a young man, Caroline was accompanied by her parents and brother and settled in the village of Hazardville, Connecticut, later known as Enfield.

On April 3, 1854, Frederick and Caroline were married by a clergyman; they went on to have six children. Only one did not survive. The oldest was Bowles's grandfather August Frederick Winnewisser, who assumed the head of the household and the running of the farm after his father drowned at fifty in the Connecticut River. August was twenty-one when he claimed his inheritance and set out alone on horseback for Rockingham, Vermont. It was here that he met Henrietta Frances Barker, whose family had been New Englanders since the 1620s. After a brief courtship, they were married on Christmas Day,

1877. Henrietta and her siblings were the sixth generation of Barkers born in New England, all descended from Richard Barker and his wife, Joannah, who had left Yorkshire, England, in 1623 and settled in Andover, Massachusetts.

Of August and Henrietta's eight children, five survived infancy: Emma, Rena, Ulla, Frederick, and Paul. The family lived first in a large wood-frame house at 48 Canal Street in Bellows Falls, just above the river and two doors from the general store that August had established before his marriage. A successful merchant, he soon moved his business a hundred yards above the river to Westminster Square, where the town hall, opera house, theater, shops, doctors' offices, and library were situated.

A Bellows Falls historian reported that Winnewisser "believed in the 'nimble sixpence' rather than the 'slow shilling,'" and sold "at bottom prices." Large signs affixed to the front of the store featured its wares of furniture, crockery, paper hangings, carpets, silver, plated ware, glassware, and picture frames. Soon Winnewisser was joined by two of his brothers, who opened shops of their own.[13]

Rena and her brother Frederick attended preparatory schools in Exeter, New Hampshire, while Emma, their oldest sister, was studying painting in New York City. With only Paul and Ulla at home, Winnewisser moved his family to a new two-story brick house on School Street, at the top of a wide bluff that had a sweeping view of the town and river. Had their home not been next door to the Immanuel Episcopal Church, an imposing edifice of stone and stained glass, and across the street from the First Baptist Church, Winnewisser, an atheist, would have relished even more his new location.

A decade later, after being thrown from a horse, Winnewisser retired from merchandising and moved his family, first to Brooklyn, then to Lockwood, New York, where they lived briefly, and finally, to a farm outside the tiny community of Brimfield, Massachusetts, just off the Boston Post Road. A two-story clapboard house overlooked 165 acres of rolling, forested hillsides, a large apple orchard, and a deep-running brook that emptied into the Connecticut River. Although the farm had been abandoned for over a year, Winnewisser and his sons soon made the house livable, scraping and painting a room at a time, rebuilding windowsills and doorjambs, replacing broken glass, installing flues, and settling in before the first snow; moreover, Henrietta performed tasks she had never anticipated: supervising the canning and preserving of food from the garden, harvesting apples, overseeing the curing of meats, and cooking for her family and two hired hands.

Each January, between snowfalls, she packed a valise and left the men to their own devices to spend three weeks with each daughter—all now married—who in turn left their husbands for a spring vacation with their parents at what they now called Happy Hollow Farm. At Christmastime each daughter returned to the farm with her husband and children.[14]

Bowles was ecstatic when at the age of three he rode the train with his parents to Springfield, but the fun did not begin until after his father had deposited them on the farm and returned to New York. Each summer Bowles and his mother spent two weeks at Happy Hollow Farm, which he cherished since it meant being free to roam as he saw fit. One summer his grandfather summoned him and two cousins who also were visiting and demanded to know if they believed in God. Having already decided that God was an invention by adults in order to manage their children more easily, Bowles said nothing, but his cousins answered quickly with enthusiasm: "Oh yes, Grampa, of course we do!"

"Pah! There's no god," countered Winnewisser with a grimace. "It's a lot of nonsense. Don't you believe it."[15]

Bowles had no idea until several years later that he had been christened at the age of one by his great-uncle the Reverend Henry Green, a Unitarian minister. "Of course my christening made no sense," declared Bowles, who suspected that his parents had consented to it to humor Green. "I am sure they feared I would grow up a heathen. I could not help sympathizing with Gramma Winnewisser, who obviously worked harder than anyone else at Happy Hollow

Farm. I surmised that she was a heathen, too. I can't say that I loved Gramma, but I liked her and respected her. It even occurred to me that she would have made a nice mother, yet the thought itself seemed irreverent since I already had a mother."[16]

Although Bowles usually visited his father's family in Elmira, New York, each summer after leaving the farm, he knew little about them except what he observed. At seventeen he was surprised when his mother mentioned that he and his father were related to several generations of distinguished publishers and newspaper editors in Springfield, all named Samuel Bowles. The first Samuel was twenty-six when he founded a weekly newspaper, the *Republican*, which his son took over and converted into an evening daily, the Springfield *Daily Republican*. As the *Springfield Republican*, under the editorship of the third Samuel Bowles, the paper became the preeminent daily in the country for its advocacy of the ballot to every *man* regardless of creed or color, and also for its promotion of women's suffrage.[17] Bowles had no desire to know more about the Samuel Bowleses, since they were links to his father.

He was only vaguely interested when he learned that still another antecedent, Harvey Edward Bowles, his great-grandfather, was a medical doctor in New Jersey before moving to Northampton, Massachusetts, for the birth of his son, Frederick Theodore, Bowles's grandfather. Frederick Bowles became a traveling salesman for the Corticelli Silk Company, and for a time his route included Elmira, New York, which held promise as a site for the harvesting of raw silk, mulberry trees having once dotted the town's Chemung River landscape as far as the eye could see. In 1833 the Chemung Canal opened to river traffic, and the burgeoning town became readily accessible to upstate New York by way of Seneca Lake and the Erie Canal. "My only interest in that regard was in the geography of the area, but I much preferred to create my own," said Bowles.

Frederick's wife, Ida Twiss Bowles, shared her husband's disdain for organized religion and thought it ironic when they moved to Elmira that they lived on Church Street, which cut a mile-long swath between a dozen blocks of impressive three-story houses of Queen Anne and Tudor Revival design. Characterized by tall, asymmetrical rooflines, towers, turrets, and multiple porches, each house was set off by manicured lawns and gardens. It was the Church Street house that Bowles remembered visiting as a child, and it was here where he first met his paternal grandparents, whose "solemn, tight-lipped, and strait-laced" demeanor reminded him of his father.[18]

Frederick and Ida Bowles disavowed religion in any form and demanded that their three children follow unswervingly their mandates of restraint and practicality. Prattle was unacceptable and privacy sacrosanct. Bowles gathered that his own tendency for secrecy evolved from his father's side of the family.

By the time Claude graduated from the Elmira Free Academy, his brother, Shirley, had finished his own program at the Philadelphia Dental School and was practicing dentistry in Washington, D.C. Claude reluctantly followed suit and entered the same dental school from which Shirley graduated. It was Bowles's impression that his father suffered a mental breakdown halfway through his program and found refuge in Montevallo, Alabama, where his half uncle, Charles Frederick Robbins, arranged for him to be a foreman of a railroad work crew. "I am sure my father's railroad work was meant to be constructive therapy, but he never spoke of it to me," said Bowles. After several months of recuperation, he returned to dental school, graduated in the spring of 1901, and practiced for two years with his brother in Washington, D.C., until moving back home to practice dentistry with Dr. Carl Waples, whose office was walking distance from Church Street. The last mention of Claude Bowles, Doctor of Dentistry, in the 1907 *Elmira Business Directory* was that he had given up his practice with Dr. Waples and relocated in New York City.

It was the same year that Rena Winnewisser left Boston and moved to New York. Upon graduation from Robinson Female Seminary in Exeter, New Hampshire, Rena moved in with her sister Emma in Boston to attend Simmons, a private women's college, bent now upon enrolling in a professional program leading to certification in domestic science. After graduating from Simmons, Rena began teaching domestic science at the New York State Normal School in Jamaica, Long Island, where she met Claude Dietz Bowles, whom she perceived as steadfast, hardworking, and intent upon marriage. Bowles concluded later that his father was smitten by his mother's trim figure, playful personality, pretty face, and luxurious brown hair, which she brushed carefully and pinned up each morning.[19] For two years Rena taught at the New York State Normal School, then returned to Vermont to prepare for her marriage. On October 16, 1909, the weekly *Bellows Falls Times* reported the event in her parents' home as a "charming, Saturday morning wedding" at which the bride was "becomingly gowned in a gray traveling suit" and given away by her father.

Upon their marriage, the couple moved into a cramped third-floor apartment on Fulton Avenue, a thoroughfare that eventually stretched through the business district of Jamaica to the easternmost reaches of Long Island, New York. It was here that young Bowles spent his formative years. "When I finally learned to walk, having put it off as long as possible, I hated being made to go outside, yet invariably, out I went into the fenced backyard for an hour of play and what my father called deep breathing." From there, Bowles could see only the roofs of other buildings, the windows of his father's office on the second floor, and the windows of his family's living room on the third. "I knew nothing of swings, slides, or sandboxes with which most children distracted themselves during outdoor play. I had no friends and knew only my own backyard, which I hated," said Bowles. If his mother looked out the window and noticed him standing idly or staring at the clock, she rapped on the pane and gestured that he should move about and play. Bowles obeyed by galloping back and forth a few times, an activity that prompted his father to shout down from the window of his office: "Calm down, young man!"[20]

Bowles's most overarching feelings of childhood were his abject loneliness and sense of deprivation. One event he remembered was his mother's having told him that he must stay in bed because she needed to go out alone for a few minutes. "Of course I stayed. But I felt as though there was no one else in the world, and at that moment, for me, there wasn't. My mother returned, but to a six-year-old at home alone, she stayed away much too long."

Bowles found solace in a rag doll named Jimmie that his aunt Emma had made for him. "I was devoted to Jimmie, who was as big as I was and had a huge, hideous painted face. I also had a small doll named Kitty Campbell and a dog with hound ears that I called Nippie. I remember being two when I named a scarecrow Donty Be. I was always naming things. I suppose it made me feel less alone."[21]

When his hour in the backyard was up, he was allowed to play in the dining room, where his father insisted that his toy box be kept. "I had no idea why I couldn't have my toy box in my room, but had it been there, my father could not have monitored it. Since we ate in the dining room, everything with which I occupied myself throughout the day had to be put away by 6:00 p.m., when my father usually appeared. If he should find anything outside the box, I was convinced it would be confiscated. It was not that anything actually *was* confiscated. The important element was the threat that hung over the toys."

Bowles sat in the living room with a book until his father summoned him to the table. "Other than Poe, there was a dearth of books in that third-floor apartment compared to what I discovered later in my grandfather's library in Elmira," Bowles recounted. Of his grandparents, it was his paternal grandfather who interested him most because his library was filled with volumes of Balzac, Dumas, Hugo, and Zola. "My Grandfather Bowles, whom I called Daddypapa, taught himself French and Spanish so he could read books in their original languages. My grandmother read, too, but Daddypapa's books were not her 'cup of tea,' she told me." Daddymama was particularly critical of her grandson's desire to be alone so much. "It is unnatural," she told his mother.[22]

In their day-to-day lives at home in Jamaica, Claude relied upon Rena to live within a well-defined budget. Bowles remembered his mother's careful planning of each meal and her preparation of the dishes his father especially liked. "She was a good cook, baked all of our bread, and served us special breakfasts on weekends. When my father seemed irritable at the end of his workday, which was often, he found fault with almost everything Mother cooked. 'We have to make allowances for his temper,' she told me. 'He's under a terrific strain.'"

From the sidelines, Bowles pondered why he and his mother had to make allowances for his father's temper and the nature of the strain from which he suffered, but he reached no satisfactory conclusions. He also watched silently as Rena coddled her husband, with whom she seemed infinitely patient despite his own impatience and moodiness with them. "I saw her try every trick imaginable to lift her husband from his doldrums. Perhaps my father's brittle exterior was a means of disguising his depression and latent anger that always seemed on the verge of exploding," Bowles concluded.

Since his parents were never demonstrative of any affection that may have existed between them, Bowles did not know what to think when he heard little cat sounds and purrings made by his father one afternoon when he walked into the house. "Sometimes he called out in imitation of a tomcat: 'Ow row! Ow row!' My mother replied with a purring sound loud enough to be heard no matter where he was in the house. Their feline dialogue ended only when they sat down to dinner, often to be resumed after they had gone to bed. In my naïveté I never thought anything of it." There was no such thing as sex in Bowles's consciousness then. As a child, it did not occur to him that there was anything singular about the sexes, although he did notice that his maternal grandmother had a more ample chest than most men. "I never saw either of my parents in any state of undress. They kept the door to their bedroom locked when they were in it, and I was instructed to lock the door to the bathroom when I went in. Of course I was told never to lock my bedroom door," said Bowles, who gathered that if he did, there would be dire consequences.

Whereas Claude sometimes interrupted his wife with a "little pitchers have big ears" refrain if she were recounting something in front of their son that did not bear repeating outside of the home, Rena was inclined to address such issues head-on. "You mustn't tell anyone you saw Daddy in bed with Aunt Emma," she instructed, Bowles having walked into the guest room one Sunday morning without knocking, curious about the shrieks of laughter he heard from within. He saw his mother leaning over the footboard of his aunt's bed "holding her sides from having laughed too much," and his aunt "squealing and shrieking" in the bed. "My father, still in his pajamas, was giggling and lying in bed beside Aunt Emma. When he saw me he leapt to his feet and exclaimed: 'Let's get to those buckwheat cakes.'"

Whereas Bowles thought little of the incident, he was taken aback when his mother insisted later that he never speak of it. "I grew up believing that one should hide everything." He was four when he wrote a poem for his aunt to cheer her up and printed it out by hand:

Poor Aunt Emma, sick in bed
With an ice-cap on her head.
She's very sick, but she's not dead.

Touched by her nephew's offering, Emma laughed as she read it, then hugged him. "Why did you laugh?" he asked.

"Because I like the poem. You do love your old aunt, don't you?"

Already uncomfortable with any expression of emotion directed at him, and disquieted by his aunt's expectation of an emotional response, he averted her glance and replied softly, "Of course," then retreated from the room.[23]

Bowles had become increasingly aware that not only was he his father's enemy, but also that his father was his enemy. Intuitively, Bowles refined his subtle strategy of passive aggression, having learned from both parents that he must never be demonstrative since being demonstrative meant showing how he actually felt.

When an argument erupted between his parents regarding some aspect of child rearing, his mother's authority was a fat green book by a Dr. Riker called *Child Psychology*. "My father was annoyed that my mother spent so much time with Dr. Riker's book and tried to impose Riker's philosophies upon him. She went to great pains to keep me from seeing the book, which made me even more curious about its contents."[24] By this time he knew to avoid displaying overt curiosity about anything in which he took a special interest.

Bowles's skill at manipulating language and deflecting questions that made him uncomfortable or seemed irrelevant characterized his behavior. Although such evasiveness may have been calculated to avoid offending an interrogator, more often it was a means of matching wits or engaging in subtle gamesmanship with an opponent. The desire to keep the other person off balance, to provoke uncertainty, to perpetuate an air of mystery—all became inordinately satisfying to him and were traits that Bowles curried throughout his life.

Since his mother and father seldom informed him in advance of any activity in which he, too, might participate, Bowles knew that a trip was imminent only when his mother appeared at his bedroom door with a valise and began packing his clothes. His paternal grandparents owned three cottages a few miles north of Elmira in the town of Glenora, and vacations there were the highlight of Bowles's summer. Although he had no idea which cottage they were to occupy until they arrived, he was fondest of the Boat House since it stretched thirty feet over the lake. It had boat slips on the first level, a kitchen and servant's room on the second, and the family's living quarters at the top. On all levels the rooms abutted the bare shale cliff behind it, the shale itself forming the back wall of the structure. From the top floor, a large open porch extended across the back of the house, and from it, two more flights of stairs provided access to the woods and ridge above. Across a narrow road to the rear was a cottage named Red Rough, and southwest of the road was Horseshoe Cabin, where his paternal grandparents usually stayed.

One of Bowles's favorite pastimes at the lake was inventing lists of place-names for his imaginary railroad. He drew maps and prepared timetables so that his train would arrive on schedule and depart each station without keeping its passengers waiting. One afternoon he printed the names of each station on small squares of paper and anchored them at intervals under bits of shale. Just before dark, he hurried back to Horseshoe Cabin to wash up for dinner, all the while taking exquisite pleasure in visualizing his railroad. What he had not anticipated was his father's discovery of some of the slips of paper during his own excursion beside the lake. Certain that he had stumbled upon a code of some sort, Claude confronted his son and demanded an explanation.

"He was right. I had violated the unwritten rules of the community: that one must refrain at all times from scattering any kind of litter along the paths in the woods," said Bowles. In the manner of a prosecuting attorney, Claude presented his case to the family, now seated around the dinner table. First he exhibited the square of paper on which was printed the word *NOTNINRIVO*. Having found it at the edge of a dry creek bed above the lake, he announced glibly that the word obviously meant "nothing in the river."

"That's not what it means," his son interrupted, incensed by his father's intrusion.

"What does it mean then?" Claude demanded.

"You wouldn't understand," Bowles replied. "I had no intention of revealing to anyone that *NOTNINRIVO* was merely the name of the preceding station spelled backward."[25]

Claude seized his son and shook him. "It's just a bid for attention," he snapped, and again demanded an explanation.

Bowles fled the house to reclaim his treasures, his game having soured. He retrieved each slip, ran to a remote cove down the shore, and burned them, then pounded the smoldering embers into the ground. In a final solemn moment, he selected three flat rocks of shale amidst a bed of leaves and stacked them carefully to mark the shallow grave. Making his way back to his grandfather's cottage in the dark, Bowles vowed anew to conceal from anyone who attempted to intrude upon his private life the slightest evidence of anything that mattered.[26]

Upon the family's return to Jamaica, Bowles hid each notebook, more aware than ever before that he had entered a new phase of stealth and subterfuge. In one notebook he had recorded such names as Shirkingsville, 645th Street, Clifton Junction, El Apepal, Hiss, Ickerbona, Norpath Kay, Wen Kroy, Snakespiderville–scores of names, his imaginary world expanding in spurts. Yet his life in the real world of mealtimes and hostile, intrusive adults continued as though his interior world of magic, mystery, and inversion did not exist. In another notebook, Bowles created a planet on which he drew land masses and gave names to its four continents–Ferncawland, Lanton, Zaganokword, and Araplaina–and to the seas that surrounded them. He drew maps of rivers and tributaries, hills, mountain ranges, deserts, towns, cities, and the railroad lines that linked them. Bowles insisted that he never connected himself in any way with his maps of the world, nor did he inhabit any of the continents he invented. The whole point of the imaginary world was that it allowed him *not* to exist.

Despite his resolution to exercise caution at every turn, Bowles unwittingly invited disaster by drawing in his notebook before breakfast, an act he had hoped to conceal by locking his door. "I listened to a blue jay complaining loudly, and for a time I was that blue jay. I wanted to draw houses to add to my real estate collection and had just opened my notebook when my father bounded up the stairs and tried to get into my room. . . . I hid my notebook under the bedcovers, and he stormed in and made me show him what I had been doing."

"Just for that I'm going to give you a good hiding."

"I offered no protest, whereupon my father asked between slaps if I had had enough." Bowles made no reply, and again his father demanded to know if his son had had enough.

Again, the youth made no reply.

"Now?" Claude scowled as he again raised his belt.

"Whatever you say," answered Bowles, his voice unwavering.

"Give me every notebook," his father hissed.

One by one Bowles extracted each notebook from his closet and laid it out on the bed.[27] "I was convinced that I was seeing them for the last time, but I would not allow myself to grovel for their continued existence." He was astonished that his father confiscated them for only two months. "It was the shortest sentence my mother could wangle for me, and almost the only time she interceded for me. It was also the only time my father actually beat me, and it began a new stage in the development of our hostilities, for I realized that I could take any verbal abuse or physical punishment at the hands of my father and not shed a tear." Bowles realized, too, that power was the significant ingredient in their conflict. As soon as Claude discovered something that his son wished to do, he withheld permission.

At five Bowles was old beyond his years, having developed the art of feigning enthusiasm through facial expression and gesture for anything he disliked and to express disgust or abhorrence for whatever he might secretly desire. "I was convinced that dealing with my father was merely a question of holding out. To endure was to win. I also vowed to devote my life to my father's destruction, even though it could mean my own," said Bowles. "For many years it was my sole obsession."[28]

CHAPTER TWO

Bowles's Move to a New Neighborhood and His Discovery of the Arts

(1917–1927)

"My imagination was horribly active when I was a child, and for weeks at a time I had no glimpse of reality."

—Paul Bowles to Bruce Morrissette,
Jamaica, New York, January 14, 1930

Bowles was six when his parents moved from their apartment on Fulton Avenue to a three-story, two-family dwelling in a nearby residential neighborhood. "I never knew just how it came about that my father decided to move, but we soon found ourselves living at 307 DeGrauw Avenue, which even my mother liked. Our house faced south, and there were no houses across the street or on either side." From the high windows of his bedroom, Bowles could see hundreds of maples, pines, elms, hemlocks, and oaks. In the spring, dogwood blossoms dotted the landscape, and robins, thrushes, blue jays, and woodpeckers jabbered and signaled to him long before his father's summons each morning. Although Bowles was no fonder of his father in the new house than he had been in the old one, his compensation was that his father had to move his dental office to a building some distance from their home.[1] The architect of the house lived on the first floor, the family's dining room and living quarters were on the second floor, and Bowles had the entire third floor to himself. Bowles gave names to the rocks and moss-covered boulders he encountered as he made his way along virgin paths and memorized the landscape, then recorded in a notebook the names he assigned each object. He could hardly bear the interruption when his mother summoned him for dinner.[2]

An onerous new rule imposed by his father coincided with their move. Having recently heard of the teachings of Dr. Horace Fletcher, Claude insisted that Bowles begin at once the process known as Fletcherization, which required that everything in one's mouth be well seasoned with saliva before being swallowed. Followers of Dr. Fletcher were supposed to chew each bite forty times and could not swallow until the food was reduced to a liquefied mass. If Claude detected that his son was swallowing prematurely, he slapped him in the face with his damask napkin and ordered: "Keep chewing! Keep chewing! You haven't made your bolus yet!" At the table Claude sometimes counted aloud as though he were a metronome setting the pace. "Oh, how I hated that!" exclaimed Bowles.[3]

One day his mother drew him aside to say that nothing was as much fun as the games he could play in his own mind. "You make your mind a blank and not imagine anything or remember anything or think of anything, not even think 'I'm not thinking,'" she instructed, and told him that she often played the game herself to shut the door to the outside world. The whole concept of another plane of existence that he himself could control fascinated Bowles, who could hardly wait to follow his mother's instructions. "I used to lie in bed after lunch to rest, but the object was never to sleep, although sleep sometimes followed, but to retreat into a blank state that I could hold indefinitely."[4]

Bowles was six when his father informed him that he would soon be starting school. Not even his cousin Elizabeth Robbins, who was already in the third grade, had mentioned school to him. He remembered being taken by his father to an Italian barber for his first haircut, then scooping his shorn hair off the floor and stuffing it into the pockets of his blue flannel jacket. Later, Bowles was not sure why he had saved his hair, but the haircut itself seemed still another betrayal by his father, and he vowed to get even.

The next day he was enrolled in Jamaica's Model School, a training school for teachers three blocks from his home. In an interview to determine his grade level, the principal presented Bowles with a book and asked him to read a few passages aloud; then he was given paper and instructed to write something and to work a few problems in arithmetic. Bowles had no idea how to write in script and knew nothing about arithmetic. He considered himself fortunate to be assigned to second grade. Since any authority figure reminded him of his father, he rebelled by refusing to sing, and on each report card he was marked "Deficient in Class Singing."[5]

On November 11, 1918–the morning of the Armistice–Bowles and his classmates were sent home to get combs, and upon their return were coached in the melody of "Marching Through Georgia," which they hummed and blew repeatedly into their combs. At noon, every student and teacher present that day marched in orderly fashion from the playground into the center of town while gathering crowds smiled and waved small American flags on sticks. Although the whole affair made little sense to Bowles, he enjoyed it since no one noticed whether or not he was singing.[6]

"I wasn't," he said.

Bowles recognized at once that he could read, write, spell, add, and subtract better than any of his classmates, thus saw no reason to participate in group activities. Miss Mabel Crane, his teacher, was patient with her new pupil, having concluded that the child was abnormally shy, but when he told her point-blank that he had no intention of doing *anything* she asked of him, she suggested that a conference with his parents and a daily *D* in deportment might induce him to change his mind. Bowles remembered smiling back at her as he sauntered down the aisle from her desk to his own.

His next ploy was turning in every assignment written backward, for which he routinely received a zero. Finally, unwilling to put up with such insubordination another moment, Miss Crane summoned him to her desk, shook a sheaf of papers in his face, and demanded to know what he meant by such nonsense. "There are no mistakes," Bowles declared, his voice sweet with innocence.[7]

On the playground, he refused to play soccer or to talk to anyone during recess. Never a team player of anything, he had no desire to make friends and discouraged such relationships by making slighting remarks to selected classmates who were likely to effect some kind of physical reprisal. Bowles recalled that he "always took punishment stoically and ecstatically, never on any occasion wept," and when the fury of his attacker abated, he got to his feet, dusted himself off, and if he still felt the desire to be hurt, leveled new abuse to his face.[8]

Although Bowles usually managed to keep obvious displays of anger in check, he found himself on several occasions slumping beside his desk as though he were about to faint. "I even ground my teeth and turned blue in the face, or so I was told. I don't know if my latent anger had anything to do with such attacks, but when the event was reported to my parents and our family doctor, I was told that I probably had suffered some sort of epileptic seizure."[9] Bowles did not recall suffering such attacks in subsequent grades.

"I may have been relieved from these attacks upon my discovery of music," said Bowles, who was seven when he became aware of hearing it for the first time. From his room on the third floor he heard "magnificent sounds from downstairs" and rushed to investigate. He found his parents seated side by side on the living room sofa in front of a Victor gramophone listening spellbound to a recording of the Philadelphia Orchestra in a performance of Tchaikovsky's Symphony no. 4 in F Minor, opus 36, conducted by Leopold Stokowski. In awe, Bowles sat down and listened, too, convinced that he had been transported to another land. Although his father warned him not to touch the recordings or the machine, he had no intention of obeying him.[10] Impatient to buy records of his own and to play them while his father was at work, Bowles purchased first "At the Jazz Band Ball" and "Ostrich Walk," performed by the original Dixieland

Jazz Band, songs that had been recommended to him by a classmate he tended to trust. Never before had he heard such music, and he played it for hours at a time. His mother paid no attention, but one day his father came home unexpectedly and caught him at the machine.

"He plays the other music, too," she offered, yet knew that her son's being told *not* to do something by his father was the very thing he intended to pull off without detection. Determined now to save enough money so that he might buy his own gramophone and play it in the privacy of his room, Bowles began making calendars embellished with designs in crayon to sell to visiting relatives and friends of his parents, who appeared not to object since he was subtle in his pandering. Even Daddypapa Bowles, his paternal grandfather, concealed money under his napkin for his enterprising grandson, who was ambivalent about its source since he inevitably discovered the bills in his father's presence and felt obliged to observe how he might spend them.

Other than having played a comb on Armistice Day, and later, a zither given him by Daddypapa, the child's only access to what he considered *real* music was his father's gramophone until he discovered a stack of sheet music in an antique cabinet given to his family by a relative to help furnish the new house. Although Bowles had no idea what the notes meant as he pored over the sheet music, it occurred to him that he might compose something of his own. At seven he began making up lyrics, copying out melodies to go with them, and creating a story line to tie it together. He called his first composition "Le Carré, An Opera in Nine Chapters" and played it on a zither that he tuned with a skate key. "I knew I was not writing a real opera, but I was amused by what I did write." Its plot revolved around two husbands who schemed to swap wives. When the women realized their husbands' infidelities, they plotted revenge. Although Bowles's opera did not survive, a seven-line soprano aria from it, which turned up later in a collection of his manuscripts, began:

Oh lala,
Oh daba,
Oh honeymoon![11]

Bowles was also writing poetry at the age of seven as still another means of amusing himself. An early poem that survived intact began:

Give me wine
That comes from a vine
Hanging in a garden of thine.
Oh, no. You'd get drunk.
Yes, you would, you rank old skunk.
. . .
I'll give you some molasses
Served in little glasses,
But never any wine.[12]

At seven, Bowles also began working at what he called his "secret chores," which involved making daily entries in his notebooks and creating a newspaper in which he meticulously recorded the fictitious news of the day. "Today we landed at Cape Catoche" began one entry recounting a sea journey undertaken by a group of correspondents. Bowles's imagination was fueled by the huge world atlas in his home over which he pored for hours trying to decide the kinds of people who might inhabit such strange lands.

Whereas Claude and Rena paid little attention to their son's antics upon joining a country club in the neighborhood, they were annoyed by the criticism of Claude's parents, who sometimes visited for several days at a time and concluded that this new sociability had adversely affected their parenting. Since neither Daddypapa nor Daddymama drank liquor or gambled with dice or cards, they were distressed to find their son's integrity compromised by his and Rena's drinking bootleg scotch, sitting in a circle on the floor with other couples, and playing poker for hours at a time. When the Eighteenth Amendment was ratified on January 16, 1919, followed by the Volstead Act nine months later, Frederick Bowles expressed sharply his condemnation of those who disobeyed the law by drinking.

Bowles was eight when he noted the expressions of disapproval of his great-aunt Mary Robbins Mead when she stayed with them in Jamaica. "Upon observing my mother's drinking cocktails before dinner, smoking cigarettes, and using cosmetics, Aunt Mary minced no words in registering her antipathy. 'They are unnecessary, vicious habits, each a separate insult to the body, and thus to the entire being,' she declared."[13] As a child, Bowles avoided his great-aunt as much as possible and took her comments as a warning of what might be in store for him if his parents did not "mend their ways."

Bowles noted, too, that when Grandmother Winnewisser came alone for her usual two-week visit, she was never disapproving of anything she witnessed. "I loved having my grandma visit, although she sometimes surprised me. She once offered me a dollar to beat up Buddy, a neighborhood bully who taunted me while I shoveled snow. I told her I didn't know how to fight, but Grandma assured me that he did not know how to fight either, a possibility I had never considered. The next time I saw Buddy, I walked straight toward him, and when I was about three feet away I jumped on him and knocked him down leaving him motionless in the snow. Never before had I fought willingly with the idea of winning."[14]

Bowles was relieved when at the age of seven he learned that he needed to be treated by an orthodontist and would be allowed to leave school early to go into the city. "Dr. Waugh told my mother that he not only had to straighten my teeth, but also broaden the upper and lower jaws to make room for their realignment. I found the entire process a most excruciating form of torture and would not have objected to having every tooth in my head pulled. It was a fair trade since I cherished my freedom in the city. I also started taking piano lessons that winter. Since my mother and her sisters had studied piano privately and played until they went off to college, my father agreed to order a grand piano from Wanamaker's."[15]

Bowles assumed that his mother had insisted upon a grand for its attributes as a piece of furniture, rather than for its qualities as a musical instrument. Each Friday afternoon, Bowles was given private lessons in piano technique by Miss Dora Chase, a neighbor, whom he liked far better than his teachers at the Model School. On Tuesdays he participated in her obligatory Tuesday afternoon group lessons in theory, solfeggio, and ear training. "In the process, I learned musical notation and could render my own musical ideas on paper–in effect, to compose. If the group lessons had been optional, I would have avoided them," said Bowles.[16]

During his second year of lessons with Dora Chase, the piano's soundboard buckled, and his father insisted that Wanamaker's pick up the instrument and void the purchase. "I had no piano until Daddymama sent us her ancient upright Chickering that she no longer played. By this time, Mrs. Chase had moved her studio to Brooklyn and invited me to continue working with her there."[17] He relished the thought of being in Brooklyn since the Hoagland sisters–Anna, Jane, and Sue–lived there during the months they were not in their summer home in Glenora. After his piano lessons on Fridays, Bowles often walked to the Hoaglands' home for dinner and was invited to spend the night. "They treated me to movies and symphony concerts at the Brooklyn Academy of Music and took me to the Brooklyn Museum. I remember seeing *Nanook of the North* twice with them and several of Harold Lloyd's films."[18]

When the New York Philharmonic Orchestra launched on January 16, 1924, a new series of Young People's Concerts at Carnegie Hall on Saturday afternoons, Bowles, now thirteen, was permitted to go unaccompanied. Later he attributed much of his early musical knowledge to these special programs, which included commentaries and humorous designs by conductor Ernest Schelling to illustrate musical notation and musical form. He also watched slides of portraits of composers whose music was being played that day, pictures of instruments, and title pages of famous editions of classical music. "The drabness of the auditorium contrasted strangely with the glamorous sounds that filled it, and any orchestral sound was a delight. Nineteenth-century works made up the programs until one day they played *The Firebird.* I would not have expected an orchestra to be able to make such sounds," he said. After the concert, Bowles bought his own Victor recording of *The Firebird* and played it constantly on his victrola in the privacy of his bedroom.[19]

During his solo ventures into Manhattan to see his orthodontist, Bowles sometimes visited his father's widowed sister, Adelaide Maltby, who was a librarian at the main branch of the New York Public Library and shared an apartment in Greenwich Village with her friend, Anne Carroll Moore. Moore was the director of the children's section of the New York Public Library, and Bowles was exceedingly fond of her. She wrote a children's column, "The Three Owls," which appeared regularly in the *New York Herald Tribune* Book Review, and sometimes she presented him with children's books inscribed by their authors.

Bowles was devastated when he learned that his aunt Adelaide had died during the influenza epidemic of 1918–19. "My mother's blunt words caught me off guard: 'Your Aunt Adelaide has gone away. You'll never see her again.' At first I did not comprehend her meaning." When Bowles demanded an explanation, his mother left the room without a word. "I understood that my Aunt Adelaide was dead and felt a blind rage which, needing an object, fastened upon Mother for being the bearer of the news and, above all, for giving it to me in such a dishonest fashion. Things were never the same between us again."[20]

Until his aunt's death, Bowles was unaware that there even was an epidemic. When a second flu epidemic swept the Northeast shortly after the first subsided, both he and his parents were stricken. Whereas Bowles and his mother recovered rapidly, his father's condition was critical. Unwilling to be hospitalized, Claude insisted upon being treated at home, demanded that nurses report to his bedside in eight-hour shifts, and that his doctors make daily house calls. Worried that Paul might become reinfected, Rena sent him alone by train to stay with her parents at Happy Hollow Farm. Astonished by his good fortune, Bowles traipsed the hills and meadows, gathered eggs from the henhouse, fed the horses, and thrived on grown-up conversations with his grandparents and uncles, who treated him as someone whose thoughts and opinions they valued. In the evening Bowles sketched, wrote in his notebooks without fear of interference, and went to bed whenever he chose.

Suddenly, his maternal grandparents were stricken, too, and he was sent to Northampton to be supervised by Guy Ross, the husband of his aunt Emma, who went to the farm to nurse her parents. Ross was a registered nurse, and Rena was confident that her son would be treated expeditiously if he showed any sign of illness. Bowles was surprised when he discovered that Emma and her husband lived in separate apartments in the same building, and that his uncle often walked the corridors dressed in Japanese kimonos and burned incense in his apartment. He kept his aunt and uncle's living arrangement to himself. Each morning Ross ascertained that his young charge had enough reading material at hand with which to entertain himself, then left for several hours to attend a terminally ill patient who also lived in the building. "I was delighted with my uncle's apartment and imagined it as a setting for a murder mystery. As if to reinforce this impression there were a few Sax Rohmer novels on the table beside my bed, and at night I made the acquaintance of Dr. Fu Manchu."[21]

Bowles had seen only three movies in his life when his uncle began taking him to the Academy of Music, where two films were shown daily. "I remember seeing Mary Miles Minter, Charlie Chaplin, Viola Dana, William S. Hart, and other stars of the silent screen with a sharp and delightful awareness of the degree of disapproval Mother and Daddy would feel if they knew what was going on. Uncle Guy promised he'd never tell them, and I certainly wasn't going to."[22] Sometimes Ross invited Bowles to accompany him to an import shop that was also the home of his friend Mr. Bistany, whose walls, floors, and couches were covered with soft Turkish rugs. Mr. Bistany seemed "even busier with his incense than Uncle Guy was," Bowles concluded.

Since he considered Ross a friend, Bowles was perplexed upon being informed one afternoon that he must eat early and alone, then go to bed. Ross explained only that he was giving a party in his wife's studio, and that his nephew was not invited. Offended by the exclusion, Bowles did as he was instructed, but on some vague pretext after dinner wandered in his bathrobe through the building to the door of his aunt's apartment at the end of the hall. He could hear dance music being played on a piano and a great racket of voices and laughter. Regretting that he was missing out on something that obviously was fun, Bowles cracked the door and peered into the room, then stepped inside. In the living room he saw young men dancing together. Ross spotted his nephew at once, spun him around, and marched him back to his own apartment. Thrusting the youth inside, he declared in a steely voice, "I told you not to come, and now I'm going to lock you in."

Humiliated yet unrepentant, Bowles retreated to the guest room and glowered at the face of a "pretty girl with an inviting smile" in a framed photograph on the wall that he had never noticed before. He had no idea who she was, nor did he care. At that moment, she was his enemy, and he rammed his fist into her face. "I never paid Uncle Guy for the damaged frame, nor was the roomful of dancing men ever mentioned again by either of us," declared Bowles, who recognized that if he were to survive in the adult world, his defiance must be unobtrusive yet unmistakable. Upon Emma's return to Northampton, Bowles wrote a pleading letter to his mother requesting permission to stay longer, but she was steadfast in her refusal.

"I don't want you to bathe me, and I don't want you in the bathroom with me when I take my bath," Bowles announced testily when his mother followed him into the bathroom the night after his arrival home. To Bowles, everything had changed.

Rena replied casually, "Oh, you don't have anything Mother doesn't know about."

"I *said* I don't want you in the bathroom while I'm in here," Bowles said, glowering, and his mother withdrew.

Things were different for Bowles at the Model School, too. Although he had missed most of his first semester of fifth grade, he was promoted to sixth grade in the middle of the second term, his teacher having persuaded his mother to allow him to join Miss Miller's class of sixth-graders. Bowles resented her interference and was furious because he had done nothing to earn the promotion. At the end of the school year, Miss Miller invited the class to stand and applaud her new student's extraordinary achievement of having made the highest marks in the class.[23] Bowles was mortified.

He was eleven when his father announced that they were moving again, this time to a three-story house of their own on Terrace Avenue, not far from the house they had been renting on DeGrauw. Compared with their two former homes, the Terrace Avenue house was enormous. Bowles remembered trucks arriving almost daily from Lord & Taylor, Altman's, and Wanamaker's, unloading rugs, sofas, tables, and countless accessories purchased on approval. His bedroom was on the second floor, next to the guest room, but the area he coveted, and eventually was given, was at the top of an open stairwell on the third floor, which he petitioned to use as a clubhouse.

Impressed by their son's sudden interest in doing things with boys his own age, his parents agreed, but cautioned him to avoid the stairwell since it still lacked railings. Bowles's desire to have the top floor to himself had nothing to do with organizing a club or making new friends. His actual motive was to retaliate against Gordon Linville, a classmate with whom he had been on unfriendly terms for over a year. Bowles had engaged Linville in a rock fight and injured him, then felt guilty about the altercation and tried to make amends, but the offended boy wanted nothing more to do with him.

Having learned from Edgar Allan Poe the art of subterfuge, Bowles could hardly wait to arrange Linville's fate by inviting him to join the Crystal Dog Club. There was no Crystal Dog Club, but Bowles created letterhead stationery on a small printing press to give it a semblance of truth and invited a few prospective members from the neighborhood to attend the initial meeting. To avoid suspicion, he asked Linville's two brothers to deliver the invitations and suggested that they mention the homemade ice cream—"as much as they could hold"—to be served at the first meeting.

"Everything happened as I anticipated," Bowles reported. "The Linville boy demurred when I casually suggested that he be the first initiate. His objections to the blindfold and having his hands tied behind his back and a long rope wrapped around his waist were taken by the others as an unseemly lack of courage, but he went along with it despite his blubbering." Though Linville feared that he was about to be dropped three floors from the clubhouse window to the ground, Bowles had no such intention. It was merely the sound of his opening the window that conveyed a verisimilitude befitting the occasion. "It took four of us to help lift him to the edge of the stairwell, and now, having already determined the appropriate length of rope that would allow us to check his fall before he hit the landing below, we pushed him over the edge. None of us anticipated his being such a deadweight, and he bellowed as he fell."[24]

Bowles's parents heard the thud and raced upstairs in anticipation of the worst possible scenario. "We were astonished that he continued to scream even though Daddy and Mother went over him carefully and found no broken bones or other injuries. My father insisted that he was suffering only from shock and offered to escort him home to explain to his parents what had happened. When he returned, the rest of us were in the kitchen eating ice cream, just as our invitation had promised. My father burst in upon us demanding an explanation. I was amazed that the others took up for me. It was my first encounter with any camaraderie on my behalf. Of course our club was disbanded, and the next thing any of us knew was that Linville had been sent off to a boarding school. All we could think of was 'good riddance.'"[25]

"I want to get you away from home as soon as possible," Bowles's mother announced after the disbanding of the Crystal Dog Club. She said she had already registered him at Phillips Exeter Academy, the private school in New Hampshire that her brother Fred had attended.

Claude opposed Rena's plan from the first, calling Exeter a snob factory and an unjustified expense. "Mother did her best to convince my father to send me there, but he refused to change his mind," said Bowles, who was amazed that Claude appeared to be on his side. Continuing to live at home seemed a small price to pay for the privilege of making regular forays into the city, but he knew not to act as though he wanted to stay in New York or his father would side with his mother.

To humor her, Bowles agreed to spend a week during the summer of 1925 with the Greens, his mother's aunt and uncle, in Exeter. It was the Reverend Green who had christened him, and he knew that living under the same roof with the Reverend Green for four years would be "like being in church night and day." The visit was not entirely unfruitful for Bowles, however, because he wrote a short story there, which he read to his uncle. "I suppose that my purpose was to shock him, in addition to my thorough enjoyment at having an audience of any size," said Bowles. "'Hadeized' was set in a small town not unlike Exeter, and if its residents tasted even a drop of liquor, they were instantly transported to hell. Invariably they did, and soon the entire town was *hadeized.*"

Although his uncle appeared fascinated by the story, he left the room to get from his study a leather-bound copy of Emerson's *Essays*. "You are old enough for these now," Green declared, thrusting the book at him. Bowles read Emerson's essays as instructed, but was more intrigued by the books of Arthur Machen, which he had discovered in the school's library. Machen's fictional world depicted in *The Great God Pan* and *The Hill of Dreams* was "sinister and labyrinthine, filled with secret codes, necromancy, alchemy, torture, terror, and death," and it reminded Bowles of Poe's writing. Bowles had been especially intrigued by Machen's autobiography, *Far Off Things*, on one level the haunting portrait of an only child coming of age in late Victorian Wales, and on another, the dawning of Machen's own creative senses. "Naturally I identified with Machen. *Far Off Things* was not a story with a plot in the ordinary sense of the term, but an interior tale of the soul and its emotions," said Bowles, who declared that he hoped to be able to write that kind of tale himself someday.[26]

Bowles's favorite literary project during the summer of 1924 was writing a series of loosely related crime stories about a mysterious character named Volga Merna, who was rumored to be on hand when various people began dying without any apparent reason. Although there was nothing to confirm Volga Merna's participation in their deaths, the puzzled characters speculated on her possible involvement. Just as the fictional characters were drawn into the mystery and attempted to solve it themselves, so, too, were the Hoagland sisters, to whom he read his stories every day on the porch of their summer cottage in Glenora. Bowles was similarly intrigued by their houseguest, Mary Crouch, who had just arrived from Cape Town, South Africa, with her two teenaged children.

Everything about Mrs. Crouch was different from anyone he had ever seen, especially her eyes, which "seemed to crackle with darkness." She seldom moved from the chaise longue and pounded the floor with a cane when she wanted the maid. When Bowles overheard Daddypapa refer to her as "an immoral woman," and Daddymama declare that she was "an unscrupulous adventuress who had a stranglehold on poor Sue Hoagland," he liked her even more. By now Bowles's external surroundings and interior world were so entwined that he could seldom distinguish where one ended and the other began. "Daily I read aloud each episode of what I now called the *Snake Woman Tales* to Miss Sue and Mrs. Crouch, who were convinced that I was a sort of medium and that the tale or poem I read to them came 'from the other side.' I must admit that I rejoiced in their rapt attention."[27]

Before graduating from eighth grade at the Model School, Bowles was invited to read a few of his stories to the class, some of which were so long that he was asked to read them in installments. Finally, after three weeks of daily readings, Mrs. Woodson, his teacher, suggested that he read his stories after school so that attendance could be voluntary. "These readings, too, were a great success until I was overheard telling another boy that one of the girls in our class had a mustache between her legs. Mrs. Woodson made the entire class stay after school so she could interrogate a few of us at a time. Finally, I was the only one left. I am sure her questions were prompted by her own curiosity regarding the amount of sexual information to which I was privy, and how I may have come by it. Of course it was none of her business, but I wisely said nothing. Actually, I knew nothing, either."[28]

Bowles did admit to his mother that year of having learned "something about how mammals were born," yet claimed to be curious still since babies were sometimes described as "looking like the father" despite their having come from the mother.

As usual, Rena hedged. "It is a great mystery some people claim to understand, but no one really knows just how it works." Bowles resented his mother's evasiveness. "She said such stupid things that I was often embarrassed by our private conversations," he added. One evening at dinner while several guests were present, Bowles asked his mother what the word *circumcision* meant. He said he had heard a girl whispering that she could not come to her friend's party because she was "going to a circumcision."

Bowles's father appeared to take no notice of the question, nor did the others at the table, but his mother summoned Bowles to the kitchen when she got up to serve dessert. "You want to know about circumcision?" she asked. Then she explained that "sometimes when a baby boy is born, they take the little penis and cut a piece off the end of it."

"What for?" cried Bowles, wondering vaguely who *they* could be.

"Some people think it's cleaner."

Unable to imagine how "civilized people could agree to practice such a barbarous act on helpless babies," Bowles conducted his own investigation with a needle. "The pain was not so intense as I expected, but I never experimented in such fashion again."[29]

Bowles was thirteen when he learned that his maternal grandmother had died while on a camping expedition in north Florida. On January 21, 1924, his uncle Fred wrote Rena that their mother had had a slight stroke. A week later, a telegram arrived from their father declaring that she was "hopelessly ill." A second telegram was delivered while Bowles was playing mah-jongg with his parents and Fanny Fuller, their housekeeper.

"Is she dead?" asked Fanny, handing Rena the unopened telegram. Bowles had no idea what their housekeeper meant by such a dire question and turned to his mother for an answer. Rena merely glanced at the message, tossed it upon the game board, and left the room without a word.

"You'd better get up to your homework," his father growled as he followed his wife upstairs. Bowles was incredulous when he reached across the table and read the telegram for himself: MOTHER DIED THIS AFTERNOON. LETTER TO FOLLOW. FATHER.

Bowles pondered how everyone else in the room knew that his grandmother was dying, yet he had had no inkling that anything was wrong. It occurred to him now that the grudge he had held against his mother for not having told him of Aunt Adelaide's death five years earlier was now strangely mitigated. "I realized that my mother was incapable of dealing with death, except summarily, and in that regard, I suppose I was not unlike her."[30]

At fourteen, Bowles was elated when he and Elizabeth Robbins, his seventeen-year-old cousin, were invited by Mary Robbins Mead, their paternal grandmother's sister, to spend two weeks without their parents at Holden Hall, in Watkins Glen, New York. "We traipsed through the corridors and rooms of the old hall, our imaginations feeding upon the gothic trappings, shadowy observation tower, remote storerooms, and hundreds of bats hanging silently in the gloom before emerging noisily on their nightly forays for food. Since Holden Hall was not wired for electricity, we carried lamps wherever we went."[31]

After dinner one evening, Bowles was taken aback when his aunt informed him that he looked tired and should go to bed early since she and Elizabeth were "going to talk in the library." Bowles could not imagine why she had said such a thing. "I retired as instructed, but got up a few minutes later and opened the door into the hall in the hope of getting a scrap of their secret conversation. 'Paul has all the earmarks of a boy who has started on the *downward path,*' she said."[32]

The next morning, Bowles confronted Elizabeth: "What does she think I'm doing, robbing banks?"

Elizabeth replied that their aunt thought he had the wrong friends, "the sort who hang out on street corners and whistle at women going by." Bowles was astonished and insisted that he had no friends. Then he concluded that his father had turned his aunt against him or that Aunt Mary had heard about the practical joke he had played on a classmate when he brought to school an empty vial marked *morphine* that he had found in the wastebasket of his home. "I was unaware that Aunt Emma was being treated for morphine withdrawal during her month-long stay with us, and having overheard a boy in the cafeteria holding forth on dope fiends and claiming that cocaine was a powder and morphine a liquid, I interjected that 'morphine comes in powder form, too.'" Since his classmates scoffed at him for entering a conversation about which he had no apparent knowledge, Bowles filled one of the discarded vials with a concoction of baking soda and dusting powder and took it to school the next day.

"You could be arrested for having this in your possession," whispered the boy to whom he handed the vial. Another student snatched it from him and disappeared into the principal's office.

"We know it's just talc. What we want to know is where you got the bottle," insisted the principal in his interrogation of Bowles.

"At home, out of the wastebasket," he replied casually.

Although Rena confirmed her son's statement when telephoned, the principal insisted upon speaking to Bowles's father. "Now, just what was all that about? You certainly can be counted on to do the wrong thing in a big way," sneered Claude when his son returned from school. Fearful that her husband's knowledge of the event might trigger new leverage in his argument to have Emma treated for her addiction at a hospital, Rena, too, reprimanded their son: "Yes, whatever possessed you?"

Until now, Bowles knew only that his aunt was "a veritable skeleton," and that she suffered endlessly from severe headaches, her moans and screams rising and falling "like sirens wailing." Since the guest room was next to his own, he could hear through the walls everything that went on, but had no idea what was wrong. Finally, by eavesdropping, he gathered that his father feared that he would lose patients if they thought he was housing a dope addict. When he asked his mother about his aunt's condition, she replied vaguely that the doctors were obliged to give her shots regularly because when they wore off, the pain in her head was unbearable. "If instead of lying, they had only told me the truth about her, I should not have done what I did. My hindsight was good, but my foresight was often abysmal," Bowles allowed.[33]

Over the years his mother displayed a curious lack of sensitivity in the practical jokes she sometimes played on him. One afternoon when he arrived home from school, Bowles was dismayed to find neither his mother nor a note telling him where she had gone and feared that something terrible had happened to her, or that someone might be hiding inside. He cautiously checked the windows and doors for signs of a forced entry, then peered into closets, behind drapes, and under tables, chairs, and beds. Finally, in the guest bedroom, he glimpsed a figure on the floor beneath the dust ruffle and cried out in alarm. He heard his mother's hysterical cackle as she slid out from the far side of the bed, still giggling. "Hannah and Anna had to go out, so I thought I'd see what you would do if I disappeared, too. You wouldn't like it much, would you?" she observed lightly.[34] To Bowles, his mother was unbearably insensitive, and he went to his room without a word.

In the fall of 1924, Bowles entered high school, but instead of registering at Jamaica High School, which most graduates of the Model School attended, he announced to his parents that he wished to go to Flushing High School, fifteen miles away. "It was here that I made the startling discovery that there were two sexes. It had never occurred to me that there was a significant difference between boys and girls until we were dissecting frogs in my biology class when I was a sophomore. In all good faith, I asked the teacher if these differences applied also to human beings. Everyone else in the class giggled. 'That's enough out of you—I'll see you after class,' she snapped."[35]

After completing three semesters at Flushing High, Bowles transferred to Jamaica High. "I know why he wants to switch schools. Because here they don't know yet what a damn fool he is," Claude retorted. Bowles was tempted to say, "And you don't know what a damn fool *you* are," but he kept the thought to himself. Since Jamaica High was hugely overcrowded, Bowles usually perched upon the sill of a broad window, along with one or two other students. During his first semester there, he joined the staff of the literary monthly, the *Oracle*, and was soon appointed humor editor, "not because I was considered funny, but the post was suddenly vacant."[36] Given considerable leeway to develop his column as he saw fit, he created first what he called "By the Way," a jumble of little-known quotations, quips, snippets of literary interest, and recommended readings. As a senior, he wrote "How We Read It," a column to which he invited other staff members to contribute. Determined to write only about books he recommended, Bowles endorsed Willa Cather's *Death Comes for the Archbishop*, two books by Christopher Morley, *The Arrow* and *Pleased to Meet You*, H. L. Mencken's *Selected Prejudices*, and André Gide's *The Counterfeiters*.

It was Gide's book that intrigued him. One of its protagonists was a boy who left home clandestinely at the age of seventeen and wandered the streets of Paris for six weeks, then returned home "as unexpectedly as he left." An earlier book by Gide that made an even deeper impression upon Bowles was *Les Caves du Vatican*, which he read in French. By this time, Bowles had taken three semesters of both French and Latin and could read most of Gide's writings without a dictionary.

As poetry editor of the *Oracle*, the post to which he was named next, Bowles was also president of Kinsprits, the school's poetry society. He cherished being recognized as a poet, a determination enhanced now by his discovery of a slim volume of ancient Chinese poetry translated by Arthur Waley, a prominent English-born linguist. In Waley's "compact little pellets" of *One Hundred and Seventy Chinese Poems*, Bowles discovered the "existence of a whole series of other purposes for which the poetic process could be used" and was fascinated by such limitless opportunities. He soon found himself looking anew at his familiar external world with the idea of defining it in as few words as possible. He sometimes interrupted his homework to "tackle the problem of foghorns" rising from Long Island Sound or "the rustle of poplars and birches" outside his window.[37]

By the end of his senior year, Bowles had published more poems in the *Oracle* than had any other student in the history of the school. "More than half of my poems were written without conscious intervention," he noted. "To my astonishment, I could type a whole page without any awareness of what I had written." Bowles said later that his automatic writing had been a natural progression from his writings in childhood when he saw himself as a registering consciousness that merely received and recorded what came to him with the same psychic mechanism at work. He was reminded of his mother's teaching him to empty his mind before entering his "blank state" and to refrain even from thinking that he was *not thinking*. By then he had conceptualized an even more satisfactory way of not existing, "by viewing the entire unrolling of events as the invention of a vast telekinetic sending station," a process by which he could view, rather than participate in, his own existence.

Coincidental to his pursuit of poetry in high school, Bowles discovered an avant-garde review published in Paris titled *transition*. As a reader of the *New Yorker* almost since its founding in 1925, Bowles had learned of *transition* through Janet Flanner, whose "Letter from Paris" appeared regularly in the *New Yorker*. Flanner noted that while she was not impressed by James Joyce's "Opening Pages of a Work in Progress" (*Finnegans Wake*), she did find in the magazine's first issue several pieces to her liking. Bowles combed Lower Manhattan for its first issue, and upon reading it declared that it had not only altered his style, but increased his output of poetry.

Later, Bowles wrote: "Quite apart from the frontal assault of Surrealism, the existence of which I had not even suspected, I loved the magazine's concise format, the strange muted colors of the soft paper they used as covers, and the fact that the pages had to be cut with a paper knife." Reading *transition* also gave Bowles the illusion of being in Paris. "The feeling of the city I got from reading its pages coincided with my own idea of what Paris must be like, where the people were desperate but sophisticated, cynical but fanatically loyal to ideas. Paris was the center of all existence. I could feel its glow when I faced eastward as a Moslem feels the light from Mecca, and I knew that some day I should go there and stand on the sacred spots."[38]

Telling no one, Bowles submitted two poems, "Spire Song" and "Entity," to *transition*, both products of automatic writing, and hoped that nothing in his presentation would suggest that he was still in high school. He also assembled a grouping of twenty-nine poems that he intended to submit to a publisher as a book. Taking the title from two of his poems written at the age of twelve, "Air" and "The Sea," Bowles called his manuscript *Air to the Sea* and made a pen-and-ink drawing for the cover that depicted a boat at sea with its sails full to the wind. Accompanying each poem was his age at the time of composition.

When publishing his poems in the *Oracle*, Bowles had signed himself *Paul F. Bowles*, *Paul Frederic Bowles*, or, occasionally, *P. F. Bowles*. On his birth certificate, his parents had spelled his middle name with a *k*, but at the age of sixteen Bowles much preferred the look of *Frederic* without the *k*. He may not have thought consciously that his dropping the *k* was also a means of distancing himself from the other Fredericks in his family, but concluded that "on some level, it did have that effect."

Included in the senior number of the *Oracle* was a list of extracurricular activities and honors of each graduate of the mid-year class of 1928, and also "The Class Chart," rendered anonymously. With some amusement, Bowles read:

He is
A day dreamer;
He thinks he is
A poet; he'd like to be
A futuristic artist; always seen with
A dazed expression; hobby literature.

Bowles's principal had the last word when he entered his own assessment upon the school's official record before sending it, at Bowles's request, to the registrar of the University of Virginia:

Intellectual Promise:	Very good, high along literary lines.
Seriousness of Purpose:	Pronounced in lines in which he is interested.
Personal Character:	Erratic–aloof–no mixer.
Class Standing:	First quarter of his class.
Other Facts:	Thoroughly capable of doing college work. Needs a little more play in his makeup.[39]

CHAPTER THREE

Paul Bowles, a Runaway to Paris

(1928–1931)

"It had not occurred to me to attend the University of Virginia, or any other any college; I was only marking time until I could run away to Paris."

—Paul Bowles to Virginia Spencer Carr,
Atlanta, May 10, 1994

Bowles had selected the University of Virginia at the urging of Anne Carroll Moore, who reminded him that Edgar Allan Poe had been a student there until his gambling debts got out of hand. Besides the lure of Poe, Bowles considered the university's main attraction to be its remoteness from his parents' home. "The anticipation of living for a few months in the bucolic setting of Charlottesville while I considered my next move contributed to a new sense of well-being, a feeling enhanced by my orthodontist's having released me from the torturous wires to which my teeth had been subjected for a decade."[1]

Excited by his awareness that he was on the cusp of a new adventure, Bowles cast about for something pleasant to do during the spring and summer of 1928 and chose a four-month program at the School of Design and Liberal Arts in New York, which he paid for with his own savings. The School of Design and Liberal Arts occupied the third floor of a run-down building at 212 Central Park South, where Bowles joined a half-dozen painting students in front of broad windows overlooking the park. Until the models arrived, Bowles had never viewed a naked body and was astonished that the women were "so repulsive looking" and that the male models were covered with body hair. "I was too repulsed to look closely or to feel any embarrassment," he concluded.

Of the six female students enrolled that spring, Bowles paid attention to only one, Venetia "Peggy" Drake, whom he thought strikingly beautiful. Until Bowles met Drake, who had arrived from England only a few weeks earlier, he had never been interested in her country except to note its existence on a map, but to Daniel Burns, who taught French and Latin at Boys High School in Brooklyn and was spending the summer of 1928 in London, Bowles wrote that he viewed America as an alien entity and England as his true home.

It was the Hoagland sisters who had introduced them, and had Bowles not been physically attracted to Burns, he allowed later, he would not have participated in an amateur repertory production by the Phylo Players, a local theatrical group who performed regularly at the Percival Vivian Studio Playhouse not far from Burns's home. It was Burns who had urged him to join the group, and Bowles agreed since the play in question, titled *Kis-A-Mis Alley: Three Episodes in the History of That Surprising but Little-Known Thoroughfare Faithfully Recorded by Walter Phylo*, was scheduled for only a two-day run. Looking back on it, Bowles could not imagine having played such comedic characters in the three episodes, but he rehearsed with the group and appeared onstage in all three. In "The Washday of Kis-A-Mis Alley," he played a character named Teen; in "The Twinkled: A Drama of the Difficulties of Domestic Life," Bowles was the Hoodlum Who Shouted "Hurrah"; and in the "Last Harlequinade," a play within a play, he was the Second Harlequin. Bowles had never acted onstage in anything while he was in high school, and his only concern now was that his parents might get wind of his role in the production and insist upon attending. "It would have been hard to live down my father's snide remarks that were sure to follow if they saw it. Fortunately, they didn't, and my acting career ended practically before it began, thank god."[2]

Bowles sometimes invited Drake to dinner, then accompanied her to her room in Greenwich Village, where they smoked cigarettes and laughed about the various subjects that each brought up. "I never imagined how much fun it would be to have a friend like Venetia, and I was comfortable in the relationship since we were not romantic, although I did write outrageous letters to her for a time."[3] Bowles insisted that he never kissed her and downplayed any potential romantic relationship with her. "She was merely the first girl I liked well enough to allow myself to get to know, but it would never have occurred to me to do such a demonstrative thing as kiss a girl, or a boy for that matter." When Bowles was in high school, he did not date girls, but chose instead to admire from a distance "one superlatively beautiful and equally unapproachable girl at a time" since nothing concrete could be expected of him.

From London that summer, Burns asked Bowles to report to him regularly what he was reading and insisted that he keep up his study of French by translating French poetry and writing poems in French. Bowles replied that Thomas Mann's *The Magic Mountain* was high on his list despite his having to read an English translation of it, and that Mann's *Children and Fools*, also in translation, attracted him, too. From Charlottesville, Virginia, a month later, Bowles wrote Burns that despite James Branch Cabell's *Jurgen* being called "the darling of his professors and classmates," he preferred Djuna Barnes's *Ryder* and hoped that he might eventually meet Barnes, who represented to him both modernism and surrealism.[4]

Bowles was still studying painting at the School of Design and Liberal Arts when he returned home one afternoon and discovered a small parcel with French postage on it. He had imagined the moment so many times that the reality itself seemed a déjà vu. The newest issue of *transition* (#12), dated December 1927, listed the contributors on the cover, and his name was among them. "I took a paper knife from the desk beside me, sat down quietly, and slit the pages until I found my contribution somewhere in the middle, a long surrealist effort called 'Spire Song.'" In a note inside, the magazine's co-editor informed him that his other submission, "Entity," would appear in the summer issue.[5]

Bowles insisted that both "Spire Song" and "Entity" were written without conscious intervention, a technique he had earlier discussed with Sue Hoagland and Mary Crouch. Since Hoagland was skeptical of the process, she inquired if he could write something worthwhile at that very moment. Delighted to have a chance to prove himself, Bowles disappeared upstairs for ten minutes, then returned and read aloud the twenty-four lines he had typed, which began:

Everything is too late
We are all unbecoming to each other
Come doors shriek doors we are all too late
Everything is unbecoming to everything else
Come steel lizards pounce on us all
We are all too late.[6]

The two women looked at each other in disbelief and concluded that Bowles was a medium who defied explanation.[7]

In mid-September 1928, his mother accompanied him to Charlottesville, where he successfully opposed her insistence that he accept a room assignment on campus instead of installing himself in private housing. Bowles knew that in a dormitory he would be expected to keep his door unlocked, having heard the rumor that anyone who locked his door was spending his spare time masturbating. Bowles acted as though he did not know what they were talking about. "But of course I did. I had been doing it since I was fourteen and managed things quite nicely," he added.[8] He ate his meals in a boardinghouse near campus and enjoyed as never before the "pleasures of hunger and its satisfaction." He said that he had not expected his new regime of eating without Fletcherizing to be accompanied by a gain of twenty pounds. "Of course my weight gain had nothing to do with my not Fletcherizing," he admitted.[9]

Many of Bowles's letters to Daniel Burns that fall were written without capitalization or punctuation.[10] He also sprinkled his letters with French phrases to demonstrate that he was keeping up his French. Bowles especially liked his geology field trips, but refused to identify and memorize the hundreds of rocks to which he was exposed. It was one thing for him to have given names to countless rocks and moss-covered boulders he had encountered at the age of six when he moved with his family to DeGrauw Avenue, but quite another to identify rocks that someone else had named for which a grade would be assigned. "Why continue to clutter my mind when there are more interesting things out there," he asked himself upon dropping geology in the fourth week. The only course he thoroughly enjoyed was music history.

Each afternoon Bowles took brisk walks along unpaved roads, country lanes, and up and down railroad tracks on the outskirts of Charlottesville. Another pastime was finding bootleg liquor, which required a certain amount of stealth on his part since one could easily be spotted carrying empty gallon jugs across the countryside and returning with them full. The liquor still required aging, which he handily accomplished by draining off the fusel oil, then adding dried peaches and a bag of charcoal. By the next evening, his concoction was ready to drink. Another fad of Bowles and his classmates was inhaling ether.[11]

In another letter to Daniel Burns, he noted: "Still *seventeen*, although the happy part of it is that down here everyone believes I'm nineteen. Not that I've told anyone such a lie. In fact, I deny it vigorously." Sometimes his classmates ran their fingers through his thick, curly hair and asked how he managed to get a comb through it.[12]

A new friend was Bruce Archer Morrissette, who attended the University of Richmond, majored in French, and shared Bowles's interest in literature and music. He also edited the university's literary magazine, the *Messenger*, to which Bowles was invited to contribute, and later, to guest-edit an issue of his own. They spent a number of weekends together, alternating between Richmond and Charlottesville. Bowles considered Morrissette far more interesting than Daniel Burns and had no desire to introduce them to each other.

Despite his having dropped geology and paid little attention in the classes he did attend, Bowles was astonished to learn that he had made the dean's list in his first semester. Being on the dean's list meant attending only the classes he chose, although he did have to take and pass his final examinations. Although Bowles relished the accompanying privileges, he became aware of an increasing restlessness. "I returned to my room one afternoon at dusk and upon opening the door knew at once that I was about to do something explosive and irrevocable. . . . I shut the door and gave a running leap onto the bed, where I stood, my heart pounding. I took out a quarter and tossed it spinning into the air. 'Heads!' I cried out with relief. Tails would have meant that I had to down a bottle of Allonal and leave no note. Heads meant that I would leave for Europe as soon as possible."[13]

At this point, Bowles gave no thought to whether he should go; he knew only that he was going, and that he must be on his way to Paris before anyone missed him. Selling everything he had bought for his room except his bed and a Persian rug might have alerted some observers, but no one seemed to notice or care. Bowles was skeptical that the stationmaster could get the train to stop at 4:00 a.m., or even to be awake when it thundered through. "But everything proceeded according to plan." Upon arrival in New York, he checked into a Ninth Avenue hotel, and rode the subway to Brooklyn to enlist the help of Sue Hoagland and Mary Crouch, who congratulated him for showing such initiative and offered to do anything they could to help.[14] On his own, Bowles managed to get a photostatic copy of his birth certificate so that he could get a passport. Mrs. Crouch passed herself off as his aunt and declared that his parents were sending him to school in Europe, but were indisposed and unable to apply for a passport in person. "We perjured ourselves!" exclaimed Sue Hoagland proudly.[15]

After buying a one-way ticket to Boulogne-sur-Mer, Bowles was left with fifty dollars in his wallet but hoped that Mrs. Crouch or Sue Hoagland would donate some additional cash with which he could buy francs until he found a job. Instead, they handed him an armful of books and three letters of introduction to friends in Paris. Bowles was far too excited to be apprehensive about what might lie ahead since it was never his way to regret a decision or to look back at anything.

Of the eight passengers aboard an ancient Dutch ship making its last voyage, four accompanied him in a bobbing rowboat outside the port of Boulogne-sur-Mer. One was a young pregnant woman, Christine de Guendulaine, who wanted her infant delivered on French soil. Although she was traveling alone, her husband, the Comte de Guendulaine, had promised to join her later in her family's home in Paris. Bowles accompanied Christine on the boat train to Gare St. Lazare, where her family met her and invited him to their home for lunch. "After lunch we sat on tiny gilt chairs drinking coffee and liqueurs, and Christine's brother, who called himself the Duc de St.-Simon, gave me a cigar. I hoped he would not guess that I had never smoked one before."[16]

That evening in a small residential hotel, Bowles reviewed the letters of introduction written by Mrs. Crouch, but whom to approach first? he pondered. Miss Lynch was an osteopath who practiced in the heart of Paris; Madame Daniloff was a Russian aristocrat whose husband had served as a general under the czar; and Madame Caskie was an Irish actress ensconced on the Left Bank, whom he concluded would be the least likely to help. "Perhaps later, if I still need her," he reasoned. Choosing Miss Lynch, whom he visited the next day and found friendly and responsive, he was turned over to her receptionist, who took him to the Paris office of the *International Herald Tribune* for a job interview. Bowles's proficiency in French qualified him to be a switchboard operator, a position the operations manager was desperate to fill since the present operator had just resigned. Since Bowles was an American citizen and the *International Herald-Tribune* an American firm, he was assured that not having a work permit would present no problem. He was put to work immediately.

"My job involved listening to numerals via a distorting acoustical apparatus, then repeating them to the central operator. I dreaded making a mistake," said Bowles. He became even more nervous when he learned that Eliott Paul, a coeditor of *transition*, worked as a proofreader in the editorial department upstairs. "I would see him, complete with beard and cane, going in and out, since everyone had to pass the telephonist's cage in the entrance hall. I used to imagine ways in which I might get to speak to him."[17] For a time Bowles considered going directly to the *transition* office and presenting himself as "the American poet Paul Frederic Bowles, whom they had published in *transition* #12 and *transition* #13," but feared that the absurdity of the situation would render him tongue-tied. One day during his lunch break he walked some distance to the building in which *transition* was produced and waited outside the door of the office for several minutes without knocking. Then he feared being discovered and accused, perhaps, of eavesdropping, so he left immediately.

Now that he had a job, Bowles decided it was time to present Mrs. Crouch's letter to Madame Daniloff, whose husband still basked in the success of his biography of Ferdinand Foch, an eminent French field marshal. Whereas the general retreated to his study when Bowles appeared, Madame Daniloff welcomed the young American warmly, appreciated him as a personable diversion from her usual activities, and invited him to dinner repeatedly.

Everywhere Bowles went, he walked: to work, to the homes of other new acquaintances who also invited him for meals, to the gardens and museums, then up and down crooked streets and wide boulevards from one end of the city to the other, enchanted by the raw beauty and grandeur of Paris. Charmed by the fountains and streetlights, by the city's gargoyles and architectural wonders, and by its fashionably dressed men and women, he found himself smiling everywhere he went.

Since his salary of 250 francs covered too few of his needs, Bowles admitted, finally, to Madame Daniloff the financial and emotional strain he had been under of late and confessed his clandestine flight for Paris. He told her that he had received no letters from his mother while he was in Charlottesville, nor had he written any to her either, having rationalized that if he wrote either parent he would have intruded upon what may have become a peaceful coexistence. More pertinent to his actual situation was that he not care what either of his parents thought.[18] Madame Daniloff concluded that Bowles was ill, both emotionally and physically, and insisted upon taking him to her doctor, who gave him a number of tests, then asked if he masturbated. "Once in awhile," Bowles admitted, annoyed that he had allowed Madame Daniloff to put him into such an embarrassing situation. Still concerned for Bowles's health, she wrote his mother that he needed to go away for a few weeks "for a cure."

Rena said nothing to her husband, but inferred that her son was addicted to drugs and wrote to inform him that he must use willpower to break his habit, and that she had nothing else to offer him. He had gotten himself into such a predicament and must get himself out of it, she reasoned. Madame Daniloff was shocked that Bowles's mother seemed impervious to the plight of her only child and regretted what she had said in her letter. Bowles did not enlighten her to what he considered the New England mentality, which required "one's transgressions to be accompanied by appropriate retribution."[19]

At this point, lacking funds of her own to assist her young friend, Madame Daniloff wrote Mary Oliver, Mrs. Crouch's daughter, of the situation, which prompted Oliver to send money to Bowles to tide him over until he could find less taxing work. Instead of looking for another job, he thought only of leaving Paris as quickly as he could and coasting along as far as he could with his newly acquired funds. To quit his switchboard job was his first action; then he set out on long walks about the countryside, each time covering new territory and walking farther and farther from the heart of the city. Finally, he left his clothes, suitcases, and a few personal items in a storage locker at the train station and departed the city dressed only in boots and the clothes on his back to hike through the Swiss and Tyrolean Alps. Bowles said that he walked from village to village "in a state of semi-euphoria induced by the unfamiliar countryside" until he found himself composing a prelude at a piano in Orsières, Switzerland. From there, he took a train to Nice and stayed until his mail caught up with him. It included a letter from Mary Oliver announcing that she and her husband, Jock, were on their way back to Paris and were eager to see him.[20] His odyssey over, Bowles hastened to be on hand when they arrived.

At the Hôtel de la Trémoaïlle, Oliver took advantage of her husband's brief absence from their luncheon table to empty her purse of its francs and pounds. "Put it away fast!" she commanded, thrusting at Bowles a wad of bills. In their ensuing conversation, he spoke of his dilemma. It had nothing to do with money, he said; he was merely trying to decide whether he should be a writer or a composer, or "perhaps even both," he added. After lunch, Bowles invited Oliver to accompany him to meet Madame Daniloff, whom he had not seen since his return.

Relieved that Bowles was back in Paris, Madame Daniloff forgave him his untimely departure and arranged a meeting with Sergey Prokofiev, with whom she hoped Bowles would study since he already had made it clear that he did not wish to work with Nadia Boulanger. Although Bowles agreed to the meeting, he was convinced that Prokofiev would find nothing worthwhile among his compositions and perhaps even decline to work with him. At the precise moment of his appointment, Bowles was not on Prokofiev's doorstep, but at Gare de l'Est preparing to board a train to Saverne, France. "Clearly I felt that my action precluded the necessity of making a choice, and that once I was on the train there would be no question of my having to decide anything one way or the other."[21]

In Saverne, Bowles walked straight through the town, then on and on until he reached the historic city of Strasbourg, where he crossed the Rhine and wandered for a week in Germany's Black Forest. When he returned to Paris, his money having diminished to a few francs, he did not visit Madame Daniloff, knowing that her inevitable questions about his failure to keep the appointment with Prokofiev were unanswerable. This time, on his own, he found a job on the teller line in the Foreign Exchange Department of Bankers Trust.

This job, too, was short-lived. During his second week, Bowles gave a customer ten times the amount of francs he should have paid out for the hundred-dollar bill she presented him. Saying a word to no one, he left the bank, went immediately to the address of the unsuspecting customer, and recovered the overpayment before she was aware of the error. When Bowles returned to the bank with the money, he left it at his teller cage and told no one of his mistake. Then he walked through the front door, knowing that he would never again take a job that involved the handling of money.

The following afternoon he sat on the terrace of the brasserie Le Dôme and pondered his next move. This time fate, as he thought of it–he did not yet know the efficacy of the phrase *Mektoub . . . it is written*–intervened in the form of a young woman who approached his table, introduced herself as Hermina d'Orangeon, and invited him to join her and two friends for a drink. He also accepted their invitation to accompany them on a camping expedition. That night he slept with his companions in one large tent and bathed in the Seine when they awoke. After lunch Hermina suggested they take a walk in their bathing suits. The others had their own itinerary.

As Bowles reflected upon the event, nothing occurred that he could have anticipated and avoided. When they ran into a patch of stinging nettles, he was sure they were being attacked by angry wasps. Bowles admitted later that his nettle stings were not the only initiatory experience that afternoon. "There among hundreds of excited ants that rushed over us while Hermina declaimed such sentiments as 'I'm the flower, you're the stem,' I had my first sex."[22]

He was still recovering from his nettle stings and ant bites when Sue Hoagland and Mrs. Crouch wired him to meet their boat train in Paris. Mrs. Crouch declared that other than the loss of a few pounds, he had not changed since she saw him in New York, then added, as though he were not present: "If he returns home I shall be very much disappointed in him. But neither should he continue taking money from Mary."[23]

The next day the women invited Bowles to lunch and said that they would be joined by Madame Daniloff and a mutual friend, Katherine Muir Cowen, an anthropologist who had just arrived from Morocco. Cowen had spent several years at the Sorbonne, then two years in Paris working for the League of Nations, and was ready now to do something else. While Mrs. Crouch argued with Madame Daniloff about the Bolshevik Revolution of 1917, Bowles talked with their visitor, whom he liked at once. Single, self-assured, and twelve years his senior, Katherine Cowen was the daughter of William Cowen, a former editor of the *Baltimore Sun*. Cowen told Bowles that she was on her way now to visit her family, but would return to Paris in a few weeks. Then she asked him if he would like to accompany her to visit Tristan Tzara, whose poems he had read in *transition* but never dreamed of meeting. Bowles could not mask his eagerness to meet such a famous poet.

In his memoir of 1972, Bowles recalled still another sexual initiation two weeks after his deflowering by Hermina d'Orangeon, this time by a man he identified as Uncle Hubert, but whose actual name was William Hardy. Bowles had known Hardy in Elmira, and saw him later from time to time when Hardy visited his parents in Jamaica. "The story I always heard was that Daddymama and Daddypapa brought him to New York from somewhere in Alabama to be a companion to my Uncle Shirley when he and my father were young boys. His parents were dead, we were told. Although Uncle Billy was never formally adopted, he lived as one of the family until he left home as an adult to set himself up in business. Uncle Billy, as we knew him then, became one of the first American *couturiers* and had a salon off Fifth Avenue. I remember his coming to our house in Jamaica dressed in spats and fancy silk shirts and wearing jeweled cuff links of sapphire, ruby, emerald, or amethyst, depending on the color of his silk shirt. He once took my paternal grandmother to Paris on a buying trip, and when they returned I recall her being dressed in an outfit he had designed. 'Isn't the piping exquisite!' she exclaimed to my mother."[24]

Bowles and Hardy had not seen each other in more than a decade when Hardy discovered him in Paris and invited him to his hotel for a drink. Puzzled at first by Hardy's awareness of how to reach him, Bowles realized that in giving Katherine Cowen his mother's address and phone number, Cowen having wanted to assure Rena that her son was well and happy in Paris, his mother, in turn, had given Hardy his address. After drinking several cocktails with his new benefactor at the Hôtel Daunou, having been assured that the evening would cost him nothing, Bowles moved with him into the Hôtel Daunou and received what he termed later "a further sexual initiation."[25] Bowles's understatement was not unlike the casualness of the circumstances and attendant description of his first sexual intercourse with a woman. As he saw it, in both instances he was the passive victim. Bowles's insistence that he never made plans and that his actions depended unfailingly upon who came along confirms his reluctance to be an initiator of anything, regardless of the act in question.

Hardy told Bowles that Claude had given him a two-hundred-dollar check with which to buy clothes for Paul, but that he had destroyed it since he intended to buy Paul's clothes himself and take care of all his needs. With a chauffeur, they set out in a rented open car for Saint Moritz for several weeks of holiday. "On one hand, I was dazzled by my adventures with Uncle Billy, but quickly became bored," admitted Bowles. "He was such a show-off and thrived on taking credit for other peoples' decisions." Upon their return to Paris, Hardy suggested that Bowles consider going home to see his mother for a few weeks. "The SS *Paris* is leaving Le Havre on Monday. Why don't you take it?" asked Hardy. But for Bowles, to return home now was not an option. In a casino he gambled at *petite boule* and won $250 while Hardy lost $4,000 at baccarat. "Uncle Billy did not seem depressed by his loss, but I was scandalized. It gave me a sick feeling to see money treated so lightly, and I was at a loss as to what to do." At lunch the next day, Hardy announced that he still had the check

Bowles's father had given him and would use it to buy his ticket back to New York.

"I'll take the *Paris* on Monday," Bowles replied numbly.

"My, my! How glad your people are going to be to see their boy. And to think that Uncle Billy is responsible for it."

Bowles glowered at Hardy and said nothing. During the five-hour drive to Le Havre, he tapped relentlessly upon his knees, first with the right hand, then the left. "I was annoyed that Uncle Billy should take credit for my decision and I never wanted to see him again."[26]

When he arrived in Jamaica and the house he had once considered home, Bowles thought that his father was genuinely glad to see him. "Apparently my parents had agreed not to ply me at once with questions," he observed. While alone with his father, Bowles was not surprised to hear him declare sharply: "That was a terrible thing you did to your mother. You've noticed her hair has gone gray as a result." Bowles said that he had not.

"Well, notice!" Claude snapped. "You're so busy thinking about yourself and what *you* want. There are others in the world, too, you know."[27]

Bowles did not reply. He had not set out to offend his mother. "I always managed not to feel a sense of obligation to anyone," said Bowles, "no matter what our relationship was. When I left America the first time, I thought Paris was the center of the world, which it was then. Once you've been free, you don't want to go back to jail again," he insisted.[28]

Despite his avowed desire for independence, Bowles still relied upon the advice of those he trusted. As he declared later, "If a composer said to me: 'You are a composer,' that would be all right. Or if a poet said: 'You are a poet,' that would be acceptable, too. But somebody had to say something." Bowles thought repeatedly about the things Katherine Cowen had told him about Morocco and knew that it was only by imagining future adventures that he could bear the thought of remaining in New York for even a few weeks. Of Tangier, Cowen reported that it was a European town in which more than half the population was Arab, and that her pension was only a kilometer from the edge of the Arab quarter. Below was a huge Arab market where hay, wood, vegetables, chickens, slaughtered sheep, and donkeys were sold and camel saddles were made while potential buyers watched. She told him, too, of the abject terror she felt when six men ran shrieking toward her and jumping rhythmically while they beat with their fists upon black drums to drive away sickness, devils, or bad luck. Apparently fond of jewelry, many men wore a single huge earring and bangles on their arms and necks. The women wore embroidered yellow dresses over white blouses, and yellow veils covered their faces. A number of the people she saw on the streets of Tangier were English, Spanish, or French, and she communicated with them freely.

"Paul, you must go there yourself someday," urged Cowen. He would not have been surprised had she showered him with money and declared, "Here are the tickets, here are clothes that will enable you to fit in, here are books and stationery so that you can read and write me when the mood strikes you. You must not be timid or you will be very unhappy."

Now back in Jamaica, Bowles found it difficult to distinguish fact from illusion, but his father's accusatory outbursts confirmed that he could stay no longer at home. His words were ominous: "Don't think you're going to spend the rest of your life lolling about the house. I have something to say in the matter, too," he shouted.

For another ten days Bowles carefully avoided his father by disappearing each evening before he arrived home. One morning he left the house without a word to his mother and took his clothes and luggage with him. Although he had left to take a job at Dutton's Bookshop on Fifth Avenue, his parents suspected that he had already returned to Europe without telling them. It was Rena who heard that he was working at Dutton's and suggested that she and Claude check on him in person. Startled to see his parents out of their normal environment, Bowles told them that he had merely tired of the commute and moved into a place of his own. His mother suspected that he was again seeing Drake. "I was, but I chose not to confirm it in my father's presence and changed the subject. Later, I told my mother that we saw each other occasionally, but that it was nothing serious."

Rena stopped in again at the bookstore, this time without her husband, to inquire if he and Drake were married. Again, Bowles assured her that the "very idea of being married to Peggy [Drake] or to anyone else I knew at the time was absurd." Moreover, whatever infatuation it may have been had played itself out in a few weeks.

While living on Bank Street that winter, Bowles renewed his acquaintance with Dorothy Baldwin, whom he had met as a child in Glenora. Through Baldwin, married then to Maurice Becker, he was invited to celebrate his nineteenth birthday with Glenn Coleman, Stuart Davis, and John Marin, three of New York's best-known painters at the turn of the decade. Bowles also was introduced to Henry Cowell, who agreed to talk with him about his music and to listen to him play. "Certainly there is no one in America I would rather learn from, and whose music I think more of than Cowell's," said Bowles, who did not mention his admiration of Aaron Copland, whom he had never imagined meeting. Cowell invited Bowles to his studio to play for him and to show him some of his music; and, in turn, Cowell played some of his piano pieces for Bowles. "I was highly intrigued by Cowell's demonstration of the piano's unsuspected sonorous possibilities," said Bowles, who was even more dissatisfied with his own "unsensational little numbers." He left Cowell's apartment with a note Cowell had scribbled to Copland and suggested that Bowles deliver in person. "Since it was not in a sealed envelope, I read what he had written," Bowles admitted. "'This will introduce you to Paul Bowles. His music is very French, but it might interest you. See you soon, Henry.'" Despite his enthusiasm to meet Copland in person, Bowles was annoyed by what he took to be Cowell's condescending tone. He stood outside Copland's door for several minutes trying to decide if he should knock; then he heard a note being struck from time to time on the piano. "'Aaron will be back in a minute,' said the man who answered the door without identifying himself."[29]

Copland greeted Bowles warmly when he arrived a few moments

later and introduced him to Roy Harris, who had invited him in. "I had no reason to recognize Harris, but I knew that he wrote chamber music and had composed an orchestral piece titled *American Portraits.*" Copland laughed when he read Cowell's note. "You know I don't teach," he said. But he did read Bowles's score and invited him to play it for him at Steinway Hall, where he was giving a concert that evening.[30]

"I was nervous, but overall the session went well, and after still another meeting Aaron suggested that I might come to his apartment two or three days a week 'for an hour or so' to go over my music. I was amazed that he agreed so readily to meet with me. We began by studying Mozart's piano sonatas, which I had to learn to play, and at the same time, to analyze formally. We also talked about music and the history of music. It was easy to learn from Aaron because he wasn't teaching; he was just talking," said Bowles. For several months during the winter of 1929–30, Bowles had a harmony lesson with Copland practically every day. By this time he had given up his room on Bank Street since it had no piano and returned to his parents' home to work on the old Chickering piano when his father was not present.

Later Copland declared: "From the start Paul was not a student in the sense of being a beginner. Working with him was more like showing things to a professional friend. He was born to be a composer. He had an alert, quick mind, and he was knowledgeable about many things, not just music."[31]

Bowles was still working at Dutton's Bookshop when he began writing what he hoped would become a novel. He called it *Without Stopping,* which he thought appropriate because he feared that if he stopped to exercise choice or judgment, he would throw it out or stop writing altogether. "Seeing the number of pages grow gave me the illusion of being on my way somewhere, without stopping."[32]

In addition to studying regularly with Copland, reporting daily to his job at Dutton's Bookshop, and working on *Without Stopping,* Bowles resumed his writing of poetry, which he submitted to a number of avant-garde reviews in both Europe and the United States. In the autumn of 1929, he informed Daniel Burns that two of his poems had just been published in the September issue of *Tambour*, which he described as "that little brown French-English review you liked so much." A month later, *Tambour* accepted and published four additional poems.[33] Although Bowles's poetry did not exhibit the genius that later characterized his music and fiction, it fit perfectly within the burgeoning surrealist tendencies of the age and was published widely in a number of small journals. "It was a heady experience to have editors ask for my poems," said Bowles, who was particularly interested in *Blues*, subtitled *A Magazine of New Rhythms*, which had recently been founded in Columbus, Mississippi, by sixteen-year-old Charles Henri Ford. As Bowles saw it, Ford's "combination of naïveté and nerve" allowed him to solicit contributions from a number of notable avant-garde figures. With coeditor Parker Tyler, who lived in Greenwich Village and convinced Ford that he should move there, too, the two men collaborated on such advertisements as the one Bowles spotted in Lincoln Kirstein's *Hound and Horn*, which declared "AT LAST IN AMERICA A MAGAZINE THAT DARES, BLUES."

Elated by the response of their readers, Ford and Parker staged a public poetry reading in Greenwich Village and invited each of their contributors to participate. Bowles deliberated carefully before deciding what to read since it was his first time to do so in public. "I was relatively certain that few in the audience would know French, so I read 'Gravure sur eau,' 'Chanson,' and 'Les Villages du Midi,' which had been accepted by a new magazine published in Belgium, *Anthologie du Groupe d'Art Moderne*. I'm afraid I was shamelessly uninhibited at this point in my life."[34]

Still working at Dutton's Bookshop, Bowles lamented that he had no time to read the books on the shelves around him and decided to take a few of them home with him each night. "I took only what I might reasonably read in an evening, and I often gave them to other people." Bruce Morrissette was appalled when Bowles mentioned to him his purloined books, which prompted Bowles to reply: "You force me to the admission that the theft of the books was accomplished, then justified."[35] Bowles abhorred being asked to justify himself regarding anything he had done. He concluded later that he got on well with Gertrude Stein because she did not clutter her mind or conversation with anything that smacked of an expectation of any justification of an act, nor did she expect it of others. What Bowles craved was reinforcement of what he already was doing. If only someone could tell him *who* or *what* he was, he would consider the matter settled. Otherwise, he feared his ongoing tendency to rush from one creative canvas to another without focus.[36]

To Morrissette, Bowles declared that he had "stabbed into everything: linoleum cuts, woodcarving, primitive design in the three primary colors, making boxes, furniture, photographs, automatic writing." He also sent Morrissette what he identified as a *photographicomposition*. "It is merely a little statue I made, photographed against one of my machinery motifs." Bowles said later that the statue was his "only try at sculpture."[37]

Burns and Morrissette continued to serve as sounding boards for the propagation of Bowles's urges and developing tastes. To them, Bowles knew that he could do or say anything he wished without fear of derision or condemnation. When Morrissette suggested that he would like to meet Burns if he came to New York, Bowles replied: "You would like Daniel Burns after you had known him for at least three years. His pompous seriousness would repel you at first." Bowles made no attempt either to compartmentalize his friends or to go out of his way to introduce them.

A few months earlier, Bowles had mentioned to his mother that he might wish to return to the University of Virginia, hoping that she would be supportive so long as his actions did not precipitate problems for her and his father. To Dean Page of the University of Virginia, Bowles wrote: "In March of 1929 I became nervous and went to France. Now that I am back I should like to know if it would be possible for me to complete my year by taking the third term next March. Otherwise, my last year's work will be negligible. Please let me know whether I can do a thing like this, or whether I shall have to start in again on my first year at some other school."[38] Bowles had no intention of beginning a program elsewhere, but he had made his point.

On March 24, 1930, he returned to the University of Virginia, rented a furnished apartment in Preston Court, and invited a student he knew only slightly, Rosser Reeves, to share it with him. "Rosser liked music and books, and we talked a lot about what we were reading." When John Widdicombe, another UVA student he met that spring, tried to interest him in D. H. Lawrence's *Sons and Lovers*, Bowles declared that he had already skimmed through "Lawrence's excrement," *Lady Chatterley's Lover*, and had not been successful, either, in reading *Sons and Lovers*. He allowed, also, that he knew enough of Freud to believe that the sex urge was an important mainspring of life, and that "defecation and copulation were two activities which made a human being totally ridiculous. At least the former could be conducted in private, but the latter by definition demanded a partner."[39]

It was Widdicombe who suggested that he and Bowles hitchhike to Philadelphia to attend the premiere of Igor Stravinsky's *Le Sacre du Printemps*, to be performed by the Philadelphia Orchestra. In Philadelphia they were joined by Harry Dunham, a wealthy Princeton student who invited them to lunch, along with a friend of Dunham's, the editor of *Argo, An Individual Review*, who mentioned that he wanted to publish new fiction in his magazine. Upon his return with Widdicombe to Charlottesville, Bowles mailed a few pages from *Without Stopping*, which was accepted for *Argo*'s second issue.

Also that spring, Copland visited Charlottesville at Bowles's invitation, which gave Bowles a measure of recognition, too. "Unfortunately, Aaron's concert did not come off as I expected. He played a movement of his Piano Concerto, which he spoke of as a work of jazz, but many guests stirred uneasily and concluded that his performance was a hoax. I have no idea why." Whereas Copland appeared not to notice, or if he did, to be indifferent to his audience's reaction, Bowles vowed never again to expose his mentor to such crassness.[40]

Copland returned the next day to New York, and after taking his final examinations, Bowles left, too. Although Copland urged him to return at once to Paris and study counterpoint with Nadia Boulanger, Bowles was unwilling to work with anyone else. Meanwhile, Copland, now in Saratoga Springs at Yaddo, the artists' colony, prevailed upon Elizabeth Ames, its director, to invite Bowles there, too. For Bowles, the attraction to Yaddo was enormous since it meant his seeing Copland daily, a supportive environment in which to work, a studio of his own with a piano, comfortable sleeping quarters, and it was free. "I had a large, airy room in the mansion, and Aaron lived and worked in a studio in the woods. After 4:00 p.m., we were free to visit other guests, but those who abused their privileges received one of Mrs. Ames's 'blue notes' of polite chastisement. I never got one, but I am sure she was nervous when Aaron suggested that I be invited back a few months later. 'Yaddo comes to most guests only once in a lifetime,' she told Aaron, and I was certain that she had me in mind when she made the observation."[41]

Upon his return to New York City, Bowles declared that he would never live and compose at home again, and would never again ask his parents for money. When Harry Dunham offered to tap early into his trust fund, Bowles accepted several hundred dollars, which he insisted was a loan that he would repay as soon as possible. "When Harry's mother learned that I was the reason for his getting money early from his trust fund, she made no effort to conceal her dislike of me. Her accusations were never explicit, and there was nothing I could say to counter her impression."[42]

When Bruce Morrissette invited Bowles to guest-edit an issue of the *Messenger* and assured him that he could solicit poems from anyone he wished, Bowles wrote immediately to Gertrude Stein and William Carlos Williams.

By return mail, he received poems from each. Williams declared in his accompanying note: "yessir, wow! But you m-u-s-t keep everything else *mon dieu* because as I say it is I who shall receive the damns if it isn't a modishlooking mag."[43]

Nancy Cunard replied with a scenario in French; and both Richard Thoma, an editor of the *New Review*, and Edouard Roditi sent poems.

Since four of his own poems had already been published in the *Messenger*, Bowles declined to include one of his own. He had tried repeatedly to have a poem accepted by Harriet Monroe for publication in *Poetry*, but each was returned on the basis that it did not "seem like poetry." Finally, at year's end, Monroe accepted Bowles's poem "Extract," which prompted Bowles to declare that he was more proud of having this poem published in *Poetry* than anything else he had written before his twentieth birthday.

Upon his return from Yaddo, Copland suggested that he and Bowles go together to Berlin so that they might work with fewer distractions and could enjoy an intimacy that life in New York did not afford. "I was far more keyed up than I had imagined, but that does not explain what I did next. I hurled a meat knife at my father's head. Why, I am not sure. My act preceded any conscious decision to behave in such fashion. In my frustration to deal effectively with whatever verbal attack my father had just launched upon me, I simply let my guard down and retaliated. I felt no remorse at the act itself. What I did regret was that I had lost control so easily."[44]

At this point, Bowles may have been unaware of the degree of his devotion to Copland, and that their relationship meant far more than either surmised or dared to admit. Bowles said later that his father may have intuited what Copland meant to him, and even alluded to it, but at this point he was "simply blind with rage." The meat knife was at hand, and he hurled it. To Bowles, at this point "nothing was real."[45]

CHAPTER FOUR

Bowles's Return to Europe

(1931–1933)

"I am very eager to leave New York, not America, because I love America a great deal. The only trouble is that I have always had to live in New York, which is not the same thing at all."[1]

—Paul Bowles to poet Edouard Roditi,
New York City, March 4, 1931

Bowles liked corresponding with interesting people he had never met, such as Edouard Roditi, whose manuscript he had accepted in 1929 for the *Messenger*. He and Roditi had written countless letters to each other, sometimes two or three a week. Roditi also wrote letters of introduction for Bowles to carry to a number of his friends in Berlin. Three weeks after his letter to Roditi dated March 4, 1931, Bowles, now twenty, was aboard an American freighter, the SS *McKeesport*, bound for Le Havre, France. This time he carried with him practically everything he owned, convinced that he was leaving New York for good. After the knife-throwing incident, he had managed to avoid his father and hoped never to see him again, but both of his parents saw him off as though they were saying good-bye for the last time.

The crossing itself was wretched. Bowles fought off seasickness by walking the deck for hours in the wind and rain. At one point, he was sure the ship had reached the coast of Cornwall, but the captain declared that they were merely south of Newfoundland. Arriving in

Le Havre on April 8, Bowles spent the night, then proceeded to Rouen to take the boat train to Paris.

In Rouen he delighted in the early signs of spring while exploring the crooked streets and ancient cemetery nestled behind the churchyard just off the square. Here lay the bones of playwright Pierre Corneille, who had died in Paris in 1684. Corneille's remains lay close to the grave of Gustave Flaubert, a citizen of Rouen for many years. "Until then I had never read Flaubert, but now that I was back in France, I made up my mind to apply myself seriously to the reading of French literature in its original language."[2]

Before leaving New York, Bowles had received a letter from Richard Thoma, a wealthy San Francisco expatriate now living in Paris from whom he also had solicited poems for the *Messenger*, but had not met. Thoma, well known for his hospitality, greeted Bowles upon his arrival at Gare St.-Lazare and insisted that he stay with him. Another poet who offered lodging to Bowles was Georges Linze, who lived in Liège, Belgium. Bowles had discovered Linze's work in the *Anthologie du Groupe d'Art Moderne*, in which three of his own poems were published.[3] Everyone who met Bowles thought him both beautiful and charming, and he was never surprised when new acquaintances offered to put him up.

Eager now to meet Gertrude Stein more than anyone else with whom he had corresponded, Bowles called upon her on his second day in Paris, unaware that a visitor did not simply drop in. Stein's maid answered the bell and declared that Mademoiselle was busy. "I could hear the sound of women's voices coming down from the stairwell, and I said I had just arrived from America and must see her if only for a moment." She was just as he imagined her, except that her expression seemed more pleasant than she appeared in her photographs.

"What is it? Who are you?" Stein asked.

"I told her, and heard for the first time her wonderfully hearty laugh. Then Alice Toklas came downstairs, and we sat in Stein's studio hung with Picassos. 'I was sure from your letters that you were an elderly gentleman,'" said Stein.

"'A highly eccentric elderly gentleman,'" added Toklas.[4]

Stein invited Bowles to dinner the next evening to meet Bernard Faÿ, an urbane French historian who had studied at Harvard and the Sorbonne and was named chair of American Civilization at the Collège de France. As they talked and became better acquainted, Stein announced that *Paul*, a Christian name, was unacceptable, and that *Freddy* suited him much better. Since Frederic was his middle name, Bowles delighted in what promised to be a unique relationship, and he hoped that it would last.[5] He beamed modestly when Stein exclaimed "Ah! Freddy, Freddy, Freddy," smiling broadly, her mellifluous voice dropping several notes as she repeated his name in its descent down the scale. Stein's gnomic and sparsely punctuated phrases and triplets of identical words rolled effortlessly from her lips and were obviously intended for emphasis and dramatic effect. Bowles loved every aspect of her mannerisms and was certain that in time he would love her as well.

At dinner a few evenings later, Bowles brought up Ezra Pound, whom he had just met through Richard Thoma. It did not occur to Bowles that Stein and Pound may not have been friends, but he soon learned that such assumptions could get one into trouble. "Oh, I won't see Ez anymore. All he has to do is come in and sit down for a half hour. When he leaves, the chair's broken, the lamp's broken," said Stein.

"And the teapot, too," reminded Toklas, who presided over tea no matter how many guests were present.

Having gathered that Stein's tendency was to dismiss people whose offenses were usually inadvertent, Bowles was determined to do nothing to offend either woman. Stein prided herself upon her steel-trap memory and seldom forgave a perceived iniquity. It was Bernard Faÿ who informed Bowles that Pound was not the only intimate of Stein's circle with whom she had fallen out of late. To mark the occasion, she sometimes sent the offender a formal announcement to the effect that "henceforth Miss Stein would do without so and so's friendship." Both composer Virgil Thomson and painter Pavel Tchelitchew, to whom Bowles was introduced several days after his initial visit to Stein's atelier, testified that they, too, had received such notices. Thomson's dismissal, dated January 21, 1931, declared: "MISS GERTRUDE STEIN declines further acquaintance with Mr. Virgil Thomson."[6] Eventually, Thomson was reinstated when she realized that she needed him to write some music for her, but never Tchelitchew.

"I believe you've published some of Freddy's things in *transition*," declared Stein upon introducing Bowles to Maria Jolas, whose visit had unwittingly overlapped with Bowles's one afternoon. Jolas's husband, Eugene, had founded *transition*, but it was she who financed the venture and wrote the checks. She pretended to know neither Bowles's name nor work, which prompted Toklas to ask upon Jolas's departure: "Freddy, you didn't by any chance ever write and ask to be paid, did you?"

Bowles allowed that he had been paid promptly for "Spire Song," his first poem published in *transition*, but had received nothing for "Entity" and "Delicate Song," even though these poems, too, had been published therein. He said that he had written to request payment when his finances were practically nonexistent, and that a check arrived promptly. "Surely there was nothing wrong on my part in reminding her of the missed payment," ventured Bowles.

"That's the end of *transition* for Freddy," declared Stein, who basked anew in her contribution to the education of Freddy Bowles.[7]

When Eugene Jolas announced a few weeks later, in *transition* #19/20, that he was suspending the magazine indefinitely since he could no longer afford the expenditure of time and labor necessary to its preparation, he thanked many of the journal's contributors, but Stein and Bowles were not among them.

Committed to meeting everyone of note as quickly as possible, Bowles welcomed the opportunity to introduce himself to such other writers as André Gide, who attended, as did Bowles, an opening of an exhibition by American artist Eugène McCowan. "I was so elated by the idea of being face to face with the master that I could recall nothing pertinent that he said. What I treasured most was the event itself. I don't know why I was so obsessed by the idea of meeting such notables, but I was, and I kept track of each one I met and wrote little notes to myself to remind me of our conversation."[8] To be able to write Copland that he already had met Stein, Gide, and Cocteau rivaled the experience itself. Unlike Ernest Hemingway, whom Bowles once met in Paris, it was not that he wanted to be a part of any artistic community in Europe; he simply wanted to meet those who were. "I suppose I felt that I was taking pot shots at clay pigeons: 'Pop! Down goes Gertrude. Pop! Down goes André Gide. Pop! Down goes Jean Cocteau!' It was silly of me, of course."[9]

Later, to meet Manuel de Falla, one of Spain's most important composers, Bowles took a train to Granada, knocked on de Falla's door, and was invited in. "He didn't know me. One might expect a young man of twenty to have progressed beyond such naive behavior, but not I," observed Bowles.[10]

Although Copland, still in New York, worried that his pupil was getting little work done in Paris, Bowles assured him that despite appearances he had completed a two-movement sonata for flute and piano and was working then on a nocturne. Faithful throughout his life to his habit of making all sorts of lists, Bowles recorded, in addition to the people he met, the concerts he attended and his reactions to them. In one entry he wrote: "Milhaud gets worse. He has a propensity for mixing his major and minor chords, and that's his most distinctive feature." On another page in his diary, he declared: "Prokofiev is hopelessly meaningless." Not to have kept his date with Prokofiev before fleeing Paris in 1929 was fortuitous, insisted Bowles, who could not imagine the kind of life such study, had he pursued it, might have entailed. His only regret was having upset Madame Daniloff since it was she who had arranged the meeting with Prokofiev. For a time, Copland wanted Bowles to study with Nadia Boulanger, but the idea did not appeal to him. Bowles insisted that it was only Copland with whom he wanted to work.[11]

Meanwhile, the prospect of being on his own in Paris *without*

Copland assured Bowles of time to pursue his interests as he saw fit. His new idol was Jean Cocteau, whose theatrics were constant during the several occasions to which he was witness. It was as though Cocteau were playing charades and illustrating his remarks through mime and caricature. Bowles was highly amused when he witnessed Cocteau crawling across the floor in imitation of a bear; on another occasion, Cocteau was a succession of disdainful ushers at the new Paramount Theatre in Paris. Bowles likened the constant agitation of Cocteau's hands to a choreography perfectly devised to mimic his speech.[12]

Bowles was invited to tea a second time by Samuel Putnam and Harold Salemson, founders of the *New Review*, a journal in which he, too, had published. Since Charles Henri Ford, who also had published in the *New Review*, was now in Paris, Bowles asked Putnam if he might bring Ford along with him. Hearing nothing to the contrary, they arrived on the appointed day. "We did not enjoy ourselves," said Bowles. "Putnam served us no tea, and we had made a rather long trip to Fontenay, where he lived. I never knew what to make of his inhospitality since it was he who extended the invitation." Bowles surmised that Putnam may have had a date that evening, or that Ford had inadvertently offended him, such as turning down something submitted by Putnam to *Blues* before Ford shut it down and followed Djuna Barnes to Paris. Although Bowles appeared to take disappointment lightly, he worried endlessly later about some gaffe on his part.[13]

Bowles's commitment to the arts continued to be fueled by Roditi, whose poetry had appeared in some of the same issues of *transition* and *Tambour* in which Bowles's work had been published, and Bowles was immensely fond of the poems he had solicited from Roditi for the *Messenger*. Roditi, too, was surprised at how much they had in common. Both were born in 1910, their natal hours marked by breach births and forceps deliveries. Also like Bowles, Roditi played the piano, painted, wrote poetry, and manifested so many talents in his youth that he was single-minded about none. He, too, had been a restless undergraduate student and told no one when he left Balliol

College at Oxford. Roditi admitted being drawn sexually to men, but he also liked women and sometimes went to bed with them. Bowles, too, was attracted sexually to men, but at age twenty-one had "played around" only with Billy Hardy and did not consider such encounters copulation.[14]

Upon Copland's arrival in Paris in mid-April 1931, Bowles could hardly wait to tell him of their invitation to dinner by Stein and Toklas. Although he was convinced that Copland's and Stein's attraction to each other would be mutual, he also knew that Stein had no interest in his or Copland's music unless she, too, could be involved in some way. Bowles recognized that it was the theatrics of the event, rather than the music itself, that she found engaging.

A week later they arrived in Berlin, where Copland stayed in a well-appointed flat on Steinplatz and Bowles in the private home of the Baronin von Massenbach, an impoverished Englishwoman who allowed him to work on her Bechstein in the music room and served him breakfast trays of hot chocolate and freshly picked strawberries topped with whipped cream. Bowles concluded that he was laying the foundation for the liver complaints that plagued him later, but the breakfasts of the Baronin were among the "high points" of his Berlin sojourn.

Each morning before presenting himself at Copland's door to begin their two-hour lesson, Bowles dressed carefully in a suit, white shirt, and tie, then meticulously arranged a monogrammed white handkerchief in his breast pocket. After his lesson, he accompanied Copland to the Café des Westens to join Christopher Isherwood, Stephen Spender, and cabaret singer Jean Ross, to whom Roditi had already written letters of introduction. Bowles was offended that his new acquaintances, despite the introductory letters, seemed to treat him with good-humored condescension, whereas they tended to hang on every word of Copland's without question. "I suppose I was somewhat jealous," admitted Bowles.[15]

Despite his intention to study German formally, he soon abandoned that idea. The Germans he saw on the boulevards and in the cafés took him for a native with his fair skin, blue eyes, and golden hair, and his unwillingness to talk with them they attributed to shyness. He merely nodded agreeably, a habit he had developed successfully over the years whether or not he agreed with what was being said. Bowles also found himself seeking out "details of behavior that goaded them into angry expostulation," such as tapping a fast rhythm with a coin on a café table or resting his foot on the rung of a chair opposite his own. "Anything they were not used to seeing or experiencing infuriated them because it was not in their manual."[16]

In Berlin, Bowles had the feeling that all of life was being directed by Austrian film director Fritz Lang. Life in Germany during pre–World War II seemed sinister "because of the discrepancy between those who had it and those who didn't. The 'haves' were going hog-wild while the 'have-nots' seethed with hatred. A black cloud of hatred was over the whole east end of the city, and one felt catastrophe in the air," observed Bowles. Whereas Copland was impatient to return to Paris, convinced that he could work there with less stress, Bowles insisted that there still were "too many people he wanted to meet elsewhere in Europe" and was not ready to go back even though it meant forgoing for a time his study with Copland.

One person he wanted to meet was Carlo Suarès, a wealthy Egyptian architect who had moved to Paris to become a banker. Bowles had heard of Suarès through *Carnets*, a theosophical journal devoted to the writings of Krishnamurti, who lived in southern Holland. Suarès was presently the guest of Krishnamurti at Kasteel Eerde, and Bowles was invited to join them. Since only Indians could stay within the castle gates, he and Suarès slept in an apartment outside the compound and took their meals with their host. Exhilarated by the philosophical conversations of Krishnamurti and Suarès during their daily walks, Bowles listened carefully. He had glimpsed Krishnamurti's face many times in a photograph that Mary Robbins Mead kept on her desk at Holden Hall since she, too, was a theosophist, and he now felt privileged to know Krishnamurti personally.

Meanwhile, from Paris, Copland complained to Bowles about

his apparent lack of seriousness as a composer and urged him to settle down. Bowles refused to feel guilty. In a postcard to Roditi posted in Munich, he wrote of his joy at having attended a performance of Stravinsky's opera-oratorio *Oedipus Rex*, and from Heidelberg he wrote of exploring the castle with a flashlight under a full moon.[17] In Hanover he met sculptor Kurt Schwitters, whom he accompanied by trolley in search of refuse for the sculptures he was constructing. The bowl of a tin spoon, a broken thermos, a square of wire screening, mosquito netting, bits of paper and rags, broken metal objects, a stiff hospital bandage, shards of milk bottles, china, and glassware, all became a part of Schwitters's creations.[18] Schwitters also composed vocal sonatas, which he called syllable poetry. One such poem Bowles relished and recited to Copland began:

Lanke trr gll.
Pe pe pe pe pe
Ooka. Ooka. Ooka. Ooka.
Lanke trr gll.

Later Bowles notated the words, rhythm, and vocal inflections of Schwitters's recitation and used it without change as a frame for the theme of a rondo movement of a sonata for oboe and clarinet. It was this sonata that Copland presented in December 1931 in London's Aeolian Hall.[19]

From Roditi, Bowles learned of two recently published magazines that especially interested him: *Le Grand Jeu*, founded and edited by several dissident surrealists, and an "anti-literary journal," *Cahiers de l'Étoile*. By return mail, Bowles sent Roditi his own new poetic prose piece, untitled, which began: "Somewhere there is a furious vermillion hiding for you at the top of a flight of stairs. In Crimea on docks at dawn it stoops sighing for you."[20]

Another writer whose work fascinated Bowles that year was Bob Brown, who solicited from him a contribution to his "Readies" for Bob Brown's Reading Machine. Bowles was amazed upon learning of

Brown's reading machine in an article published in the June 1930 issue of *transition*, which declared that there was a critical need for his invention, which Brown described as a "light-weight, simple apparatus that one could attach to an electrical outlet and read novels of 100,000 words in ten minutes. The printing was done microscopically by a new photographic process on a transparent roll able to carry the contents of a book on something as small as a typewriter ribbon." In soliciting contributors, Brown advised them to eliminate articles, pronouns, adjectives, and other connectives since most readers could get the gist of a piece without them, and to use, instead, dots, dashes, and other signifiers of missing words and phrases so that the thrust of the piece could move smoothly.[21] Intrigued by Brown's invention, Bowles and many other expatriate Americans living in Paris at the time, some thirty-nine in all, contributed pieces unlike anything they had created in the past. Bowles called his own piece "June-Twelve-Dirge," having written it on June 12, 1931. The opening paragraph established his unique text, form, and tone, and the seventy-six lines that followed looked much like the first six:

> *IS-there-depth-to-beginning . . while-below-worm-turns . . turning-in-hedgerows-turning-?-? . . asparagus--helms-us-into-bed . . bridges-of-asparagus . . hey----nonnynonny-no . . IS-there-plumb-for-sores-silksores--while-blowing-thousand-roses . . WHITE-while-wilmy --grillows-wail-?-satinflirks-upyawning.*

"It's not a poem, of course. It doesn't mean anything, but I had fun writing it," he informed Brown, who published at year's end three hundred copies of "Readies."[22]

Shortly after his return to Paris in August 1931, having left Copland in Berlin, Bowles was invited to join Stein and Toklas in the country home they had recently leased outside Belley, in the hamlet of Bilignin, France. Bowles described the house as a miniature château with thick walls and floors slanting in various directions. "If you went straight through the house, you came out into a garden whose farther edge was a parapet, and below was the Rhône Valley, checkered with planted fields." At Stein's insistence, Bowles dressed himself in short pants and romped with Basket, her standard poodle. Although Bowles was twenty, Stein viewed him as a prepubescent adolescent, and he, in turn, thought of her as "a sort of very loving grandmother, very warm and motherly, and lots of bosom."

Bowles had been in Belley less than a week when he received word that Copland was arriving the next day and would need to be fetched at the station in Culoz. Their plan was to stay three days with Stein and Toklas, then leave by bus from Aix-les-Bains to Grenoble and proceed to Nice for the remainder of the summer. To Daniel Burns, he wrote that he was "getting a light on Miss Stein's own works," and that she had set him "right." There was "nothing in her works save the sense."[23]

Bowles was astonished several years later to hear that Stein had declared him the "most spoiled, insensitive, and self-indulgent young man she had ever seen," and that his "colossal complacency in rejecting all values appalled her."[24] Although he did not take issue overtly with her pronouncements, he suspected that what she said was true. Years later Bowles regretted not taking Stein's advice when she first offered it. He thought her "superb at setting the stage for other actors, then retiring from view, knowing that she would hear about their performances later and be entertained again."[25]

Whereas he and Copland had planned to spend the late summer in Nice a few days after Copland's arrival from Berlin, Stein urged them to go instead to Tangier, where rents were cheap, and pianos could be had "for practically nothing." They must stay at the Hotel Villa de France since that was where she and Toklas had stayed twice. After a final week with Stein and Toklas in their home in Belley, Bowles and Copland left from Marseilles aboard the SS *Iméréthie II* despite a series of mishaps that almost caused them to miss their ship.[26] Upon boarding, they learned that Tangier was not a scheduled port of call in Morocco, and that they would have to leave the ship at Ceuta in Spanish Morocco and travel overland to Tangier.[27] "The journey itself was unforgettable," said Bowles. "On the second day I went on deck at dawn, saw the rugged line of mountains of Algeria ahead, and felt a great excitement. It was as if some interior mechanism had been set in motion by the sight of the approaching land. As I stood in the wind looking at the mountains ahead, I felt a stirring of the engine within, and it was as if I were drawing close to the solution of an as-yet-unposed problem."[28]

Years later Bowles admitted that everything he had written about his crossing to Morocco with Copland was true, but that his words were layered and conveyed a deeper meaning. To his biographer, Virginia Spencer Carr, he declared: "At this point in my life I had never had what I considered real sex with anyone, male or female. On our first night out, Aaron seduced me. I hated it, and I vowed that never again would I allow myself to be abused in this manner. Even worse, Aaron was my teacher, and sex should not have been a part of our relationship."[29]

The passengers whose destinations were Ceuta and beyond were able to leave the ship in Oran while supplies and cargo were hoisted aboard. Although ambivalent about going ashore, Copland gamely agreed to explore the city with Bowles. Suddenly they found themselves looking down the barrel of a rifle in the hands of an Algerian soldier who ordered them to halt, turn around, and return on foot to the boat. When Copland voiced relief that they would not be staying in Algeria, Bowles replied: "Morocco's much wilder." Until their arrival in Ceuta, neither had set foot on Spanish soil. In Ceuta, Bowles had the impression of "something great and exciting happening somewhere offstage." Alfonso XIII had fled Spain on April 14, 1931, but did not abdicate until ten years later. The agitation observed there was part of the general euphoria evident throughout Spain.[30]

From Ceuta they traveled by train alongside the rugged Rif Mountains to Tetuán, a town settled by Moorish exiles from Spain in the sixteenth century. Bowles noted that the Moroccans of Tetuán seemed even more excited than the Spaniards in Ceuta, and that each gave the impression of performing in a huge drama. When Copland exclaimed that the whole country was a madhouse, Bowles replied: "It's a continuous performance, anyway."[31]

Kristians Tonny, a surrealist Dutch painter educated in France and a former friend of Stein, was already in Tangier with a girlfriend when Bowles and Copland arrived there. At one point, Tonny drew Copland aside and asked if the young man with him (Bowles) was "slightly off his head." Copland reported Tonny's comments to Bowles, who decided at once that he liked Tonny even better for having made them. Still looking for a place to stay for at least a month, Bowles came across a run-down villa near the top of what the locals called the Old Mountain, a heavily forested area three kilometers from town. His challenge now was to convince Copland that the house was desirable despite its lack of running water. The rent was feasible since it included a servant who fixed breakfast and lunch, shopped daily for food, tended a well-established garden, and collected water in pails from nearby wells on the property.

To bathe, Bowles and Copland took a footpath across the road and down a steep incline to a level beach, where they disrobed and slipped into the clear blue water of the Strait of Gibraltar. There was no doubt that Bowles enjoyed being with Copland more during their few days together in Tangier than ever before.

Although Stein had assured them that finding a piano to rent in Tangier would be no problem, the one they finally located was delivered on the back of a donkey that balked at the entrance gate and dropped its load upon the ground. To Stein, Copland wrote: "We have an African piano that sounds like hell! We tried one man who put it more out of tune than it was before he touched it. These are problems you are happily free of, but they make my stay somewhat precarious." Copland did not mention to Stein that the furniture they rented was delivered a few pieces at a time in a horse-drawn cart. To Bowles, Copland admitted privately that he would have preferred to be on the Riviera, but he agreed to stay on for a month.

Upbeat as usual in most of his letters to friends, Bowles wrote Bruce Morrissette that the piano was not as bad as they feared, and that the house was "swell, with palms and olives waving in the second-story windows and a view toward the mountains far away south; the town itself is too beautiful for words."[32]

Bowles also began writing long and entertaining letters to his mother as though he were addressing an intimate friend. At least twice a week he wrote in great detail of almost everything he saw and felt. Meanwhile, each morning Copland continued giving harmony lessons to Bowles, who worked lying in a deck chair in the lower garden of the house to avoid what he called Copland's "chordal laboratory" while composing his *Short Symphony*. Bowles had the piano to himself each afternoon while Copland napped upstairs. By mid-September, Bowles had finished his sonata for oboe and clarinet and was doing copy work for Copland, who insisted on paying him ten francs a page.

"Aaron may direct a chamber music concert in London in December, and I am trying to get him to have my piece played at it," Bowles wrote his mother. "He also wants me to write a string trio for the League of Composers, but I am not sure I could do it before next summer."[33]

Although Copland was impatient to return to Berlin, he agreed to accompany Bowles to Fez, an eight-hour train trip. Upon checking into the Hotel Ariana, situated within the ancient gates of the city, they ate a leisurely dinner then explored their new environs by moonlight. Each morning they had coffee and croissants on the ramparts just outside the windows of their rooms, and ate their other meals in a Jewish restaurant in the Mellah. Although Copland made clear his impatience to leave Fez, he agreed to stay a fifth week, his low-keyed demeanor in sharp contrast to Bowles's exuberance.[34]

Harry Dunham, the student at Princeton whom Bowles had met in Philadelphia at a performance of Stravinsky's *Sacre du Printemps*, envied his rootlessness and regretted his own need for accountability to his parents, who believed him to be in Dresden studying dance and expected him to call home from there on his twenty-first birthday. When he learned that Bowles was in Morocco, Dunham wired him that he was "on his way" and clamored for "untold adventures."[35]

To Copland, who returned to London shortly after Dunham appeared, Bowles wrote: "Harry's money disappears visibly, daily. I wonder how long it will hold out inasmuch as I am living entirely on it. Living with him in such a manner is a ticklish business. His strange behavior and fits of temper are quite irrational."[36] At this point, Bowles was not explicit to anyone that he had been involved sexually with Dunham, but friends who knew them both did not doubt the nature of their liaison.

In Marrakech, Dunham had singled out an Arab youth, Abdelkader, who was being mistreated by his employer, the manager of the hotel in which he and Bowles were staying. Abdelkader's job was to lie across the doorway to the street until dawn to guard the guests against the "dishonesty and savagery in Morocco." When Dunham asked indignantly if the youth could not at least have a mat on which to lie, the French proprietress replied: "He's already so spoiled he's no good. I'd fire him except that he owes me two months' work for one of my husband's shirts he ruined trying to iron it. He's an animal, that one!"[37]

Dunham already had initiated the essential paperwork for Abdelkader to leave the country, but Bowles was charged with completing the task, viewing it as a payback for all that Dunham had done for him. To his mother, he wrote: "Of course, I was wrong. The whole process is maddening since it means endless daily trips to the police station and to notaries to confront and satisfy those who insist that they have a lien against the youth."[38] Bowles thought it prudent not to elaborate.

Finally, Abdelkader was allowed to leave the country with Bowles serving as his surrogate guardian. Crossing over to Spain, they made their way to Seville, where they were invited by a Western couple to attend a cabaret with them. They were sitting at their table when Abdelkader suddenly reached out and touched one of the dancers as she swirled past them. Astonished that he felt actual flesh, he practically swooned at the realization that she was not a projection upon a screen. In Morocco he had seen dancing girls only in films. When they visited the Prado, Abdelkader was disappointed that the figures in the Francisco de Goya paintings did not move off their canvases; similarly, upon viewing the Hieronymus Bosch paintings, Abdelkader was convinced that Satan was causing the figures to move. In Paris he was horrified when he mistook the currant jelly on the brioches for congealed blood. Bowles was sufficiently fascinated by Abdelkader that he could hardly wait to introduce him to Stein and Toklas, certain that they would consider him a worthy specimen to examine under their microscope.

"You must come tonight and bring your young man," Stein insisted, adding that Joan Miró and a few other guests would join them. Never having met Miró, Bowles was eager to have a private conversation with him while Abdelkader sat beside Toklas as she engaged in verbal intimacies and presided over the teapot and cups. Bowles said later that when he told Miró about Abdelkader's behavior at the Prado, the artist agreed with Abdelkader about the Bosches. "They did, indeed, move," said Miró.[39]

On December 8, 1931, Bowles left Paris for London to attend the rehearsals of his Sonata for Oboe and Clarinet in Aeolian Hall, and to meet, at last, Edouard Roditi, whom he described as "tall, suave, and polyglot."[40] Copland was to play his own *Piano Variations* and perform Carlos Chávez's Sonatina for Piano since Chávez himself could not come from Mexico; Roger Sessions was to play his Piano Sonata No. 1, and Virgil Thomson was to arrive early enough to coach the singers of his cantata based on Stein's text *Capital Capitals* and to play the piano part at the concert. Also on the program was Israel Citkowitz's "Joyce Songs."

In his review of the concert for *Modern Music*, Henry Boys declared that Copland's piece was the only interesting one on the program, although he did mention Bowles's Sonata for Oboe and Clarinet and liked the composer's "sure sense of style."[41] Although Bowles did not agree with Boys's review of the concert as a whole, and certainly not of his own composition, he was delighted that it had been commented upon at all.

After the concert, Bowles met Harry Dunham's sister, Amelia, who observed that she disliked the entire program. "For some reason my piece, even more than the others, incurred her wrath, perhaps because it had been described in the morning newspaper as pagan," said Bowles. Later they found themselves on the same ferry crossing the English Channel to return to Paris. "Amelia said to me, 'If I had a little boy and he wrote a piece like that, I'd know what to do with him.'"

"What would you do?" Bowles asked.

"I'd see that he got hospital treatment," she replied.[42]

Upon Bowles's return to Paris, he put Amelia's annoying comments out of his mind and was delighted when he met an attractive French artist named Anne Miracle Mannheim who did tiny Klee-like engravings. "We sat in Montparnasse bars and talked so much about skiing that before we knew it we were in a third-class coach on the train to Torino, drinking large quantities of red wine. I had been spending many sleepless nights, and the one on the train was one too many." In Torino, Bowles went directly to the hospital. "Anne wired Harry Dunham, and he came too. When I was able, Anne and I went up to Clavières, where Anne did some skiing while I recuperated. Of course she had no idea of the true nature of my illness," said Bowles, who suspected that he had contracted syphilis, but was uncertain whom to blame. In addition to Copland as a possible source of his illness, Bowles thought that it could have been Dunham from whom he had contracted it since Dunham had learned in London that he, too, had syphilis. Dunham, in turn, was furious because he suspected Bowles to have been the source of his illness and probably had informed Amelia of that possibility. If so, that information may have accounted for her animosity toward him, and for Dunham's going immediately to Torino to learn if Bowles's illness was syphilis.

Bowles returned to Paris with Anne Miracle Mannheim, who invited him to recuperate in her flat, where she promised him regular and nutritious meals. "Then we heard that her husband might return from Germany any day. She did not live with him in Paris, but he always came to see her. It was no pleasure, living in expectation of his imminent arrival," said Bowles, who was troubled, too, because he had not heard from Copland since leaving London.

In mid-January he heard at last from Copland and replied immediately that his letter had helped clarify the situation. "It is rather difficult to be among a great many people and to feel rotten and not be able to tell anyone so, and why." He told Copland, too, that he also suffered from acute tonsillitis and awoke each morning with a swollen neck. "I gargle and can scarcely walk certain days after *piqûres* [the doctor's injections], and yes, I am miserable."[43]

To Roditi, Bowles wrote from Boulogne-sur-Seine: "I daresay I feel better but not awfully much. Everyone must surely think I am mad, but there is nothing I can do about it save to make a great many confidences I have no desire to make."[44]

Bowles worried relentlessly over his predicament and told Copland that he kept wondering how he got sick, "how long it had been that way, how long it will be that way, why it hurts, and several dozen other wonderings. I see very little use in anything. My fury at being ill has abated, and I accept it as one of the conditions under which I must live, but when I put all the conditions together, the fury returns." Still ill in February 1932 upon his return to Paris, Bowles seethed and could do nothing constructive except to write to those who knew of his situation. Then he discovered that he had been maligned to Stein by both Dunham and his sister. "Gertrude never changed her mind about anything. She did not have a mind that could be changed. This time when I telephoned her, she said: 'Why don't you go to Mexico? You'd last about two days there.'"[45]

Bowles was astonished when Dunham again invited him to share his flat in Paris, but reasoned that he needed Bowles as a buffer between Abdelkader and Amelia, who had moved into her brother's flat upon her return from London. "Obviously it was a trade-off. Neither could stand the other, nor could I," said Bowles. "But at least it was a place to stay, and the piano was handy."

At lunch in Paris with Carlos Suarès, whom he had last seen with Krishnamurti in Holland, Bowles confided that Amelia Dunham had demanded that he submit to a spinal tap in the hospital to determine if he was syphilitic. Suarès urged Bowles to move in with him while his wife was on a pilgrimage with Krishnamurti, and Bowles accepted the invitation. "Be careful, that woman's mad," warned Suarès when he learned that Bowles was still working each morning at the piano in Dunham's flat. Bowles was engaged then in composing the lyrics and music for a suite of six songs to be performed in the spring at Yaddo. The work was going well until the morning he discovered Dunham's flat in disarray and most of his clothes missing. When he heard Amelia come in, Bowles ran downstairs to inform her of what he had concluded was a robbery, but when he saw her face, he realized that she knew about it already.[46]

With a smirk, she declared: "Abdelkader wanted to go to Africa, so he went. I took him to Louis Vuitton and bought him some luggage, and he went."

"And my clothes?" Bowles shouted. "And all of Harry's?"

"If you have street Arabs in the house, you expect to lose things, don't you?" she replied. "I told him to fill his valises, and then I took him to the Gare d'Orsay."[47]

Several weeks later, a Frenchman newly arrived from Marrakech told Bowles that he had seen Abdelkader day after day in Djemâa el Fna "selling his booty, piece by piece, to passing Moroccans."[48]

"I did not throw up my hands in despair," said Bowles, "but I trusted that I had seen the last of that scoundrel."

Despite the disruption, he finished his songs for Copland and sent them to New York in time for Yaddo's 1932 spring concert of contemporary American music. Since Bowles had no intention of attending the concert himself, he asked Copland, with whom he was again on good terms, to give copies of his songs to Claire Reis, director of the League of Composers.[49] Bowles knew Reis only through letters, for she had asked if he would be interested in translating several French articles for publication in *Modern Music.* Four months before the Yaddo concerts, Reis published two of Bowles's translations in *Modern Music* (Arthur Hoérée's "The Renaissance of Choral Music" and

Raymond Petit's "Latin Gaiety Today"), and in the same issue Virgil Thomson's invited essay on Copland. As editor of *Modern Music*, Reis had chosen Copland as the most fitting contemporary subject to initiate a new series of essays by composers on other composers, and later chose Bowles to write an essay on Thomson.[50]

It was important to Bowles that Copland understand his rationale for returning to North Africa instead of going to Yaddo for the concerts or remaining in Paris. "I object heartily to Paris and have no desire to go on living there," he began. "I do not want to live in any city, but as far away as possible from all of them."[51] Before leaving Paris, Bowles took a few lessons in orchestration from Vittorio Rieti, an Egyptian-born Italian composer who had moved to Paris in 1925 to write ballets for Diaghilev. Although Bowles considered him "quite the best for orchestration," he was convinced that the "only good composer, with the exception of Bach, was Stravinsky."[52]

Bowles might not have left Paris when he did had he not met, through Virgil Thomson and Charles Henri Ford, John Trounstine, a literary agent from Cincinnati who was celebrating the sale of the film rights to William Burnett's novel *Little Caesar*, based on the life of Al Capone. The mood at dinner was jubilant, and before the evening ended, Bowles had accepted Trounstine's invitation to travel with him through Spain and Morocco.

"Virgil and I marveled at Paul's ability and ease in reeling in a new patron," declared Ford, who admitted having little money himself those days and so would have welcomed such a patron. "But Paul was charming and good company, so it was a balanced trade-off,"[53] he added. Two days after meeting Trounstine, Bowles was seated beside him on a train bound for Barcelona, and from there to Valencia, Alicante, Elche (an ancient Roman colony held for centuries by the Moors), and eventually to Tangier and Fez. Whereas Bowles had no desire to linger in Tangier, he wanted to accompany Trounstine to Fez in order to introduce him to Abdallah Drissi, who, with his brother, claimed to be the sole remaining direct descendants of the founder of Morocco and had entertained him lavishly in 1931. "I was walking ahead with Abdallah, and Trounstine was following with the Arab escorts when he suddenly started shouting and accusing me of telling Abdallah that he was a Jew. I had no idea what he meant, but he kept shouting, and finally, enough was enough. Without a word, I strode the dozen paces that separated us and struck him solidly on the mouth. We had no words. Trounstine checked out of the hotel that day and I never saw him again. Fortunately he had already bought me a return ticket to Paris, to which I returned in mid-May."[54]

Temperatures were still mild in Paris, but Bowles felt cold and light-headed and feared that he was getting sick again. He had been back a week when Carlos Suarès noticed that his face was flushed. "I've seen a lot of typhoid in Egypt, and I think you have it, Paul. You probably contracted it in Morocco." Since Bowles was an American citizen, Suarès was able to check him into the American Hospital of Paris in Neuilly-sur-Seine, a few miles northwest of the city, where doctors diagnosed that he had contracted typhoid A, for which there was no drug to counteract the disease. The standard treatment was to withhold food, give the patient cold baths, and pack him in ice while the fever ran its course. During his first two weeks in the hospital Bowles was too sick to know who may have visited his bedside, but eventually he was allowed to sit up briefly when callers were announced. To his amazement, his first visitor was Amelia Dunham, "wreathed in smiles." Then she declared: "At last I've got you where I want you!" Bowles seized a glass of water from his bedside table and hurled it at her.

"I had no idea why she came, and she never returned. It was the last I saw of her."[55]

When Virgil Thomson visited his hospital room, Bowles gave him the three movements to his cello and harp piece that he had already completed before the onset of his illness and asked that he try them at home. When Bowles's mother wrote that she wanted to come to Paris to help nurse him, he suggested that she wait until he was able to leave the hospital. Rena wrote sparingly of "things at home," and focused, instead, upon her son's health, his composing, and their possible trips together when he was well enough to travel.

Bowles hoped to be fully recovered when his mother arrived so that they would be free to travel. Bruce Morrissette, now enrolled at the University of Grenoble, declared that he would check Bowles out of the hospital and take him to the cottage he had rented in Grenoble, where his mother could join them. In Palma de Mallorca, in Spain's Balearic Islands, Bowles spent two days recuperating from sunstroke while his mother read Richard Hughes's *A High Wind in Jamaica* to him. "It was like being a child all over again," he admitted, basking anew in her attention.[56] By mid-September they were back in Paris, where to Bowles's consternation, Abdelkader appeared unexpectedly at the door of his hotel room. "My mother and I had just finished having tea, and out of politeness I let him in. To my utter astonishment, upon being introduced to her, he sat upon her lap, and like a child, began playing absently with her pearls." Bowles got rid of him shortly, which prompted his mother to ask: "Do you think he is all right in the head?" Bowles shook his head, but spared her the details.[57]

Upon her departure, Bowles hurried to the Mediterranean coast to spend a few days with Maurice Grosser and Virgil Thomson on the Île de Porquerolles, where they had vacationed together in the past. From Monte Carlo, Bowles dropped a note to Thomson to acknowledge what he had been up to of late: "I have dinner tonight with a charming gent, King Alfonso's cousin. I may go to Paris with him later for a week or so. He suggested going to Cairo, but I am trying to sell him on Timbuktu in January. I know you detest dead places, but I still enjoy them."[58] Bowles then took a bus to Cagnes-sur-Mer to see George Antheil and his Hungarian wife, Böske, whom he called upon as usual without an appointment. "Once again I was gratified by a friendly reaction to my importune behavior. It would have been so much simpler for them to put me off, but they asked me to dinner. Then George sat at the piano for hours reading and singing the scores of Kurt Weill's *Three Penny Opera* and *Mahagonny*. He was engaged in a propaganda campaign to interest composers in writing operas, which he claimed was the musical form of the future."[59]

In a letter, Bowles asked Virgil Thomson if he would be willing to take another look at his arrangement of the tango he had reworked for clarinet, bassoon, violin, cello, and piano after showing it to him in the hospital. "Aaron writes glowing praise of the third part of the flute piece [Sonata No. 1 for Flute and Piano], which I have just finished. He gets quite wild and puts me at the top of his list of younger composers, but pleads that I complete my studies of counterpoint and orchestration. Perhaps next year it would be best to go back to him, because he says: 'Sometimes I flatter myself to think I am your only possible teacher.' Certainly no one else has as much interest."[60]

Bowles knew that he would not study counterpoint and orchestration with anyone but Copland, yet even if his mentor were willing, he was not ready to return to New York. Instead, he boarded a French ship bound for Algeria. For Bowles, there were still too many unanswered questions where Copland was concerned, and his own urgent desire for adventure took precedence.

CHAPTER FIVE

A Lovesick Bowles in Algeria. Disillusionment, Estrangement, and Success in New York

(1933–1936)

"Writing music is a means of wishing away time. . . . I want to see you. It will cease to be life and death once I hear from you that there is some way I can return and live."[1]

—Paul Bowles to Aaron Copland,
January 1933, Laghouat, Algeria

More than anything, Bowles wanted to resume a pupil-teacher relationship with Copland, but his letters indicated a desire for a more intimate relationship. "I live in hopes of hearing from Aaron, but he never writes, and I have no idea even what country he is in," Bowles wrote his mother from Laghouat.[2] The ink from his pen was barely dry when he received a letter from Copland saying that he was en route that very moment to New York. Copland made no mention of being accompanied by Victor Kraft, a young violinist, who had been with him throughout his stay in Mexico. At this point, Bowles's own wanderings and overwhelming passion to see far more of the world than he presently knew contributed to his decision to spend the next few months in the Algerian Sahara.

In the bar his first night aboard a French ship bound for Algiers,

Bowles was told by a French soldier of a "marvelous oasis, Ghardaïa," in the heart of the Sahara that one reached by way of Laghouat. Bowles was determined to go there, too, but as usual, liked having a friend at his side. To Charles Henri Ford, who, like Bowles, loved exploring new places so long as he had someone to explore them with, Bowles wrote of the long ride across mountains and desert from Algiers to Laghouat, but assured him that Ghardaïa would be worth it. "One can't even buy a bar of chocolate there, but ah! the *palmeraie* is magnificent!"[3] When Bowles thought that Ford might actually join him in Ghardaïa, he implored Ford to bring him a copy of *The Young and Evil*, which Ford had coauthored with Parker Tyler, his collaborator on *Blues*. "I have nothing to read save Proust, Stein, and Lautréamont, and all that is a bit rarified."[4]

Finally, in Ghardaïa without Ford, Bowles was welcomed by the regional commander of the military outpost there and informed that the only house available was at the edge of the desert. The commander took it upon himself to send a prospective servant to Bowles, whom he chose not to hire because the man failed to look him in the eye during the interview. A second candidate, Aazous, was blind in one eye, and Bowles hired him on the spot. He knew shortly that he had made the proper choice when Aazous saved him from carbon monoxide poisoning, Bowles unwittingly having burned his terra-cotta brazier inside with no ventilation. Bowles's only recollection of the event was being led ten kilometers across the wasteland in a blinding sun to the commander's house, where he recuperated and was offered the use of his host's piano.[5]

To his mother Bowles wrote that the outpost's commander knew every trick of survival as well as gracious living, having lived in the Sahara for eleven years. He also wrote of an extraordinary festival he had happened upon by the light of a great bonfire of dry palm branches. On one hand, life in the desert was full of surprises, but on the other, it was a matter of putting one foot down, then another, then another and another, and the days passed without incident. Finally, the silence got to him to the point that he returned to Laghouat to reclaim from a storage locker his luggage, clothes, and books, having taken with him only Proust's *Remembrance of Things Past* and something of Stein's, then to find a piano and resume his composing.

Virgil Thomson had written Copland that what Bowles was most interested in learning was how to write for all the instruments, not just the piano, and to compose in free form. "He is learning by doing, and all the lessons he needs he gets from you and me and others by showing the finished piece and asking: 'What's wrong here?' He shocks Bernard [Faÿ] and Gertrude because he refuses to lead the conventional life of a young man of talent. He prefers the life of a *poule de luxe*, and lives quite well that way."[6]

In Laghouat on Christmas Day 1933, Bowles dined on oysters on the half-shell, filet beefsteak, roast turkey, peas, cheeses, fruit, and rosé wine. "One feels like a Russian nobleman before the war, with his six hundred slaves!" he wrote his mother.[7] He was even more impressed, in a ghastly way, by the food being gulped down raw, enormous red grasshoppers "with wings as thick as autumn leaves," by natives whose shriveled arms and legs were as black as coal. Many walked like spiders or dragged along like crabs. He described, also, the dark streets and houses decorated with bones, skulls, hooves, and horns, which he told his mother would make her shiver and perhaps even cry. Bowles could not remember ever seeing his mother cry. He also described to her a woman who resembled their first cook. The woman stood in front of his hotel, covered from head to foot with the tops and bottoms of tin cans. "Hundreds of bright discs hung from wires she had made into a girdle, which she constantly removed, examined, and put on again, talking all the while. Then she bent down to great clanking, and had a conversation with a mound of dust."[8] Bowles said that his mother loved his letters because he told her things she never could have imagined. He had already decided that if he could not find a piano in Algeria he would return to America; yet the thought of such an eventuality made him almost ill since he still had received no word from Copland that might assure him of a warm reception if he did go back home. To his surprise, Bowles discovered a harmonium in a missionary chapel, which the curé gave him permission to use daily if he wished, and just as suddenly the cantata he had been composing for weeks in his head now had a form of its own. Within a fortnight Bowles completed three movements of *Cantata: Par le Détroit* [By the Strait], a title he attributed to his preoccupation with dreams while living beside the Strait of Gibraltar. Later he concluded that *Dream Cantata* would have been a more fitting title since he had composed several sections of the work while he slept. Since early childhood Bowles had fantasized dreaming something in such detail that he could bring it "across the frontier intact," and now he had done that very thing.[9]

Still awaiting Ford in Ghardaïa, Bowles wrote Copland of what he had accomplished of late, which he juxtaposed with his complaint of how "dreadfully discouraging" it was to write him without any expectation of a reply. "I suppose it is like addressing one's self to a deity of whose existence one is not quite sure of. But Good God, I am desperate!"[10] Bowles insisted that he "must hear a bit of music, see someone, talk to someone, have a purpose other than making his francs go another week by getting himself invited to some frightful person's house."

To his mother Bowles wrote two or three times a week and made no attempt to disguise his feelings. In one letter he admitted being continually haunted by the passing hours, days, and weeks without any significant sense of accomplishment. He also feared being trapped under his father's roof and hoped that Copland would assure him that they might work together without interference, "at least for a time." Adding to his discouragement at this point was having been turned down for a John Simon Guggenheim Foundation grant because his application was late; even more devastating was a rejection letter for a second residency at Yaddo, where he had hoped that Copland would give him an hour or two during their leisure after dinner.

To address his dwindling finances, Bowles decided not to return to the house he had rented on the outskirts of Ghardaïa, but to move into a native hotel catering to itinerant drivers of produce trucks. Here he met George Turner, an undergraduate at Northwestern University who had taken a year off from his studies to travel. They began eating at the same table, and it was not long before they agreed to make a trip together. Once again Bowles had someone at his side who would take the initiative in their planning and make things happen. As Bowles insisted again and again, he did not make plans; it was a matter of who came along.

Bowles's contribution to his departure with Turner was selling the few pieces of furniture he had acquired of late and packing his books and a few cherished personal items. In Algiers, their first destination, Bowles and his companion spent hours each night exploring the Casbah and talking about where they should go next. Only once did Bowles venture alone into the Casbah, then outside the walls for what he hoped would be an extended hike in the moonlight along a country road. "It wasn't long before I realized that a yokel from the Casbah was following me, shouting imprecations against foreigners. I paid no attention, and bore the noise for a long time. At one point I did a rapid about-face and walked at my regular speed toward the man, colliding with him head-on. At that moment I drew back my fist and let him have it in the nose. Then I turned and continued to walk. He continued, also, but crying and shouting that I had broken his face. 'Now is when he'll throw a knife into my back,' I was thinking. When I heard him threaten to report the incident to the police, I relaxed. Algeria was a French colony, and the denizens of the Casbah took great pains to avoid any contact with the police. I felt doubly triumphant when I made it back to my room; I had defied the police, given an Algerian a bloody nose, and come away unscathed."[11]

Although Bowles eventually was able to rent a piano in Algiers, he seldom had access to it because it was in a piano shop that was usually closed. After three weeks in Algiers, they were ready to move on, but at this point *where* was of no particular concern. It was Bowles who came up with the idea to hire a driver and two camels to escort them across the northern tip of the Great Eastern Erg to El Oued, a three-day journey. Instead of saddles, they sat on blankets atop cartons containing food and water until the motion of the camel's gait became unbearable. Bowles preferred to trudge on foot. At night they slept on blankets a few feet from their driver and camels at *bordjes* that had been established by the French military a day's journey apart.[12]

In El Oued they dismissed their driver, then rode a Caterpillar tractor-truck to Nefta, which Bowles likened to a prolonged ride in a roller-coaster over the tops of dunes and down again. Finally, they emerged from the desert in the outpost town of Kairouan and went directly to a bank to cash traveler's checks, but the transaction was inexplicably declined. Traveling next to Tunis, they learned that Roosevelt had temporarily closed the banks in an attempt to derail the country's inflation. Officials at the American Embassy in Tunis confirmed the problem and advised them to borrow from friends.[13]

"What friends?" Bowles and his companion exclaimed, looking incredulously at each other. After wiring Morrissette to request enough money to cover their hotel bill, Bowles returned alone to Algiers, and Turner went north by ferry to Sicily. They parted company regretfully, but were confident that they would see each other again.[14]

In Algiers, Bowles learned that Copland would play Bowles's Sonata for Flute and Piano at a private concert in New York. Cheered considerably by the news, Bowles was optimistic that with his mentor's support his music would now be played in concert with increasing frequency. Copland also arranged for Bowles's Sonatina for Piano to be played and aired over the radio in midsummer. "Why don't you come, too, and hear it," suggested Copland. Bowles declined, having no assurance that Copland would be willing to work with him in an extended relationship. Before leaving Algiers, Bowles reported to Copland what he had completed of late: his Sonata for Flute and Piano, Sonatina for Piano, and a chamber piece, *Scènes d'Anabase*, derived from Saint-John Perse's *Anabase*, an epic poem depicting an extraordinary trek across the Gobi Desert in Asia.[15] He also mentioned having just read André Gide's autobiographical account of his expedition through Algeria and Tunisia. Even the thought of such a journey was exciting, and he longed to meet someone like George Turner who would travel with him. Meanwhile, he learned that Charles Henri Ford was already in Tangier and had no intention of joining him in Algiers and proceeding with him to Morocco as they had originally planned. Bowles went on to Tangier and rented a small house near the top of the cliffs on the Marshan. Except for its greatly diminished size, it was similar to the one that he and Copland had rented on the Old Mountain. It, too, had no running water, but, with its stunning view of the city and harbor beyond, he was delighted by his choice. Bowles intended to use it only as a studio, and to sleep and keep most of his belongings in a small hotel room in the Medina. Feeling responsible for Ford's being in Tangier at his encouragement, Bowles offered him the use of his sparsely furnished studio for sleeping, the only condition being that he was out by 1:30 p.m., Bowles's usual hour to begin work.

"Contrary to what Paul led me to believe, I found nothing exotic about Tangier, but it was cheap and Djuna Barnes joined me there," Ford reported later. "I was still in love with her and would have done anything for her. She was working on *Nightwood*, and I told her I would type it for her. I felt much as Paul did, that almost anything would be better than returning to America. Besides, I loved the beach and the sun once it stopped raining, and the weather was getting warm enough for me to swim and to dance on the beach."[16]

Bowles was astonished when he heard later that Ford had reportedly told a number of people that he and Djuna were charged a thousand francs for the several weeks they slept in his studio. "The very idea was preposterous. I gave it to them free, although they accepted it with the understanding that they would be nowhere around when I arrived in the afternoon to begin work. The arrangement was fine for about three days, after which I invariably found them still in bed."

"Oh Paul, you come so early," Ford called out in answer to Bowles's poundings.[17]

"I had a key, of course, but did not want to barge in on them.

Finally they moved into another house only a few hundred feet up the lane, where they lived Moroccan-style, on the floor."[18]

Bowles's habit that summer was to buy lunch in the Medina and eat it on the cliffs opposite his studio. Here he worked until 5:00 p.m., then packed up his materials in an attaché case and strode with it back into town. If his insistence upon prolonging his wanderings was compulsive, no less so was the fanatical manner in which he forced himself to work regularly each day.

Finally, in late May 1934, having reconciled himself to returning to New York, Bowles purchased a third-class ticket in Cádiz, Spain, for passage to San Juan, Puerto Rico. From there he wired his parents to let them know he was back in the Western Hemisphere, then stored his trunks and valises in a hotel and took a bus into the hills to a village called Barranquitas, where he settled in for a week with a piano and composed three new pieces, then jotted a note to Copland to announce that he was on his way to New York. "I want to see you terribly. Will it be possible for me to live in the city?" Then, more tenuously, he asked, "Is there hope for a happy life or not? These things you will tell me when you see me, but the questions are asked in case there is still an opportunity to accomplish something between the time you receive this, and the time you see me."[19] Bowles closed his letter with a few words in French: *"Mon cher, si tu savais combien je tiens à te voir!"* [My dear, if you knew how much I need to see you!]

Upon arrival in New York, Bowles found Copland polite but elusive. To Virgil Thomson, now in Paris, Bowles lamented that he had been back three weeks "and sick three weeks, naturally. Certainly nobody hates New York as much as I do. Aaron of course has a new pet so there is no snuggling there."[20] To Gertrude Stein, Bowles wrote similarly: "Aaron has a new pet, and since he was my only reason for returning, I feel deceived." Thomson was in Paris orchestrating Stein's libretto of *Four Saints in Three Acts*, in collaboration with her, and neither took time to address Bowles's laments.

Upon Bowles's return to New York, Copland downplayed their personal relationship and tried to engage him in activities that would help further his career as a composer. One of Copland's suggestions was that Bowles make an appointment with John Kirkpatrick, a concert pianist from Syracuse who had agreed to look over some of his music, and if he liked it, to play it over the air. In addition to his Sonatina for Piano, Bowles gave Kirkpatrick five new solo pieces he had written for piano: *Impasse de Tombouctou*; *La Femme de Dakar*; *Guayanilla* (composed during his spurt of creativity in Barranquitas); *Tamanar* (inspired by his visit to Agadir in 1931); and one simply titled *8*. Kirkpatrick told Bowles that he was not impressed by *Tamanar*, but asked for copies of the others.[21]

At loose ends again after a brief stay with his parents, Bowles was encouraged by Emma Ross to spend the summer with her in Westhampton, Massachusetts, where she was living with Orville Flint, a widower whose wife had recently committed suicide. Bowles's father had never been fond of Emma or her husband, whom she had divorced, and declared it fitting that his son move in with her.[22]

To Thomson, still in Paris, Bowles described his new environment and his adaptation to it. "Utter silence, utter country. And chastity, moreover! Since Morocco, without one break. It gets on one's nerves."[23] To Copland, to whom he continued to write but seldom saw, Bowles declared: "As to love, I am waiting to find some. So far it has really been buying and selling. I have tried to gyp wherever I could."[24] In another letter on the same topic, Bowles accused Copland of exaggerating when he claimed "that sex is here," then countered with an exaggeration of his own: "Where in this country can I have 35 or 40 different people a week, and never risk seeing any of them again? I hate America because I feel attached to it, and I don't want to feel that way." When Copland suggested that Bowles join him in a vacation house on the south end of Lake George, which had been offered him for the late summer, Bowles replied on September 2, 1933: "Would love to come," but "when?" The indefiniteness of Copland's several invitations was maddening, he declared.

Although Copland had hoped to spur Bowles into finishing his symphony in time for Yaddo's Second Festival of Contemporary

American Music, he admitted that the selection of music for the festival would not be his alone to make. It had never occurred to Bowles that his piece might be turned down, given the fact that Copland himself headed the Central Music Committee, which supposedly selected the program. Then he learned that the committee must collaborate with regional representatives before making its final choices.

To Thomson, who had been named a regional representative while working with Stein in Paris on *Four Saints in Three Acts*, Bowles complained that he had just been turned down by the Central Music Committee and was furious. "I should not have minded if the objection had been that I had no métier, or that it was badly arranged, but for the Committee to argue that it was *cheap* really is too much." Thomson replied that he himself had submitted a composition before learning that he was to be a judge, and that his entry, too, had been rejected.[25]

Since there seemed to be no one else whom he could hold accountable for the decision not to select him, Bowles turned to the third movement of his symphony, now scored for flute, oboe, clarinet, bassoon, trumpet, trombone, piano, tambour, violin, viola, cello, and bass, and renamed it *Suite for Small Orchestra.* Later, to composer Phillip Ramey, Bowles summarized what he had done: "The *Pastorale* is made up of simple and repetitious North African melodies that I remembered from my trip to Algeria in 1933. It's lyrical and very brief. I composed the *Havanaise*, the longest of the three pieces, in Agadir, in 1932. It's a tango. The *Divertissement* is a fast piece that obviously is in a Latin American style. I recall what Elliott Carter, at his meanest, wrote: 'Bowles's procedure is to take folk tunes and deprive them of their meaning.' But I never used Latin folk tunes; rather, I invented melodies in the manner of Latin folk music. Of course they are deprived of meaning because they never had that meaning in the first place."[26] Bowles hated having someone ascribe to him something pertaining to his composing that was totally false.

For a time he considered studying harmony with Roger Sessions and sought Copland's advice. "Of course learning anything significant meant studying, yet I foolishly thought I could do it without any rigorous training. For me, short, simple pieces were the most satisfying. I didn't know how to appreciate long, complex ones. I knew intuitively why I put down every note and saw no reason to study harmony or counterpoint with anyone in any formal arrangement, especially not Nadia Boulanger."[27] If it were not Copland with whom he could continue discussing harmony, then to compose as he saw fit, Bowles declared that he might as well be in a monastery.[28]

In an article titled "America's Young Men–Ten Years Later," Copland complained to his fellow composers that there were those "who refuse to see in Bowles anything more than a dilettante," and that Bowles himself "persists in taking a militantly non-professional air in relation to all music, including his own." Then he cautioned: "If you take this attitude at its face value, you will lose sight of the considerable merit of a large amount of music that Bowles has already written, music which comes from a fresh personality, music full of charm and melodic invention, at times surprisingly well made in an instinctive and non-academic fashion." Copland concluded by saying that he much preferred an amateur like Bowles to a "well-trained conservatory product."[29]

Bowles was still working on Emma Ross's piano in Westhampton when Copland proposed that he and a number of other young composers who had been out of the country for a time would benefit by getting together regularly to discuss one another's music and to discover what had been written in their absence. Although Bowles rejected the idea of being a "joiner" of anything, he soon found himself a part of Copland's Young Composers' Group. He was twenty-three, and except for Copland, everyone else was twenty-five or younger. "What it boiled down to was that I needed a place to live, the group needed a place to meet once a week, and the studio apartment Aaron had found on West Fifty-eighth Street had a grand piano in it and was fully furnished. Aaron paid half the rent, and I paid the other half."[30] Most of the time Bowles had the apartment and grand piano to himself.

The timing was perfect, he allowed, having just been expelled from Harry Dunham's apartment in which he had expected to spend the winter. Dunham had given Bowles his flat before going to Samoa to make a film, but when his father heard of it he threatened to cut off his son's allowance if Bowles did not move out immediately.[31] In the spring of 1934, Dunham returned from Samoa and asked Bowles to compose the music for his film, but cautioned that there would be no money in it, "or very little." To Morrissette, Bowles wrote several months later that the Samoan film, its name having been changed from *Siva* to *Bride of Samoa*, was "marked by a leering commentary" meant to help distribution and was atrocious.[32] Bowles said later that he had no idea that his composing the music for Dunham's *Bride of Samoa* would lead to his composing incidental music for both Broadway and Hollywood. "They were miles apart, of course, but it *was* a beginning, and I was optimistic for the first time in more than a year."[33]

It was a heterogeneous assortment of composers who came to the first gatherings of the Young Composers' Group, and Bowles was skeptical that he would fit in. Bernard Herrmann thought both Bowles and his music were absurd, but remarks by the rest of the group were tactful. Henry Brant and Israel Citkowitz, who had been students in Paris with Nadia Boulanger, met regularly with the group, as did Arthur Berger, Lehman Engel, Vivian Fine, Irwin Heilner, Jerome Moross, Elie Siegmeister, and two or three others who appreciated the opportunity to get together under Copland's sponsorship. Bowles found the group articulate, vociferous, and combative. In February 1935, several of its members signed on for Roger Sessions's harmony class, and Bowles was one of them. "Once the group ceased meeting in my apartment, Aaron told me that he could not continue paying half the rent, so I paid the next two months' rent by myself, then broke the lease," an action for which Bowles was later sued for the rest of the year's rent.[34]

Bowles's impatience to leave the city was intensified when he moved next door to a factory that pressed Decca records and operated twenty-four hours a day. The windows opened upon a courtyard of noise, grime, and gloom. "I tried to drown my melancholy in work, but I was obsessed by memories of the air and light of North Africa and knew that I would have to return, but *how* was always the question," he admitted.[35]

The opportunity for change came unexpectedly in the person of Colonel Charles Williams, an American in charge of a philanthropic foundation in Fez dedicated to the prevention of cruelty to pack animals, and he needed someone to work for him. As usual in such circumstances, Bowles had no clear plan when he called upon the colonel, but declared that he was well acquainted with Fez, knew its resident administrator of the American Fondouk there, and wanted to do anything he could to help.[36] He was advised to apply through the president of the American Society for the Prevention of Cruelty to Animals, which oversaw the American Fondouks abroad, but was cautioned that if he were hired, he would have to pay his own way to Gibraltar and get home at his own expense. Bowles considered the entire operation a superb opportunity to return to North Africa.

As usual, he saw no reason to finance the entire trip himself, and again, fortuitously, he presented himself as a personal travel guide to a Wall Street stockbroker who wanted to spend several weeks in Spain. Although there was no salary involved, the stockbroker agreed to finance the entire trip himself. Soon they were first-class passengers aboard a deluxe Italian liner, the SS *Conte di Savoia*, and upon arrival, Bowles found himself with ample spare time to do as he chose. After considerable roaming in Algeria and Morocco, Bowles met Colonel Williams in Gibraltar as agreed and proceeded with him to Fez. As both had anticipated, their work was over in six weeks, and Bowles considered his next options. He had not planned to return to New York so soon, but almost before he realized it he was back in Cádiz and boarding the only ship leaving within the next few days for any port in the Western Hemisphere. The ship was the SS *Juan Sebastian Elcano*, the same ship on which he had traveled a year earlier. Feeling increasingly ill his third day at sea, Bowles sought haven in the ship's infirmary, where he spent the rest of the journey on a diet of rice, eggs, and apricot jam. The one book he had brought with him was Marcel Proust's *Le Temps Retrouvé* [*Time Regained*], which he dreaded finishing. "For that reason I read sparingly, and reread rather than going ahead. Gertrude says everyone during his youth finds one great book which influences more than any other; hers was *Anna Karenina*. Mine was *Le Temps Retrouvé*, which I read in French."[37]

In December, Bowles's ship steamed into San Pedro Bay, California, where the sprawl and smog that later characterized the Los Angeles/Hollywood area was only beginning to emerge, and large portions of the region were relatively pristine and unspoiled. From the ship, Bowles wired Shirley West Bowles, his father's brother, to inquire if he might spend a few days with him and his family before setting out for New York. Bowles's uncle had established a home on the side of a mountain in a Los Angeles suburb. "I had not seen Aunt Elizabeth, Uncle Shirley's wife, or his children, Dwight and Barbara, since I was five, when our holidays in Glenora and Watkins Glen overlapped. When I saw Uncle Shirley this time, I could hardly believe that he and my father came from the same family. He was not at all neurotic." Bowles thought him a nicer person and much better natured than his father. "He was also better looking. I wondered if my mother thought so, too, but she rarely saw him. My father saw to that."[38]

To Morrissette, Bowles wrote cryptically: "I shall go up to San Francisco in January, where Henry Cowell will be master of ceremonies," by which he meant that Cowell might be willing to help redirect his career since Copland had proven elusive. "After visiting Uncle Shirley, I traveled up the coast to San Francisco to see a distant cousin on my paternal grandmother's side whom I had never met." Bowles also looked forward to exploring the Bay Area and hiking among redwoods beyond the Golden Gate Bridge. He told Morrissette that he would have been "more open to the region's amenities" (again his reference to sex) had he not received what he considered a ridiculous letter from Daniel Burns. "'You will surely come to love it. You will think you're in Amsterdam or Copenhagen or England or Vienna or Paris or a provincial town of France. You will eat excellent food and hear good music and meet interesting people,'" wrote Bowles, who concluded that Burns "ought to do the sop for the Chamber of Commerce. There is nothing like that here."[39]

Had Bowles not been confined to bed with fever for almost a month, he would have left the home of his relatives sooner. "Aunt Jessie was an inveterate Christian Scientist and wanted to invite a practitioner to commence treatment. I suggested seeing a doctor, but she prided herself on the fact that neither she nor her daughters had ever been examined by one, and she did not want one in the house now. I was relieved when her daughters quietly opposed their mother's harsh proscriptions and smuggled in medicines and goodies via the Swedish housekeeper."

Bowles was impatient to recuperate, too, so that he might spend a few hours with Henry Cowell, who was teaching at Stanford University. Upon sitting in on several of Cowell's classes, Bowles realized that they shared an obsessive interest in rhythm. Cowell had devised a piano technique of playing tone clusters in which adjacent notes were played by his forearm and the flat of his hand that resulted in violent and colorful dissonances. He also pioneered such musical innovations as plucking the strings of the keyboard of a piano and muting them with cardboard and metal.[40] Cowell had studied at the University of California, Berkeley, with Charles Seeger, who encouraged him to "codify the unorthodox rules he was making for himself."

When Cowell asked to see some of his visitor's unpublished music, Bowles showed him the text of a letter from Stein from which he had made a song for voice, piano, and oboe and called *Letter to Freddy*; he also gave Cowell his *Café Sin Nombre*, a piano solo; parts four and six from *Danger de mort*, which contained six songs for voice and piano and lyrics by Georges Linze; and part three from *Scènes d'Anabase*, with lyrics by Saint-John Perse.

After leaving the Bay Area, Bowles stopped in Evanston, Illinois, to visit George Turner, whom he had not seen since they parted in Tunis while both were down to their last several francs. Bowles had hoped to spend three or four weeks with Turner since at this point his own funds were practically nonexistent. To Stein, he confessed later: "I think my welcome was worn out quite a while before that and so I moved on to Morrissette in Baltimore."[41]

To Morrissette, before leaving Evanston, Bowles wrote with unrestrained glee: "T[urner] tells me that Gertrude was a total flop and has canceled her lecture tours. In Chicago, it was suggested that the audience try listening to *Four Saints* with 'blank minds.' I am pleased with Gertrude's fiasco."[42] Bowles's ambivalence regarding Stein had prompted him to observe to his mother: "I want to take every poet and shove him down into the dung-heap, kick all his literary friends in the ass, and try to make him see that writing is not word-bandying, like Stein and the thousand legions of her followers, but an emotion seen through the mind."[43] Despite his remarks now about the failure of Stein's opera and his uneven feelings for her upon being told by her that he was "no poet," Stein was often in his thoughts.

Although Bowles made a number of negative comments about Stein to others, he continued to write her cordial letters and chose his words carefully when he requested permission for Henry Cowell to publish her "Letter to Freddy" and told her that already he had made songs out of two excerpts from her book *Useful Knowledge*, "Red Faces" and "The Ford," which he wished to publish as "Scenes from the Door." Actually, Bowles had already printed privately, with neither her knowledge nor her permission, one hundred copies of "Scenes from the Door" under his own imprint, Éditions de la Vipère, a publishing venture financed largely by Harry Dunham. "I hoped that Gertrude would never see them since the copies had not been circulated."[44] From Copland, Bowles learned in the spring of 1934 that Cos Cob Press had discontinued publishing altogether, and he was even more convinced that he could make money from his own publishing venture. "I saw myself as a viper residing in an American nest."[45]

Bowles was still in Evanston when Morrissette wrote that "just the kind of job you need awaits you in Baltimore." It was a live-in position that required him to read to a bedridden patient with encephalitis. The patient, whom Bowles knew only as Mr. Fuhrman, was a wealthy Austrian who lived in an exclusive area occupied by families with old money. Except for the requisite reading, Bowles would be free to come and go as he wished. Even better, Morrissette pointed out, Fuhrman had a grand piano on which Bowles could work. It seemed a perfect setup. Bowles was close enough to New York to go there when he chose, and he reasoned that he would make enough money in Baltimore to live on without calling for help from either his mother or Harry Dunham. To his parents, writing music was an avocation, not a profession, and they could not envision his ability to support himself. "What will become of you if you do not take a *real* job?" they asked during one of their son's rare visits home.

In Baltimore, Bowles accompanied his employer on chauffeur-driven rides into the Maryland countryside and conversed with him in French and Spanish about the books he read aloud to him. To Bowles, Fuhrman was a captive audience and no different from anyone else to whom he had read his tales over the years, except that now he was getting paid to read whatever he chose.[46] In Baltimore he became acquainted with two wealthy maiden sisters, Etta and Claribel Cone, friends of Stein who collected modern art. When Bowles told them about Eugene Berman's extraordinary pen-and-ink drawings and offered to bring some down after his next visit to New York, they were delighted to have a new source for their collection. They also introduced Bowles to the curator of the Baltimore Museum, who bought most of Berman's remaining drawings.

By this time Bowles was well into Éditions de la Vipère, for which he was now publishing his own scores and music as well as those of others. To show his appreciation to his old friend, Berman asked to illustrate something new by Bowles before it was published. Bowles chose his musical portraits of Katherine Cowen and Bruce Morrissette and offered Berman, also, the opportunity to do the covers for Bowles's music of Cocteau's *Memnon*.[47] Earlier, while visiting his uncle in Hollywood, Bowles had seen Richard Thoma, whose *Green Songs* he had liked especially, and asked for permission to publish "Grass," "Farewell," and "Silence" under his Vipère imprint. Bowles also published songs by David Diamond and Erik Satie. Much of the music he published was illustrated by Anne Miracle Mannheim and by Bowles himself.[48]

When he was not composing, reading to Fuhrman, or being driven about the city by his employer's chauffeur, Bowles began visiting the headquarters of the American Communist Party, also in Baltimore. Here he met the brother of Earl Browder, who was nominated in June 1935 to lead the Communist Party ticket. Much of Bowles's political consciousness at this point was inspired by Katherine Cowen, with whom he exchanged letters regularly. On December 12, 1935, he wrote of his resentment at her insistence that he was a Fascist. Since Bowles hardly knew at that point what a Fascist was, he decided to research the topic. "But you were not right, of course! Since then I have read at least fifteen works on the subject and thought each day and dreamed each night of naught but the subject."[49] The developing crisis in Europe in 1936 and 1937 contributed to Bowles's horror at Cowen's observation, and he returned to the subject in letter after letter. In some he appeared to be a devout student of communism and launched into extended technical discussions of the revolution that he feared would follow; in others, he insisted that he cared little for the principles of the party, and that its chief value was as a harassing instrument.[50] Bowles told Stein that he would be voting for Roosevelt in 1936, "not because he is any good himself, but because his staying in will keep a Republican out."[51] When Morrissette wrote that he intended to study at the newly established Workers' School in Mexico City and suggested that the two of them go together, Bowles assured him that he had no intention of doing such a thing.

In the fall of 1935, Bowles left Baltimore to return to New York, this time to copy scores for Vladimir Dukelsky, a Russian-born composer he had met through John Latouche who later went by the name Vernon Duke. "I did it for a fraction of what Dukelsky would pay had he hired a union copyist to do the job, but any money came in handy then." Virgil Thomson lectured Bowles that music was a commodity that must be paid for, and that a composer who gave away his music was simply a scab. A. Everett "Chick" Austin Jr. agreed with Thomson and hired Copland, Thomson, Antheil, and Bowles to perform in Hartford at a party given by the Friends and Enemies of Modern Music, an organization Austin had founded. Bowles's suitcase disappeared in the "general drunkenness that followed the breakup of the evening," and he borrowed a suit, shirt, tie, and socks from his host rather than return to New York in white tie and tails.[52]

On another occasion, Bowles, Marc Blitzstein, Copland, and Thomson were hired to play at a party given by Mrs. Murray Crane, and they were given their checks before leaving. Bowles said that he felt "horribly ashamed at that moment" for it seemed "a bit like accepting payment for moving one's hostess's chair for her. But Virgil's indoctrination asserted itself: 'A composer is a professional, and professionals get paid.'"[53]

On April 12, 1935, Bowles wrote Morrissette that he had just composed the music for a composite piano portrait parodying the styles of five of his fellow composers: "Virgil smiling sweetly, Aaron remembering the world, Roger [Sessions] looking careful and honest, George Antheil in a hurry to go, and Israel Citkowitz being as pleasant as he can."[54] Bowles had no desire to publish his parodies, but allowed that they were fun "to dash off."

Bowles was delighted when Henry Cowell returned to New York, this time to teach at the New School for Social Research. Together on several occasions, Cowell was especially impressed by Bowles's Chleuh collection and asked if they might make copies of some of his recordings for use with his classes. In return, Cowell provided Bowles with recordings of Central African music from his collection and offered to help Bowles find recording equipment to take back to Africa with him, "whenever that may be," Bowles lamented, his impatience mounting in anticipation of recording the indigenous music of Morocco before it disappeared.

To Morrissette, he wrote: "The happiest part of the sudden late acquaintance is C's [Cowell's] promise to provide me some sort of recording equipment to take to Middle Africa. He agrees that the territory to explore is the Niger Valley, Tchad, and Mauritania."[55] Cowell had asked Bowles if he would be willing, also, to make a set of records for Béla Bartók, who collected and edited Hungarian folk songs after fleeing his native Hungary and moving to Pittsburgh. Cowell told Bowles that Bartók was incorporating the Chleuh material in a piece, and "sure enough, when I heard the Concerto for Orchestra, there was the music, considerably transformed, but still recognizable to me since I was familiar with each note of every piece I had copied for him."[56] By 1936 Bowles had established himself as a spokesman for non-Western music and militantly argued for its viability as a replacement for Western styles, which now seemed "stale and outdated." Part of his respect for Cowell stemmed from his obvious familiarity with the music of North Africa.

To music historian William Treat Upton, who was in the process of revising his *Art-Song in America: A Study in the Development of American Music* and had asked Bowles for a comment, he replied: "My own approach to all music is preeminently an instinctive one and precludes any consciousness of method. Art music will get what it needs not from new subjects to sing about . . . nor from technical devices (quarter tones and careful rhythms), but from new ways to sing."[57]

Bowles's appetite for music beyond the mainstream of American high culture led him to continue, also, his exploration of American jazz, having met and corresponded with jazz/blues collector John Hammond, whom he visited often in 1936 to listen to his jazz recordings. Hammond had asked Bowles to accompany him to Harlem to hear jazz pianist Teddy Wilson, who was embarking on what gave promise of a brilliant career.[58]

Bowles was ecstatic when, on April 2, 1936, a concert of his music was given considerable attention in the *New York Times*, this one presented by the Composers Forum-Laboratory, a quarterly program funded by the Federal Music Project which featured each quarter the work of several American composers. The headline read: "MUSIC OF BOWLES HEARD: His Compositions Comprise the Twentieth Forum-Laboratory Bill." The program included his Sonata for Violin and Piano; Trio for Violin, Cello, and Piano; *Scènes d'Anabase*; Suite for Violin and Piano; and several solo piano pieces. Also on the program was the premiere screening of Harry Dunham's film *Venus and Adonis*. Bowles remembered Dunham's censoring the nude scenes by holding his hand in front of the projector, and after the concert there was a question-and-answer "heckling session." "The Leftists were against the music on principle since it depended on style rather than socially relevant content," and the audience was "an unprecedented mixture of anonymous people attracted by the prospect of a free concert."[59]

Bowles had invited his parents to the concert and was astonished that they came, but not surprised by their comments later. "And this is where our tax money goes now. My God!" exclaimed his father. His mother observed that "at least they can't un-give the concert now that they've given it. If it were trees they'd been planting, they'd be digging them up again tomorrow."[60] Bowles lamented that his parents seemed to be growing more alike every day.

Colin McPhee reviewed the concert in the May–June 1936 issue of *Modern Music* and praised Bowles's music for its "allure and melodic individuality," but called Dunham's film "incredibly stupid."[61] Although modest in his reactions to favorable criticism, Bowles disliked comments taking him to task for what he had not done or had no intention of doing. To Bowles, his most accurate critics so far as music was concerned were Aaron Copland, Virgil Thomson, Peggy Glanville-Hicks, Ned Rorem, and Phillip Ramey.

Bowles's music received positive exposure, too, when director Joseph Losey asked him to compose the score for a privately financed benefit stage production titled *Who Fights This Battle?* At this point, upon Franco's invasion of Spain, Bowles was asked to become a founding member of the Committee on Republican Spain to raise money for the Madrid government. Kenneth White wrote the story line, Joseph Losey directed the production, Bowles wrote a score for the chorus using trumpet and organ, and Earl Robinson was musical director. "The play's polemic had a staunchly anti-Fascist coloration to get its point across that what was going on was a foreign invasion."[62] The play raised two thousand dollars, which was sent directly to the minister of education in Madrid.

On August 22, 1936, Bowles wrote Cowen that he had gone to an exciting rally at Madison Square Garden for the defense of Spain. "The meeting was packed with coatless men, and they collected well over five thousand dollars. Only the *Daily Worker* is of interest since it prints nothing but the Spanish government's bulletins without censoring them." Bowles also admitted to Cowen that if he were to survive as a composer for the serious concert hall, as well as for the theatre, he would need more than just "an occasional gig" that paid.

Under the auspices of the Works Progress Administration, Federal Theatre Project 891 had just been launched to employ playwrights, composers, and musicians. According to Bowles, everyone received $23.86 a week. For a time, Virgil Thomson was involved in a federally funded all-black production of *Macbeth* in Harlem, for which he was solicited by John Houseman and Orson Welles, the latter a precocious youth of eighteen. "The play was incredible," exclaimed Bowles, who persuaded Houseman and Welles to undertake a production of Eugène Labiche's *Un Chapeau de Paille d'Italie*, directed by Edwin Denby and adapted and translated from the French as *Horse Eats Hat.*[63]

Denby was a Swiss poet, critic, and dancer who had recently returned from Europe and was well known in theatrical circles abroad. For this production, Denby expanded Labiche's text and devised a horse ballet, in which Denby appeared as the rear half of "the offending beast who ate the hat." The bridegroom, played by Joseph Cotton, was on his way to get married when his horse ate a woman's hat, which had to be replaced before the owner's husband discovered the loss. Orson Welles played the bride's father, and Welles's wife, Virginia, was the bride. Bowles was dismayed that *Horse Eats Hat* required an unusual amount of music, yet already was in rehearsal. "Whereas my earlier compositions were conceived and arranged for small chamber forces, the pit orchestra for *Horse Eats Hat* required thirty-three musicians, a grand piano in each of the lower boxes, a pianola, a female trumpeter, and a gypsy orchestra–all multiple units with which I had no experience. Yet I did manage to compose for the occasion two long pieces 'of continuity,' three overtures, the horse ballet, and several songs, including the 'Father-in-law's Lament.'"

Houseman explained that "for the rest, the dances, the marches, the chamber music, the piano solos, and some added songs," they were able to use "existent compositions by Bowles or pieces from the public domain."[64] Never having learned how to orchestrate pieces of music for anything other than a limited number of musicians, Bowles appealed to Thomson to help with the orchestration, and the play opened officially on September 26, 1936.[65]

According to Ned Rorem, Orson Welles's production of *Horse Eats Hat* was "the first of some two dozen plays for which Bowles provided the most distinguished incidental scores of the period. The Broadway theatre accounted for a huge percentage of his musical output, and for the milieu he frequented for a quarter of a century. Indeed, the intent of his music in all forms is to please, and to please through light colors and gentle textures and amusing rhythms, novel for the time, and quite lean, like their author."[66] The success of *Horse Eats Hat* led immediately to additional work in the theater for Bowles. When Houseman collaborated with Welles in a production of Christopher Marlowe's *The Tragical History of Doctor Faustus*–also through Federal Theatre Project 891 of the WPA–Welles directed the production himself and played Faustus.

In the spring of 1936, Lincoln Kirstein commissioned Bowles to compose the ballet score for *Yankee Clipper*, which he described as a "character ballet in one act." Choreographed by Eugene Loring, it was performed by the American Ballet Caravan, a ballet school founded in Manhattan by Kirstein and operated by George Balanchine. Although the program notes of *Yankee Clipper* declared the composer the "foremost of younger American musicians," Bowles himself identified with the roving New England youth of the ballet who embraced randomly a companion in every port–and was ready to move on as the wind and scenery changed. "None of my friends had a loose foot that matched my own; moreover, the only woman I knew well who shared my adventuresome spirit and many of my convictions regarding war and revolution was Katherine Cowen."[67]

Writing in French after spending a leisurely week with Cowen and her family in Baltimore, Bowles asked: "*Quand la guerre arrivera, viendras-tu à New York aider tes camarades dans leur travail?* [When war breaks out, will you come to New York to help your comrades in their work?]" Although Bowles wrote often to Cowen in French, his tone was more intimate than usual as he concluded his letter. "I would have liked to stay very long with you. It [the visit] was beautiful, and you are a person who eats the time. Your mother is so nice, and you are lucky to have a witty brother. In short, yours is the only family in which I would have liked to be born, for families annoy me."[68]

CHAPTER SIX

Paul Bowles Meets Jane Auer. They Fall in Love and Marry

(1937–1940)

"Paul, There is a fantastic girl I want you to meet. I'll bring her around."[1]

—John Latouche to Paul Bowles,
New York City, Winter 1937

The only fantastic woman Bowles knew during the winter of 1936–37 was Katherine Cowen, who had never met John Latouche, and he wondered who his friend had in mind for him now. It was raining heavily when they met on the appointed date outside the Plaza Hotel, where Bowles spotted Latouche huddled under an umbrella with two women. One he recognized as Erica Mann, the daughter of German novelist Thomas Mann and the wife of Wystan (W. H.) Auden. The other was Jane Auer, whose bright red hair, pointed nose, and slight limp attracted him, although it was immediately obvious that the interest was one-sided. Latouche escorted them to an apartment in Harlem where guests paid an entrance fee, sat on the floor, and smoked marijuana cigarettes. Mann's marriage of convenience to Auden in 1935 enabled her to travel freely wherever she chose, and she, too, loved meeting new people. Mann was in New York now because her anti-Fascist revue, *The Peppermill*, was being translated by Latouche for a revival production at the New School for

Social Research. "Wystan enjoyed seeing Erica when their paths crossed, which was usually by happenstance," noted Bowles.[2]

A few days after their initial meeting, Bowles saw Jane Auer again, this time at 5 Patchin Place in the apartment of Marion Morehouse, who most people assumed was married to E. E. Cummings, although that was not the case. Patchin Place was a small tree-shaded court near the old Jefferson Market at Sixth Avenue and West Tenth. Many people with literary interests wandered into the court on Sunday afternoons in hopes of being spotted by Cummings or Morehouse and invited to join them. As Bowles saw it, the real draw was the heady conversation one encountered during such informal gatherings. Cummings's studio was upstairs, where he stayed when he wanted to be alone. During their drop-in parties on weekends, he played host with Morehouse.

Jane Auer was Latouche's guest, and Bowles's guests were Kristians Tonny and his new wife, Marie-Claire Ivanoff, who had just arrived from Paris. To Bowles, Tonny was full of vague complaints about America, an annoyance stemming primarily from the fact that he and Marie-Claire appeared to be the only ones present who did not speak English.[3] They drank wine brought by Bowles and talked in French about Mexico, where Tonny was determined to travel next. Bowles decided on the spot that if they actually did go, he would like to accompany them. They were amused when Jane announced that she, too, would like to go to Mexico.[4]

Bowles was astonished when Jane handed him the telephone and said that her mother was on the line. "If my daughter is going to Mexico with a man, I think I should meet him, don't you?" she asked. Within the hour, Bowles found himself seated with Jane and her mother in their apartment in the Hotel Meurice. "I found it hard to believe that Mrs. Auer had accepted her daughter's sudden caprice so completely," said Bowles, who learned shortly that even though Mrs. Auer was set upon having an eligible Jew for a son-in-law, she encouraged Jane to keep her options open. "I soon realized that the more Claire Auer insisted that her daughter behave in any prescribed manner, the more determined Jane was to comport herself precisely as she chose."[5]

Mrs. Auer declared that her daughter must stay at the Hotel Ritz in Mexico City, no matter where the others wished to register. She also insisted upon Jane's having a new wardrobe for the trip.[6] Bowles was skeptical that Jane actually would accompany them. Years later, when invited to write an autobiographical sketch for *World Authors 1950–1970*, Jane said that the night she and Bowles met she recognized him immediately as her *enemy*.[7] When Bowles asked what she meant by such a ridiculous assessment, she described him as more inimical than anyone she knew, which he saw as having nothing to do with his being "an enemy."

"Why, we hardly knew each other," countered Bowles. "Enemy, indeed! Jane *was* strange, and that appealed to me, of course."[8] It did not occur to him that she may have considered him a threat to her lesbianism. "On our trip to Mexico we were usually in the company of others, and before that, we were with Cummings. It was never a question of either of us 'coming on' to the other," said Bowles, whose most memorable picture of Jane for many years was of her smoking Cuban cigars, wearing bright red lipstick, and coloring her short hair to bring out the red. "She invariably attracted attention even when she was not actively seeking it. She was impish and mischievous, and I never knew whether to believe what she said or not. . . . Her extraordinary stage presence and awareness of audience were endlessly entertaining. I discovered later that writing was her means of being both on and off stage simultaneously."[9]

Although Jane became increasingly important to Bowles in the weeks that followed, he was scarcely aware of it. To resign from the Federal Theatre Project meant giving up his first regular paycheck since working at Dutton's Bookshop, but of that fact he had no second thoughts. When he told his parents that he was resigning to go to Mexico, they did not object, having been critical of his affiliation with the Federal Theatre Project, which they saw purely as a left-wing welfare agency. Bowles already had concluded that Trotsky's assassination was only a matter of time and that he might do something concrete to speed up the process short of wielding the hatchet himself.[10]

Before leaving New York for Mexico, he commissioned a printer to make up flyers proclaiming in Spanish that Trotsky was "an immediate danger!" and "must not be allowed to remain in Mexico!" Other flyers exclaimed that "Trotsky must die!" Bowles expected to get help from several Stalinist groups who were alarmed that Trotsky had been granted asylum in Mexico after being ejected from the Communist Party.[11] At this point, despite Bowles's tentative support of communism, he had no desire to join the party. "For the Communist Party USA to have meaning, it would have to be driven underground," Bowles insisted.[12]

On March 1, 1937, Bowles set out for Baltimore by bus with Jane, Tonny, and Marie-Claire. His only reservation at this point concerned Tonny, who he doubted had sufficient money to remain more than a few weeks in Mexico. Bowles feared having to dole out his own money to offset Tonny's and Marie-Claire's expenses. In Baltimore, where Etta and Claribel Cone had purchased many of Eugene Berman's drawings, Bowles showed the Cone sisters several of Tonny's pen-and-ink drawings, which they purchased with enthusiasm, as did the curator of the museum. Their mission accomplished, the foursome headed south, stopping two nights each in fair-sized towns in which they could count on finding decent hotels and seeing the sights. "It took us two weeks to get to New Orleans, and another week by way of Houston and Laredo to reach Monterrey," said Bowles. In Houston he jotted a cryptic message to Virgil Thomson declaring that they had stayed three superb days and nights in New Orleans. "So far Janie has lost her makeup case, her sandals, her disorder, and that's all."[13]

Seated together on the bus and exploring towns along the way gave the couple considerable time to get acquainted. Other than with his mother, Bowles had never traveled with a woman before, and he was amazed upon crossing into Mexico that they had become friends in the process. "We talked for hours each day, in French mostly, telling each other as much about our lives as we thought the other wished to hear. . . . She did admit to still being a virgin and said that she intended to remain one until she married."[14] It was Tonny's having made a sexual pass at Jane one evening in her hotel room that provoked her to tell Bowles as much about herself as she did, including her preference for romantic friendships with women. Even her mother knew of the several lesbian relationships Jane had flaunted since she was sixteen.

Bowles learned, too, during their trip to Mexico that Jane's memories of her father, who had died at forty-five, were extraordinarily dear to her, and that she felt cheated not having been able to tell him good-bye. She also admitted hating her middle name, Stajer, because it was her mother's maiden name. "That's why I refuse to use it. Its being a Jewish name has nothing to do with it," she told Bowles, who was not surprised to learn that Jane and her mother were usually at odds no matter what the topic.

Claire Auer feared that her daughter's disdain of "nice Jewish boys from good families" would put off eligible suitors, and she had already decided that she would not remarry until Jane herself was well situated in marriage. "The pressure exerted upon me by my mother was almost unbearable, and I could only deal with it through laughter," said Jane, who also shared with Bowles the details of her two-year treatment in a clinic in Leysin, Switzerland, that stemmed from a fall from a horse. "I remember Jane's telling me that a leg that would not bend was nothing to cry over. She always selected an aisle seat so she could extend her right leg into the aisle, and she joked about tripping any fellow-passenger who did not look where he was going," said Bowles, who considered Jane a good sport no matter how serious the problem.[15]

Finally, exhausted from their first three weeks on the road, they took rooms in a ramshackle hotel in Monterrey, Mexico, where Bowles went alone the next morning to the local college to find students who wished to distribute his flyers calling for Trotsky's death. That evening Jane joined him in a public demonstration against

Trotsky, and the next day they set off with Tonny and Marie-Claire for Mexico City.

To Jane's dismay, the highway narrowed to an unpaved roadbed pitted with rock, and the hairpin curves as the bus ascended to the higher reaches of the Sierra Madre Oriental range terrified her. At one point, she bolted from her seat and crouched among the Indian women with their babies and bundles in the back of the bus. Nothing that Bowles said cajoled her out of her misery, which intensified when she was overcome by diarrhea and refused to use the primitive toilet facilities where they had stopped to take on more passengers. In Mexico City at last, Jane bolted from the bus, retrieved her luggage by herself, and flagged down a taxi while Bowles and the others looked on dumbfounded from the curb.

Frantic upon learning of her failure to check into the Ritz, Bowles searched for Jane for three days before finding her at the Hotel Guardiola and recovering from a flash fever that had confined her to bed since her arrival. Bowles was skeptical when she told him that as soon as she could walk, she would take the next plane to the United States, but when he arrived the next day to take her to lunch, he learned that she already was on a plane bound for San Antonio, Texas.[16]

"Good riddance," declared Tonny and Marie-Claire upon learning that Jane had left Mexico. Bowles said nothing in her defense. For three weeks the trio traveled through Guatemala, then returned to Mexico City and moved into a pension in the countryside. In his new environment, Tonny began painting with fantastic intensity and produced dozens of drawings. "They were beautiful, and I was stunned both by his output and his imaginative treatment of subject matter, which I liked even better than those he had drawn in Morocco," said Bowles.[17]

Other than Katherine Cowen, whom he now called Kay and to whom he continued to write regularly, the only woman he cared about intensely was Jane Auer, who reappeared in New York a few days after his return from Mexico with an invitation for him to visit her at Deal Beach, New Jersey, where her mother had rented a house for the summer. "I went, and we had a wonderful weekend. There were many people present, including Virgil Thomson and Jane's mother, who, so far as I could tell, was a perfect hostess. There was plenty to eat and drink, and she didn't stand over us like a hawk waiting for one of us to do something wrong."[18] On Saturday night Bowles took Jane to the black section of Asbury Park and bought marijuana cigarettes, then returned to the house in Deal Beach and stayed up most of the night talking and playing charades with the other guests.[19]

Several weeks later Bowles asked her if she would spend the night with him in his parents' home since they were out of town. "She came, and that's when I tried to get her to go to bed with me. Actually, we *did* go to bed. We had been necking, and we took off all our clothes and lay naked under the covers. But when I began to caress her and made it clear that I wanted to have sex, she addressed me in French, as she usually did, and declared: 'I am not in the act of going to bed with you.' I could tell that she was still intent on remaining a virgin until she got married, so nothing else happened. By now I was crazy about her," said Bowles, "but it did not occur to me that we might get married someday."

When Tonny and Marie-Claire returned to New York a few days earlier than they had expected, having run out of money in Mexico, Bowles invited them to spend a month with him in the home of Emma Ross in Westhampton. "I wanted to help Tonny sell some of his paintings, but I was also tired of lending him money and resented his doing little to help himself. We got along fine except when he and Marie-Claire argued over some imagined offense."[20] Several weeks later, Bowles was astonished when Virgil Thomson casually mentioned that he had seen Tonny in New York, and feeling generous, had lent him enough money for him and Marie-Claire to return to Paris. Thomson also suggested that Tonny repay him first since Bowles "was not hurting" for money just then. Shocked by Thomson's admission, Bowles wrote him a scathing letter regarding his handling of the entire "Tonny affair." Thomson replied with an angry eight-page missive of his own. At the fund-raising concert for the *New Masses*, neither spoke although both were on the same program, nor did they speak at the founding meeting of the American Composers' Alliance when forty-eight composers of serious music signed on as members.[21]

"Virgil was right," allowed Bowles. "We were really quite outrageous in our comments to each other. We had wasted our time and energy fuming and feuding when we should have been composing and concentrating on our music. I don't remember just how Virgil and I patched up our differences, but we did. Soon we were writing to one another in much the same vein we always had. Of course I never did get any money back from Tonny or see either of them again, and I doubt if Virgil did either."[22]

At the time, Bowles was writing music for Charles Henri Ford's libretto *Denmark Vesey*. Its subject was an abortive slave rebellion led by Vesey, a former slave who bought his freedom with money he won in a lottery. Bowles already had scored the first two acts and was well into the third when he told Ford that he wanted the Juanita Hall Choir to present the first act in a fund-raising concert for the *New Masses*, and that he would play the piano for the first act. Although apprehensive at first, Ford was soon responsive to Bowles's urging since it meant the production of a work in progress from which they both would benefit. "Actually, we were a good team, and the choir was appropriately responsive too," said Bowles, who rented two large connecting rooms at 2 Water Street, Brooklyn, in which to rehearse the nine-member choir and its three principal vocalists. On February 6, 1938, the concert was presented at the Forty-sixth Street Theatre, and "judging from the applause and remarks out front, everyone in the audience considered it a huge success," said Bowles.[23]

Almost before they were aware of it, Bowles and Jane began talking about getting married, thinking first of how amusing it would be to their friends and family. "Then we began to talk seriously about the possibility, and Jane seemed very much for it. When we told her mother that we had decided to get married, she was ecstatic. I think she had given up on Jane's ever getting married and was desperate to get married herself to ease her own financial needs."[24]

When Bowles informed his parents that he was going to marry Jane and made it clear to them that she was a Jew, Claude reportedly remonstrated: "It's not enough that we have a crippled kike in the White House, but you have to go and marry one." On the other hand, Jane's mother was quite reconciled to her daughter's marrying a Gentile and spent what Bowles considered an "outrageous amount of money" on expensive clothes for their honeymoon. "I could not imagine her wearing everything, but she did, eventually. Jane had great style, and she loved dressing up. . . . She was enormously funny, and we laughed practically the whole way to the courthouse to pick up the license the day before her twenty-first birthday."[25]

The justice of the peace secured two employees from his office to witness the civil ceremony on February 21, 1938; then they walked to a small Dutch Reformed Church around the corner for what Bowles termed "a more proper wedding ceremony" to which their parents were invited. "Jane wore a street-length dress and I wore a gray suit. I didn't give her flowers. I didn't know I was supposed to since it was the first wedding I had ever attended. I didn't give her a ring, either, but she insisted that a ring did not matter either. I'm sure she knew I couldn't pay for one just then. We had some kind of a meal after the wedding, which our parents attended, but I don't remember much about it."[26] Bowles was surprised that his father attended either event.

Charles Henri Ford was taken aback when he answered a knock on his door that evening and found Jane and Paul Bowles standing there, "laughing so hard they could hardly talk, but I heard them say that they were getting on a ship and sailing to Panama. When I asked Paul what he was running away from, he assured me that they were not 'running away' from anything, and that they had just been 'married properly' in front of their parents."[27]

"We didn't stay long at Charles's flat. I don't remember his even offering us a drink, but that didn't matter," said Bowles. "We were still laughing when we walked out the door. I'm not sure where we stayed that first night. We were going to Central America, and it was a matter of when the ship sailed. Also, I wanted to attend a concert in New

York two days after our wedding, when some of my Mexican music was being played, this one a lively three-movement piece that I called *Mediodía*, for which I played the drums."[28]

On March 1, 1938, Bowles and his bride boarded a small Japanese freighter, the SS *Kano Maru*, with two wardrobe trunks, twenty-seven suitcases, a typewriter, and a record player. "There was no grand send-off. Jane's mother was already busy with her own wedding plans, but my parents came to the ship, and John Latouche brought champagne." Although Bowles and Jane were seasoned travelers, neither had encountered a ship like the *Kano Maru* with its two state rooms on the main deck for passengers and two state rooms for the captain and first mate. Such an arrangement in itself was not surprising, but what they had not anticipated was communal bathing. On their second day out, the captain walked in on Jane while she was bathing, greeted her nonchalantly as he disrobed, then climbed into the other tub.

"I beg your pardon! I beg your pardon!" she exclaimed, expecting him to apologize for his intrusion and leave the bath area immediately, but the captain continued bathing as though nothing was amiss and volunteered several observations to her regarding the ship.

"That's the last bath I'll take on this ship," Jane snorted as she stomped back to their cabin. Bowles allowed that he could not imagine anyone's being more modest than Jane. "If I had let her, she would have taken the rest of her meals in the cabin, but I managed to cajole her out of her embarrassment." They continued dining at the captain's table, but Jane refused to meet his eye or react to anything he said.[29] The rest of the voyage was uneventful. "In an American bookstore in Panama City we bought a complete set of the works of Lewis Carroll, and I discovered later that Jane had taken Charles Henri Ford's book, *The Young and Evil*, without paying for it. I don't think either of us felt a tinge of guilt."[30]

In Balboa they boarded a small craft that was once the private yacht of ex-Kaiser Wilhelm of Germany and proceeded to Puntarenas in Costa Rica, a town situated at the mouth of the Gulf of Nicoya. From there, they traveled by train to San José, the capital, where an earthquake routed them from their beds. "We ran around the room not knowing what we should do, but the tremor ceased shortly and the walls did not tumble in upon us, despite Jane's fears, so we went back to bed." They did not linger in San José.

Upon their return to Puntarenas, they were invited by a cattle rancher to visit his ranch in the province of Guanacaste, which required traveling through inland lagoons, then up a narrow winding river under dense, hanging vegetation while crocodiles sunned themselves on the banks. At the ranch, they rode horseback daily for hours. "These were not pleasure rides, but to accompany our host while he examined different regions of his immense property. At first Jane urged me to go without her, but before long I think she liked it even more than I. To Jane, being out with a group of any size was always preferable to staying indoors if it was just the two of us."[31]

In Guatemala City they were in a café talking and drinking with a group of students Jane had met earlier, but after two hours of inconsequential conversation, Bowles suggested that they ought to be getting back to their hotel. "Certainly not," Jane insisted. Her response did not surprise him.

He observed casually that since she knew the way she could stay as long as she wished, but that he was leaving. "I did not mean to imply that I was giving her *permission* to stay on without me, but I think that's how she took it. I read for a while and listened for what seemed like hours for her to come in. I must have dozed, but woke up when I heard her. I could tell by her voice that she was upset, but she offered no explanation, saying only 'I almost never got back at all.'"[32]

Bowles gathered later that Jane had suggested to her drinking companions that they visit a brothel, thinking it would be amusing since she had never done such a thing before. The excursion ceased to amuse her, however, when a patron invited her to a private room. Although the madam spoke up on Jane's behalf, the customer was not appeased. As the chief bodyguard of Guatemala's dictator, he was not accustomed to being rejected, especially since his own bodyguards were at hand, too, and had witnessed her refusal. "When Jane told me later that the prostitutes themselves had helped her escape, I reproached her for having put herself into such a predicament, an observation to which she did not take kindly."[33]

From Antigua Guatemala in April 1938, Bowles wrote his friend Dorothy Norman to explain his not doing the article she had asked him to write for *Twice a Year*, a journal she edited that was devoted to literature, the arts, and civil liberties. "I didn't mean to leave you without a word," he began and explained that he and his bride were on their honeymoon in Central America and would soon leave for France. Bowles also told Norman that they were being accompanied by a parrot named Budupple, which he expected to leave behind along the way. "But I shan't care very much, as it is omnivorous and has eaten its way through toothpaste, a pair of Jane's glasses, a copy of "I LOVE" [a Russian novel], a copper cage meant to keep it in, and a large mahogany armoire."

One of Bowles's earliest essays was about parrots. "My wife and I had been riding all morning with the *vaqueros* in Costa Rica and were very thirsty. At a gatehouse between ranch properties we asked a woman for water. When we had drunk our fill, rested, and chatted, she motioned us into a dim corner. There, perched on a stick, were seven little creatures. She carried the stick out into the light, and I saw that each of the seven tiny bags of pinkish-gray skin had a perfectly shaped, hooked yellow beak, wide open. And when I looked closely, I could see miniature brilliant green feathers growing out of the wrinkles of skin. We discussed the diet and care of young parrots, and our hostess generously offered us one. Jane claimed she couldn't bear to think of breaking up the family, so we went on our way parrotless."[34] A week later, while waiting fifteen hours for an overdue boat in the hamlet of Bebedero, they bought a full-grown parrot and named him Budupple. In Antigua, Budupple ate its way out of a second cage and escaped to the top of an avocado tree behind their pension. "We never saw him again," Bowles declared.

Owning Budupple, even for a short time, gave rise to a new game conceived by Jane. "The persona she created was named Bupple Hergesheimer, a young man who thought he was a parrot. Naturally, I was Bupple, and since I was dangerous, I had to be kept in a cage because I bit the furniture. Jane was a multiple character. When she wasn't Teresa Brawn, she was Teresa's mother or aunt or the governess of the young man who thought he was a parrot. Jane, the Teresa character, would hold out her hand to Bupple, and I would take hold of it the way a parrot does and wouldn't let go. Then Teresa shouted at me, 'Bupple, Bupple, let go! Let go!' And I would go 'Squawk! Squawk!' 'Back into your cage!' Teresa commanded as she unfastened the door so that Bupple could return to his cage. I could not tell whether Jane was launching into a new game or telling me something that had actually occurred, but we laughed a lot."[35]

In May 1938, Bowles and Jane left Guatemala City and traveled to Puerto Barrios to board the SS *Cordillera*, a German ship overrun with Nazis. By this time, German troops had crossed into Austria and were bent on war. At each Colombian and Venezuelan port, more Germans boarded, for the ship served, also, as a polling place. "Finally, after stops in Port of Spain and Barbados, we headed for the French coast. I could hardly wait to show Jane Paris."[36]

During their honeymoon in Central America, Bowles had been inordinately happy, and despite Jane's rebellious nature, she was more devoted to him now than he could have imagined. "Early in our marriage, Jane was an ideal companion, and given her needs, I think I was, too. We slept together and had what I considered very good sex."[37]

"Eventually, 'having very good sex' became part of the problem for Paul and Jane," observed Hall Winslow, who met Bowles upon his return to New York and saw much of him in the 1940s and 1950s. "I gathered from things he told me that Jane wanted to be with him all the time and liked 'having sex' too much."[38]

To Bowles, Jane's lesbianism was more whim than reality, a phase she merely was going through. "For her, the anticipation and chase were far more viable. Jane declared again and again under a variety of circumstances that she loved me, and as much as I understood about love I am sure I loved her, although I cannot say unequivocally that I was *in* love with Jane. I find the word *love* bantered too much in the lyrics of popular songs and films, and when I hear a declaration of love between casual acquaintances or mere friends, I find the word objectionable. If to make love is the same as having sex, the word is a misnomer."[39] Before their marriage, Bowles and Jane had agreed that each should be free to be with other people, even sexually, yet their commitment to each other was far stronger than either could have imagined.

Bowles considered the crossing from Barbados to Le Havre a bad omen. The weather was unseasonably cold and the sea so rough that they could hardly keep their footing on deck. In Port of Spain, Trinidad, Bowles had bought calypso records and he played them on deck on his portable phonograph after the weather cleared enough for them to sunbathe, but the dozens of Germans on board found the music distasteful and could not bear to hear it, even pianissimo, and lectured the couple on "the insidious spread of such degenerate forms of music."[40] Both Bowles and Jane loved the new music, marked by improvisation, syncopation, a strong percussive element, and contrapuntal melodies sung in patois, but to play such music in their cramped quarters below deck in the privacy of their cabin was not pleasurable, and they got on each other's nerves. Jane became cross, a side of her Bowles had not seen, and he could say little that pleased or amused her. They seldom left their cabin except for meals, and sometimes ate in their room before walking about the deck, separately, and retired early. "Jane was unwilling to talk about the novel she had begun in Central America and complained that she made no progress. Out of curiosity, not censure, I occasionally asked her questions about it, and she accused me of snooping. Later, I accepted that *I* was the problem. By the time we reached Paris, she was remote and engaged begrudgingly in conversation on any topic."[41]

Jane insisted upon going off on her own almost as soon as they arrived and lost no time checking out the bars and nightclubs. When

Bowles suggested one evening that he accompany her, she replied that she wanted to be with *her* friends, a comment that made no sense, he insisted, since they had only just arrived. "I realized later that I was much too possessive of Jane and had no right to be."[42] Bowles had hoped to introduce her to Gertrude Stein, but when he telephoned to suggest a meeting, Stein replied that she and Alice Toklas were busy packing to leave for Bilignin the next day. Having been summarily rejected, Bowles was determined not to call either of them again. Like many of Stein's former friends and admirers, he knew that he had fallen inadvertently and irrevocably from her favor. "I chose not to grovel, which was never my way in any circumstance," said Bowles, who had long since ceased thinking of the trip as an extension of their honeymoon, although he tried from time to time to revive Jane's occasional flourishes of interest or their desire for each other physically.[43] When he discovered an all-Stravinsky concert scheduled a few days after their arrival, he invited her to go with him, and to his surprise, she accepted. The Stravinsky program included the first public performance of the *Dumbarton Oaks* Concerto with the composer himself conducting. Bowles saw it as an occasion for them to be together, yet not alone, and he was dismayed when she told him the day before the concert that she had invited some new friends to join them.

Brion Gysin and Denham Fouts were the interlopers and had not guessed that Bowles was annoyed by Jane's having included them in what had been, until now, an exclusive invitation. "Jane said things without thinking, and it was often to the detriment of our relationship," said Bowles, who liked Gysin at once, but had no use for Fouts, whom he saw as a playboy. Gysin had just completed his studies at the Sorbonne and was painting.[44]

Each morning Jane left their modest hotel room on the Left Bank and worked on her novel in a café near the rue Bonaparte. At cocktail time, she moved to Le Monocle, a bar and nightclub in Montparnasse, where she perched for hours on a bar stool or at a table with other patrons. "It was understood that I was not to come along or look her up later," said Bowles. Most of the patrons of Le Monocle were lesbians who wore their hair parted, slicked back, and close-cropped, and dressed in white shirts, ties, and men's suits or tuxedos. Others dressed in feminine attire, as did Jane. Long after the fact, Jane told Bowles of her infatuation with the proprietress of Le Monocle, whom she described as "the most masculine woman" she had ever seen, and that she had sat at the bar night after night "drunk as a lord" because she did not want to go to Africa with her husband.[45]

Bowles hoped that Jane might change her mind about staying in Paris and accompany him to Tangier or Fez, but she had no interest in doing either. Since the weather was hot and muggy in Paris in June, he suggested their going first to the south of France, then to North Africa. "If you can't work here, that's your problem. I'm staying in Paris," she insisted.

Bowles went alone to Saint-Tropez, but after a week wired Jane to meet him in Cannes if she were so inclined. To his surprise, she came.[46] Although he had promised himself not to intrude upon her space or to criticize her about anything, Bowles became increasingly annoyed when all she seemed to want to talk about were her friends at the Monocle, women he had no interest in hearing about, or knowing. "Jane's playfulness, her delicious sense of humor, her word games in which we both delighted, her tenderness when I least expected it–all were gone. Finally, I made it clear to her that her behavior was tiresome and her lesbian friends inconsequential to me.

"'Kill-joy! Kill-joy!' she sang out. I lost all control and slapped her, hard, on the face."[47]

Bowles was stunned by his behavior. When he threw a knife at his father, he hated him, but he hated even more having lost control of himself. "Yet here I was, displaying anew my vulnerability that I had vowed never again to reveal to anyone. I apologized to Jane, but knew that I had behaved so outrageously that I had no right to expect forgiveness, or that she would eventually forget the incident. She fell across the bed and began sobbing 'It's all right. I still love you just the same.' But I knew that she did not love me, could not love me *just the same*."[48]

On the surface, they behaved with each other as usual. Bowles tried not to impose his wishes upon her or to be judgmental, but he usually ate alone and felt sorry for himself. At first he used to rush back to the room in the hope of finding her there or a note suggesting that they meet somewhere, but to no avail. Occasionally, Jane told him of some little happening that she thought would amuse him, such as the night "an obscene and lecherous man" tried repeatedly to entice her to his hotel, but he rarely found her tales amusing. A few months later, upon their return to New York, Jane was surprised to see in the window of a Fifth Avenue bookshop a picture of the "lecherous man" who had annoyed her. It was Henry Miller, and his picture was displayed prominently beside his new book, *Tropic of Capricorn*.[49] "We looked at it through the window a long time, but had no desire to buy it," said Bowles.[50]

Given the uneasiness of his relationship with Jane and other distractions to which they both were susceptible in Paris, Bowles had little heart for writing incidental music for the theater or for films. Instead of crossing over to Tangier in mid-July 1938, as he had hoped, Jane agreed to accompany him to Eze, a French village that had been built upon high rocky cliffs overlooking the Mediterranean, near Nice. "Jane still had a good bit of money left that she had come into when she turned twenty-one, and I had some from Aunt Adelaide's estate that I had squirreled away, so we leased a villa and contributed mutually to our expenses there."[51]

They had been in Eze scarcely a week when Bowles asked Jane if she would like him to invite his friend Kay Cowen to join them for a few days. "I had told Jane enough about Kay to pique her interest, and since she was both witty and intelligent, I thought they would be a good match. Also, I needed time to myself to compose in my detached studio behind our villa, and Jane needed other people around her."[52]

Before Cowen's arrival, Bowles was invited to dinner by the wife of Samuel Barlow, who had developed and owned half the village, but she failed to include Jane in the invitation. "Although hers was the initial gaffe, the gaffe was mine, too, since I accepted and went without her. Jane was furious, of course, because she had missed out on meeting new people, which caused a further breach in our relationship. It was stupid and inconsiderate of me," he allowed.[53]

On August 1, 1938, Cowen wrote her mother: "Paul and wife Jane are in Eze, near Nice, and want me to come there–swimming in the Mediterranean, etc. I do want to see them, and I am very pleased with the suggestion. They have two rooms in somebody's villa, and if I go there I can eat all my meals with them." A week later, Cowen announced her arrival in Eze on a picture postcard to her mother: "You can see at a glance how easy it is to go for a swim. Twenty minutes straight down until your knees break and three quarters of an hour straight up until your lungs burst. Tonight there is a full moon, and tiny lights twinkle on Cap Ferrat. It is incredibly beautiful." Cowen described Eze as "a sweet little mediaeval village until an American named Barlow bought the chateau and twelve surrounding houses, and incorporated it all into a dwelling for himself and his wife and daughter. Then a man who led a gypsy orchestra in Belgrade went to New York and married a lot of money, and did the same sort of thing. So between them they own the village and seem to be the sole support of its inhabitants."[54]

In one letter to her mother from Eze, Cowen described Jane as an immature woman who enjoyed attracting attention to herself. "She certainly won't be much help to Paul ever, but he likes her. I hope she won't hurt his work. They are sailing this very day for America because he suddenly got a telegram asking him to do the music for a Victorian revival that is to open September 25. Their departure was characterized by such disorder as I have never seen. And Jane did nothing about anything."[55]

Bowles had already interrupted his work on *Denmark Vesey* to write a chamber piece for six winds and strings, piano, and percussion, which he called *Romantic Suite*. Bowles wrote Charles Henri Ford, "We left Eze abruptly, and I think this piece got left behind. Obviously I shouldn't say anything about Jane's losing things. I've had my share of things going astray."[56] He grumbled about having to give up his studio overlooking the sea, but Jane was delighted by the prospect of returning to New York sooner than they had anticipated. To forfeit the unused rent they had paid upon signing the lease was of little consequence to Jane, but to Bowles the financial loss was considerable. The only ship they could take on such short notice was the SS *Europa*, a German vessel leaving from Marseilles.

In contrast to their trip over, they found the return voyage almost pleasant. "There were mostly French and Italians aboard, and a few Americans like us hurrying home. This time we played our calypso records on deck, and Jane was cheerful throughout the voyage, in anticipation, I am sure, of being once more with her friends."[57] Bowles noted that they had been away for almost six months, and despite their efforts to act as though nothing had changed, both knew that the honeymoon was over.

The play for which he was summoned home, *Too Much Johnson,* was already in production, with Joseph Cotton in the lead role and Arlene Francis and Ruth Ford in supporting roles. A gifted actress, Ruth was Charles Henri Ford's sister. Welles's wife, Virginia, his coproducer, John Houseman, and Marc Blitzstein played minor roles. "I might have been smitten by Ruth Ford had I not been married to Jane," Bowles allowed later. "She was beautiful and sophisticated and more generous-spirited than any woman I knew," said Bowles.[58]

"There's a hell of a lot of music to compose for it," he informed Charles Henri Ford to explain his interruption on *Denmark Vesey*.[59] As originally staged, *Too Much Johnson* was a Victorian adaptation by William Gillette that had evolved from a still earlier play, *La Plantation Thomassin*, set in Santiago, Chile. Having read Gillette's production of *Too Much Johnson*, director Orson Welles was determined to present a different play through rhythm, momentum, and lighting. *Too Much Johnson* was to have been Welles's means of breaking free of the confines of the stage altogether, and to this end he introduced film segments juxtaposed with the actors onstage.[60] Bowles was grossly disappointed when he learned that the music he had been called home to compose for the entire play would be used now only as an accompaniment to two short cinematographic sequences presented between acts.

In an interview, Bowles declared that Welles was a genius and the czar of the production. "He did costumes, sets, everything."[61] Bowles appreciated the fact that despite Welles's knowing little about music, he was intelligent enough not to interfere except once. "The musicians were rehearsing and he suddenly said, 'Yes, yes, I like this bit, but couldn't they play it in some sort of minor key?' I couldn't explain to him that it was impossible." Bowles was taken aback when John Houseman informed him that he and Welles had decided that *Too Much Johnson* was inappropriate as an opener for the second season, and that they had already selected a different play, *Danton's Death*, to take its place. "But my music would not be at all appropriate for *Danton's Death*," Bowles countered, having assumed that the music he had written for *Too Much Johnson* would be used for *Danton's Death*.

Houseman's response was that since the company had finished its first season with a profit of forty thousand dollars, he could not risk the success and health of the group on what he now saw as a "trivial, tedious, and under-rehearsed play." Whereas *Too Much Johnson* was originally scheduled to open on Broadway, Welles and Houseman compromised by agreeing to present it as an interim production in a regional theater in Stony Creek, Connecticut. Bowles was not appeased. What no one realized at the time was that Stony Creek's fire regulations prohibited the use of nitrate film in a projector because it was highly flammable. Upon learning that, Welles informed the cast that the film footage was canceled and that the play must run without it. To Bowles, the production was pitiful. *Too Much Johnson* closed after three performances.[62]

Angry and resentful that he was given only a hundred dollars for his "work and trouble," Bowles complained that it had cost him and his wife twenty times that amount to abandon their villa in Eze and establish themselves once again in New York. "Ultimately, my complaint resulted in no additional payment, and I had only myself to blame. Yet I rejoiced that one good thing ultimately came out of it, a small suite for clarinet, trumpet, piano, and percussion derived from some of the numbers, which I called *Music for a Farce.* Some people said they liked it better than anything else I had done."[63]

Whereas he and Jane had checked into the Hotel Chelsea and rented a good-size room with a private bath for fifteen dollars a week, they now felt obliged to look for cheaper quarters. Finally, for a room with kitchen privileges in a ramshackle building on Seventh Avenue at Eighteenth Street, they paid five dollars a week. Their alcoholic landlady, whom they knew only as "Lady Saunders," divided her time between building fireplaces and bookshelves for her lodgers and drinking wine with Jane and a few odd characters from the neighborhood.[64] In January 1933, Bowles wrote Charles Henri Ford that a fire had routed them from their room and forced them to camp out in unheated rooms until their fireplace could be rebuilt. When word of their plight reached John Becker, a friend of Bowles, he gave them two rooms in his Sutton Place apartment and insisted that they stay as long as they wished.[65]

Already Bowles had resolved to go on relief if he could establish his eligibility, but instead of seeking advice from the Federal Emergency Relief Administration, he visited the Communist Party USA headquarters, where he was advised, unofficially, to take a room in an impoverished area of the city, then to present himself to the nearest Workers' Alliance Hall so that a relief examiner could determine if he were eligible for help from the federal government. Unless his name could be added to an official federal relief roll, he would be denied employment on the Federal Music Project, which he now desperately sought. When Bowles had worked previously on the Federal Theatre Project, being on relief was not a requirement, but the rules to participate had tightened in the meantime.

"I still had the studio apartment at 2 Water Street in Brooklyn Heights, for which I had paid a year's rent in advance, and the same old upright piano was in it that I had used while working on the first act of *Denmark Vesey*. Since I was working now on the second act, I thought it fitting to establish myself there while I awaited review," said Bowles. The federal relief examiner who presented herself to Bowles's door on Water Street was sympathetic when he told her that he had a wife to support and very little money. Then he played and sang for her from the first two acts of *Denmark Vesey*. "I could tell that she was impressed, and within a week she delivered my card in person. Each week Jane went with me to my relief board in Brooklyn and together we carried home great sacks of food and sometimes even suitcases full of sugar, butter, flour, and other staples. When my father learned of my new status, he was incensed. 'Good Americans are paying their taxes so that a lot of parasites like you can live without working. What's happened to America's moral sense?'"[66]

As though in reply, Bowles delighted in telling his father that he and Jane had recently joined the Communist Party USA.[67] "My father was flabbergasted and demanded to know how a member of the party could continue to accept groceries and government funds. I assured him that I had no problem with it. I did not add that I had always found it exciting to get something for nothing, and that we were not actually living on Water Street in Brooklyn but with my friend on Sutton Place."[68]

At party headquarters, Bowles was asked the name he would like to use in joining the party.

"How do you prefer it?" he replied.

"Oh, we'd rather you use your real name, of course."

"So we went in as Paul and Jane Bowles. Later I discovered that many new members used pseudonyms. For example, we both knew that John Latouche was a member of the party, but he was cagey and did not admit it."

For several weeks Bowles and Jane attended a class in Marxism-Leninism that met at the Workers' School in Manhattan. "Jane only went because I went. 'I don't know what I'm reading,' she complained when she studied our textbook. I knew what I was reading, and that made it worse." To compensate for their lack of devotion to the principles of Marxism-Leninism, they saw every Russian film they could.

Later, Jane tried to renew her American passport in Lisbon, but first had to sign a deposition that she was never a good Communist and had joined the party only because she wished to show her independence of her family. She also declared that since she was vehemently opposed to Hitler, as were the Communists, it was the right thing to do.[69] Her deposition read in part: "I was willingly dropped from the Party because it was stated I was not serious enough. I attended a possible eight meetings before leaving the Party. After this I had no further contacts with any of the other members. I completely lost all belief in any of the ideals or promises of the Party. During my membership I never heard any mention of the overthrowing of the United States Government and I certainly never advocated any such procedure."[70]

In the spring of 1939, Bowles rented a two-story farmhouse outside Prince's Bay, on the remote south end of Staten Island, for which he paid five months' rent. "I suspected it would be good for Jane, too, if she were less distracted by certain friends whom I considered a bad influence, and also by the various goings on in the city which distracted me as well." The timing was right because Bowles had just been commissioned by director Bobby Lewis to write the music for William Saroyan's *My Heart's in the Highlands*, scheduled as a workshop production by the Group Theatre. This time a condition of his acceptance was that Lewis would provide him with a good piano on which to work. "I was given the keys to Clifford Odets's apartment since Odets was to be away for six weeks, which was my deadline, also. 'Odets doesn't have a piano, but he has a lovely Hammond organ,' said Lewis."

Reviews were mixed upon the play's opening on April 13, 1939, at the New York Guild Theatre on Broadway, but after laudatory pieces by Brooks Atkinson, George Jean Nathan, and John Mason Brown, it was extended five weeks. Atkinson's reviews in the *New York Times* were generally well regarded by play-goers, who agreed that Bowles's music "notably sweetened the occasion" and concluded that *My*

Heart's in the Highlands was the "finest new play put on by the Group this season."[71]

Bowles recalled reviewer Burns Mantle's observation that the "play's meaning, sense, or excuse eluded him," but that attendees might "still get something for their money, and possibly for their minds as well." Of Bowles's music, Mantle observed it was "probably good, being a little weird."[72] Odets's play was still running on Broadway when Bowles and Jane moved to Staten Island, where a stream of visitors followed them on weekends. One of their first guests was composer Colin McPhee, who had recently returned from Bali. "Colin prepared for us some lovely Indonesian meals while Jane looked on in wonder and decided that she, too, would like to learn to make such exotic dishes," said Bowles. "Leonard Bernstein might have stayed longer, but he was allergic to Jane's cat and sneezed all night. Harry Dunham and Latouche brought their fiancées, Marian Chase and Teddy Griffis, an engagement that surprised everyone since we knew that both usually preferred men as their sexual partners." Judy Holliday, who was appearing with Betty Comden at the Village Vanguard Club, was another overnight guest, as was Elsie Houston, a Brazilian singer they had met in Eze. Their most difficult houseguest was Mary Crouch Oliver, who turned up unexpectedly, widowed a year earlier upon Jock Oliver's death, and needed a place to stay.[73]

Bowles asked Jane to draft a welcoming letter to Oliver and her maid, and she did, but it was not a letter he wished to send, and he was horrified when he read it. "It was Jane at her wittiest, and everything she said was true, but I asked her not to mail it. Instead, I wrote a carefully worded letter of my own, which conveyed our frugal life at present, then sent Jane's letter to Kay Cowen for safekeeping. Kay wired me that she, too, wanted to come to Staten Island and was not put off by my tales of Mary's uncontrollable thirst for alcohol, or the state of our household no matter who else was present."[74]

Bowles also told Cowen that he had taken a room in town because Latouche had caused such extraordinary chaos and havoc during his fortnight with them that he could not work there, but hoped that she would come anyway. "We now have a nice German woman who comes every day to clean and pick up the mess. It is probably a crucial moment in Jane's life. But only one among many, I suspect!"[75]

To Bowles's surprise, Jane's progress on her novel while they were on Staten Island was impressive, which he realized when she gave it to him in small segments to read. "Everything seemed disconnected, but it was funny, too, given her odd way of looking at things. In a sense, I envied Jane, whose tools were always at hand, whereas I was constantly required to have a piano and a place to put it. She could write anywhere and liked doing it with a great hubbub of activity surrounding her. Her distractions and the background noises were a part of her writing process and the end result as well. I don't recall precisely what triggered it, but I did write a short story myself in the fall of 1939 after I left the farmhouse and stayed alone in Brooklyn Heights. I called it 'Tea on the Mountain,' and it was set in Tangier."[76] Bowles had no idea that he was about to launch himself into a new career as a writer.

Meanwhile, Mary Oliver and her maid remained with Jane on Staten Island until mid-November; then the three of them moved together into a leased apartment on West Thirteenth Street. Bowles was amazed that Oliver had managed to lease the apartment without presenting any rent money up front and had furnished it on credit from Wanamaker's. "She apparently had warned the manager at Wanamaker's that she intended to furnish an entire apartment, whereupon he assured her that she should buy whatever she wished. He had seen the British passport of her husband and had no idea that he was dead. Jane was fascinated by Mary Oliver's maneuvering, having cherished for years the tales of clever people adept at getting something for nothing."[77]

On January 3, 1940, Bowles informed Bruce Morrissette that he, Jane, and Mary Oliver all lived separately now. "It works better that way. Jane and I get more work done."[78] He did not speculate on how Mary Oliver was managing. To Kay Cowen, Bowles wrote that Jane was happier now that they were living separately. "Everyone seems dead broke, at least all of my friends."[79] By then, Bowles's relief case had come up for review. In an effort to check out the allegation that Bowles still needed to be on relief, an investigator presented himself at the front door of his client's childhood home in Jamaica, New York, where Bowles's parents were still living, and was quietly astonished to be told by a housekeeper that he must present himself at the service entrance. "Not in present need," the investigator reported, and recommended that Bowles be dropped immediately from both the relief rolls and the Federal Music Project.[80]

It was Cowen to whom Bowles expressed most frequently his views regarding the political scene in America in 1939–40. Although neither a Communist nor a fellow traveler, Cowen engaged Bowles in long discussions about party politics and the various goings-on to which he was privy. From Staten Island he wrote Cowen of his disenchantment by the Communist Party USA primarily because of the inconsistency of various messages conveyed by the *Daily Worker*. "I would be more pleased with the *Worker* if it would say what it means instead of clinging to the idea of democracy on page two, and making it evident it isn't interested on page three, praising Roosevelt on page one, saying he is worthless on page five, then blaming the Soviet Union's present policy on page six, and concluding on page four that it would save peace and bring war faster," he wrote Cowen during the late summer of 1939.[81]

Sometimes Bowles telephoned various party members to see what they thought of a particular situation, then reported to Cowen what he had learned. "They seem to think the Party should divorce itself from Moscow. I think that would be the most asinine procedure they could follow. Those people should be expelled, and the Party reduced to those members who understand what it's all about, and who are ready to follow the lead of the Soviet Union. Were you ever taken in for a minute by [Roosevelt's] Democratic Front?" Bowles had just read in the *New York Times* that the Soviet Union and Nazi Germany had signed in Berlin a seven-year trade agreement providing the Russians with extensive credits with which to purchase German-manufactured goods in exchange for Russian grain and raw materials. On August 22, 1939, the Soviet news agency Tass announced that Germany's foreign minister, Joachim von Ribbentrop,[82] would fly to Moscow to sign the Non-Aggression Pact between Germany and the Soviet Union. The next day the Communist Party's political committee assembled in emergency session. Bowles followed such events each night on the radio, read regularly the two newspapers of the party, the *Daily Worker* and *Freiheit*, a Communist Yiddish daily, and reported to Cowen whatever he thought would interest her.

In one letter he said that a piece of his was being played in concert at the 1939 New York World's Fair in Flushing Meadows, and that he had taken the event as an occasion to go out early to talk with a few of the musicians about the Ribbentrop-Molotov Pact since all were either Communist Party members or sympathizers. "Well, where do we go from here?" one musician asked Bowles.

"We [go] straight ahead as though nothing has happened, because we [will] see it later as a Soviet ploy to crush the Nazis," replied Bowles.[83]

Looking back upon the heady and disturbing years of 1939 and 1940, Bowles declared that since he was not a writer but a composer, he had nothing to do with the League of American Writers, but knew many of its members and followed as best he could what was going on. "Ultimately, I knew that it was time for me to leave the Party. Communist writers under Party discipline were expected to take on the literary assignments that would be most immediately beneficial to the revolutionary cause, and I would never have been willing to comply. As a composer, I had avoided such expectations and remained on the edge of the fray. Meanwhile, I was given definite assignments as a member of the Federal Music Project, but naturally they were not political. I remember composing a piece for eight clarinets for a group in the Bronx, some piano music for children in elementary school, and a few choral pieces for adult groups. Most of the time I was free to do my own work. After the relief investigator checked on my family's circumstances in Jamaica, all of that stopped."[84]

In the spring of 1940, William Saroyan asked Bowles to compose the music for *Love's Old Sweet Song.* "Bill was terribly naive as a playwright. I remember that Dorothy Norman wanted to meet him, so I arranged for the three of us to meet for lunch at the Russian Tea Room. Throughout the meal, he hardly spoke except in response to something that either Dorothy or I said. 'I want to put that down,' he would say, then dived into his notebook and began writing. In fact, he wrote all through the meal. I couldn't believe it. Dorothy and I looked at each other suspiciously while this was going on, and I knew that she, too, was wondering if we would end up as characters in his next play."

With money in his wallet once again, this time for his contract to compose the music for *Love's Old Sweet Song,* Bowles and Jane returned to the Hotel Chelsea, but their living arrangement quickly wore thin. "Jane stayed out inordinately late, her habits reminiscent of those during our honeymoon. One evening I discovered our apartment filled with noisy strangers." Clearly annoyed, he told Jane that it was late, and that he had to be up early the next morning to work on his show; then he retired to the bathroom to await the guests' departure. To his astonishment, he discovered a strange woman lying in the tub wearing one of Jane's dressing gowns. In a steely voice, his temper mounting, Bowles strode into the front room and instructed Jane: "Get these people out of here and get that woman out of the bathtub!"[85]

"These are my friends," she retorted. "They'll leave eventually."

"There was no mistaking her meaning," concluded Bowles. "Her friends would leave when they were good and ready. We had a heated exchange in front of the remaining guests, who left, finally, and as in Cannes, Jane reproached me for being a killjoy." Angry beyond measure, as before, he struck her a solid blow on the cheek. "Again she told me that she forgave me and still loved me. Although the marriage had all the earmarks of a union irretrievably broken, as they say in the courts today, I was wrong. We did make love in Albuquerque a couple of times during the spring of 1940, then, as suddenly as it had commenced, that was the end of it. After that, I stopped trying, and we never made love again."[86]

Bowles was ambivalent about his feelings for Jane, and he regretted his impatience and sudden rages directed at her. No matter how forgiving Jane appeared to be, Bowles readily admitted that he should never have taken his anger out on her in any physical way. "I should never have slapped her, and the fact that I had slapped her twice was unforgivable, no matter how forgiving she appeared to be in return. I was abjectly ashamed of myself, but that did not change things," he admitted.[87]

Bowles was scheduled to go to Albuquerque, New Mexico, to write a score for the film *Roots in the Soil*, a documentary about the Rio Grande Valley commissioned by the Soil Erosion Service, and he assumed that he would be going alone. Then Jane suggested that she go too, providing she could invite a friend of hers to join them. It was Robert (Boo) Faulkner, who worked regularly for the *New Yorker*, but planned to quit his job if he were allowed to go with them. Although taken aback by her proposal, Bowles knew that he would rather be with Jane, on her terms, whatever they might be, than not at all. Later, she told him that his view of life depressed her to such an extent that when they were together "everything seemed hopeless." Her nickname for him at this point was "Gloompot," which he thought appropriate, but with Faulkner along, "who laughed more or less continuously," Jane hoped to find in him a counterbalance.

Upon finishing the film, Bowles had every intention of going to Mexico and staying as long as possible, but he also worried that the upcoming Mexican elections might trigger a civil war and close the borders before they had a chance to cross. In six weeks he finished the film, and they boarded a train to Mexico City. Ultimately, Bowles was relieved that Faulkner was along to keep Jane company. "Once we were safely across the border, I was in no hurry to get anywhere, and for the first time in many months Jane was in excellent spirits."[88]

Glenora, New York, July 1912. "From my mother's photo album—I have never seen my mother look so fetching, or my father so relaxed."
(Photo courtesy of Paul Bowles)

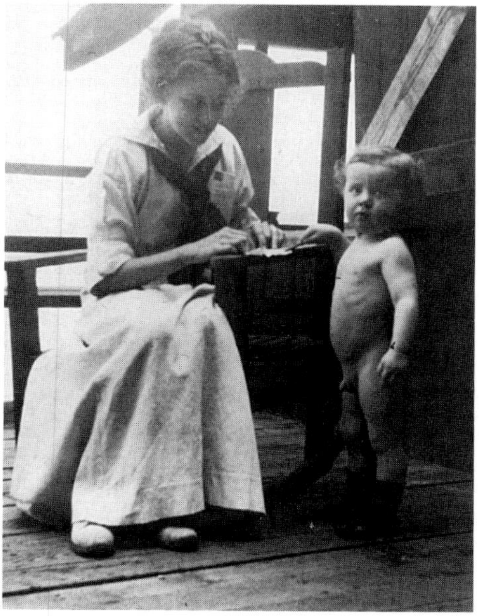

Paul Bowles in the nude at eighteen months, July 1912. "I have no idea where this picture was taken, or by whom. I seem to be holding a writing instrument of some sort—perhaps that was the point of the picture. I found this snapshot in my mother's photo album."
(Photo courtesy of Paul Bowles)

Drawing by Paul Bowles at age sixteen as cover for his manuscript of poems published individually in the *Oracle*, Jamaica High School, Jamaica, New York.
(Courtesy of Photography Collection, Harry Ransom Humanities Research Center, University of Texas at Austin)

Paul Bowles at sixteen, Jamaica, New York.
(Photo courtesy of Betty Ann Austin)

"My aunt Emma's husband, Guy Ross. He always looked like something out of the *Gentleman's Quarterly*."
(Photo courtesy of Harold Wesley Danser III)

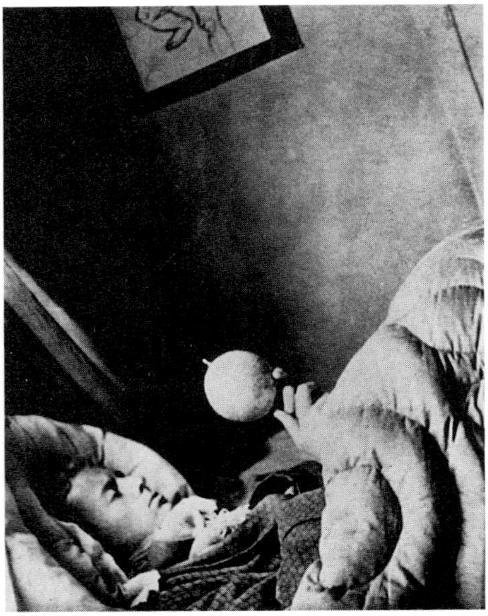

Paul Bowles, Paris, 1931.
(Photo courtesy of Paul Bowles)

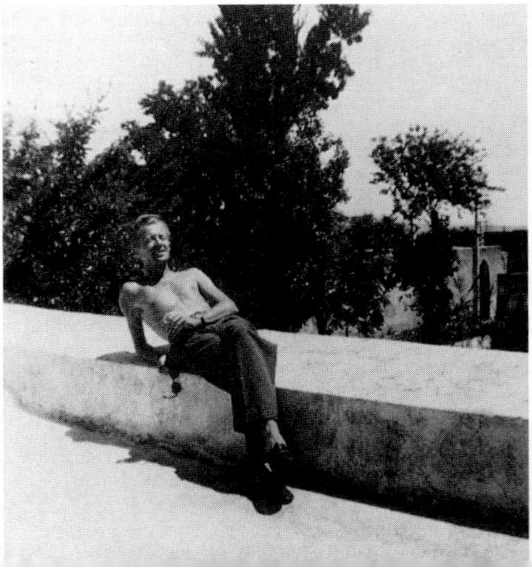

Paul Bowles in Morocco, 1949.
(Photo courtesy of Paul Bowles)

Oliver Smith with Jane and Paul Bowles, New York.

(Copyright 1950 by Irving Penn, courtesy of Vogue*)*

Paul Bowles and Tennessee Williams during Williams's first visit to Morocco, January 1949.

(Courtesy of Photography Collection, Harry Ransom Humanities Research Center, University of Texas at Austin)

Left to right: Emilio Sanz de Soto, José (Pepe) Cárleton Abrines, Truman Capote, Jane Bowles, and Paul Bowles with Cotorrito, his Amazon parrot. El Faharar, Tangier, October 1949.

(Photo courtesy of Emilio Sanz de Soto)

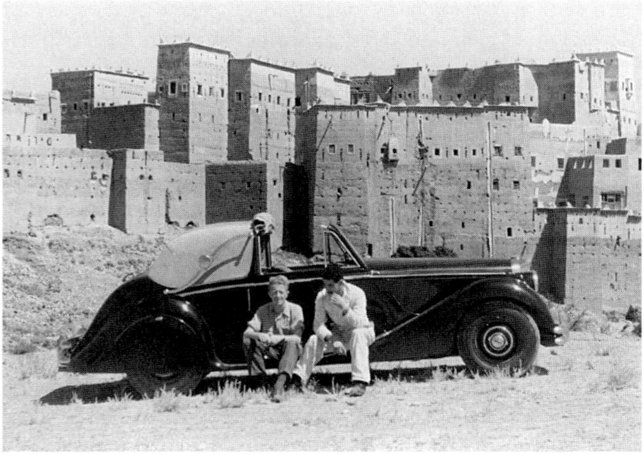

Paul Bowles with his driver, Mohammed Temsamany, outside the Casbah of Ouarzazate, in the High Atlas, autumn 1950.

(Photo by Brion Gysin, courtesy of Photography Collection, Harry Ransom Humanities Research Center, University of Texas at Austin)

Paul Bowles, Tangier, 1954.
(Courtesy of Photography Collection, Harry Ransom Humanities Research Center, University of Texas at Austin)

Paul Bowles on the roof of his house in the Casbah.
(Photo by Emilio Sanz de Soto, courtesy of Emilio Sanz de Soto)

Outside William Burroughs's room in the Villa Muniriya, Tangier, summer 1961. From left to right: Gregory Corso, Paul Bowles, Ian Sommerville, Michael Fortman, and Burroughs.
(Photo by Allen Ginsberg, courtesy of Allen Ginsberg)

Jane Bowles crossing the Atlantic with Tennessee Williams from New York to Málaga, Spain.
(Photo courtesy of Paul Bowles)

Libby Holman, a popular American torch singer, asked Bowles to marry her and suggested that Jane could live with them, an invitation that he did not accept.
(Photo by Marcus Belchman, courtesy of Photography Collection, Harry Ransom Humanities Research Center, University of Texas at Austin)

Virgil Thomson and Jane Bowles, Tangier.
(Courtesy of Photography Collection, Harry Ransom Humanities Research Center, University of Texas at Austin)

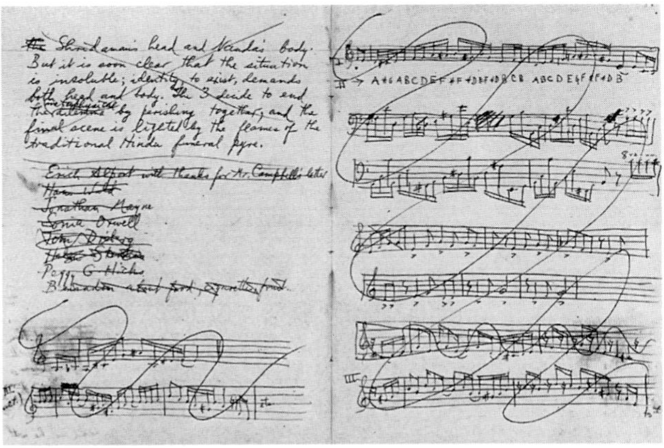

A page from Bowles's notebook, Tangier.
(Courtesy of Photography Collection, Harry Ransom Humanities Research Center, University of Texas at Austin)

Paul Bowles with his mother,
Rena Winnewisser Bowles,
Tangier, 1956.
(Photo courtesy of Paul Bowles)

Paul Bowles by the Kelani Ganga,
Sri Lanka, 1950.
*(Courtesy of Photography Collection,
Harry Ransom Humanities Research Center,
University of Texas at Austin)*

Paul Bowles and Abdelouahaid Boulaich
at the pet cemetery, Tangier, 1994.
(Photo by Cherie Nutting, courtesy of Cherie Nutting)

David Herbert on his terrace, date unknown.
(Photo courtesy of Jdaoudi Med. Nourredine)

Cherie Nutting to Paul Bowles: "If you were an animal, what would you be?" Bowles: "A cat or a macaw." Paul Bowles in Tangier, 1987.
(Photo by Cherie Nutting, courtesy of Cherie Nutting)

Paul Bowles with Joseph A. McPhillips III, March 1998, in Bowles's study, listening to his latest music for a production at the American School of Tangier.
(Photo by Cherie Nutting, courtesy of Cherie Nutting)

CHAPTER SEVEN

Paul and Jane in Acapulco, Where They Meet Tennessee Williams

(1940–1943)

"I brought one novel down here with me called The Heart Is a Lonely Hunter *by a young girl named Carson McCullers. It is so extraordinary it makes me ashamed of anything I might do. What a play she could write!"*[1]

—Tennessee Williams to Bennett Cerf,
September 1940, Acapulco, Mexico

Tennessee Williams, still a fledgling playwright, was on the rebound from a Cape Cod romance gone sour when he met Paul and Jane Bowles in Acapulco. The Mexican border was still open, and Americans crossed over as they saw fit. Among the names given to Williams by his friends in New York was Paul Bowles, to whom he presented himself at once. On the day he arrived, Bowles and Jane were just leaving the hacienda they had rented to spend the afternoon at the beach. In a whispered aside, Jane urged her husband to get rid of him; instead, he suggested that their visitor make himself at home until they returned. "Here is the house. Here is the patio. Here are hammocks. Here's a new bottle of rum, and there's plenty of Coke. You just call the servants and they'll bring you sandwiches or whatever you need." Upon their return, seven hours later, they found Williams still ensconced, having partaken of the amenities and stretched out now in a hammock reading *The Heart Is a Lonely Hunter*. For two weeks they saw one another daily.[2]

To various people upon his return to New York, Williams described his new friends in Acapulco as "an odd and charming couple"; however, his memory of their "one evening together," which he mentioned later in his memoirs, was chiefly of Bowles's stomach, diet, pet names for Jane, and dyspeptic humor. "Oh, Bubbles, if you'd just stick to cornflakes and fresh fruit!" Williams quoted Jane as saying.[3]

Surprised by Williams's recollection of having spent only a single evening with them in Acapulco, Bowles retorted: "Certainly I was never Bubbles, although Jane sometimes called me Bubble. More often she addressed me in letters and notes as Bup, Buppie, Bupple, or Budupple, the name we assigned our first parrot. Budupple was also the persona I assumed when we pretended I was a parrot she was ordering back into its cage. It was all a great game, and nothing we would have shared that first night with Tennessee, who conflated our several encounters in Acapulco to make it suit his design."[4]

Williams's recollection of Bowles's dietary concerns stemmed from the incipient nausea he experienced upon arrival in Mexico City. Whereas neither Jane nor Faulkner was bothered by the rarified atmosphere of Jajalpa, a remote village thirty-five miles southwest of Mexico City to which they traveled next, Bowles spent much of his time in bed. Since Jane was unpredictable except in her inconsistency and inability to make a decision, or if she made one to stick with it, Bowles worried that she would find the isolation unacceptable. Yet through it all, she was determined to finish her novel.

To Bowles, the vastness of the landscape had a paralyzing effect. He was reminded of Thomas Mann's observation that "being in the presence of a great natural spectacle impedes the desire to create." It also impeded Bowles's desire for food. He was convinced that if he could get to the sea, his health would improve, but he wanted to see Mexico City first.[5] Here he visited the Communist Party headquarters to offer, vaguely, his services, whereupon a party official suggested that he allow sightseers to inspect the property they were renting since it was one of the few old-fashioned working haciendas in the area. The house itself consisted of twenty rooms wrapped around a giant courtyard; outside were barns, a chapel, some eighty cows that required milking daily, and several hundred sheep. As a result of Bowles's visit to party headquarters, a swarm of tourists, mostly Americans, came twice to Jajalpa, gawked and exclaimed appropriately at what was promised in a promotion brochure, then were served lunch, which Jane organized since she liked observing the tourists from the vantage of the kitchen. "Finally, it got too much for all of us, and we agreed that I should hire a car and go alone to Mexico City, then on to Acapulco, where Jane and Boo Faulkner would join me later."[6]

Although Jane worked daily on her novel and spent considerable time in the kitchen adding significantly to her repertoire of recipes, the isolation was overwhelming. Writing, drinking with Faulkner, interacting with the servants and tourists, all were of little consequence unless someone else was at hand with whom she could be on intimate terms, preferably another woman. Jane wired Bowles in early September that she was leaving immediately with Faulkner and two servants, and that he must find a house in Acapulco in which they all could stay.

Bowles did as Jane instructed, but the servants were homesick and wept as they worked. After a month, she bought them bus tickets and sent them home. The house Bowles had rented in Acapulco was not in itself extraordinary, but the birds and mammals who took up residence in the garden were. A large patio at the rear of the house, shaded by avocado and lemon trees and surrounded by a high wall, discouraged most two-legged visitors, but other creatures came and left at will. A half dozen rooms opened upon a wide, covered corridor off the patio, where six large hammocks were strung. "As I think back on it, the setting of *Night of the Iguana*, which Tennessee Williams started as a short story, then rewrote as a play, was not much different from the house we were renting when he visited us in September of 1940."[7]

When Jane decided that she had had enough of Acapulco and

wanted to move somewhere else, preferably to Taxco, it was Bowles who collected the birds and animals and transported them there. It would not have occurred to Jane to want a house in Taxco had she not accompanied two friends from New York, Morris Golde and Gordon Sager, who invited her to ride with them to Taxco. "Janie was thrilled to have found a large community of expatriate Americans who had lived in Taxco for some time and seemed far more interesting than those she encountered in Acapulco," said Golde.[8]

It was not that Jane wanted to put down roots in Taxco, but she wanted to be with people who already had. Bowles himself had no desire to live there, having concluded during an earlier visit that the mountain air of Taxco was oppressive, yet from there he could return relatively easily when summoned to New York.[9] By the time he arrived in Taxco with Jane's menagerie, he found her already enamored of Helvetia Orr Perkins, who had settled in Taxco with her daughter, Nora, to wait out the war. Perkins was forty-five, sophisticated, and divorced. Born in Switzerland, she grew up with several sisters in Evanston, Illinois, attended private schools in the East, traveled abundantly abroad, and lived in Paris with Nora before joining the community of expatriates in Taxco.

Despite his discovery of Jane's new romantic attachment, Bowles was more concerned that he had composed almost no music during the summer and fall of 1940. Nonetheless, he decided to turn to poetry and wrote a sequence of poems, which he titled *Scenes*.[10] In his introduction to a manuscript of poems, *Air to the Sea: Collected Poems, 1923–1977*, Bowles commented upon the circumstances from which his *Scenes* evolved: "In the summer of 1940 came the abrogation of the Ribbentrop-Molotov Pact and the German army's attack on the Soviet Union. For some reason American sympathies were with the Russians rather than the Nazis, and this eventually made the Soviet Union America's ally. It seemed to me an intolerable situation, and I felt that there was no hope for mankind." Bowles declared that the series of scenes, dated September 1940, illustrated his disinclination to accept the Russians as friends. Although he was still a card-carrying member of the party, he had decided that Stalin and Hitler were "two tyrants" he had no reason "ever to think about again."[11]

Bowles had been in Taxco less than a month when the Theatre Guild summoned him to New York to write a score for *Twelfth Night*, scheduled to open on November 19 at the St. James Theatre. Air travel was "pleasant in those days," said Bowles, who marveled that he had his own cabin as well as a bed. Coincidental with his summons to New York to work on *Twelfth Night* was an order to report to his draft board there, the United States Congress having enacted on September 16, 1940, a Selective Service Act requiring all men between the ages of twenty and thirty-six to register for the draft. Bowles was twenty-nine.

Although he passed the physical examination, he was declared 4-F by the induction psychiatrist. "I told him I could not sleep in a room or barracks with other men, and that I had always, without exception, slept alone with my door locked. No matter how they asked their questions, I was unwavering in those two requirements. Had they threatened me with jail, I would not have answered otherwise. I'm sure they knew of my affiliation with the Communist Party of the U.S.A. and concluded that I was up to no good. The induction psychiatrist also was dumbfounded that anyone could be a composer. On his report he wrote 'Paul Bowles. Writes symphonies. Rejection recommended.'"[12] Tennessee Williams told Bowles that he, too, had been declared 4-F. "I'm not sure why Tennessee was turned down, but I assumed it was his poor eyesight. I am sure he did not have my hang-up about locked doors."[13]

Twelfth Night, starring Helen Hayes as Viola in her first Shakespearean role on Broadway, and Maurice Evans as Malvolio, opened to considerable fanfare in mid-November 1940. Critics termed Hayes's performance "superb" and Evans's rendering of Malvolio "Shakespearean acting at its best." Brooks Atkinson, who described the play as "rowdy, dry-humored, and briskly paced," singled out Bowles's music for "its freedom from Elizabethan affectation and more in a spirit of loveliness than of innocence." John Mason Brown applauded the production's "uncommon charm which fittingly moved to the measures of Bowles's music." Virgil Thomson, too, wrote positively of Bowles's music in the *New York Herald Tribune*: "Bowles's gift as a composer of theater music [is] so precise in its functional design and accurate in its adjustment to the subject of each play that it hits his audience squarely in both ears and rings the bell for the play at every music cue. With six musicians–flute, oboe, harp, imitation harpsichord, percussion and, very occasionally, a muted trumpet–he makes a rich and ancient-sounding ensemble that is more sufficient than a larger group would be of more disparate sonorities." Then Thomson described what he called the "Bowles formula":

"He writes no brassy pit-music, no off-stage realistic sound-effects. He does what nearly every musician in the world would say, on principle, can't be done. He writes chamber-music to accompany large theatrical productions, and he aggravates his supposed error by putting [his musicians] in the pit. . . . His emphasis comes from contrast of tune and timbre, from structure and harmonic progress, never from weight. He leaves that to the actors. . . . Were it not for Shakespeare himself and Miss Hayes's and Mr. Evans's faithful and absorbed public, Mr. Bowles might easily have walked away with *Twelfth Night*."[14]

After touring with *Twelfth Night* in New Haven and Boston and attending its opening in New York, Bowles was asked by Theresa Helburn to write the music for *Liberty Jones*, whose script Philip Barry had just finished. Bowles could see that *Liberty Jones* would be a musical extravaganza and require an enormous amount of work, so he wired Jane in Taxco and told her to come to New York. "I don't think she took my summons amiss. Her coming up from Mexico simply made sense. Certainly there was no 'please, Jane, wouldn't you like to come to New York, and I will book you a room at the Chelsea, where I am staying?' That was not our way. Besides, she liked New York far more than I did. I wasn't thrilled to see Boo Faulkner so soon, but he came, too, and stayed at the Chelsea."[15]

Jane had a room of her own, and they saw each other daily. "I missed her when we were apart, and in our own way we nurtured each other and continued to have a wonderful time together. She made me laugh–I mean really laugh–whereas with others I might chuckle a bit, smile, and wear a pleasant face. I seldom begrudged her desire to have other people around. I understood her needs and could usually anticipate them. Jane arrived on Christmas Day and was joined a few days later by Helvetia Perkins."[16]

Bowles saw much of Leonard Bernstein, who was studying that winter at the Curtis Institute in Philadelphia when *Liberty Jones* opened there. To Bernstein he complained that he was so busy trying to fit the 158 musical cues to *Liberty Jones* that he had no time to orchestrate two scores for a ballet company in New York that were due almost immediately. Bernstein offered to orchestrate the ballet scores for Bowles since he was so busy, whereupon Bowles paid him his own commission of three hundred dollars. Bowles concluded later that Bernstein had arranged the instrumentation in a "perverse and unlikely fashion, giving to the brass those passages which lent themselves to strings. It was not at all what the ballet company wanted, he told me subsequently, and with glee" since only Bowles's name appeared on the scores.[17]

Liberty Jones provoked a barrage of hostile criticism from reviewers upon its opening at the Shubert Theatre on February 5, 1941. "Although the play was not a huge success that night, Jane was. At the party afterward, she was introduced as 'Paul's delightful little Mexican bride,' and she acted the part, accent and all. Jane was a wonderful mimic and got a kick out of role-playing. If she were the butt of a harmless joke, she ran with it. Jane's resilience was only one of the things I admired about her."[18]

Despite the poor reception of *Liberty Jones*, Bowles was asked next by Herman Shumlin to write the music for Lillian Hellman's *Watch on the Rhine*, a request he readily accepted. By mid-March 1941, the play was ready for tryouts in Philadelphia, and a week later it opened at the Ford Theatre in Baltimore before premiering April 1 at the Martin Beck Theatre. Everything about Hellman's play pleased its audiences. The

New York Drama Critics' Circle Awards judges declared it the "finest American play of the season," and reviewers in general described it as "stunning," the "first great anti-Fascist drama," and a "vital, eloquent, and compassionate play about an American family suddenly awakening to the danger threatening its liberty." Bowles's music was declared "delicate," "wistful," and "hauntingly beautiful" in its mirroring of "the fragile yet determined hopes of the anti-Nazi movement." Donald Kirkley, writing for the *Baltimore Sun*, called *Watch on the Rhine* the "anti-Nazi play for which democracy has been waiting many years" and concluded that the show proved "that art is the best propaganda."

Succinct by nature in everything he wrote or composed, Bowles gave short shrift to the film version of *Watch on the Rhine* upon discovering that he had received no credit for his music. "When I saw the screen credits, I was dumbfounded since my name was not among them; instead, the musical accompaniment to the film was given to Max Steiner, who, someone pointed out later, had done the score for *Gone With the Wind*. I had to hire a lawyer before I received any compensation, and even then my name was never added to the credits, which was what I wanted in the first place."[19]

Virgil Thomson played the role of expert witness and declared that he had seen recently the film *Watch on the Rhine*, and that not only was the song sung by the leading male character Bowles's song, without appropriate credit, but also the same melody and harmony used during the screen credits and many times during the film itself, all of which were the property of Bowles. Thomson also pointed out five notable instances during the action of the film when the song was quoted at length. "I am sure I would not have gotten my money had it not been for Virgil's intervention. Despite our differences over the years, I could not have had a better friend. I never got over loving Aaron, but it was Virgil whom I knew I could count on."[20]

Bowles had just finished writing the music for Hellman's *Watch on the Rhine* when he persuaded Jane to move with him into a boardinghouse at 7 Middagh Street in Brooklyn Heights. He had heard about it from Lincoln Kirstein, who wanted to collaborate with him on an opera. Since Helvetia Perkins had returned to Taxco, Jane was amenable providing they could have two rooms. "Gypsy Rose Lee had stayed there briefly while writing *The G-String Murders*, and having finished the manuscript, moved out, which enabled Jane and me to move in," said Bowles, who described the house as "a model of *Gemütlichkeit*" filled with oddments that George Davis had picked up on Third Avenue and Brooklyn's Fulton Street. "When we were there, George lived on the first floor, Jane and I on the second, Benjamin Britten, W. H. Auden, and Peter Pears on the third, and Thomas Mann's son Golo in the attic. Our communal living worked well largely because Auden ran it. He would preface a meal by announcing: 'We've got a roast and two veg, salad and savory, and there will be no political discussion.' He had enough of the don about him to keep us all in order."[21]

Writer Michael Meyer remembered being invited by Peter Pears to 7 Middagh Street to celebrate Britten's twenty-seventh birthday. "It was a marvelous house, a broken-down house, in which we played children's games most of the evening: charades and 'ghosts' and things like that. Gypsy Rose Lee once sat on my lap with a gin bottle in her hand, and when I had to act out 'You Can't Take It with You,' I did so by trying to carry Carson McCullers across the threshold. It was very easy to carry her because she weighed practically nothing."[22]

Another friend of Auden's, Louis MacNeice, came to New York as a guest lecturer at Cornell University and visited the Middagh Street house, which he described as "a warren of the arts: Auden writing in one room, a girl novelist [McCullers] writing with a cup of sherry in another, a composer [Britten] composing, a singer [Pears] hitting a high note and holding it, and Gypsy Rose Lee coming round for meals like a whirlwind of laughter and sex. It was the way the populace once liked to think of artists—ever so bohemian, raiding the icebox at midnight and eating the cat food by mistake. But it was very enjoyable and at least they were producing."[23]

No matter how dictatorial Auden was, said Bowles, he "exercised a peculiar fascination over Jane," who was fond of him and offered to do his typing. "He accepted, and of course did not pay her. I don't think she ever typed for anyone else. What she did with her time was her own business, but I thought she ought to be working more on her novel. Of course she would have never gotten up at 6:00 a.m. to work on *Two Serious Ladies*. Her writing was far too sporadic for that. She and Auden worked together for about three hours each morning, calling out to the kitchen from time to time for more coffee. By 9:00 a.m., they had stopped working, and most of us had come to the table for breakfast. If we were late, we didn't eat."[24]

Bowles's sojourn with Jane at the Middagh Street house lasted four months. "We might have stayed longer had Auden not casually remarked that he would be requiring my room over the weekend," a definitive remark that annoyed Bowles no end. Later, he commented:

> I was just getting over the measles and had no intention of moving out and told him so. It was mid-winter, and I got grippe immediately after my recovery. I always kept a room to escape to, around the corner, on Columbia Heights, and it was to this room, I suppose, that Auden imagined I would go. "I have a friend coming from Michigan, and he will go into your room," he said. When I stated clearly that I was not giving up my room to anybody for any reason, Auden turned very white and went downstairs and out into the street, slamming the front door violently. I decided Auden disliked me because I was a Stalinist. From then on I would not let anything be said at the table without giving the Party's viewpoint on the subject; I knew this would annoy my antagonist more than anything else. It certainly made for unpleasant meals, and thereafter we did not speak, although Jane and I stayed on in the house until I finished my ballet. By this time, she, too, was ready to get back to Mexico and Helvetia.[25]

They were still at Middagh Street when Bowles received word that he was one of six composers being awarded a Guggenheim Fellowship. When the awards were announced on March 25, 1941, in the

New York Herald Tribune, Bowles was pictured on the front page with Carey McWilliams and Oliver LaFarge, a fiction writer known chiefly for his novel *Laughing Boy*. "I don't know how many times most composers, poets, and writers usually apply for a Guggenheim, but this was my third try at it. This time I proposed writing an opera for which William Saroyan had already written the libretto, which he called *Opera, Opera* and admitted later that he had never been to one. I was more interested in composing music for which I was offered commissions, yet attempted, upon my return to Mexico, to do something with Saroyan's libretto. By then, the whole idea was stale, so I turned my attention to García Lorca's *Así que Pasen Cinco Años*, having decided to make of it a *zarzuela*. The new work became my passion."[26]

Before leaving New York this time, Bowles secured the services of a Fifth Avenue theatrical agency, Matson and Duggan, to keep track of his commissions and earnings, negotiate his contracts, and prepare his tax returns since he was out of the country more than he was in it. Whereas Bruce Morrissette had managed to keep up with Bowles's music archives, he had scrupulously avoided any involvement in the financial end of things. Bowles was in Acapulco when his agent wrote: "I am enclosing herewith a statement of monies earned by you through us during 1941. It is too bad that I have not been able to get you a show recently; however, your Mexico residence is a very definite obstacle. The managers want to talk to you, but they will not send for you and they will not take the responsibility of your making a trip here just to consult. On the other hand, there has been very little 'incidental score' activity this season."

Bowles's 1941 royalty statement listed two payments by the Theatre Guild, one for *Twelfth Night* for $1,125, the other for *Liberty Jones* for $1,000; his commission for *Watch on the Rhine* was $1,200. The royalty statement also listed a $500 retainer to compose the music for *Pastorela*, which Kirstein had hoped to tour in Latin America; and $1,050 upon completion of the work. Still another commission was to orchestrate the score for Richard Hepburn's *Love Like Wildfire*. "I remember setting to music five of Hepburn's songs: 'Owl,' 'Spring,'

'Violet,' 'Moonbeam,' and an untitled song. I was paid $200 for the batch of them, but the show itself was never produced and the music was eventually lost. I also received that year a $5 commission upon publication for my song 'A Little Closer, Please,' which originally had been titled 'Pitchman's Song.' It was one of the songs from *Love's Old Sweet Song* for which I wrote the music and Saroyan the lyrics."[27]

After the agency's 10-percent fees were deducted, Bowles's portion that year came to $5,080, a sum that, coupled with his Guggenheim Fellowship of $2,500, eased his money worries considerably. Jane's only concern was that her novel, which she was determined to finish in Mexico, would not be any good.

By the time Bowles returned to Mexico in the spring of 1941, he had already published in *Modern Music*, at the request of editor Minna Lederman, a number of informal essays titled "On the Film Front," essays that concerned themselves only with film music, not the dialogue, quality of acting, plot, sound effects, or anything else that normally contributes to a film's success or failure. In his first column, Bowles established his premise that "music is to good choreography what the visual action of a film should be to its sound-track. Regardless of the music's form, the dance springing from it must have a recognizable pattern, a logical design, and an indisputable sense of direction."[28] In subsequent columns Bowles recommended films that he found satisfying for their scores, but withheld favor when the musical content seemed amiss or lacked synchronicity with the picture as a whole.

Whereas his earliest pieces in *Modern Music* were translations into English of articles by French and Italian composers and musicologists with such titles as "The Renaissance of Choral Music," "Latin Gaiety Today," "Italy's New Recruits," "More Italian Operas," "Exotic and Contemporary Music," and "Malipiero and Pirandello at the Opera," Bowles's first original essay was an appreciative piece in *Modern Music* on Virgil Thomson's *Mass* and other choral works. Impressed by Bowles's wide-ranging knowledge of contemporary music, Lederman gave him free rein to write on any subject he chose. Although he had continued to compose incidental music for a number of Broadway plays, Bowles appreciated the opportunity to write about music and film.[29]

In 1939 Lederman published his "Anatomy of Jazz," "Negro and Non-Negro Music," and his first "On the Film Front" essay, then commissioned him to write a regular column. This time his essays bore such titles as "Spirituals to Swing," "Calypso-Music of the Antilles," "On Mexico's Popular Music," and "Letter from Mexico." Bowles was reminded anew of the satisfaction he felt at sixteen when writing his column "By the Way" for his high school paper. Again, he relished having one of his own that he could shape without restriction.[30]

In a second "On the Film Front" essay, Bowles concentrated upon sound tracks and a series of nonfiction films being shown daily at the Museum of Modern Art. One, *The Song of Ceylon*, traced the influence of Western civilization upon native life. In it, he appreciated the recordings of actual native music with street calls and songs superimposed upon the score itself, which reminded him of the cinematic techniques of John Dos Passos's *U.S.A.* trilogy of the 1930s. In *The Song of Ceylon*, conversations in English and Hindustani were relieved by sound effects, a chorus, and gongs and bells. Hearing it, Bowles was determined to go to Ceylon himself to check out if what he had written were true. Bowles's most positive comments were for Ernst Toch's score of *The Cat and the Canary* and the scores for two films by Dmitri Kabalevsky: *Short* and *The Peasants*. He also recommended Silvestre Revueltas's *Redes* (The Wave), then wrote glowingly of Revueltas's work in a memorial tribute in the fall of 1940, which prompted him to declare later: "Writing about music by Mexican composers and performers was one thing, but the thought of being in Taxco myself, despite my dislike for it previously, now appealed to me enormously. Even Jane complained about how little she had done on her novel, given her countless distractions in New York, and I knew that she, too, looked forward to our return."[31]

On April 1, 1941, they boarded a steamship for Veracruz, then proceeded inland to the village of Fortín, where the entire valley reeked of gardenias. Their hotel had a ritual of strewing each morning hundreds of gardenia blossoms over the swimming pool. "Jane, too, loved the heavy fragrance, which permeated our clothes as we walked in the garden. Then it suddenly occurred to us to cover our bed with the blossoms. We bought many sacks of gardenias and strew them over our bed, then stripped ourselves naked and stretched and rubbed our bodies over the crushed petals and giggled and snuggled and laughed like little children until we fell asleep. At this point I was confident that Jane felt no alarm at our being alone together. We knew that we loved each other no matter who else might be in our lives. I was no threat to her independence or preference for female companionship. If I provoked Jane, it was unintentional except when I urged or cajoled her to work on her book. We cherished our privacy, and I learned, finally, not to pry or meddle in her affairs. Although we continued to compartmentalize our lives to a great extent, it was no longer to the exclusion of the other. We respected each other's needs and missed each other inordinately when we were apart, no matter how brief or long our absences were from one another. Jane wrote wonderful letters to me, filled with wit and humor and marvelous details involving whatever she thought would amuse me at the moment."[32]

From Fortín, Jane went alone to Taxco to join Helvetia Perkins, and Bowles to Mexico City to work without interruption on his score for *Pastorela*. "I was satisfied with it when I sent it to Kirstein, but I don't think he was."[33] Performed on July 1, 1941, by George Balanchine's ballet dancers, it was one of six presented during its six-month tour of Latin America.

When Bowles rejoined Jane in Taxco, he grumbled upon finding Boo Faulkner still ensconced in their house and complained that he had no place to which he could retreat and work without distraction. "Taxco life is so much more amusing in one's own house than in a hotel or pension, and we are having a very good time making ours beautiful," Bowles wrote Kay Cowen. "The only thing I lack is a piano in the house, but I have the use of one all day at Tamara Schee's house, so it's not too bad."[34]

Bowles was working then on a commission for Richard Hepburn's play *Love Like Wildfire.* "Inasmuch as harmony rather than melody was the pivotal element in my musical thinking, I was unable to compose without having access to a keyboard instrument since I can hear clearly only up to five simultaneous tones on my mental keyboard. After that I falter. The actual composition of the music went well, but the countless hours I spent orchestrating and copying were not easy. I needed absolute privacy for that, and it was not available at home."[35] Finally, after several tedious excursions by horseback down the mountain, Bowles found an adobe hut and strung a hammock from corner to corner of its thatch-covered veranda. "Each afternoon when everyone else was at siesta, I got astride the little rented horse and rode down to my hut to work for three hours. When tired of orchestrating, I threw myself across the hammock and listened to the far-off hollow sound of the invisible waterfall, which reminded me of the sound of the waterfall in Glenora."[36]

While Bowles was off composing, almost every morning Jane sat outside on the terrace in Taxco working on *Two Serious Ladies* until she heard Perkins's station wagon coming up the drive. "I never saw her so serious before about her writing," said Bowles, who was comfortable around Jane's lover and sometimes accompanied them on their forays for fruit, vegetables, and pottery before riding down the mountainside to his adobe hut.[37] Faulkner had moved out, finally, after he and Bowles argued about his late-night routines. "With Faulkner no longer an ever-present entity in our house, Jane concentrated on enlarging her circle of acquaintances. There were cocktail parties and dinners practically every night, at which almost everyone drank too much. Most of the time Jane was either drinking or writing, and I saw no reason to interfere."[38]

In the home of Gilberte de Charentenay, a French countess, and her companion, a Spanish marquesa, Bowles and Jane were introduced to Ned Rorem, who at seventeen was already composing music. "I remember first seeing him [in July 1941] when we were invited to the home of Natalie Scots for lunch. It seemed to me that she 'ran' Taxco. Young Rorem was there with his father, who spent much of his time consulting with hospital supervisors. He was conscious of his good looks and assumed, I thought, that everyone admired him for his handsome appearance."[39]

Rorem remembered the countess and the marquesa as "a pair of handsome forty-year-old European ladies sitting out the war in Taxco" who had invited him to tea and informed him that they would be joined later by Paul Bowles and his wife:

> The name rang a bell. Except for [Leo] Sowerby, I had never met a recognized composer, nor anyone whose reputation preceded him. But since I did not know his music I was not intimidated. Bowles did not look like a composer, i.e., a somber, thoughtful, bearded nineteenth-century German. His direct Americanism, the blond thirty-year-old good looks, and informality despite the necktie in July, made him seem accessible in the extreme. An ivory cigarette holder was his sole exotic accoutrement. Paul invited me to his studio the next afternoon, as one musician to another. I don't remember seeing him again that trip, although Jane was ever in view, usually in the station wagon of an odd-looking "older woman" named Helvetia Perkins.[40]

Other visitors to Taxco that summer included Oliver Smith, Smith's mother and stepfather, Ivan Bernkoff, and Antonio Álvarez, a young Mexican painter for whom Bowles developed great fondness. "Incidentally, please don't think that I have to be 'enamored' of someone to have sex with him (or her) a few times," said Bowles. "A sexual relationship with a friend is quite different from simply 'having sex,'" he added.[41]

After the others returned to Taxco, Bowles stayed another week in Acapulco with Álvarez, then left with an ocelot cub as a gift for Jane. "When *Life* magazine heard about it and sent a photographer, I could not watch the routine they had devised: This consisted of letting a white pigeon loose on the terrace (its legs were tied together, so that it walked with difficulty) and allowing the ocelot to stalk it." The denouement of the filmed episode was the delayed killing and eating of the pigeon.[42] "Jane was horrified, and I was not amused," said Bowles.

After being diagnosed with jaundice he ended up in a British hospital in Mexico City. "I could not bear the thought of returning to Taxco, so I urged Jane to get rid of the furnishings and move into an apartment in Mexico City, where I would join her when I was well enough to leave the hospital."[43]

In the sanatorium outside Cuernavaca to which he was moved several weeks later, Jane brought him what she purported to be the finished manuscript of *Two Serious Ladies*. "I doubt that I told her how much I admired it. Perhaps I did. I hope so, but I found great fault with it for its orthography, grammar, and rhetoric. 'You can't let anyone see such an abject manuscript!' I shouted.

"She was very calm abut it. 'If there's a publisher, he'll take care of those things,' she assured me, adding, 'They don't publish a book because it has perfect spelling, Gloompot.'"[44]

From Mexico City, Jane confirmed that she had spent two months "in a very bad humor, drinking and writing and rewriting and throwing at least half of it away. After awhile it was fun but the beginning was dreadful." She had intended to go with Helvetia Perkins to New York to try to get it published, but had no idea where to begin since the United States already was at war. "If you know of anyone who does things about books, will you smile at them for me if you still love me?" she asked Virgil Thomson.[45]

Jane also inquired about the cost of a room with bath at the Chelsea ("if possible without salon") and declared that she was "riding up with a friend" and hoped that she could "persuade Paul to come too. I shan't write about the parrot as I'm sure Paul has written you *plenty*. I am bringing a fluffy kitten."[46] Since gas was now rationed up and down the Atlantic seaboard, Jane and Helvetia postponed their departure until the end of March.

Already Bowles had petitioned the Mexican immigration officials for a month's extension of his tourist card on the basis of his jaundice treatment and the early effects of liver disease. On March 30, 1942, the Mexican immigration authorities summoned Bowles to appear before them to clarify his status in Mexico. In response, he presented documents signed by his dental surgeon which affirmed that he had operated on Bowles for a tumor, and by his doctor in Cuernavaca, who declared that he was helping Bowles to get over a "nervous ailment that needed further treatment."[47] Although he was granted still another extension, the immigration section of the Mexican Department of the Interior ordered him to leave Mexico within ten days regardless of his physical condition. Two days later, according to Bowles's FBI file, he "departed Mexico at Nuevo Laredo, Mexico."[48] Bowles had no idea how closely he was being monitored, but he was not surprised to learn that the FBI's interest in him stemmed from his membership in the Communist Party USA, from which he had tried repeatedly to resign.[49]

By mid-April 1942, Jane had arrived in Palm Beach with Helvetia Perkins at the home of Henrietta Simms Wyeth, Perkins's sister, to await Bowles's instruction to proceed directly to Holden Hall in Watkins Glen, New York, since it would cost them nothing to stay there. Meanwhile, Bowles had no intention of taking his Mexican companion, Antonio Álvarez, to New York City, despite his pleas, until he learned that Álvarez had attempted suicide by taking an overdose of Nembutal capsules. Bowles remembered that Latouche had a "miracle-working doctor" named Max Jacobson who could be used in desperate cases. "As soon as I was well enough to travel, Antonio now having recuperated, also, the two of us left together," said Bowles.[50]

Meanwhile, before leaving with Helvetia Perkins for New York, Jane had written Bowles that she had shipped his luggage and a few crated items to the Hotel Chelsea and left the rest of his things in a locked storage compartment of the Hotel Carleton in Mexico City. Bowles immediately replied: PLEASE WIRE WHEREABOUTS OF DRUM STOP SCHWAB CLAIMS NOT IN BODEGA.

The FBI had kept tabs on both Bowles and Jane throughout their stay in Mexico and were well aware of her going to Watkins Glen.

Bowles's cryptic telegram to Jane made no sense to the FBI agents who had intercepted it and concluded that the message was a code for something entirely different, whereas Bowles had explained while still in Mexico that the manager of the Hotel Carleton, a pleasant German named Oskar Schwab, had allowed him and his wife to store a number of crates and boxes at the hotel, including a native drum that was now missing.[51]

When the two agents arrived at Holden Hall and were admitted by the maid to the library, they began shuffling papers while Jane looked on innocently and Perkins took the back stairs to her room, locked the door, and began burning letters in her fireplace. When the agents smelled smoke, which was now filling the fireplace in the room they were in, one observed to the other: "It's a rather hot day for a fire, isn't it?" Jane shrugged and said vaguely that they were testing the furnace.[52] The interrogation became more intense when they asked Jane to explain the telegram and the drum. She said that the drum, merely a native drum, had finally turned up safely in New York at the Hotel Chelsea and was nothing to be concerned about. Then they demanded that she identify the person referred to as "Schwab" and tell them the precise route she herself had taken to Bodega. Jane explained that *bodega* was not a geographical location, but a storage facility. Undaunted, the agents pressed further: "Who is Friedrich von Winewitz, Mrs. Bowles?"

"No one at all," she replied. "It's a made-up name based on a joke my husband and I shared with a friend whose mother was Jewish, and who pretended to believe that my husband's mother was Jewish, too. In that mood, their friend sometimes called him Friedrich von Winewitz."[53] The agents continued plying Jane with questions until, finally, she declared that she was unable to remember the answers to such remote questions.

When they asked why her husband "traveled so much," she replied: "I don't know. He's nervous, I guess." Finally, failing to learn anything of note, the agents left.

Perkins explained later that she had been burning letters from "an acquaintance who had just received a very long prison term for accepting $75,000 from the Japanese 'to do propaganda work in the United States,' and that she was terrified the FBI might discover the letters, consider her an accomplice, and arrest her."

"This grotesque confrontation in my absence had its counterpart after we arrived in Watkins Glen," said Bowles. "Antonio took long walks through the gorges and on the hills roundabout. Wherever he went, people hidden behind the curtains of farmhouse windows rose and went to their telephones. Even I was arrested twice, once at gunpoint, and held for questioning until Uncle Charles could come to Holden Hall and identify me." Xenophobia had reached such a pitch that in public they dared speak only in English, and to Antonio they whispered in Spanish since he spoke no English.[54]

Despite the distractions at Holden Hall, Bowles found the music room spacious, cool, private, and ideal for his work on *The Wind Remains*, which he intended to finish before returning to New York City. "In the meantime, even the two brief visits by my parents to Holden Hall were not unwelcome," he added. "Mother and Daddy sometimes brought bourbon and gin, but never wine, which held more interest for gourmet-minded Jane and Helvetia."[55]

Meanwhile, Álvarez proceeded alone to New York City to stay with John Latouche, who had arranged for him to undergo treatment with Dr. Max Jacobson. Bowles had also convinced Betty Parsons, whom he and Jane had met in Taxco, to stage an exhibition of Álvarez's paintings in the small gallery she had recently opened in the city. "By this time, Antonio was feeling quite well. After selling a number of paintings at Betty Parsons's gallery, he was ready to return to Mexico, cured, and with a little money," declared Bowles. "Unfortunately, I learned shortly that he had disappeared while exploring the distant lagoons beyond Pie de la Cuesta and never returned. Those who searched for him concluded that he had met with foul play, suffered a fatal accident, or committed suicide."[56] Bowles was convinced that his friend had acted out his "own death wish."[57]

A number of months later, Jane told Bowles that she herself had made a halfhearted attempt to commit suicide by slashing her wrists. "She told me that it 'didn't mean anything,' that she was simply angry at Helvetia and did not want me to know they were having any problems. I knew that Jane's drinking antagonized Helvetia, who was inflexible in her expectations. I don't know how they stuck it out together for as long as they did," said Bowles.[58] In October 1942, they were still at Holden Hall when Perkins proposed that the three of them take a motor trip through southern New England to observe the turning of the maple leaves, but Bowles declined, having no desire to be a party to anyone else's mission, itinerary, or timetable. "I felt as strongly then about my not being a *tourist* as my protagonist Port did in the novel I eventually wrote, *The Sheltering Sky*. The seeds for that scenario were planted and watered when I was a child."[59]

Bowles was now writing music reviews for the *New York Herald Tribune* and needed to stay in the city. Despite Thomson's having recommended him, Bowles was dubious about his ability to turn out a literate critical report in forty-five minutes. "For a few weeks I suffered; then, like most things, it became a matter of habit. During the years that I wrote for the *Tribune*, I was continuously engaged in writing incidental music for Broadway plays, which provided an income of sorts. I also made thirty-five dollars a week no matter how many concerts I reviewed. Later, at Virgil's suggestion, I joined the union and made fifty dollars a week."[60]

On March 30, 1943, Bowles's opera *The Wind Remains* was presented in a single performance at the Museum of Modern Art, a program in three parts conducted by Bernstein, in his premiere as a conductor, against a set designed by Oliver Smith. The first, "Homage to García Lorca," was by Bowles's friend Silvestre Revueltas; the second, *The Wind Remains*, was described in the program notes as a "*zarzuela* in one act, after García Lorca and adapted by Bowles." In it, choreographer Merce Cunningham also danced solo as the clown; the Harlequin, a tenor, was performed by Romolo Di Spirito; and Jeanne Stephens, a soprano, was the Girl. "*The Wind Remains* has remained one of my favorite compositions of my entire life," said Bowles.[61]

The third number of the evening, *El Café de Chinitas*, was a ballet based on a folk song of the nineteenth century recorded by Lorca. Among its dancers was José Greco, and the guitarist was Carlos Montoya. The entire series was organized by the Marquise Yvonne de Casa Fuerte, whom Bowles knew originally as the organizer of the musical society La Sérénade in Paris.[62] She had come to New York with her husband to launch a similar series later in the season and had asked Bowles to let her produce *The Wind Remains* as soon as it was ready. "Although I had hoped it could be produced first on Broadway, she convinced me to let her do it. She and Jane had become friends, based largely upon their interest in food, Yvonne having come recently from Europe where food was scarce. Later, she and Jane took turns preparing meals with what one could get at the Washington Market, and we continued to eat well."[63]

By this time, Bowles was staying in a studio penthouse owned by Friedrich Kiesler, in whose home he had worked several years earlier while composing *Too Much Johnson*. "I moved a piano into the penthouse and went on working. By then, Jane and Helvetia had taken an apartment together on Waverly Place, and I spent much of my spare time with them. We were not a bad threesome, and I became rather fond of Helvetia. Although she had a selfish streak, I always thought she had Jane's best interests at heart."[64]

Since Bowles's only regular income in 1942 and 1943 was his salary as a music critic, he asked to be released from his contract with his agent, Harold Matson. In a letter dated May 20, 1943, Matson wrote: "Please accept this letter, then, to mean that if you come by an assignment or a contract of a deal of any kind of employment of your services without benefit of my office, then I shall have no claim whatsoever against you."[65]

It was John Latouche who gave Jane's manuscript of *Two Serious Ladies* to Harold Ober, a literary agent who arranged for its publication by Knopf on April 19, 1943. "Unfortunately, Jane's novel was greeted by largely negative reviews. As I recall, the novel scarcely made a hundred and fifty dollars during the first year, which was grossly disappointing to us both," said Bowles.[66]

Typical of the early reviewers of *Two Serious Ladies* was Edith H. Walton, who wrote in the *New York Times Book Review* that "to attempt to unravel the plot would be to risk, I feel sure, one's own sanity."[67] Most reviewers concluded that the novel was incomprehensible and found little positive about it. According to Bowles, what upset Jane most was that the reviews were beside the point. Although she had dedicated her novel to "Paul, Mother, and Helvetia," he was convinced that Helvetia thought the book "too obviously lesbian, as did Jane's family and my own, but as I saw it, it was Jane's business what she wrote and I supported her and her book vigorously when I got the chance."[68]

Bowles continued to live frugally and to keep his finances separate from Jane's. If they ate out together and others were present, Bowles calculated how much each person should pay. "It was the only arrangement that made sense since much of the time we were a trio or a quartet. Had Jane not had her own money once her novel was published by Knopf, naturally I would have supported her with whatever it took. It may not have appeared to be that way, but we were a team," said Bowles.

Although Jane was reticent about giving out copies of her book, Bowles loved *Two Serious Ladies* and presented it to almost everyone he knew. Years later, after Jane's death, a visitor to Bowles's flat in Tangier asked if he would object to inscribing Jane's book to her, which she told him she had read and admired enormously.

"I would feel privileged," he replied. "I wish I had written it."[69]

CHAPTER EIGHT

Writing Music Reviews, Music for Broadway, Fiction, and Translations

(1943–1947)

"What's in a story or a novel is not important to me. It's how it is told, how the words go together. After all, there's nothing in writing except words, patterns of words."

—Paul Bowles to Virginia Spencer Carr,
Tangier, September 9, 1989

Despite Jane's immense disappointment at the critics' response to *Two Serious Ladies*, Bowles encouraged her to continue writing. In 1942 when she was revising her novel at Holden Hall, he went over it repeatedly with her until each detail was as they agreed it should be. He added nothing that she herself had not written, but simply analyzed sentences and rhetoric. It was being present at the making of Jane's novel that excited Bowles and made him aware of how much he, too, wanted to write fiction. Talking with Jane, reading to each other, listening to the words, the cadences, all made him realize how much he had missed the creative process where words were concerned. The music reviews he was writing under the pressure of time afforded little personal satisfaction other than the pleasure that came from seeing his name in print, and he wanted far more than a byline.[1]

Of his new venture, writing music reviews for the *New York Herald Tribune*, Bowles declared that the only reason he could find for doing what he considered secondary work, instead of composing or writing fiction, was to augment his monthly income. At first he felt inadequate to the task, despite Virgil Thomson's encouragement, but the tension and boredom eased after a few weeks and he found himself enjoying the routine.

Bowles discovered that composing music for the lyrics of others required the same attention to patterns of words and their literary overtones that a good sentence or a paragraph demanded. "It's the *expression* of an idea that counts, not the idea itself. I've always thought the manner to be far more important than the matter in expressing an idea in words, and it is equally true in composing music. The setting of music to words and words to music is a creative process not to be entered into lightly, although the results may, of course, be light," he admitted.[2] Bowles felt similarly about the process of translating. "A translator enters into a special relationship with the work that he or she is translating, whether it's a phrase, a poem, or an entire book." Even as a student in high school he had delighted in making literary translations of poems. Although the process itself was exciting, being identified as the translator of a poem enhanced his sense of linkage to the poet whose work he had translated. "I rejoiced in such couplings. I loved translating, and still do," he insisted.[3]

It was Charles Henri Ford and his coeditor, Parker Tyler, who provided a new arena for Bowles's interest in translating and editing in their six-page tabloid, *View*. At first the issues appeared irregularly; then it became a thin magazine printed on slick paper. Bowles was convinced that had the war not caused the flight from Paris to New York of a number of important painters and writers, it is unlikely that *View* would have existed, and "without its surrealist bias it would have been a far less interesting publication. Its aim was not to shock, but to surprise."[4] By 1942 *View* averaged forty pages an issue, and its editors were now devoting entire issues to individual artists or themes. For the April 1943 issue, Ford invited Bowles to contribute a column of his own, "something on jazz, perhaps." In his first column, titled "The Jazz Ear," Bowles informed his readers that dreams were sometimes an impetus of a particular action, and that he had dreamed he began his column with the sentence: "Poets have ears, but the world of sound is unkept, chaotic and barbarous." Upon awakening, he tried to figure out what the sentence meant and concluded that whereas persons and sensibility have always agreed about the desirability of arranging the world in such a manner that the eye shall be pleased, the ear is less fortunate. To Bowles, hearing was a secondary sense and less directly connected to the intellect than sight.

Another early piece published in *View* was Bowles's "Bluey: Passages from an Imaginary Diary."[5] "Our readers loved it," said Ford, who invited Bowles to be a contributing editor and to edit an issue of his own.[6] "I hadn't done such editing since I was nineteen when Bruce Morrissette asked me to edit an issue of the *Messenger*. My problem now was that I wanted to do everything."

During the first half of 1945, Bowles covered fifty-five musical events for the *New York Herald Tribune*, translated the acting version of Jean-Paul Sartre's *Huis Clos*, wrote incidental music for Jean Giraudoux's play *Ondine*, composed many songs, and prepared an issue for *View* on the topic of Tropical Americana for which he selected, edited, and translated works from Spanish and French. In a section titled "Scrapbook of Tropical Americana," he included photographs by filmmaker Rudy Burckhardt as well as some of his own that he had taken in Central and South America.[7] "For a reason I never understood or appreciated, Parker Tyler rewrote my preface and made it mean something quite different from what I had intended. The only point totally accurate after Parker finished with it was my statement that the 'final aim of this issue of *View* is to present a poetically apt version of life as it is lived by the peoples of tropical America.' As I said, I've never objected to change so long as it was my own."[8]

For the November 1945 issue of *View*, Bowles translated from the French Francis Ponge's "A New Introduction to the Pebble," and for the December issue, two primitive myths translated from the French,

Bluet d'Achères's "The Visions of the Comte de Permission" and Jean Ferry's "She Woke Me Up So I Killed Her."[9] At this point, Bowles realized that he especially enjoyed translating tales that had evolved from myths, and little by little he began inventing his own myths from the point of view of the primitive mind. "First, animal legends resulted from the experiments, then tales of animals disguised as basic human beings. One rainy Sunday I awoke late, put a thermos of coffee by my bedside, and began to write another of these myths. No one disturbed me, and I wrote until I had finished it. I called it 'The Scorpion,' and decided that it could be shown to others. When *View* published it in December of 1945, I received compliments and went on inventing myths."[10] For the October 1946 issue of *View*, Bowles submitted another myth, "By the Water," and at this point he knew he would continue writing such tales.

In addition to his regular contributions to *View*, he was especially interested in being published in *Partisan Review*, which he considered in 1947 to be the most important magazine in America. When *Partisan Review* accepted "A Distant Episode" for publication in the January/February issue, Bowles was confident that he had been launched fittingly and knew irrefutably that he would go on writing fiction. A year later, in March 1948, *Partisan Review* published his "Under the Sky." Bowles's next submission to *Partisan Review*, "Pages from Cold Point," which he wrote aboard ship just before his arrival in Tangier in the fall of 1947, was rejected. In an undated letter to Peggy Glanville-Hicks, he wrote: "*Partisan Review* didn't like it. When they sent it back, I cut it down with a knife, having decided it was too long and discursive."[11] In the fall of 1949, the tale was published in a New York–based journal, *Wake*.[12] Bowles recognized, too, that translating the works of others would not deter him from writing his own fiction, but instead fuel it.

Under the influence of Jorge Luis Borges, Bowles began translating poetry. For the "Surrealism in Belgium" issue of *View*, published in December 1946, he translated from the French Paul Magritte's "Prose Poems" ("The Soup," "Dissertation on Rain," and "The City") and five poems by Paul Colinet, also translated from the French, known then as "The Lamp's Stories." With these translations to his credit, Bowles knew that he would continue to translate as well as to write original stories.

By this time, royalties were coming in fairly regularly from his incidental music and commissions, which prompted him to consider leaving New York and returning to Morocco. "Jane was nearby, of course, and we enjoyed immensely each other's company, but we lived separate lives for the most part. To my delight I had resumed at last an intimate relationship with Aaron Copland, which was fairly intense for three and a half years. Although I still considered Aaron my mentor, and other than Jane the most important person in my life, we seldom talked 'composing and music' at this stage of our lives. Aaron was always closemouthed about what we meant to each other, as he was about others as well. In this regard I am told that Howard Pollack's biography of Aaron is quite good. One would never know from it that our relationship had ever been a sexual one. Until I'm dead, too, I would just as soon it stay that way."[13]

There was no mistaking Jane's jealousy of Bowles's spending considerable time with Peggy Glanville-Hicks, who helped him keep track of his music and articles related to it. "We did go to bed together once, but Jane would never have asked if I was sleeping with Peggy." In his memoir, *Without Stopping*, Bowles wrote: "My almost constant companion for two and a half years was Peggy Glanville-Hicks. We were composers with much the same musical tastes, so that it was not surprising that we should enjoy being together. Her husband, Stanley Bate, a British composer in a very different tradition, had a brutal streak; when he was drunk, which he was regularly, he expressed himself by beating Peggy and tossing her around the apartment. I thought she should have divorced him. I suppose that my spending as much time as I did with Peggy stemmed, in part, from my resentment of the omnipresence of Helvetia. Of course Peggy and I had music in common, which prompted much of our correspondence."[14]

In an attempt to counteract the possessiveness of Perkins, Bowles suggested that he and Jane go to Canada on a weeklong vacation, a proposal to which she seemed surprisingly amenable. They were halfway to Montreal on the train when Bowles realized that she was ordering and drinking one whiskey after another. He knew that if he voiced disapproval, she would have consumed even more. Upon arrival, Jane was in good spirits and appeared not to be affected by the alcohol, but when they stepped off the escalator at the foot of the main lobby, she collapsed and passed out. "People in the station helped me lay her out on a bench, and someone found a cab for us. By the time we reached the hotel she was fully conscious and had no memory of the incident," said Bowles, who saw no reason to remind her. "But I was troubled by it, for it could have indicated a more serious problem than her drinking suggested."[15]

Both found their four days in Montreal duller than either anticipated, but Quebec City, to which they traveled next, was fascinating. "Despite our knowing French, it was hard for us to understand the natives there, but it delighted me to think that so foreign a place existed practically next door to New York City, and I hoped that we could return," said Bowles, who could see that Jane was impatient to get back to Helvetia.[16]

Once home, Bowles signed a contract to write music for *Colloque Sentimentale*, a ballet to be produced by the Marqués de Cuevas in collaboration with Salvador Dalí. Oliver Smith was still "learning the ropes of producing, and through no fault of his own, getting hooked up with the instigators of this ballet was one of his mistakes," said Bowles. Before committing themselves, Smith urged Bowles to meet the Marqués de Cuevas since he intended to found a ballet company. After several lunches together to discuss the ballet envisioned by the marqués, to be based on a poem by Verlaine, Dalí sent Bowles many sketches, but the marqués showed him only those having to do with the backdrop, "a garden scene with tall cypresses, gloomy and vaporous."[17]

Bowles signed a contract, composed the music, orchestrated it, then left for Manzanillo, Mexico. He declared later that he had left New York in good faith after hearing his music rehearsed for *Colloque Sentimentale*, which "sounded fine," but the ballet rehearsals themselves had not begun. Upon his return home, Bowles was inundated with concerts and other musical events and had no time to see a full rehearsal until the night before the ballet opened. "I was horrified when the dancers, Eglevsky and Marie-Jeanne, appeared on stage sporting great hanks of underarm hair that reached to the floor, while men with yard-long beards that trailed behind them rode bicycles at random across the stage. There was a large mechanical tortoise encrusted with colored lights . . . that moved unpredictably this way and that, several times almost causing upsets among the performers. I sat looking incredulously at the chaos on stage."[18] No sooner had the curtain risen on opening night than the hisses began, followed by catcalls, boos, shouts, whistles, and the shuffling and beating of feet on the floor of the hall. *Newsweek* reported that the composer's "beautiful score was wrecked by Dali's usual outlandish weirdness."[19] After the ballet had run several weeks, Bowles was curious to know if the negative reviews had prompted Dalí to change anything, so he attended again. The sounds of protest were now only simple giggles, and Bowles was not surprised that the show closed after forty-two performances. In retrospect, he thought *Colloque Sentimentale* contained some of his best orchestral music, but "loathed Dalí's dramatization of it."[20]

Despite his intentions, there were not enough hours in a day for Bowles to do everything he set out for himself in the mid-1940s and to have any kind of private life. Finally, after three and a half years of reviewing, he resigned his post on the *Herald Tribune*, but agreed to continue writing regular articles for the paper's Sunday edition.[21] Actually, he wrote nine more music reviews for the daily *Herald Tribune* in early 1946, his final review appropriately titled "'Exit Singing': Ninety-nine Minutes of 'What's Left of Jazz.'" Bowles concluded his piece with the observation: "Although it's perfectly true that not much is left of jazz right now, there is a possibility that not all of its remnants were displayed yesterday."[22]

During the height of his reviewing for the *Herald Tribune*, Bowles accepted requests to compose incidental music for ten plays, which included a revival of John Ford's Jacobean tragedy *'Tis Pity She's a Whore* (1943); *South Pacific* (1943); *Jacobowsky and the Colonel* (1944); *The Glass Menagerie* (1944); *Ondine* (1945); *Cyrano de Bergerac* (1946); *Land's End* (1946); *The Dancer* (1946); *Twilight Bar* (1946); and *On Whitman Avenue* (1946). Only Giraudoux's *Ondine* was not produced.

The first, *'Tis Pity She's a Whore,* opened on May 18, 1943, in Hartford, Connecticut, with the settings and costumes by Chick Austin. "I was named in the program for having composed the incidental music, but I don't remember the reviewers paying any attention to it; nonetheless, it was a pleasant production, and a number of New Yorkers came up to see it. Anything Chick Austin presented was considered a theatrical event, and in typical Austin fashion, *'Tis Pity* ran for five days. He had no intention of mounting the play in New York."[23]

The next play was *South Pacific*, not the musical *South Pacific* based on James Michener's *Tales of the South Pacific*, but an earlier play written by Dorothy Heyward and Howard Rigsby. In the play, for which Bowles did the music, Earl Wilson declared in the *New York Post* that "it becomes clear today that you can't fight the Japs in the South Pacific very realistically on a stage on West Forty-eighth Street." Louis Kronenberger observed: "I'm afraid it's not possible to call *South Pacific* a good play, which is a great pity. For in intention and integrity, and for that matter in its ability to hold your interest, it belongs in a different world from the slick trash and shoddy cleverness of Broadway. Mr. Rigsby and Miss Heyward have had something to say, and they have tried to say it as honestly as possible; that they have said it clumsily and confusedly at times is to their disadvantage but not their discredit." Every reviewer of note faulted the writing, and the play closed after two matinees and three night performances.[24] Not a single reviewer mentioned Bowles's music.

Bowles interrupted his work on Giraudoux's *Ondine* to compose the incidental music for Franz Werfel's *Jacobowsky and the Colonel.* "I liked Schuyler Watts, who translated *Ondine*, and I had worked with him on *The Wind Remains*, but I should not have taken on the music for the Giraudoux play before the financing and everything else was set, so I put *Ondine* on hold."[25] *Jacobowsky and the Colonel* was adapted by S. N. Behrman in collaboration with Franz Werfel, the playwright. The critics' response to its two-week run of tryouts at the Colonial Theatre in Boston made it clear that a hit was in the making. Bowles had been instructed to pack the score with nostalgia for prewar Paris. Werfel, himself a German, escaped across France to England during the war, and he knew firsthand his subject. "The play was both realistic and romantic," said Bowles. According to director Elia Kazan, the success of *Jacobowsky and the Colonel* was due to Oscar Karlweis. "I'd never heard of him before the Guild brought him to me; I was told only that he was well known in Europe as a light-comedy and operetta star. He gave one of the most deft and light-fingered performances I've ever seen. He had a magic that overwhelmed the audience."[26] The play ran almost a year on Broadway, then moved to the Piccadilly Theatre in London under the direction of Michael Redgrave, who played the Colonel.

Bowles was in Chicago preparing for the opening of *The Glass Menagerie* when it was reported that he had signed a contract to write the music for *Ondine*. "With few exceptions, I never ceased to be amazed at the lag time between being asked to compose the score for a show and signing a contract, composing it, reading what the scouts had to say about the play before it came off, and, finally, hearing it from my seat, or back stage, on opening night. *The Glass Menagerie* was one of those exceptions," said Bowles.[27]

The genesis for his being asked to write the music for *The Glass Menagerie* dated back to the fall of 1945 when Tennessee Williams appeared at the door of Bowles's flat on West Tenth Street in the company of Margo Jones and his friend Donald Windham and told him that he had just finished a new play. "Would you be willing to read it?" Williams asked. Bowles read it and liked it, declaring later that for a play aiming at a Broadway production, it was somewhat experimental, envisaging as it did the use of projected color slides to serve as comments on or asides to the dialogue and action. "The next time I saw Tennessee, the production was set, and what with the drawing up of contracts and my habitual refusal to write anything until I had stuffed an advance into the bank, I found myself with three days in which to compose and orchestrate the score."[28]

Louis J. Singer, a first-time producer who put up seventy-five thousand dollars and insisted on having his hand in every aspect of the production, agreed verbally to Bowles's doing the music for the play, but delayed giving him a contract. "I didn't like Singer and didn't trust him," said Bowles. "Finally, it was Audrey Wood, Tennessee's agent, who put her foot down and insisted that I have a contract. She told me that Singer had made his money owning and operating a string of hotels and knew nothing about the theater. During rehearsals in Chicago, he decided that the play should have a happy ending, that Laura should marry her gentleman caller, but Audrey put a stop to that nonsense by threatening to tell every critic in town about the kind of wire-pulling that was going on if he made Tennessee change the play. At first I was furious at him; then disgust set in. I have little tolerance for ineptitude and fools no matter what the context."[29]

A blizzard was raging when Bowles arrived in Chicago for the tryouts on December 18, 1944, and checked into the Hotel Sherman, where the rest of the company was staying. "It was horrible. The auditorium was cold, and Laurette Taylor was on the bottle. She had got off it during the first part of the rehearsals but suddenly the dress rehearsal coming up was too much. The night of the dress rehearsal she was nowhere to be found. Finally, the janitor spotted her behind the furnace in the basement. . . . No one thought she would be able to go on the next night, but she spruced up and didn't drink again. The night of the opening in New York, George Jean Nathan sent her a bottle of Scotch, a pinch bottle, and she sent him a little wire saying 'Thanks for the vote of confidence.'"[30] The cast settled down during the play's New York run for a total of 556 performances, during which it won the 1945–46 Drama Critics' Circle Award as "Best Play" and was named by *Billboard* as "Best Play of the Season."

In the spring of 1946, Margo Jones, who codirected *The Glass Menagerie* with Eddie Dowling, asked Bowles to compose a short score for *On Whitman Avenue*, a play by Maxine Wood that Jones was directing. It was for this play that Bowles composed the lullaby "Baby, Baby," which theatergoers commented upon favorably. After a week of tryouts at the Erlanger Theatre in Buffalo, the company moved to Detroit, Wood's hometown, where its three-week run generated favorable reviews and packed houses despite its depiction of racism, prejudice, and hypocrisy. Bowles accompanied the group to Buffalo for the tryouts, then to Detroit. Although Canada Lee, who had the lead in *On Whitman Avenue*, was good, he fared poorly at the hands of the critics, as did the production as a whole when the play opened on May 8, 1946, in New York's Cort Theatre.[31] Despite negative reviews and sagging box office receipts, *On Whitman Avenue* was still playing on Labor Day, its attendance having been boosted by Eleanor Roosevelt, who wrote in support of the production.[32] After 173 performances, the Broadway production closed on October 5, then set out on an extensive road show that was more successful than its run on Broadway.[33]

That fall, Bowles interrupted work on a commissioned piece, Concerto for Two Pianos, Winds, and Percussion, to write the incidental music for Edmond Rostand's *Cyrano de Bergerac.* "After we discussed the show for a fortnight or so, I started work on the score, using as one of the instruments a Novachord. It was a carefully planned show and also a great hit, which was a pleasant change from the succession of failures with which I had been associated of late, with the exception of *The Glass Menagerie.*"[34] Reviewer Howard Barnes urged his *Herald Tribune* readers to see for themselves the "stunning and enchanting revival" of *Cyrano de Bergerac* and cited Bowles's incidental music for its "proper magical mood" and called the play "a show to gladden the season." Brooks Atkinson's review in the New York *Daily News* ended with a benediction of sorts: "Let everyone, therefore, be well bestowed–by Melchor C. Ferrer for his direction, Lemuel Ayers for the costumes and settings, and Paul Bowles for the incidental music. Mr. Ferrer has done Cyrano in the grand manner, like a man who gets fun as well as a living out of the theatre."[35]

Bowles said little about the other plays for which he wrote scores in 1945 and 1946. Of the fantasy play by Arthur Koestler, *Twilight Bar*, Bowles declared: "It might have lived had it been properly directed and cast [it was produced and directed by George Abbott], but it died in Baltimore."[36] He described *The Dancer*, by Julian Funt and Milton Lewis, as "an obliquely melodramatic version of episodes in Nijinsky's life, although the dancer was never identified as such. The script required that the music at times slip out of its function as background music and take on the quality of concert music. These moments occurred when Anton Dolin, the dancer, began compulsively to dance. It was a new kind of problem to solve musically, and for this reason working on it was a pleasure. The show was a flop, nonetheless."[37] Regarding *Land's End*, Bowles wrote: "The only thing I recall about this production is that it ran no time at all, indeed was dead before the week was up."[38]

Bowles was still reviewing for the *Herald Tribune* when he translated Jean-Paul Sartre's *Huis Clos*. By this time, Bowles had read with satisfaction Sartre's *La Nausée*, *L'Imaginaire*, and *Le Mur* and recommended the play to Oliver Smith. "We tracked down Sartre, who was on some kind of government-sponsored tour with a group of French journalists, and arranged to meet him at the Statler Hotel in Washington, D.C., where we had a long lunch together. While we ate, he went through the script in detail, and the contract was signed over coffee." Bowles learned later that Theresa Helburn and Lawrence Langer, directors of the Theatre Guild, called on Sartre for the same purpose two days later and were "incredulous and indignant" to find the play unavailable and Sartre on his way back to France.[39]

Bowles saw no reason to rush into translating the play until the appropriate arrangements for putting it on were made. It was at this point that Oliver Smith rented the top three stories of an old house on West Tenth Street and convinced Helvetia Perkins and Bowles to sign the lease with him. Bowles took the top floor, Perkins and Jane, the second floor, and Smith, the floor in between. "A new era began once we got our respective floors furnished," reported Bowles. "Work and sleep were private, while eating and entertaining were largely communal. The cook was stationed on Oliver's floor, but since each floor had its own kitchen, she was able to serve meals on any of them."[40] By this time, Bowles was writing fiction, although he still wrote occasional reviews, and Jane was well into the writing of *In the Summer House.*

It was over a year before his translation of *Huis Clos* was ready to be produced. First, Oliver Smith had to convince Herman Levin to put up most of the money, then to secure a director, actors, set designers, and a theater. Bowles noted that Levin had hired three French actors, but still needed a woman to play Estelle and recommended Ruth Ford, Charles Henri Ford's sister. "Two of the imported actors, Claude Dauphin and Annabella, were a problem, so I gave Annabella daily lessons in English pronunciation until one could understand what she was saying. Although Dauphin was better, even he went off track occasionally and the words came out sounding as if they had been put through a scrambler. Sandwiched between the two overpowering French accents was Ruth's Southern belle intonations as Estelle, which I also worried about until opening night proved me wrong."[41]

Of his translation of the title, Bowles declared: "I'm not very good at titles. It took me six weeks to get *No Exit* out of *Huis Clos*. The Bible was open at every book; Dante was spread out on the desk too. At the end it was the Independent Subway which provided the two words."[42] Bowles found himself trying to exit the subway through the IN turnstile when he saw the words NO EXIT. "That's it! 'No Exit!'" exclaimed Bowles, who thought it a perfect title for a tale set in hell from which there was, indeed, *no exit.* "Unfortunately, the production as a whole was fraught with problems. . . . My voice was lost in the hubbub of highball clinking and free advice," said Bowles, who was certain that Sartre held him responsible for the "small mutilations" to the production since it was officially his adaptation. "He was annoyed because I was unable to keep the director from changing the script. Sartre considered that my province, which it should have been; but the point was that I didn't have a percentage in the show and he didn't know how Broadway works. I was simply the translator, so I had no rights whatever."[43]

The play opened on November 26, 1946, at the Biltmore Theatre in New York to generally favorable reviews. Brooks Atkinson set the pace in the *New York Times* when he wrote: "Being a person of agile mind, Jean-Paul Sartre has written a fascinating and macabre play about three lost souls in hell. *No Exit*, they call it in Paul Bowles' excellent English adaptation, and it was played with horrible logic and pitiless skill. With such characters, *No Exit* is a grim experience to undergo in the theatre. What redeems it is the skill of M. Sartre's craftsmanship and the knife-edge dexterity of the writing, which must owe something to Mr. Bowles' idiomatic English translation."[44]

Bowles also translated in 1946 Jean Giraudoux's play *La Folle de Chaillot* (*The Madwoman of Chaillot*). After Giraudoux's death earlier in the year, two producers had obtained the property and wanted the finished adaptation within six weeks. "Accordingly, I flew down to Montego Bay to concentrate on the work at hand without the distractions of New York City. Then I moved to Ocho Rios, where I stayed in an almost empty hotel, got the work done on schedule, and returned to New York."[45] Later, Bowles declared: "I don't know what eventually happened to my translation, but the play as I rendered it was never produced, and I received only my commission, a pittance, for it."[46]

In his memoir, Bowles wrote: "It is true that I 'produced' during those years, but in such a way that I always seemed to find myself doing what someone else wanted done. I furnished music which embellished or interpreted the ideas of others. . . . To my way of thinking I was only marking time.

"Happily, my daydreaming on the subject of escape was not given the opportunity of growing into an *idée fixe*; the decision was made for me," said Bowles.[47] "My heart accelerated, and memories of other courtyards and stairways flooded in, still fresh from sixteen years before. The Tangier to which I wandered in my dream was the Tangier of 1931. It did not take me long to conclude that Tangier was the place I wanted to be more than anywhere else. . . . I thought that Jane, too, would be excited about my going, or at least reconciled to it, but when I couldn't find my passport the day I was to leave, it turned up in the back of her underwear drawer. 'You know I don't want you to go,' she said. If we had planned on it, I would have taken her with me, of course, but she made it clear that she wanted to stay in New York, or elsewhere with friends, and finish her own novel."[48]

It was through Helen Strauss, Bowles's newly acquired literary agent at the William Morris Agency, that he signed a contract with Doubleday-Doran to write a novel, and on the strength of his six short stories already published he was given an advance against royalties. Whereas Bowles's intent had been to make a book of his short stories, an editor at Dial Press advised him that a book of short fiction, no matter how good, would have no future at all unless it was preceded by the publication of a successful novel.

Having set his mind on returning to Morocco, Bowles found "hundreds of small forgotten scenes" welling up unbidden in his consciousness. On a Fifth Avenue bus one day he thought of a song he had played on the Victrola in his family's boathouse in Glenora. "It was not the banal melody of 'Underneath the Sheltering Palms' which fascinated me, but the strange word *sheltering*." Almost at once Bowles decided to set his novel in the Sahara, "where there was only the sky, and so it would be *The Sheltering Sky*." He envisioned that the tale would be similar to "A Distant Episode," the story he had just published in *Partisan Review*. "It would write itself, I felt certain, once I had established the characters and spilled them out onto the North African scene." By the time his bus reached midtown, Bowles had decided upon an omniscient narrator, and that he "would write it consciously up to a certain point, then let it take its own course."[49]

He was reminded, too, of something he had read of Kafka's: "From a certain point onward there is no longer any turning back. That is the point that must be reached." He would write the novel "without any thought of what he already had written, or an awareness of what he was writing at that moment, or an awareness of what he was going to write next, or how the tale would end."[50]

Accompanied by Gordon Sager, Bowles soon found himself aboard a freighter bound for Morocco. To Peggy Glanville-Hicks, he wrote of a dream that he took to be an omen: "Dreams do clarify your life completely. They tell you much more than anything else could possibly tell you about what you really want and how much you're willing to sacrifice to have it."[51] He was still several days from his destination aboard the SS *Ferncape* when he felt the urge to write a short story that had been sitting uneasily upon him for some time. "The tale practically wrote itself, given its head start. I finished it the day before we reached Casablanca and called it 'Pages from Cold Point.' Then we landed and Morocco took over."[52]

CHAPTER NINE

Bowles's Departure for Morocco and Return to New York to Compose Music for *A Streetcar Named Desire* and *Summer and Smoke*

(1947–1948)

"Perhaps writing will be a means to a nomadic life for you, but I hope you won't slowly stop writing music altogether. I think you will do both."

—Jane Bowles to "Dearest Bupple,"
East Montpelier, Vermont, December 1947

Bowles found the dry scented winds of Fez exhilarating after breathing the humid summer air of the Atlantic during the ten-day crossing aboard the SS *Ferncape* to Casablanca. For two hundred dollars he had booked a large stateroom with a double bed, private bath, a huge desk, portholes on two sides of the cabin, and a double door leading to the deck. At the last moment Gordon Sager, who thrived on exploring new terrains, was able to book one of the three cabins. "It is much pleasanter than being alone," Bowles wrote Peggy Glanville-Hicks on July 8, 1947. Although Gordon Sager was ready to leave Morocco after a fortnight in Fez, he stuck doggedly at Bowles's side until a friend invited him to Marrakech.[1] Jane was fond of Sager, whom she considered far more *her* friend than her husband's, but she liked the idea of his having someone to do things with in Fez when they were not working. "I hope you and Gordon will stick close together, and please be careful of your health," she admonished. Bowles replied that Sager had already left, and that he was considering going on to Spain. "I'm sorry Gordon left you, naturally, because the whole thing now sounds incredibly gloomy. Not that it is gay here either," Jane reminded him.[2]

For Bowles, it was enough to smell the fig trees, cedarwood, and mint beds; to rejoice in the murmur of fast-running water outside his hotel window; and to hear the jingling of bells on the horses drawing his carriage back and forth between Bab Bou Jeloud and the Mellah.[3] His room overlooked the valley of Oued Zitoun, and when he wandered the paths shaded by canebrake outside the walls of Bab el Hadid, he could not have been happier. The food was good, his stomach was behaving, and he settled in to begin his novel. A mother and son whose behavior was strange enough to interest him began showing up repeatedly in hotel lobbies in Fez, Tangier, Algeciras, and finally, in Córdoba, where they parted ways until Bowles re-created them in his novel as Mrs. Lyle and her obnoxious son, Eric.

In Ronda, Spain, having recalled with fondness a hotel in which he had once stayed, Bowles worked intensively on his novel. By the time he was back in Tangier, he realized that the structure and character of the Moroccan landscape would be supplied chiefly by his imagination and, to some extent, by memory. He said that he never knew what he was going to write the next day because he had not yet lived through it.[4] Like his protagonist Port, whom he resembled more than superficially, Bowles was not a tourist, but a traveler. It seemed inevitable that many of his own habits were also Port's. Port, too, pored over maps with a passionate intensity in his eagerness to set out for the Algerian Sahara, Bowles's setting for his novel.

In a letter to Peggy Glanville-Hicks, Bowles reported that Jane was spending the summer with Libby Holman, a torch singer whom they had met in New Haven, Connecticut, at the opening of *Beggar's*

Holiday, a musical in which Holman had the starring role. Later, Bowles observed that there was something of the black widow spider or poisonous lily about Holman the night they met, but there was no disputing that both he and Jane wanted to know her better.[5] They had first heard of Holman through John Latouche, who was a frequent visitor to her palatial neo-Georgian house in Stamford, Connecticut. It was Latouche who had introduced Bowles to Jane, and they trusted him despite his occasional indiscretions. Holman's house, which she called Treetops, had sixteen bedrooms, nine bathrooms, a wood-paneled library, fireplaces in each of the main rooms, and a formal dining room that was an exact copy of the one in the Governor's Mansion in Colonial Williamsburg. French doors opened upon a wide terrace and a large oval swimming pool.

In the autumn of 1946, Bowles and Jane had been invited to Treetops, Latouche having made it clear to Jane that Libby Holman's fetchingly sultry voice and body left no doubt that she preferred the company of women despite her marriage some fourteen years earlier to tobacco heir Zachery Smith Reynolds, whose death in 1932 from a bullet wound to the head caused authorities to question if Holman herself had killed him. Although Reynolds's death was ruled a suicide, both Holman and Ab Walker, her husband's best friend, were arrested and accused of murder after Reynolds's body was disinterred and an autopsy performed. By then, Holman was four months pregnant, and no one knew for certain if Walker or her late husband was the father. Determined to establish the infant as his heir, Reynolds's father prevailed upon the prosecutor to drop the charges against both suspects.[6]

Holman named her son Christopher Smith Reynolds and called him Topper. The youth was fourteen when he told his mother that he wanted to go to Africa with Paul Bowles and have his tongue cut out. Holman was astonished that Topper had read any of Bowles's fiction, but recognized at once his familiarity with "A Distant Episode," in which Bowles's naive protagonist has his tongue cut out in the North African desert.

Bowles was still in New York when Jane flew to Cuba with Holman,

Eugenia Bankhead, and Louisa Carpenter, heir to the DuPont fortune. Carpenter was the pilot, and the plane was her mother's. "I drank heavily on the weekend, played poker, and did no work," Jane wrote her husband, adding that "Louisa C. is the most sexually attractive woman in the world, but I am, alas, not alone in thinking this."[7] Having become enamored herself of Jane during their weekend retreat, Holman urged her to break her ties to Helvetia Perkins and move into Treetops with her. As an added inducement, Holman promised that she would do everything possible to reinforce Jane's need for privacy and freedom from the mundane details about which she tended to worry. Bowles had little confidence that such an arrangement would work even if Jane agreed to it since the word *routine* or *mundane* had never applied to her. He knew, too, that tension was essential to Jane's creative life, but Holman would have to discover that on her own. As Bowles saw it, Jane's pecking at a problem until it festered bore little resemblance to the situation that had disturbed her in the first place.[8] Although her sense of self-worth was inextricably tied to how she regarded herself as a writer, more pertinent was her husband's perception of it. To that end, Bowles suggested that she report periodically on her progress while he was away, reasoning that a genial sharing and spirit of competitiveness might help her become more decisive and goal-oriented.

"Of course, my scheme backfired," he admitted.

In her next letter, Jane retorted: "I don't mind how much better or worse you write than I do so long as you don't insist that I'm the writer and not you. We can both be, after all, and it's silly for you to go on this way just because you are afraid to discourage me. I suppose I was irritated and appalled because you referred to your work as *your little novel* just as Helvetia would do. She has written more than either of us this summer, but also she has had more time. Well I hope all the novels will be good novels and published," Jane added in an attempt to end the discourse.[9]

In another letter, she lamented that she had no real news. "Certainly you would be bored hearing about Iris [Berry] and Jody

[McLean] and Louisa [Carpenter] and Sister [Talullah] Bankhead. You know it is always the same old grind with me. I think I shall simply never be interested in anyone who is Latin or Arab or Semitic." After spending ten days with her mother in New York, Jane wrote: "I did not do a lick of work and slept in a different bed every night, including I.B.'s [Iris Berry's], who was pretty annoyed to find me in her place the next morning." Berry was director of the film library of the Museum of Modern Art, and Jane's unrequited crush on her for over a decade had been without remission.[10]

As Bowles saw it, "When Jane made such comments as 'sleeping in someone else's bed,' her observation may have meant (a) that she slept in the bed alone, (b) that she shared a bed with someone who chose to keep her distance, (c) that they merely snuggled up to each other for emotional nurturing, or (d) that they were passionate lovers." Bowles never probed regarding Jane's bed mates, nor did she of his. "I was confident that she was not sleeping with a man; if she were, I would have been jealous. Naturally I wanted Jane to be happy, to be less anxious about things, and having a fit companion made her less dependent upon others, no matter what the intensity of the relationship; but I also believed that for Jane, the chase was the main event."[11] Her longing for reciprocity was far more sustaining than any reality that came out of it. What she hated most was having no prey in sight.

After two months at Treetops with Libby Holman, Jane wrote Bowles that Helvetia had already made her way into the novel and that she, too, was in it in the person of Helvetia's son. "This is good because I am usually trying to be too far removed from my own experience in writing, which can be tricked in a short story very well but not in a novel. You know what a state of confusion Helvetia has put me into anyway, so you can imagine how difficult it is for me to hammer a novel out of anything she has prompted me to think."[12]

So far as his own creative life was concerned, Bowles adhered to his conviction that one's life was programmed, and that it was simply a matter of being responsive to one's environment. In her letters, Jane habitually juxtaposed her impasse as a writer with something that

Bowles had just written her. "I realize that I have no career whether I work or not, and never have had one. You have more of a career after writing a few short stories than I have after writing an entire novel. Don't keep writing me 'come in January if your novel is finished.' Naturally I know yours will be finished years ahead of mine and will be wonderful. I seem to be completely ignored by the whole literary world just as much as by the commercial one."[13]

In September 1947, Bowles moved from his hotel on the beach in Tangier to a two-room cottage in an outbuilding of the Hotel El Farhar on the Old Mountain. "I had a fireplace and an incredible view overlooking the sea. Then I bought an Amazon parrot that giggled, and I realized at once the great difference between an empty room and one with a parrot in it."[14] He was pleased with his progress on the novel until he reached the scene of his protagonist's death from typhoid. Bowles likened his impasse to the recalcitrant donkey that had refused to go through the gate to the house he and Copland had rented during his first trip to Tangier. "Living across from that same gate sixteen years later and looking at it each time I left my cottage to walk into town I recalled that scene vividly and was confronted once again by my own immovable object."

To Peggy Glanville-Hicks, to whom he continued writing often, Bowles told of having found "a hashish almond bar [*majoun*]," which was "unbelievable in its effects, but you have to eat it carefully, like Alice nibbling the mushroom. The transportation is rather sudden, like gusts of golden wind along the vertebrae, and an upward sweep into the clouds. It leaves no ill effect that I can find. The obtaining of it is almost as much fun as the eating."[15] Under the influence of the *majoun,* Bowles climbed up the mountain above his cottage and lay on a slab of rock while it took effect. When he returned to the Farhar, the sun was low. "I [lit] a fire in the fireplace, gave a piece of banana to the parrot, and made a pot of tea. Then in the fading twilight I lay on my bed and stared into the fireplace at the flames. . . . I was trying to imagine the death of my protagonist. The next day I wrote out much of the scene. Very consciously I had always avoided writing about death because I saw it as a difficult subject to treat with anything approaching the proper style; it seemed reasonable, therefore, to hand the job over to the subconscious. I was certain that the *majoun* provided a solution totally unlike whatever I should have found without it.[16]

Having regained the flow of his narrative with the aid of *majoun*, Bowles became increasingly restless and wandered for days in the upper Medina and Casbah until he knew every street and alley. He surprised himself when he realized that he wanted a home of his own in Tangier, an idea contrary to his usual inclinations of being acted upon rather than initiating an action. He began looking at houses in the Casbah, where they ranged in price from $250 for a two-room cottage with an orchard to $2,000 for "big ones with covered courtyards." Even the cheapest had something to commend it, but to buy a house of any size was more than Bowles could manage alone, given the contents of his wallet. He wired Oliver Smith to ask if he wanted to buy it with him, but wrote nothing of his plan to Jane. Smith agreed, although he questioned its practicability. Bowles replied that he had already selected one with "the finest view of all" and urged Smith to come see it for himself.[17]

Dismayed and hurt, Jane could not understand her husband's buying a house of his own volition and not saying a word about it to her. "*I* happened to be in town when Oliver got your wire, and I of course advised him to send the $500, which you said you needed, but you don't sound as though you expected us both to come over, but only Oliver, who refuses to go without me."

Later, Bowles explained his side of the matter. "I am sure I advised Jane of my plans, but there was always such a lag between letters that it's no wonder she was frustrated. I never kept secrets from Jane. . . . But I had long since learned that Jane was such a worrier about things of which she had no firsthand knowledge that it was usually better to inform her after the fact." At that point Bowles had no intention of telling her that one had to go down the alley to a communal latrine.[18]

Jane was certain that Smith would not want to live in a house without a bathroom. "I think he might better stay at a hotel and see how he likes it before making any more expenditures. This way it is still low enough in price to come under the heading of *lark* because *lark* it is." Finally, impatient to see the house for herself, Jane admitted: "Sometimes I am in despair and sometimes very hilarious but I have a terrific urge now to go to Africa in spite of the house, although even the house I would like in the daytime I imagine. I shall naturally not mind the house when there is more than you and me in it. And it does sound beautiful because you can see the water. . . . Write me *everything*–including about the house."[19]

Although Bowles had finished some 150 pages of his novel, he told Jane that he had meant to kill off his hero halfway through the book. "He lingers on in agony instead of dying. But I'll get rid of him yet. Once he's gone there'll be only the heroine left to keep things going, and that won't be easy, either," he added.[20]

Bowles was in Fez awaiting permission to cross the border into Algeria when he wrote Glanville-Hicks that he was "in bed in the streaming sun, all windows open, birds screeching outside, the parrot's cage in the window, the city below, very slowly disengaging itself from the morning mist and smoke, while a million cocks crow at once, constantly. There is also the faint sound of water in the fountains of the palace gardens. The human voices make the most beautiful sound of all when the muezzin calls during the night, especially the one for dawn."[21] There was no one else in Bowles's life to whom he wrote more vividly.

To Kay Cowen, who had recently married and moved with her husband to Augusta, Georgia, Bowles declared that he had no particular news except that Jane was in Vermont working on a novel and a short story. "When she finishes those stints she will be allowed to come here. A trip always upsets her much too much when she's working. But so does a careless inflection in the voice. Still, she *says* she's working."[22]

Reflecting later upon his comment to Cowen about Jane's not

being "allowed" to join him in Morocco until she had written what she was supposed to, Bowles admitted that he did sound "terribly high-handed" in making such a remark. "Yet my insisting upon her finishing what she had set out to do was what I perceived, in good faith, Jane needed. I once told her that if she did not write, she would have to leave. I meant it, and she knew that I meant it. I did not intend to keep living with her if she did not write. It was the one thing in life to which she had dedicated herself, but she was too easily distracted and obsessed by her own self-doubts. Later, when Jane became too ill to write, I regretted that I had appeared so uncompromising in my expectations and demands."[23]

The same evening that Bowles wrote Cowen of his imminent departure for the Algerian desert, he commenced a more relaxed letter to Charles Henri Ford, to which he added periodically as he made his trek, first by train to Oujda, then to Colomb-Béchar, a French Foreign Legion post in western Algeria: "My parrot still refuses to talk. He used to cluck, but now he remains obstinately silent. Perhaps it's the cold and the dry climate. He was brought from South America, and I'm sure he wants to go back."[24] Bowles said that he had wound two woolen cummerbunds around its cage for warmth and sat upon his own feet for the same reason in a first-class compartment of the narrow-gauge train which had left Oujda in a blizzard.

In Colomb-Béchar, a fifteen-hour trip, Bowles waited for the weather to clear, then hitched a ride on a produce truck traveling to Taghit, another day's journey. "I don't know how my parrot survived, but he did. I regretted that he didn't have the vocabulary to tell me about it."[25] In Taghit, Bowles stayed in a tiny hotel operated in conjunction with a nearby military fort. "What made Taghit so special was its situation, overlooking on one side the rocky *hammada* with its incised, meandering river valley bristling with palm trees, and on the other side, the very high *erg* of orange-gold sand, its base only a five-minute walk from the hotel." From there he traveled to Béni Abbès and Timimoun, which he described as "Sudanese in aspect and thus spectacular." Here he was shut in for four days by a sandstorm.[26]

At practically the same moment that he was speculating how long it would take to return to Tangier at a leisurely pace, Bowles was handed a cable from Jane announcing that she would arrive in Gibraltar with Jody McLean on January 31, 1948.[27] "I can't believe it. Now I must leave. You see? Someone always saves you from your masochism. How carefully life is arranged. I approve of it completely."[28]

Bowles had worked well in Timimoun. Each morning he wrote in longhand, ate a leisurely lunch, typed whatever he had written that morning, then wrote again in the afternoon except during the period that he continued to refer to as his "blank state," just as his mother had, when he lay in the bed, emptied his mind of every thought, then napped. "I write slowly, so in spite of all my application, very little progress shows. I have nearly 200 pages typed [and] have no idea whether it's childish or unreadable or engrossing."[29]

To Ford, Bowles wrote of being greeted in Algiers by "a ridiculous, libelous article" about him in the *Echo d'Alger*, in which he was described as "distant, chilly, and eccentric. The staff of the Hotel Saint Georges seemed frightened to let me loose in the lobby, because as soon as I signed my *fiche* [bill] they all knew I was the crazy American from the desert. Of course I was really delighted. No one can ever heap enough insults upon me to suit my taste. I think we all really thrive on hostility, because it's the most intense kind of massage the ego can undergo. Other people's indifference is the only horror."[30]

Upon his return to Tangier, where Jane awaited him, Bowles introduced her to a woman named Cherifa, whom he had described as "a wonderful savage girl with a laugh like a savage and who spoke only Moghrebi. He had already determined that Cherifa was different enough from other Moroccan women he had met that Jane would find her fetching, albeit elusive.[31]

Jane's reaction to Cherifa was precisely as Bowles anticipated. "Cherifa asked Jane to have a bowl of soup with her, and she did. I left the two of them together, and the next thing I knew Jane had fallen passionately in love with Cherifa, who played harder to get, I am sure, than anyone else she had courted. Jane soon discovered for herself the truth that Arabs had accepted unquestioningly for centuries: *'Mektoub'* [It is written]."[32]

A week later, Bowles convinced Jane to join him in Fez since they both were on the verge of finishing their novels and needed no distractions. Each morning they ate breakfast in bed in Jane's room; then Bowles retired to his, but left the door open so that they could talk back and forth if they chose. At one point Jane called out, "Bupple! What's a cantilever, exactly?"[33]

Immersed in the writing of his final chapter, Bowles answered anything that seemed reasonably accurate. After three or four mornings he became aware that she was still trying to build her bridge over a gorge. "I got up and went into her room. We talked for a while about the problem, and I confessed my mystification. 'Why do you have to *construct* the damned thing?' I demanded. 'Why can't you just say it was there and let it go at that?' She shook her head. 'If I don't know how it was built, I can't see it.'"[34] It had never occurred to Bowles that such considerations entered the act of writing. "Perhaps for the first time I had an inkling of what Jane meant when she remarked, as she often did, that writing was 'so *hard*.'" Bowles was convinced that what Jane ultimately wrote was far better than what he had suggested.

On May 10, 1948, Bowles finished his novel at the Hôtel Belvedere in Fez. "I have a certain amount of correlating to do, a certain number of pages to retype because they have been corrected too often and I want the copy to be as neat as I can make it. It will all be sent off within the week. I don't quite know what I'll do next, perhaps some stories I have had on my mind for a while. But my agent [Helen Strauss] doesn't seem to be selling any, so what's the use of writing them? She sends them all to *Cosmopolitan* and *Esquire* and *Good Housekeeping* and *Today's Woman*."[35]

The same day that Bowles wrote Glanville-Hicks that he had finished his novel, Jane wrote Libby Holman: "I finished my story and am typing it in one more than triplicate (quadruplicate?), so that I will have a copy here to show you when you come. The other three go to my agent [Harold Ober], Mrs. Aswell [Mary Lou Aswell], and Helvetia. Paul has finished his novel as he wrote you, I imagine, and will turn out six stories tomorrow."[36]

Whereas Jane feared that she would never get to know well the elusive Cherifa, who claimed to be a daughter of the patron saint of Tangier, Bowles had become increasingly intrigued of late by a sixteen-year-old youth named Ahmed ben Driss el Yacoubi. Yacoubi was a *cherif*. Being acknowledged a *cherif* meant that both parents were considered direct descendants of the Prophet Mohammed, founder of Islam. Yacoubi lived in his parents' home in El Keddane, one of the ancient quarters of Fez. His father, a *f'qih* (a lawyer of religious law), was from Fez, and his mother was from the mountains.

Yacoubi's paternal grandfather was also a *f'qih*, whom Muslims accepted as the highest authority in the land. Yacoubi was taught at home by his father and grandfather, who ministered to the sick and cast out spells through the laying on of hands, the manipulation of fire, the brewing of concoctions to be used in their treatments, and the writing of sacred formulas. When Bowles met Yacoubi, his education consisted chiefly of learning the legends, songs, and dances of his region and paraphrasing the Koran.[37]

As a *cherif*, Yacoubi was a privileged and popular guest in any Muslim home he chose to visit. It was in one such home during the summer of 1947 that he and Bowles met. On this occasion, their host was Moulay Ali ben Ktiri, an elderly Fassi gentleman whose title *moulay* signified that he, too, was a descendant of the Prophet. Moulay Ktiri was highly regarded as a member of Fez's rich merchant class, and he had a wife and many sons and daughters. At tea during Bowles's initial visit to the home of Moulay Ktiri, he was introduced to a number of young men, all natives of Fez, who were attending the Collège Moulay Idriss and were destined for careers in the Moroccan government. They spoke French fluently and were articulate, charming, and witty. Yet no guest impressed Bowles nearly so much as did Yacoubi, who spoke neither French nor Spanish, languages in which Bowles was fluent, and the few words he knew in Arabic contributed nothing to their attempt to communicate. Yacoubi's Berber dialect was unique to Fez, yet through gestures and facial expressions they managed to make themselves understood. "I was determined to know him better. He was primitive, and his reactions were those of a primitive. That was what fascinated me. I don't think I'd ever known anyone so primitive, and when we became better acquainted, I encouraged him not to lose that quality. I was told that when he spoke *Darija* to Westerners it was as though he were addressing an infant, and that his dialect was entirely different when he conversed with natives of his region. Jane was learning the *Darija* unique to Tangier, and I wished to speak the *Darija* of Fez, since I was always fonder of Fez and its people than I was of Tangier. Jane wanted merely to communicate with the women in the grain market."[38]

Although Bowles was careful to acquaint himself with Moroccan protocol and customs, he drew the line when it came to learning Arabic, unlike Jane, who had spent the autumn in Paris attending the École de Langues Orientales, then hired a Moroccan tutor upon her arrival in Tangier. "I had neither the time nor the desire. I was busy working, writing, and writing music. Everything I was interested in reading or speaking was already available in languages I did know."

Bowles never forgot his astonishment when he observed Yacoubi sitting on the floor in front of a drawing he had just finished and playing his flute to it. "For a good ten minutes he sat there 'blowing life into it.' Somehow he'd heard the legend of God's bringing Adam to life after making him out of clay, and he decided that a drawing was not really alive until he played his flute to it. As a child, Yacoubi also made small sculptures, but his father insisted that he work at something else since it was 'against the religion to make idols.'"[39]

In a postscript to Peggy Glanville-Hicks after his return to Fez, he wrote: "I enclose one of a series of drawings by Ahmed ben Driss el Yacoubi. There are some incredible ones, but Jane has fallen in love with them and insists on keeping them. One, of the parrot, is the most extraordinary thing I've seen in a long time. Hilarious and very sad, all at once. He names each one. I have one called 'Three Men Running Past a Mosque in Aït Baza, 380 kilometers from Fez.'"[40]

It was Jane who first got Yacoubi to use paint, and later she took his drawings and paintings to New York to give to Betty Parsons to exhibit in her gallery. By the time he was twenty-one, Yacoubi was Morocco's best-known contemporary artist. They were in Fez when Jane met him and watched him draw pictures on the hotel stationery in their room. "You should go into the Ville Nouvelle tomorrow and get him some decent paper and India ink," Jane instructed her husband.

"It was Jane's first time to eat *majoun* candy, which Yacoubi's mother had made for us, and we waited for it to take effect," said Bowles. "Jody McLean was there, too, as was Edwin Denby, and everyone wanted to try it. Of course I warned them that they must eat only a small amount at first, then wait until it took effect. We drank tea, which I made several times, and played the phonograph while Yacoubi continued drawing, and after a while, I heard Jane say: 'Ah, this stuff is nothing.'"

When he turned to look at her, he realized that she was finishing off a still larger piece of the *majoun* candy. "It has no effect," she said.

"But I told you, the effect is delayed. Now you've taken too much."

Bowles reported that as the evening wore on, they both slept for several hours, then he awoke and found Jane in a state of extreme agitation. "She looked at her hands and could not understand what they were. When she saw her fingers move, she became paralyzed with terror. From that day on Jane remained an implacable enemy of all forms of cannabis."[41]

Bowles's own sense of the experience was that he had come upon a fantastic secret, and that he had only to spread a bit of *majoun* on a biscuit and eat it. He then began a series of experiments with *majoun* so that he might determine his own "optimum conditions regarding the quantity to be ingested, the time of day for the dose, the accompanying diet, and the general physical and psychological ambiances most conducive to pleasure during the experience." Large quantities of hot tea were essential, he said, and twilight was the best hour for taking it; "the effect came on slowly after an hour and a half or even two hours had passed, preferably at the moment of sitting down to dinner. . . . It was imperative to be unmitigatedly content with all facets of existence beforehand. . . . It is a delicate operation, the taking of *majoun*."[42]

Jane was still in Fez with Bowles, Yacoubi, and Oliver Smith when Libby Holman wired that she and her son, Christopher, now sixteen, would be arriving shortly in Tangier and hoped that Bowles could be there to meet them and to organize for them a trek into the desert. For Christopher, having read several of Bowles's stories, his mother's friend had become a hero to him. Despite their entreaties, Jane had no intention of joining them since the trip entailed crossing the High Atlas Mountains and going deep into the Anti-Atlas, far to the south. She not only was afraid of heights, tunnels, and elevators, but abhorred the idea of being constantly on the move beyond her immediate and safe surroundings. Jody McLean had already returned to New York, and what Jane wanted most now was to spend time with Cherifa.[43]

Bowles said later that Jane was wise in deciding not to accompany them into the desert. "We spent our days jealously watching one another take sips of whatever liquid happened to be in the car. It was the month of Ramadan, so the driver could not touch water until sunset. At that moment, wherever we happened to be, in the middle of a mud village or at the edge of a precipice, he would bring the car to a halt and pull out his thermos of water and one hard-boiled egg. After a few minutes of respectful silence on our parts while he refreshed himself, he would start up again and we could resume our chatter." Their most distant destination, by way of Fez and Marrakech, was Tafraoute, deep in the Anti-Atlas. "It seemed to take forever to go through the various military road checks, and we spent our nights in an assortment of roadside hotels." One night they stayed at a leopard hunter's lodge in Ksiba, and after dinner Bowles and Holman sat upon the rocks in the moonlight. "We were talking and looking at the moon when Libby suddenly proposed that we get married. I was astonished. I was already married. Then she told me that she had talked about the possibility with Jane, and that Jane had been agreeable should that be what I preferred. Libby assured me that Jane would always be welcome to live at Treetops with us, should we marry, and that we could be 'a family.' I remember staring at the moon and saying nothing. I had no intention of becoming involved with Libby beyond being her houseguest and close friend. After a while, she laughed and said: 'I don't think Jane likes the idea *really*. I think she wants to be Mrs. Bowles herself.' Neither of us mentioned it again."[44]

One of Holman's motives for coming to Tangier was to ask Bowles to find her a play that would make a "good singing and acting vehicle," then to commission him to write the libretto. Knowing that he was devoted to Lorca's work, she had already read *Yerma* and told Bowles that she admired it immensely. "I told Libby that if I were to do it, I should have to make my own translation first, and she agreed. I also knew that it was not something I could do quickly. To create incidental music for a play was one thing, to write songs, another; but to do an entire opera was quite a different matter. She assured me that there was no hurry, and I took her at her word. By the time *Yerma* was ready for production, Libby's voice was not what it once was, and the production was a disaster."[45]

Like many of Bowles's friends, Tennessee Williams had toyed with the idea of going to Morocco shortly after Bowles himself arrived. In an undated letter to Margo Jones, who had directed *Summer and Smoke* for presentation in her theater in Dallas, Williams wrote: "I have heard from Paul Bowles lately. He and wife Jane and Edwin Denby are all in Morocco, in Fez, and he urges me to visit him there. I can't right now but I will later on and I am wondering if I should ask him about doing music for *Summer*. We certainly must have some and I am sure you would want Paul to do it. The question is whether he'll come back to the States in time." Williams had reservations about Jones's directing ability and wrote Bowles that he was considering alternatives to her being both director and producer for the New York production. To his friend Paul Bigelow,

Cheryl Crawford's assistant, Williams wrote: "Margo is bound and determined to put on *Summer and Smoke*, though I am most apprehensive about its following *Streetcar Named Desire*. It is by no means as well put together. Consequently I am having to devote most of my energies to re-writing it so it will not show up too badly."[46] After another exchange of letters, Bowles accepted the commission to compose the music for *Summer and Smoke*, but questioned the advisability of his opening a new play with a relatively inexperienced director while *A Streetcar Named Desire* was still a runaway success at the box office. "What I feared might happen *did* happen. *Summer and Smoke* closed after 100 performances, and *A Streetcar Named Desire* kept on running. Yet, to my surprise, royalties dribbled in. In hindsight, ten percent of the gross was not bad," he allowed.

Commenting upon the play later, Bowles saw no serious flaws in the production of *Summer and Smoke*, but knew that it paled compared with *A Streetcar Named Desire*. Disappointed, he declared: "Other than being acknowledged in the program and on the theater posters as the composer of the music, I don't recall the critics taking any special note of the fact."[47]

In a letter to Jane shortly after the opening of *Summer and Smoke*, Bowles reported that Carson McCullers was back in Paris and had sent Jane her love. He also suggested that Jane might wish to "look in on her" since she, too, would be in Paris shortly. Jane replied that she did not care to visit McCullers now. "I'm sorry she's ill [but] why does she send me her love? She doesn't know me."[48]

"Certainly Jane was never one of Carson's admirers," said Bowles. "She was jealous of Carson, as she was of all women writers. She used to say that Carson may have been as talented as Sartre or Simone de Beauvoir, but was not a 'serious writer.' She believed that Carson wrote too easily about the freaks who were such a feature of her work, thinking to make them attractive by superficial means, whereas to Jane the more peculiar people were, the more one had to labor to make them *real*."[49]

Contrary to Bowles's intention when he came to New York to write music for Williams's play, which was to return to Tangier as quickly as possible, he ended up accompanying the show to Cleveland, Buffalo, and Detroit, then on to New York for its opening in early October. He also completed his Concerto for Two Pianos, rehearsed it with a full orchestra, and attended its premiere at Town Hall on November 18, 1948.

Meanwhile, he and Jane continued to write each other frequently and report on their various doings. Jane wrote often of her delight in almost every aspect of Tangier. "The view of the Arab town from my window is a source of endless pleasure to me. I cannot stop looking and it is perhaps the first time in my life that I have felt joyous as a result of a purely visual experience. I am just beginning to try to work now and the morning noises are very bad. It makes me frantic because I love it here. I fear that Cherifa is never going to work out. I think she is afraid of me."[50]

Both *A Streetcar Named Desire* and *Summer and Smoke* were still running on December 1, 1948, when Bowles boarded an Italian liner, the SS *Vulcania*, having convinced Williams and his companion, Frank Merlo, to accompany him to Tangier. In the hold was the playwright's new maroon convertible, in which they intended to explore Morocco for three weeks before proceeding to Rome. "It was a stormy crossing, and I stayed in my cabin most of the time. I also wrote a story during the crossing, which I called 'The Delicate Prey,' and gave it to Tennessee to read on the ship. The tale itself was based on an actual happening, but Tennessee thought I had made the whole thing up. The next day he brought it back to me and said: 'It is a wonderful story, but if you publish it, you're mad.'

"I think if you write something, you should publish it, that is, if an editor wants to publish it," replied Bowles. "Tennessee had written shocking stories himself. Think of his 'Desire and the Black Masseur.' That's pretty shocking. Or even 'The Mysteries of the Joy Rio.' No, my particular brand of shockingness shocked him more because it was mine and not his, I think. It was just a friendly admonition on his part to try to dissuade me from publishing it."[51]

Williams's own version of the incident was that it was "quite incomprehensible to Paul that I, who had published such stories as 'Desire and the Black Masseur,' should be shocked by 'The Delicate Prey.' I recognized it as a beautiful piece of prose but advised him against its publication in the States. You see, my shocking stories had been published in expensive private editions by New Directions and never exhibited on a bookstore counter."[52] Upon Williams's return to New York a few weeks later, he told his friend Jordan Massee: "It wasn't the Arabs I was afraid of while I was in Tangier; it was Paul Bowles, whose chilling stories filled me with horror." Massee concluded that Williams was being melodramatic, but he believed him.[53]

To James Laughlin, Bowles wrote from Fez on January 10, 1949: "Thanks for your letter; it arrived while Tennessee was still here. Soon afterward he left for Italy, having attempted unsuccessfully to persuade me to go along. I am perfectly content here, and there is no reason why I should leave. He, on the other hand, was violently perturbed by the Moslem scene, and couldn't leave fast enough to suit him. He's a strange one. I suppose he thinks I'm mad to like it here, although he pretends not to.[54]

Williams, having met Ahmed Yacoubi, knew at once Bowles's rationale for not accompanying him to Italy. To Williams, it was obvious that Bowles not only was intrigued by the young *cherif*; he was obsessed by him. Later, Bowles declared: "As much as I was capable of loving anyone, I loved Yacoubi with an intense passion heretofore unknown to me. With Yacoubi, it was never 'just sex.' Whereas Libby Holman had once suggested that she and Jane and I could live quite happily together as a trio, I had no intention of sharing Yacoubi with anyone."[55]

CHAPTER TEN

Bowles Returns to the Desert with Jane, and They Renew Their Dedication to Writing

(1949–1951)

"This place we're in is an oasis. We had to walk to it from a bus, with donkey carriers for our luggage. It is so beautiful up there. Nothing but mountains and valleys of sand as far as the eye can see."

—Jane Bowles to Katharine Hamill
and Natasha von Hoershelman,
Taghit, Algeria, March 17, 1949

Bowles was surprised that Jane agreed to accompany him into the desert, and even more surprised that she liked it. "The hotel here is kept up for the army since no tourists ever come," she wrote her friends in New York. "There are just Paul and me, the Arab who runs the hotel, the three soldiers in the fort, and the natives. It is very quiet, no electricity, no cars. Just *Paul* and *me*," she repeated. "We plan to be in the desert about a month and then back to Fez and Tangier, where I can resume my 'silly life with the grain market group: Tetum, Zodelia, Cherifa and Quinza.'"[1] Jane was devoted to her husband, but she also was devoted to her writing despite the distractions she encouraged, most of them having to do with the women in her life.

Before leaving the desert, Jane felt compelled to write a short story, "A Stick of Green Candy," and Bowles, delighted that she was writing again, typed it for her. Both traveled with their portable typewriters, but Jane constantly revised and he feared that she would never stop tinkering with it. Biographer Millicent Dillon saw "A Stick of Green Candy" as Jane's story of the "loss of belief in the imagination . . . a coda to all that she had done before."[2]

Upon their return to Tangier, Jane realized how much her month in the Sahara had intensified her own need for personal space, but there was little time to pursue it before she allowed herself to be caught up in a whirl of social activities being choreographed this time by Cecil Beaton, David Herbert, Gore Vidal, and Truman Capote. Beaton, an avid diarist, wrote on August 26, 1949: "Jane Bowles, who is perhaps one of the rarest talents on the literary scene (alas, she has published but little), is as wise and witty in life as she is in prose. Her appearance is likewise unique, for, although nearing middle age, she seems still to be a child with her shorn-off hair, gangling, spindly legs, and wide-eyed wonder."[3]

Bowles resented Jane's being referred to as "nearing middle age" since she was only thirty-two. "I imagine most people took her to be in her twenties. She was fetching in her naturalness and obvious good humor," he insisted.[4] In one of Beaton's photographs, Jane stood barefooted on a giant boulder at Merkala Beach, where sunbathers often gathered and swimmers braved the surf. David Herbert, his head wrapped in a towel, was seated behind her, and next to Jane was a goat wearing a hemp collar. Squatting on the rock was the Arab youth charged with the goat's care. In another, Jane was seated on the boulder beside Bowles, dressed in a short-sleeved, shirt-waist blouse, a cardigan knotted loosely about her waist, and slacks rolled to the knees.

Biographer Fred Kaplan described Tangier in 1949 as a "gathering place for traveling queens" attracted there by the weather, beaches, cheap cost of living, easy availability of drugs, and the Arab ethos that permitted every sort of sex under terms totally independent of European puritanism.[5] The town's dirt and widespread poverty, its total lack of intellectual culture, and the hovel Vidal rented in town, all were repugnant. Jack Dunphy, who had arrived in Tangier with Truman Capote, reported being greeted at the dock by Bowles, Jane, and Vidal "looking like vultures awaiting the wash-up after a hurricane." Dunphy complained, too, that despite the countless people he and Capote had met in Morocco during their several weeks there, the Arab world remained a mystery. "Of course one could always simplify the whole thing, as the British seem to do, and look on most of the citizens of Tangier as servants," he reasoned, but such a view "was sad and made one feel more of an outsider than ever."[6] Dunphy's observation was also a shot at David Herbert, the second son of Britain's Earl of Pembroke, who had settled in Tangier in 1947 with a passel of servants and played host to everyone of note.

Meanwhile, Bowles resented Doubleday's rejection of *The Sheltering Sky* that summer on the basis that it was not a novel. "If it isn't a novel, I don't know what it is," he growled. Helen Strauss, Bowles's agent, pointed out that he would not have to repay the thousand-dollar advance since it would be deducted from royalties if a new publisher should take over the contract, but he had no assurance of that happening either. Finally, Strauss negotiated contracts with both John Lehmann, Ltd., a small British press, and James Laughlin, editor of New Directions, for an American edition of *The Sheltering Sky*. "The fact that my edition came out first annoyed Mr. Laughlin no end, and he threatened to sue me," declared Lehmann, who intended to publish, also, a collection of Bowles's short stories. "Again, I got the jump on Mr. Laughlin, who failed to bring out such a collection at all." Bowles's agent then negotiated with David McDowell of Random House for an American edition of Bowles's collected stories. To promote the publication of *The Sheltering Sky* in Britain and to recognize Jane's success, too, as a writer, Lehmann invited them to London to meet the literary community there. Bowles readily agreed, but Jane had no intention of accompanying him until David Herbert extended a personal invitation for them to stay with him in his family's ancestral estate in Wilton since he intended to return there himself shortly and would drive them. "David Herbert once told Jane that if anything happened to me, he would like to marry her himself. She was flattered and believed him, as did I, but we were relieved not to have to put him to the test," said Bowles.[7]

In the late fall the three of them left Tangier aboard the liner *Koutoubia* with Herbert's Jaguar in the hold of the ship. From Marseilles they set out for England on a leisurely driving trip through France, but in Lyons, Bowles's liver flared up and delayed their journey for three days. Jane was not perturbed since both she and Herbert were bent upon partaking of the culinary delights of the area, and each evening they returned to Bowles's bedside to gloat over the delicacies they had consumed in epic portions, tales that he viewed as a ghastly trick.

In London, upon meeting Bowles for the first time, John Lehmann was struck "at once by his quiet charm and intelligence, his shrewdness about the ways of the world, and his sharp wit that did not spare his contemporaries."[8] Whereas Jane had decided to spend the winter in Paris with Jody McLean, with whom she had revived her romance, Bowles was determined to put considerable distance between himself and anything he had experienced in the past. "I needed to immerse myself in the writing of my next novel and could not afford the distractions of either London or Tangier; moreover, I was not ready to go back into the Sahara so soon," said Bowles, who had seen in one of David Herbert's scrapbooks "almost an entire album devoted to a ravishing little island where he had stayed with his parents in the mid-thirties."[9] The island was called Taprobane, and it lay just offshore in the Bay of Weligama at Ceylon's extreme southern tip. "Ah, Taprobane!" Bowles exclaimed, and the word itself excited him and reminded him of the exotic names he had made up as a child. When he learned that a Polish freighter, the MS *General Walter*, was due to leave shortly for Ceylon from Antwerp, Bowles realized that he, too, was on the cusp of a new adventure. "*Mektoub*, it is written," he declared.

To Libby Holman, Jane wrote from England: "Paul is hell bent on going to Ceylon. I think it would be fatal if he hung around until February–for Spain. It is the wrong season there, and he doesn't have any place he wants to be in winter except the Sahara where there really is no piano. He can surely find one in Ceylon. . . . He wants to meet you in Spain in the spring." Jane was referring to her husband's collaboration with Holman on Lorca's *Yerma*, which he had to finish translating before he could convert it into an opera.

The day Bowles left Antwerp, he saw his first review of the British edition of *The Sheltering Sky*. Despite the anonymous reviewer's reservations in *Time* magazine about the novel's central characters and "a plot that may be taken as a lurid, super-sexy Sahara adventure story completely outfitted with camel trains, handsome Arabs, French officers, and a harem," he called *The Sheltering Sky* the "most interesting first novel by an American all year."[10] Another early notice of the book was George Malcolm Thomson's Book of the Month Club review in the *Evening Standard*. The novel was "touched with genius, a book of challenging power and penetration, a story of almost unbearable tensions, a bitter modern drama played out against the blazing desolation of the Sahara," wrote Thomson, who was clearly intrigued by Bowles's tale and seemed envious that he, too, had not been on hand for the adventures that followed.[11]

Similarly, Edwin Muir's wholly positive review in the London *Observer* commended Bowles's "understanding of character, the significance of every external detail, of the scenery, the sounds, the changes of atmosphere, the sense that everything happens by necessity and fatality–all were wonderfully conveyed." Still another early review, this one in the *Times Literary Supplement*, on September 30, 1949, addressed the novel's "series of remarkable episodes, [which] though increasingly macabre and pointless, still retain some kind of hallucinatory logic." With such praise of his first novel, Bowles could hardly wait to start the next one.

An essay/review by Tennessee Williams in the *New York Times Book Review* awaited him in Colombo. In it, the playwright allowed that some readers would be enthralled by the book "without once suspecting that it contains a mirror of what is most terrifying and cryptic with the Sahara, moral nihilism, into which the race of man now seems to be wandering blindly."[12] In the same issue of the *New York Times Book Review*, William Carlos Williams placed *The Sheltering Sky* at the top of his list in "The Best Books I've Read This Year." A piece in the *New York Herald Tribune* Book Review on Christmas Day of 1949 was similarly laudatory. Many other positive reviews followed. Fanny Butcher, writing for the *Chicago Sunday Tribune*, applauded the novel for its "magnificence of description" and likened it to Hemingway's *The Sun Also Rises* in its "mood of existentialism." On a similar note, Florence Codman informed readers of *Commonweal* that she had found for the first time an American novelist who "met the French existentialists on their own ground and held them to a draw. From the first page to the last, the story stealthily increases in suspense and insinuation." Some forty thousand copies of the British edition of *The Sheltering Sky* were purchased before the book disappeared from the best-seller list.

Bowles wrote later of the events that triggered his second novel. "The night we sailed through the Strait of Gibraltar, I stood on deck staring longingly into the dark on the southern side of the ship. A rush of nostalgia for Tangier seized me. I went inside and got into my berth. Then I began to write something which I hoped might prove the nucleus of a novel about Tangier. The first scene was on the cliffs opposite the point we were passing at that moment. Dyar, my protagonist, stands at the edge of the cliff and looks out at the freighters going by in the strait. From that scene the book grew in both directions–backward as cause, and forward as effect."[13]

In a preface to a new edition of the novel, which he titled *Let It Come Down*, Bowles declared: "I knew I must write enough of the text to serve as an umbilical cord between me and the novel before I landed in an unfamiliar place, otherwise I should lose it all. As the ship drew nearer to Ceylon I found myself recalling Kafka's well-known aphorism: *From a certain point onward there is no longer any turning back. That is the point that must be reached.* I doubt that [Kafka] meant it to be applied to the writing of a book; nevertheless it seemed relevant to the situation. I strained to pass that crucial point."[14]

The wind and slanting rains prevalent through much of the voyage contributed significantly to the opening of his novel and to its development, its title having come from a scene in *Macbeth*:

> Banquo: It will be rain tonight.
> First murderer: Let it come down. [stabs Banquo].

The ship had encountered a dramatic storm off Cartagena, Spain, and made no progress for twenty-four hours. Bowles stayed in bed almost the entire time and wrote. "I felt much as I had in Dutton's Bookshop on Fifth Avenue when I kept adding page after page 'without stopping' for fear that if I stopped, the whole thing would be a total waste of time. I had the illusion of being about to add another country, another culture, to my total experience."[15]

Upon arrival, Bowles wrote of walking great distances and being constantly exhilarated by the light, climate, vegetation, and great quantities of rice and curry at the Mount Lavinia Hotel, situated just below the fort in Colombo. In a bookstore he met the Trimmers, an Anglican minister and his wife who invited him to their remote rubber and tea plantation and were a font of information and anecdotes about the country. Born in Ceylon, they spoke Sinhalese and Tamil, the language of many people who lived in southern India. "I never tried to learn their language since they spoke English, but I liked hearing it," said Bowles.

To Vidal, who had planned to visit him in Ceylon, but allowed that he had missed the ship, Bowles scolded: "Why the hell didn't you write long ago and let me know at least that you had not taken the boat? . . . I must say that the opportunities for happy living are greater in Ceylon than anywhere I've been so far. You never would have done any work if you'd come. . . . One is at a premium here among the collegians, and can pick and choose. The only trouble is that one chooses everyone."[16]

After a fortnight with the Trimmers, Bowles set out by train along the southern coast of Ceylon, where to his astonishment he caught a glimpse of the island he had seen in David Herbert's scrapbook. It had barely come into view as the train rounded a bend, then disappeared. In letter after letter to his mother, editors, and friends, Bowles commented upon his environment, the people he encountered, and various adventures that he hoped would entertain them.[17]

On March 7, 1950, Bowles assured his Random House editor that he was busy working on his new book, but hesitated to mention it because he wanted "to be able to throw it out" if he did not like it. At this point, he had written seventy pages. In still another exchange with McDowell regarding who would publish the American edition of his short stories, Bowles presented his side of the matter: "What if I did go into detail with [Laughlin at New Directions] in letters about the format, order of stories, and jacket. We had been corresponding vaguely about his doing the volume for the past year. At first Laughlin intended to release it only in his 'Direction' series, as he didn't think short stories should be given a more substantial format. After *The Sheltering Sky* got good reviews he consented to make a companion volume."[18]

Bowles said that he favored using the title *The Delicate Prey* for the short story volume since that was the name of one of the stories, but pointed out that the title was applicable to all of them since "the delicate prey is man himself." He told McDowell, too, that John Lehmann would not be able to use the title *The Delicate Prey* in England, or the story itself, because it was "too explicit for English censors," and that he could not use *Pages from Cold Point* for the same reason.[19]

In Ceylon, Bowles worked each morning on *Let It Come Down*, and in the afternoon on the music he had promised to write for Libby Holman. Working each day at an upright piano in one of the cottages owned by the Trimmers, Bowles observed that the "pitch of each string in the old instrument was merely a token pitch, and that the action was fairly normal" until one afternoon he found the keys strangely blocked. "I assumed that the rain had brought about a sudden further disintegration of the mechanism, and attacked *fortissimo*. Then I sprang away from the piano, knocking over the bench. A large snake was rising vertically out of the piano's open top, its black tongue flicking in my direction. In my world, to have a ten-foot serpent come out of a piano and disappear into the ceiling was an extraordinary event, but my hosts appeared only mildly surprised."[20]

In early March 1950, Bowles traveled two hundred miles by train from Madurai to Trivandrum, a seaport town near the southernmost tip of India. "South India was a place to which one could not remain indifferent," observed Bowles. In the temple at Madurai he heard such extraordinary music that he regretted not having any recording mechanism with him, for it provided the "ambience of eternity suitable to a place of worship with far greater success than the music [one] is accustomed to hearing in European cathedrals."[21]

Bowles resumed work on *Let It Come Down* in southern India in a large airy hotel overlooking the sea at Cape Comorin. Here he was the only guest, and he worked naked by the hot light of oil lamps. In the town of Tuticorin, still farther south, Bowles spent three nights in the Railway Rest House while awaiting his ship back to Ceylon. "Of all the cities I have examined, Tuticorin is the foulest," he wrote David McDowell. "There was no sewage system, and the air stank of human excrement. The ship I was finally able to board was a floating extension of Tuticorin. The walls of the cabin seethed with big shiny cockroaches, and the fiery breath of the engine room belched through the doorway from across the corridor." For fifteen days Bowles reported each morning to a district medical officer to be checked for cholera.[22]

Bowles lamented that his holiday would soon be over, but he vowed to return. "If I cannot buy Taprobane, which of course I can't afford, I'll try to rent it. I have some others in mind up-country. I found one the other day for sale for $2,000, which included four acres of jungle, a house with its own power plant, two bathrooms with real plumbing, and a garage. I've about come to the conclusion that it's the best country to settle in, from all points of view. The climate is fine, the company is even better, the countryside suits me beautifully, and the way one is taken care of by the servants appeals to me. There is no such thing as service in Europe or America after one has been attended to by Sinhalese."[23]

Bowles said later that he had no idea how colonial he sounded in his letters from Ceylon to his editors, parents, and friends in New York. "But obviously I was." From Dehiwala–Mount Lavinia, eight miles south of Colombo, Bowles wrote his editor that lightning was flashing over the sea and the thunder was rolling overhead. "The breakers are high and shake the hotel every few seconds. The fireflies are fat and bright and crawl up the walls like little electric trains in the dark. And it's hot. I've been visiting a Buddhist monastery about three hours down the coast on an island in a lagoon at a place called Dudanduwa. I'm going back tomorrow to Hikkaduwa, which is near Dudanduwa, for a few days."[24]

Bowles was enamored of the names of the various villages and towns he had visited in Ceylon and India, just as he had been enchanted by the names of places he encountered during his first journey to Morocco when he had spelled them out in letters to his mother, savoring each syllable. "I remember pronouncing the extraordinary names I encountered in Ceylon and drumming them rhythmically with my index finger, syllable by syllable, upon the leather cover of my journal as I made them my own: Du-dan-du-wa . . . Hik-ka-du-wa . . . Du-dan-du-wa . . . Hik-ka-du-wa . . . Wel-la-wa-ta . . . Mount-La-vin-ia . . . Tu-ti-cor-in . . . Ho-ma-ga-ma . . . Wel-la-wa-ta . . . Mount-La-vin-ia . . . Tu-ti-cor-in . . . Ho-ma-ga-ma . . . the sounds themselves replicating the hypnotic chants of the Buddhist monks. I may even have recited them in my sleep."[25]

By the time Bowles returned to Tangier in May 1950, John Lehmann was well into the editing of his short fiction, having selected a dozen stories for the volume. Although Lehmann did not intend to publish all of Bowles's short stories, he considered himself fortunate to be Bowles's English publisher. Despite the extraordinary success of *The Sheltering Sky*, Lehmann was convinced that Bowles's stories were without parallel in modern literature, "a gift that general opinion is likely to fight against to the last because he has the quality that geniuses, great and small, so often display, of being profoundly disturbing to the deeper conventional assumptions and patterns of value, and not merely shocking to established codes of behavior already more or less abandoned by free-thinking people."[26]

Since "The Delicate Prey" was not to be included in the Lehmann edition, Bowles agreed to George Davis's publishing it in *Mademoiselle*. He also suggested a new title, *A Little Stone*, for the collection as a whole, since it was not derived from the title of any specific story in the volume, but from an aspect of the plot in a tale he had originally called "A Spring Day." "I thought it a disarmingly innocent-sounding title, but without consulting me, George Davis changed it to 'You Are Not I.'" Bowles resented anyone's insistence on having the final word regarding his fiction. "I was always agreeable up to a point; then I charged like a Cape buffalo."[27]

Meanwhile, Jane was still in Paris with Jody McLean, who she admitted was now "both hindrance and help." Although McLean gave a center to her day, Jane resented her intrusive presence upon the few hours she had tried repeatedly to set aside to work on the revisions of her play, *In the Summer House*. "It has taken me some weeks to realize that Jody just doesn't want to have anyone else much around, though if they must be around, she prefers them to be men. Strange that when she first arrived I thought we had a whole lifetime together," she wrote Bowles.[28]

By the time he arrived in Paris, McLean had returned to New York. Later he said: "One's taste is not something that another person generally questions, but I admit to wondering what Jane saw in her. Naturally she felt similarly about some of my friends." Jane was staying then at the Hôtel de l'Université, where her residency overlapped with Carson McCullers and Eudora Welty. "I don't think Carson and Welty paid any attention to each other, but Jane rather admired Welty, who already had published five acclaimed books of fiction, and seemed not at all jealous of Welty's success, unlike her reaction to Carson." Bowles remembered that Welty lived in joyous expectation of letters from her family and friends in Mississippi, principally in order to follow the adventures of Li'l Abner. Enclosed in each letter were comic strips that had been cut from the newspapers since the preceding letter. Never having heard of Li'l Abner, Bowles found Welty's preoccupation with the comic strip the height of eccentricity.[29]

Although Bowles had hoped that Jane would return with him to Tangier since Jody McLean was no longer a presence in her life, he discovered that another woman already had replaced her. Marty Mann was an attractive woman some thirteen years Jane's senior whom she had met while Mann was working temporarily in Paris upon founding the National Council on Alcoholism.[30] On February 18, 1951, Jane wrote Libby Holman: "Marty has given me a little Hermès typewriter for my birthday and I am very happy about it. She is wonderful to me and I think really loves me. It is extraordinary that I should have found at last someone so sweet and trusting and gay and brave and beautiful. . . . As I have told you there is a great amount of pain in this situation, mostly because of Paul, but it is not insoluble and something will work out eventually. . . . Some days I am in misery because I seem to feel two equally strong destinies and one of them is to be with Paul. I miss him of course terribly."[31]

Although Jane had written Bowles that she had no inclination to go anywhere just then, he learned shortly that she already had followed Marty Mann to New York, "although she acted as though it was to pursue the production of her play, *In the Summer House,* now tentatively set for late August. I think she was devastated when Garson Kanin, who had agreed to direct the play, left the production before its scheduled opening, and of course Jane kept rewriting lines, changing them, then writing still new ones–often upon Oliver Smith's advice–and deciding, finally, to rewrite the entire third act. Naturally she was already caught up with her New York friends, and I was delighted not to be there among them."[32]

To his Random House editor, Bowles wrote from Tangier on August 13, 1951, that he intended to stay put until Jane's play, *In the Summer House,* was ready to be produced on Broadway, "in which case I shall go to New York and write the score for it." McDowell had urged Bowles to come anyway since the volume of short stories was still in production, but Bowles was just as insistent that proof sheets be sent to him in Fez or Tangier. "A lot more could be done to promote the book if you were here," his editor countered.

"And what would that be?" challenged Bowles.

McDowell replied that there would be "many opportunities for appearances on radio programs, television programs, interviews in the *Times* and *Tribune*, personal lunches with columnists, and the like. Whether you know it or not, you are the subject of a great deal of interest here: a musician, a writer, an expatriate, and a very exotic man who wanders around deep in the sands of the Sahara. I do *not* mean that the book will be a flop if you are not here. It just simply would help."[33] Bowles was not enticed, having no intention of returning to New York until he was summoned by a producer of *In the Summer House*, and that the production itself was a sure thing. The only thing that bothered Bowles at present was a rumor that the U.S. State Department was relieving Americans of their passports upon their return from abroad. "If that proves to be true, I shouldn't want to be stuck in the USA. My case might be construed in some undesirable way, given my previous political affiliations. Twelve years may not seem so long to hysterical investigators. I'm just an ancient C.P. member, as you probably have guessed. A change of heart on one side doesn't necessarily mean forgiveness on the other."[34]

When the catalog from Random House announcing new books for 1951 reached him, Bowles was appalled to discover that the title of his short story collection had been amended to *The Delicate Prey and Other Stories*. "There is something so anti-climactic, dead, discouraging, indifferent about the expression '*and Other Stories*' that I should think the mere appearance of it on a jacket or in advertising would suffice to guarantee the minimum sales. I deplore it," he informed McDowell.[35] Bowles also complained about the jacket copy.

"Don't be sensitive and so alarmed," replied his editor, who suggested that Bowles could write new jacket copy for the second edition of the book if he wished.[36] Bowles was not amused and had no intention of writing the actual text, but he did propose that a clue could be provided in the jacket copy as to what the author himself considered the stories to be: "Practically all the tales are a variety of detective story. Not the usual variety, I admit, but still, detective stories in which the reader is the detective, and the mystery is the motivation for the character's behavior. . . . If you could form a sentence or two for the jacket of that hypothetical second edition which would embody these ideas, I should be delighted," he informed David McDowell.[37]

Bowles was recuperating in Marrakech in August 1950 from a new crop of ailments, a head and chest cold, sinus complications, a liver attack, and an invasion of intestinal worms, when both editions of his short story collections arrived almost simultaneously. Lehmann's abbreviated version was titled *A Little Stone*, and Random House's enlarged edition, *The Delicate Prey and Other Stories*, which included the tales to which Lehmann had objected originally on the basis that some of them might offend his readers. The British edition appeared without dedication, Bowles having chosen to dedicate to his mother only the expanded American edition. In reply to an enthusiastic letter from her in mid-October 1950, Bowles wrote: "I didn't expect you to like the stories so much! They are just about as gruesome as I could make them."[38]

Since the British edition bore no dedication, Bowles used a quotation from Paul Valéry as a foreword to establish both the mood and manner for the volume as a whole: *Who has been torturing you? Once and for all, where is the cause of these pains and cries? Who has twisted you, and within you twisted all the order of the world, all ideas, the sky, your acts and your least distractions? It is a small object, a little stone, a bad tooth. And it made you vibrate in every fibre, like the whistle fitted over the column of steam.*[39]

Bowles also had used a passage from Valéry to introduce book two of *The Sheltering Sky*: *"Goodbye" says the dying man to the mirror they hold in front of him. "We won't be seeing each other any more."*

In mid-December 1950, the first reviews of *The Delicate Prey* arrived. "Shocked, scandalized and disapproving. And all wrong!" exclaimed Bowles. "I think some of the critics didn't bother to read all the stories about which they spoke so glibly. How could Charles Jackson [whose review appeared in the *New York Times Book Review* on December 3] make such a boner as to say that 'How Many Midnights' was 'a story about a suicide' if he had read it? There's not the suggestion of a suicide anywhere in the book, for the very good reason that the idea of suicide doesn't enter into my personal conception of the patterns of life and destiny."[40]

Reviewer Lewis Gannett declared in his *New York Herald Tribune* column of December 6, 1950, that Bowles was "in love with decay" and that his characters were "putrescent." The one story Gannett admired was "Pastor Dowe at Tacaté," which he described as an "eerie and exquisitely subtle study in the conflicts of culture." Bowles concluded that since "Pastor Dowe at Tacaté" was the second story in the collection, Gannett probably had not read beyond that point.

Upon receiving a batch of reviews of the John Lehmann edition, Bowles commented upon the disparity between the British reviews and the American ones and found no indication of the British critics being "morally outraged" and no use of such words as *decay*, *putrescent*, *revolting*, *loathsome*, *horror*, *evil*, *sensationalism*, *disintegration*. "On the contrary, they speak of strength, directness, clean writing, and being left breathless, which I must say is a damned sight more pleasant to my eyes." The American critics were "so interested in objecting to what goes on in the stories that they pay no attention to the way they are written. The criticism seems to be philosophical and ethical rather than literary."[41]

Bowles noted, too, an unidentified reviewer's observation in the *Times Literary Supplement* on November 24, 1951, that Bowles was "not concerned with the poetic possibilities of language, but with prose as a means of coming to grips as quickly and as directly as possible with the culminating unease of the human situation. Their brilliance comes from a subtle skill in suggesting a terrifying *dénouement* without actually confirming it." David Partridge convinced readers of the *New York Times Book Review* that Bowles was never for a moment "arty or otherwise pretentious. Operating with an outward calm, he creates a world in which nature is magnificent and man, on the whole, a mean little obscenity." For the most part, Bowles and his editor were pleased by the comments of his reviewers who obviously had read the book.

In an attempt to counteract some of the negative criticism scattered among the reviews in magazines and newspapers in America, Tennessee Williams addressed readers of the *Saturday Review of Literature*:

> Bowles is apparently the only American writer whose work reflects the extreme spiritual dislocation (and a philosophical adjustment to it) of our immediate times. He has "an organic continuity" with the present in a way that is commensurate with the great French trio of Camus, Genet, and Sartre. These seventeen stories are the exploration of a cavern of individual sensibilities, and fortunately the cavern is a deep one containing a great deal that is worth exploring. Nowhere in any writing that I can think of has the separateness of the one human psyche been depicted more vividly and shockingly. Even in the stories where this isolation is most shockingly, even savagely stated and underlined, the reader may sense an inverted kind of longing and tenderness for the thing whose absence the story concerns.[42]

Meanwhile, Bowles was still working three or more hours a day on his new novel, but considered that his pace was considerably off the mark. In his progress report to McDowell, he admitted that he was averaging only a page a day, and that he was now on page 193. "It ought to be complete by spring if I don't go too far away, or get too involved in the García Lorca opera. Some days I work lying on the rocks down on the beach in the sun; the rest of the time, mornings, in bed."[43] By now, his editor knew Bowles well enough to recognize such comments as "if I don't go too far away" to be confirmation that the manuscript would by no means "be complete by spring."

CHAPTER ELEVEN

Mishaps, Chance, Intervention of Fate, and Jane's Elusive Third Act of *In the Summer House*

(1952–1954)

"The critics who refer to what I have written as 'decadent' would likely be the same people who take it for granted that the U.S. has the highest moral standard in the world. In art and literature nothing is decadent but incompetence and commercialism."

—Paul Bowles to Harvey Breit,
New York Times, March 9, 1952

Bowles had no idea when he might return to the Sahara, but his priority was to finish *Let It Come Down*. He had not anticipated going sooner, but when a stranger presented herself at his door with a letter of introduction from Truman Capote and a request that he escort her into the desert, he saw her plea as an intervention of fate. Her name was Nada Patcevitch, and she said that she had been commissioned to do an article on the Sahara for *Vogue*. Capote had assured Patcevitch that no one knew the Sahara better than Bowles or would be more resourceful in an emergency. Since the weather in Tangier had been foul all winter and the sweeping rains gave no sign of letting up despite the onset of spring, the lure of spending several weeks in the Sahara sun at someone else's expense was irresistible.[1]

Unfortunately for Bowles as well as for Patcevitch, the trip seemed doomed from the onset. At their hotel in Fez, the toilet bowl in his companion's bathroom overflowed, and in the room to which she was moved, the handle to her basin flew off and hundreds of gallons of water spewed across the floor. Calamity after calamity pursued them for the next two weeks, until, finally, in Taghit—which had so delighted Jane in the spring of 1949 when she wrote "A Stick of Green Candy"—Patcevitch was overcome by the fumes of a charcoal burner she had carelessly left too close to her bed and almost died. "If she ever wrote her article for *Vogue*, I never saw it or her after we returned to civilization," said Bowles, whose his own piece, "The Secret Sahara," was published in the January 1953 issue of *Holiday*. It bore no reference to his journey with Patcevitch.[2]

In March 1951, Bowles confessed to his Random House editor that he had not worked on his novel since Christmas, and that resuming work on a manuscript that had lain fallow for so long was harder than starting a new book. McDowell urged Bowles to be more single-minded after being informed that he was considering several new projects that were bound to delay its completion even more. One was an invitation from Prentice-Hall to translate a French novel set in the Sahara by R. Frison-Roche, whom Bowles had met in the desert a few years earlier. "I'm fairly quick at that sort of thing, having done it for years," Bowles wrote McDowell. His only concern was that Frison-Roche's novel might be deemed poor by the critics and that his own reputation would suffer. Bowles regretted later not having listened more closely to his editor in view of his primary obligation, the completion of *Let It Come Down*. After translating a large portion of the French novel, Bowles found the book "incredibly awful" and the entire project more boring than he could imagine. Bowles groaned when he saw the book itself and hoped that his friends would not come across it.[3]

It was one thing for McDowell to have agreed to Bowles's translating a French novel in his spare time, but quite another to approve of his writing a travel book on North Africa with a rival firm, which

Bowles had suggested that he might do next. McDowell replied in no uncertain terms that if Bowles were "bound to write such a book, he should do it with Random House." Bowles's naïveté regarding the way things customarily worked in the publishing world astounded his editor, who resented the fact that Helen Strauss had suggested such a thing and dangled the promise of a good advance.

Also important to Bowles was promoting Jane's work that had already been published. To her editors he suggested obliquely that her fiction should be reprinted in a single collection; yet he knew that if Jane saw his hand in such a proposal she would balk and refuse to do anything herself to promote her work. Bowles was good at provoking Jane into thinking that a particular course of action was her idea all along, and he set about to help make it happen.

When Bowles complained to Brion Gysin about the unreliability of driving someone else's automobile on an extensive trip, as he had in the Sahara with Nada Patcevitch, Gysin retorted: "Well, buy one. You can afford it." Bowles was shocked by his friend's cavalier attitude since it had never occurred to him to buy a car. "The fact that I was known in Tangier as a miser was not conducive to my spending any more money than I could help," said Bowles. "I rather enjoyed living up to the name, although I was far less miserly than some people thought."[4] Whereas Jane wrote Bowles repeatedly that she had to do something to make more money so that she could spend it on her own priorities, which usually involved Cherifa and their friends in the grain market, Bowles squirreled away everything he could and was very private about what he did with it. Within three weeks of his conversation with Gysin, he found himself the proud owner of a new Jaguar convertible with a uniformed driver, Mohammed Temsamany, and on his way to the Algerian Sahara with Yacoubi and Gysin.

Back in Fez in mid-May of 1951, Bowles sought assurance from David McDowell that Random House still intended to publish his novel despite its being far later than he had anticipated. Then he reported on his progress to date: "Three books of it are completed, and the fourth not yet started, although it shouldn't take too long once I get into it." Bowles did not mention that he had obligated himself to collaborate in July with Libby Holman on the music for Lorca's *Yerma.* Having accepted her commission, he felt obliged to deal with *her* schedule rather than his own. Meanwhile, Jane recognized that she was wasting time in New York despite her romantic entanglements there without getting any closer to finishing her third act of *In the Summer House*. Her distractions now were chiefly Cherifa and Tetum, with whom she longed to establish a more intimate relationship. In June she wrote Bowles that she had been away far too long and was returning alone to Tangier.

Whereas he had intended to finish *Let It Come Down* in the village of Xauen, the distractions there were many and time-consuming, and he returned to Tangier to work on it. At this point, Bowles had completed twenty-three chapters and was certain that he would have the entire manuscript ready shortly. On August 7, he wrote McDowell that he had just typed the final paragraph. "It's hard to believe it's finished, but I can only say I hope it is, and that the end is the end for other people as well. I must thank you for being so enthusiastic about it." Bowles hoped that the book's ending would not offend too many of his readers. Dyar, his protagonist, was not unlike his creator in many respects in that both never knew precisely what they were going to do until they did it. It took several days of cogitating before Dyar initiated his final action. "He had put the point of the nail as far into Thami's ear as he could. He raised his right arm and hit the head of the nail with all his might. The object relaxed imperceptibly, as if someone had said to it: 'It's all right.' He laid the hammer down, and felt of the nail-head, level with the soft lobe of the ear. It had two little ridges on it; he rubbed his thumbnail across the imperfections of the steel. The nail was as firmly embedded as if it had been driven into a coconut."[5] Bowles's use of the word "object" and the accompanying "it" eliminated any need for an emotional response from the reader. It might as well have been a coconut into which Dyar drove the nail, but the ending of the book was even more macabre, for Dyar was left alone with the corpse.

To John Lehmann, who had expressed concern about the book for British readers, Bowles replied: "I had wondered if you wouldn't have reservations. The Americans, I'm sure, are not aware that there *is* a 'metaphysical theme,' and so the story seems all of a piece, a straight adventure story with particularly sordid trimmings, which is perfectly all right with me." He also addressed Lehmann's comment that he had found no sense of moral choice in the book: "I'm not suggesting that young people emulate Dyar; I'm only suggesting that it would make no difference if they did since all that keeps them from such behavior is the lack of opportunity and fear of the possible consequences. There are tens of thousands who would ask nothing better than the chance to live the part of Dyar's life described in the book, particularly as he is left at the end unpunished and with a considerable sum of money in his possession."[6] The text of the British edition remained unchanged.

Later, Bowles contrasted his methods of writing *The Sheltering Sky* to *Let It Come Down*: "One's first novel often writes itself: everything comes out in it and it's generally the best novel that one writes. In that sense it was autobiographical, the one I'd been hatching for ten or fifteen years without knowing it. But the next one I planned carefully. It was completely surface-built, down to the details of the decor, choice of symbolic materials on the walls, and so on. It was an adventure story, after all, in which the details had to be realistic. The entire book was constructed to lead to an impossible situation at the end."[7]

Both editions of *Let It Come Down* appeared in February 1952, Lehmann's British edition slightly ahead of Random House's, and early reviews of each book reached Bowles shortly. *Let It Come Down* was already on the *New York Times* best-seller list, and the *New York Times Book Review* devoted its entire front page on March 2, 1952, to the novel, which Robert Gorham Davis "found more continuously exciting than its predecessor." Other reviewers concluded similarly.

John Raymond, writing for the *New Statesman* and the *Nation*, contrasted Bowles's characters with Hemingway's, saying that "Hemingway's men have free will [and] are the masters of their souls, whereas Bowles's protagonists are straws on the ends of chance, puppets waiting to be jerked into disaster. Bowles is a prince of atmospheric writers and, as previously in *The Sheltering Sky*, he has been careful to leave none of the atmosphere out. The smells, sights and sounds are so oppressive as almost to swamp the toughest characters, and Bowles's characters, though sleepwalkers, are as tough as they come."[8] Bowles did not object to his characters being contrasted to Hemingway's. "I am sure that Mr. Raymond's review will help sell some books," he added.

Bowles was in Fez in early November 1951 when he wrote Peggy Glanville-Hicks of his chauffeur's being attacked by a *djinn* while driving in Fez.[9] It had seized the steering wheel, jerked it from his hand as he shifted gears, and caused the car to crash full-speed into a stone bridge. "*'Mektoub,'* say the onlookers, smiling and shrugging their shoulders. *'B'es-sahh,'* [true] you say, trying to look as unconcerned as they."[10] Given their recent brush with *djinns*, Bowles had second thoughts about his having already published a travel piece for *American Mercury* titled "No More *Djinns*."[11] Both Temsamany and Yacoubi concluded that the djinns were retaliating for his having challenged their existence.

Before embarking again for Ceylon and India in the spring of 1953, this time with Ahmed Yacoubi, Bowles answered a set of questions submitted to him by Harvey Breit, a columnist for the *New York Times*, who converted the author's response into a first-person essay that featured Bowles's observation regarding the "New School of Decadence," which he had addressed earlier in a letter to James Laughlin, saying that he had "no great objection to being called decadent, if the word is used in such a way that it is clear the user considers my work to be a reflection of the period in which it was written, a period which by every possible cultural standard is assuredly a decadent one."[12] Bowles could hardly wait to see what Breit made of a similar observation: "You ask what decadence is. I should think in art and literature nothing is decadent but incompetence and commercialism. If I stress the various facets of unhappiness, it is because I believe unhappiness should be studied very carefully; this certainly is no time for anyone to pretend to be happy, or to put his unhappiness away in the dark. You must watch your universe as it cracks above your head."[13] Bowles was relieved that his words had not been distorted or reported in error.

In mid-December Bowles reported on "the saga of Ahmed ben Driss el Yacoubi," who came up from Fez with a large portfolio of paintings and was introduced to Mme. Isabelle Gerofi, who was delighted by his work and arranged a show for him in Tangier. "The show has been on for almost three weeks, and crowds still gather along the boulevard to gape. But what is better is that he sold twenty-eight paintings, which is unheard of, considering that they are all utterly unintelligible to the people of Tangier. Ahmed says it is Allah who really does the paintings so that they would *have* to sell."[14] To gallery owner Betty Parsons, who anticipated putting on an exhibition of Yacoubi's paintings in New York in the spring of 1953, Bowles described the artist as "astonishingly gifted, a natural abstractionist, as is to be expected when there has been no tradition in the culture save that of absolute abstraction. . . . He is completely untrained."

At the port in Gibraltar, after putting Jane on a ship bound for New York with a number of large canvases painted by Yacoubi to leave with Parsons, Bowles spotted a sign in the window of a booking office that announced first-class passage to Bombay for eight pounds aboard a Polish ship, the SS *Batory*. Bowles had not thought of going to India that winter, but it struck him as an economical trip that would be even cheaper than staying in Morocco. After turning the paintings over to Parsons, Jane reported that Parsons liked Yacoubi's work enormously and wished to open an exhibition for him in April. In another letter posted on the heels of the first, Jane wrote that some people in New York who had seen Yacoubi's paintings concluded that Bowles himself had made them. "Of course the whole idea was preposterous. There is no doubt that in the process of saying 'I like this' and 'I don't like this,' I have directed his talent one way rather than another, but any good teacher would have done as much," said Bowles.

Before year's end he learned from Random House that the reprint rights to *The Delicate Prey and Other Stories* had been sold as a Signet book to the New American Library with a minimum guarantee of $7,500. "Given how little I had received already, I was skeptical as to how much money I would eventually see from it, yet I was impressed by its press run of 244,000 copies. *The Sheltering Sky* had a comparable press run, but I think that most of the money derived from that sale went to James Laughlin to pay back his advance."[15] On October 31, 1952, Bowles's royalty statement from Random House for *Let It Come Down* for six months revealed that despite 824 copies having been sold at a 15-percent royalty, he was still in debt to his publisher for $431.30. Sales were scanty during the same six-month period for *The Delicate Prey and Other Stories*. Bowles could hardly believe his eyes when he read that the forty-eight copies reportedly sold had netted him only $14.40. "I paid rather close attention to the royalty statements concerning each of my books for the first six months following publication, but the income from my writings, overall, seemed paltry at best."[16]

Meanwhile, Jane was invited by Oliver Smith to spend the winter of 1952–53 in the spacious home he was renting in the Hollywood Hills, California, and Jane, in turn, invited Marty Mann to join them. "I didn't realize until later that Jane's affair with Miss Mann that had begun in Paris was still viable then," said Bowles. "The complicating factor for both of them was that Miss Mann had been living for many years with another woman [Priscilla Peck], and had no intention of breaking that off. I said nothing negative about the arrangement, certain that in time Jane would tire of the arrangement and break it off."[17]

On the island of Ceylon, to which he and Yacoubi traveled after crisscrossing central and southern India by train, Bowles thought many times of the photographs he had seen in David Herbert's scrapbook of the strange-looking house situated on its own tiny island off the coast in Weligama Bay. The one glimpse he had caught of it earlier made him determined to make a visit there his priority.

From the Weligama Rest House, which faced the island, he and Yacoubi put on bathing suits and waded across to Taprobane. "When I climbed up onto the long boat dock ten minutes later, there was no sound but the lapping of the sea around the piles underneath. At the far end was a padlocked gate. I called out and a dog began to bark. Soon a man appeared out of the tangle of trees, naked save for a white sarong, his lips, teeth, and bristling mustache brick-red with betel nut. For a rupee he unlocked the gate and showed us around the estate." Bowles was told that the owner, an up-country rubber planter and racehorse breeder, occasionally passed a weekend there but was not interested in selling. "Were it mine, I would live in it every winter, for it would be summer in Ceylon," said Bowles, who hoped to be able to buy it himself someday.[18]

En route again to Tangier in May, Bowles and Yacoubi left the ship in Genoa to spend a few days in Venice at the invitation of Peggy Guggenheim. Hans Richter was there too, making a film, and he wanted Bowles, Yacoubi, and Guggenheim to be in it. "We were astonished our first day in Peggy's palatial home on the canal in Venice when a servant summoned us after breakfast to join Peggy on the terrace, where we found her sun-bathing in the nude. Yacoubi withdrew abruptly because he did not think it right for women to sit naked in front of strange men. Peggy attempted to make it up to Yacoubi by inviting him into the kitchen to prepare Moroccan cuisine, and it worked."[19]

Guggenheim extended an invitation of quite a different kind to Bowles himself. "Peggy invited me into her enormous round bed, and I accepted. She wanted to have sex, and I obliged her, but in my book, once was enough, or rather, it was too much."[20]

Still en route to Tangier, Bowles and Yacoubi were in Madrid when a message arrived from Helen Strauss dated May 27, 1952: CAN SELL YOUR MOTION PICTURE OPTION SHELTERING SKY $500 AGAINST PRICE $5,000. WRITING. CABLE ACCEPTANCE.[21] Bowles did as he was instructed, but regretted later having answered so quickly. "I practically gave my rights away. It was my own fault, of course, but I did feel pressured into accepting." Bowles's reasoning was that had she instructed CABLE REPLY he might have considered its more serious ramifications, or at least delayed his decision. "My agent declared that the original offer was $3,000, but that she had managed to get an additional $2,000. Unfortunately, other than the $5,000 from the original sale, I never saw a dime in royalties, nor did the American purchaser, Robert Siodmak, ever make a film of *The Sheltering Sky*. It was he or his partners or heirs who later sold it to Bertolucci, for which I got only a pittance to act in it."[22]

A second cable caught up with Bowles in Madrid, this one from his former host in Ceylon informing him that if he acted quickly, he could buy both Taprobane and the house with all its contents for six thousand dollars. "I was suddenly downstairs at the desk of our hotel, the telegram still in my hand, cabling my acceptance and instructing my accountant in New York to wire the money."[23]

"I think you're crazy!" declared Jane, when he wrote her of his "new lark," as she put it. "An island off the coast of Ceylon?" she exclaimed, as though it were on the other side of the moon. "How do you *get* there?"

Bowles replied that one took a ship through the Mediterranean and the Red Sea, crossed part of the Indian Ocean, landed at Colombo, and "hopped on a train which lets you off at the fishing village of Weligama. And once you're on the island there's nothing between you and the South Pole." He pictured Jane looking at him for a long moment, then saying "You'll never get *me* there."[24]

In the autumn of 1952, Tennessee Williams wrote Bowles that he wanted him to compose the score for his new play, *Camino Real*, but wondered if he had time since he was "busy writing fiction." Bowles assured Williams that he "would be delighted to write a score for the show," but needed to know an approximate date since he was still committed to working with Libby Holman on *Yerma* and on Jane's play when she needed him. Then he learned that Holman was in the hospital and would be there indefinitely. If Williams still wanted him, he would be there, Bowles assured him.[25]

After a time, hearing nothing further from the playwright himself, Bowles asked David McDowell to try to find out if the final decision regarding his writing the score for *Camino Real* rested only upon Williams and Audrey Wood, his agent, or if someone else had the authority to override them. The final approval would be up to Elia Kazan, replied McDowell. Ultimately, Bowles learned that it was Molly Thatcher, Kazan's wife and a producer of the play, who vetoed his being asked to do the music on the basis of "gross immorality" in *The Sheltering Sky*; furthermore, she insisted that her husband have nothing more to do with Bowles or to use him in any other show. "Naturally, Kazan wouldn't have admitted it, and Tennessee apparently had no say in the matter," said McDowell, who learned, also, that Cheryl Crawford was having trouble getting backers for the play, and that Bowles's being associated with it could be a liability.[26] Bowles saw no relationship between his having written *The Sheltering Sky* and writing the music for the playwright's *Camino Real*, but recognized that he could not argue when it came to money.

Then Jane cabled him from New York to come at once because a production of *In the Summer House* was imminent. "It was the first of her emergent summons for me to come to New York to write the score for her play, and each time I came. Libby Holman invited us to stay with her in Connecticut but Jane declined, still appalled by Libby's having proposed marriage to me in Africa and suggesting that the three of us could live compatibly together at Treetops. Some people concluded that Jane and Libby were lovers, but I never thought so," said Bowles, who wanted to begin work immediately on the score for *In the Summer House* on Holman's grand piano.[27] Jane elected to stay with Oliver Smith in the flat they had formerly shared on West Tenth Street, where it was far more convenient for Jane to see her friends; moreover, she did not relish being at Treetops since Yacoubi, too, would be there. When Bowles and Yacoubi arrived, they found Montgomery Clift in residence, also. "Libby had been involved in an on-again/off-again affair with Monty for months, which had ended, I thought, but his drinking had not, nor had Libby's." Upon the actor's departure, Bowles suspected Holman of shifting her affections to Yacoubi, but he paid little attention to their comings and goings since he spent a considerable part of the day composing the music for Jane's play. Bowles did notice, however, that Holman lost no time in taking Yacoubi shopping almost daily to augment his wardrobe of Western clothes, shoes, jewelry, and anything else in which he showed the slightest interest.

When Oliver Smith insisted on holding tryouts for *In the Summer House* in Washington, D.C., and rehearsing it first without music, Bowles invited Yacoubi to join them, having assumed that the nation's capital would interest him considerably, but he was mistaken. "Ahmed chose to stay at Treetops with Libby, who told me upon our return that they had become sexually involved, and that she was in love with him."[28]

Later, Bowles wrote with restraint of the play's tryouts and opening: "I wrote the score for *In the Summer House* and, leaving Ahmed with Libby, went with Jane to Washington, where we rehearsed and tried out the play. Both Judith Anderson and Mildred Dunnock were brilliant, but the direction was chaotic, and the script itself had a few equivocal spots which needed clarification. We spent New Year's Eve in New York with Judith Anderson. Since both Oliver Smith and Roger Stevens thought the director must be changed, when we reached Boston José Quintero was called in to take over, and with some difficulty he managed to pull the production together. Overnight Jane tightened the play and wrote a new scene for Mildred Dunnock. I was astonished to see the work complete the following morning, and amazed at how beautifully it played."[29]

Despite Bowles's rendering of events in his memoir, the tryouts in Washington were not a success. It was obvious to both Bowles and Smith that considerable work was still needed if the play was to open as scheduled for a five-day run at the University of Michigan's Lydia Mendelssohn Theater before proceeding to Broadway. Jane concluded that the problem was in the writing and insisted on reworking the third act. "I realized that Oliver was of more help to

Jane at this point than I was, so having done my part in writing the music, I hastened back to Treetops, where I found Hans Richter already there and eager to commence the filming of 'The Middle Game,' the second of the three surreal sequences of *8 x 8*, in which Ahmed and I were the principal players. It was an ironic turn of events. Ahmed dances, undresses, jumps, climbs trees, swims, plays the flute and smiles throughout, looking rather like a tough Sabu. Fortunately it won't be released for at least another year, by which time I hope to heaven Ahmed will be safely in Morocco. Otherwise, I can see it in my crystal ball. Hollywood would be twinkling with a new starlet. Such dynamic ego-flashing I've never before seen, except for Orson Welles and Bill Saroyan, back in the old days. The awful thing is that all kinds of people fell for it. We did the film and I stayed another week, then returned alone to Tangier. Ahmed chose to stay on at Libby's."[30]

It was this turn of events that prompted Bowles to write to Mr. Hollyman ("I never knew his first name") whom he and Yacoubi had met in Ceylon: "I am en route to Tangier, Ahmed having wanted to stay on in America. He may return to Morocco later, and he may not. I was unable to get any definite intention out of him. He claimed that only Allah knew what he would be doing, and as yet Allah had not imparted his knowledge to him. It remains to be seen whether his visa can be extended or not. To tell the truth, he departed from my care about two weeks after arriving in New York, and never returned. We saw each other often, but only as casual acquaintances, and he supported seeing me simply because he needed me for linguistic and artistic purposes, to introduce him to the proper people, make publicity for him, and arrange his shows. Otherwise he was invisible, being mostly occupied with Café Society, Cartier's, The Stork Club, The Blue Angel, Westchester, Abercrombie and Fitch, Connecticut, and Radio City Music Hall. Walter Winchell and Danton Walker talked about him in their columns because he was so often at first-nights. He met everyone, did everything, got invited everywhere."

Hurt by what he saw as Yacoubi's betrayal, Bowles blamed himself as well. It was one thing for him to be intrigued by the idea of dropping a primitive Arab from the Medina of Fez into the middle of India and seeing what happened, but it was quite another to leave his impressionable protégé with an attractive and wily older woman adept at the seduction of young men more than half her age. Bowles booked only his own first-class passage to Tangier at practically the last moment aboard the SS *Independence* for departure on May 1, 1953, and secured a ticket for Yacoubi aboard the SS *Constitution*, scheduled to leave a month later. "I did not buy him first-class accommodations. I was still angry at him. Naturally I had my doubts as to his using it, but to my surprise, he did. I learned later that Libby had upgraded him to first-class."[31]

By mid-June, Yacoubi was back in Morocco, his affair with Holman over. It was she who broke it off, he insisted, after being told by her adopted son Timmy, now seven, that Yacoubi had pushed him into the swimming pool, then jumped in and begun choking him. "I think Ahmed was trying to kill me," he told his mother. Timmy also told his mother that Yacoubi had come into his bedroom one night and "played with his pee-pee."[32] Horrified by both reports, Holman confronted Yacoubi, threatened to have him arrested, and insisted that he leave immediately. Yacoubi denied both accusations and attributed the reports to the child's imagination. According to Holman's biographer, Jon Bradshaw, "What *actually* happened was not entirely clear. Ahmed was subsequently expelled from Treetops, and Timmy was dispatched to his psychiatrist."[33] Yacoubi's version was that the entire alleged incident was a misunderstanding, and that it was *he* who decided to leave. He told Bowles that on the day he left, he collected the suits and garments bought for him by Holman, cut them into tiny pieces, and threw them into her bathtub.

As Bowles saw it, their reconciliation a few weeks later was inevitable. "It was not that I believed Yacoubi's story, but I was still fond of him and wanted to see how the whole scenario played out." With Bowles's approval, Tennessee Williams invited Yacoubi to accompany them to Rome, where Bowles had agreed to collaborate with him on the English dialogue for an Italian film being produced by Luchino Visconti. "I am simply not in condition, nervously, to undertake a job of this sort. It might be worth your while if you are looking for 'loot,'" Williams wrote Bowles. "Visconti does not know your work as he cannot speak or read English but I spoke of your books. He wants me to act in a supervisory capacity, which means that I would lend advice and assistance if needed."[34] Although ambivalent about traveling overland to Italy, Bowles agreed to the assignment. "Tennessee was very generous to his friends and especially good to me, and to Jane, over the years," said Bowles.[35]

On July 28, 1953, Williams wrote Donald Windham that he and Bowles were at that moment en route to Rome in tandem in their almost identical Jaguars, and that Bowles had "two Arabs with him, his lover Ahmed (stolen but now relinquished by Libby Holman) and a chauffeur." Bowles worried that Yacoubi would not receive the proper credentials to allow him to cross the border on such short notice; therefore, Williams suggested that he fly ahead to Rome with Yacoubi while Frank Merlo drove his Jaguar and Temsamany drove Bowles in his Jaguar. Reunited in Rome a week later, Williams reported: "We all live on the same floor of this apartment building, a top floor which has only a trickle of water for us to divide among us. The Arabs smoke kif and eat majoun, which is some sort of drug that tastes like date preserves, and Paul sweats and fumes over constant anxieties and discomforts which I find rather endearing as I do the same thing. He has some liver trouble and is down to 115 pounds. Ahmed is torturing Paul by not sleeping with him."[36]

For six weeks Bowles worked with Williams on the film *Senso*, but reported later that upon being introduced to Visconti, he was handed a story by Camillo Boito and instructed: "I see a movie in it, and here is a script that somebody else has done, and it's not what I want." Bowles conceded that he could have worked much faster had his Italian been better. "Tennessee ended up having to rewrite two important love scenes after Visconti told me that they were not 'tender enough.' We shared the credits on the film, and I was paid $500 a week. I have no idea what Tennessee was paid because I never saw any of it."[37] By late September they had finished the shooting in Vicenza, Verona, and Venice, after which Bowles announced that he needed to go at once to Turkey to fulfill an assignment by *Holiday* magazine before rejoining Jane in New York.

Although Bowles remained in Tangier when Jane's play opened without music for its five-day run at the University of Michigan, Williams, now back in the States, and other friends of Jane were there to show their support. Eager to promote *In the Summer House* before leaving for Europe, his own play *Camino Real* having recently closed after sixty performances, Williams wrote a short promotional piece for the media: "A piece of dramatic literature that stands altogether alone, without antecedents and without descendants, unless they spring from the same one and only Jane Bowles. It is not only the most original play I have ever read, I think it also the oddest and funniest and one of the most touching. Its human perceptions are both profound and delicate; its dramatic poetry is both elusive and gripping. It is one of those very rare plays which are not tested by the theatre but by which the theatre is tested."[38]

Williams's remarks about Jane and her play had little effect upon the reviewers, who had their own ideas and were less than enthusiastic. A typical response was Harvey Taylor's in the *Detroit Times* on May 20, 1953: "All the efforts of a splendid cast and lively direction failed, in our estimation, to keep *In the Summer House* from degenerating into a verbose plea for understanding on the part of the playwright, and into a pointlessly morbid study of the psychic difficulties of as useless a bunch of characters as we've ever seen assembled on a stage." The *Detroit News* reviewer was particularly damning of the third act: "All those female crackpots, plus two men, get into complications which rather delightfully involve a roistering Spanish family. But not 50 funny Spaniards could save *In the Summer House* from going down its dreary course, from a fair beginning into pretentious, wordy nonsense."

In Hartford the play reopened under the direction of John Stix on November 26, 1953, after further revision to the third act, which Jane reworked more times than Bowles cared to remember. Three days later, *In the Summer House* opened in Boston, where José Quintero took over the directing since the play was still fraught with problems. It was at this point that Jane cabled Bowles to come at once to write the score. "Although I wasn't there for the Hartford opening, I was told that Stix's directing was chaotic. He was obviously intimidated by Judith Anderson and seemed relieved when Quintero replaced him in Boston. I was astonished to see how beautifully it played."[39]

On December 29, 1953, *In the Summer House* opened at the Playhouse Theater on Broadway. Bowles insisted that Jane sit out front, and he and Oliver Smith sat with her. There was nothing she could do to change things, they insisted. "I knew that she felt dreadful and seemed on the edge of tears, but there was a certain spunkiness to her, also, and she laughed from time to time," said Bowles.[40] Virgil Thomson also had seen the play on opening night and devoted his next "Music and Musicians" column in the *New York Herald Tribune* to the incidental music in the play, which prompted in turn an immediate and accusatory response by Bowles, followed by a tongue-in-cheek apology by Thomson. "Despite Virgil's apology, his sarcasm was unmistakable," said Bowles. "The fact that Jane's play did not survive had very little to do with the play itself. Jane was ahead of her time, and her play required a great deal more of her audience than they were willing to give."[41]

After fifty-five performances, *In the Summer House* closed on February 12, 1954. According to biographer Millicent Dillon, "Those who cared for the play—and by now there was almost a cult—hearing of the closing, rushed to the theater and fought for seats. During the performance there was much laughter; at the final curtain there was great cheering. Following the performance there was a wild party. To an interviewer from *Vogue*, as she prepared to leave the United States and return to Morocco, Jane said, 'There's no point in writing a play for your five hundred goony friends. You have to reach more people.'"[42]

After the play closed, Jane cabled Bowles and said that she would be staying on in New York for a few more days. "You can imagine my surprise and pleasure when I received a second cable saying that she would be home by month's end. No, she didn't use the word *home* in her cable to me, but that's the way I took it, and I was very pleased."[43]

CHAPTER TWELVE

Burroughs in Tangier and Bowles's Several Visits to His Island off Ceylon

(1954–1959)

"Paul Bowles is here, but kept in seclusion by an Arab boy who is insanely jealous and given to the practice of black magic."[1]

—William S. Burroughs to Allen Ginsberg,
Tangier, February 9, 1954

William Burroughs and Allen Ginsberg had been friends for a decade as well as occasional lovers. In 1953 they shared a flat in Manhattan on the Lower East Side until Burroughs decided to accompany a new friend to Europe, poet Allen Ansen, whom he had met recently in New York. In Rome, they headed in separate directions, Ansen to Venice and Burroughs to Tangier.[2] By then Burroughs had read both *The Sheltering Sky* and *Let It Come Down* and looked forward to meeting Bowles himself eventually. He also had read "The Delicate Prey" in the Tangier-based magazine *Zero*, in which he hoped to publish too. By this time, Burroughs had already published *Junky* under the pseudonym of William Lee and was working loosely on what became *The Yage Letters* and a novel, *Naked Lunch*.

Burroughs had assumed that the American and European community would leave him alone in Tangier, having taken it to be a live-and-let-live society in which almost any behavior was considered normal, but he did not like being ignored. "I like Tangier less all the time. No writers colony here or they keep themselves hid some place," he groused.[3] Although Burroughs paid twenty cents a day for his room and ate in the native quarter, he found it hard to make ends meet since boys and narcotics were his priorities.[4] His fortieth birthday on February 5, 1954, was no cause for celebration either. "At an age when most men are solidly established in their careers, he was still being supported by his parents, and his future as a writer was uncertain," observed biographer Ted Morgan.[5]

In 1954 Burroughs suffered increasingly from paranoia, imagining that people he had never met and saw only on the street had taken a violent dislike to him. The few writers he did meet appeared to want nothing to do with him.[6] To writer Jack Kerouac, Burroughs complained that Bowles "invites the dreariest queens in Tangier to tea, but has never invited me, which, seeing how small the town is, amounts to a deliberate affront."[7] In the spring, when they finally did meet, Bowles was recuperating from paratyphoid.

Of that encounter, Bowles wrote that during his convalescence he had been visited by a tall, thin man escorted by Eric Gifford, who seemed to know everyone in Tangier. His name was William Burroughs, and he had just written a book titled *Junky* and sold it directly to a paperback company, Ace Books. "There was something about the contract that bothered him. He wanted to get out of his *Junky* contract because his publisher was holding back $350. I told him that if he had signed the contract there was no way to change it."[8] Bowles and Burroughs continued to cross each other's path and nodded in recognition.

In the fall of 1954, upon his release from a Tangier hospital to which he had committed himself for drug addiction, Burroughs refrained from asking Bowles's opinion on something else, the bits and pieces of a manuscript that eventually became *Naked Lunch*. He was depressed, also, upon learning in mid-December that Bowles had departed with Jane and Yacoubi for Taprobane, the tiny island he had recently acquired off the coast of Ceylon. Burroughs regretted not having been more aggressive in pursuing a friendship. He liked Bowles and sensed that the feeling would be mutual if they gave it a chance to develop.[9]

Someone else who wanted to know Bowles better, too, was an English writer, Richard Rumbold, who kept a daily diary throughout his journey aboard the SS *Orsova*, the same ship on which Bowles and his companions were traveling. On December 15, 1954, Rumbold entered in his journal that he liked Bowles immensely, and that they had stayed up late several nights in Jane's cabin while she drank enormous quantities of gin. Rumbold was fascinated by the way Jane "looked *into* things, rather than *at* things," and concluded that she expressed more through a slight gesture of the shoulder than in words. He also spent time separately with Bowles talking about *The Sheltering Sky* "and of his feeling when he wrote it, of the nothingness of everything, and that the world has no reality except what we choose to invest it with; and when we are too tired, like his hero Port, to invest it with anything, then it becomes a blank."[10]

Once they had settled themselves on Taprobane, Bowles and Jane invited their fellow passenger to visit them on their island. Of it, Rumbold wrote: "To reach it one has to wade out in bathing-slips or an old sarong, holding one's watch and cigarette-case and other belongings above one's head, and then to clamber on a wooden jetty and walk up through the garden to the house. An unbelievably romantic spot. The house is octagonal, with a circular living-room in the centre, from which the bedrooms radiate, divided off by curtains. It is like some eighteenth-century folly. The garden is densely planted with tropical plants and shrubs, some of them rare, and although it is small one could get lost in it because the paths, flanked by tall hibiscus hedges, are intricately planted. Here and there, in a open clearing, one can sit on a stone bench and enjoy a vista of shimmering turquoise."[11] Bowles learned that the island had been owned for many years by a Frenchman, Comte de Mauny-Talvande, who built the house in 1926 and wrote a book, *The Gardens of Taprobane*, about the gardens he had planned and planted there.

Jane was not enamored of Taprobane and still considered her husband's purchase a lark, just as she had his co-ownership with Oliver Smith of an ancient house without plumbing in the Medina of Tangier. Although she had enjoyed cooking in Tangier and always prepared fancy meals for guests, she showed little interest in food of any kind and barely ate anything until they were invited by several welcoming couples to their homes for dinner. As Bowles recorded later, "When we first got to Weligama and she saw the island of Taprobane there in front of her, a mere tuft of rain forest rising out of the sea, she groaned. Then we came to the gate, and she looked up the long series of stairways through the unfamiliar vegetation, toward the invisible house. 'It's a Poe story,' she said, shrugging. 'I can see why you'd like it.' A newspaper photographer sent by the *Ceylon Times* caught Jane's frown before they crossed over to the island."[12]

He had prepared Jane for the fact that there was no electric power on the island and that the house had only one bright oil lamp to illuminate the thirty-foot-high ceiling, but he worried that she would find the nightly invasion of bats disturbing. After the first night Jane confessed that she had not expected so many, or that they would have such huge teeth and wingspreads of three feet. She was amazed, too, that scarcely a day went by when they were not besieged by a variety of Ceylonese who sent telegrams and letters asking to visit, to work for them, or to sell them anything they might need. One even offered to tell Bowles's fortune. Buddhist priests, teachers, town officials, government employees, doctors, lawyers, and a gamut of others arrived almost daily. Peggy Guggenheim petitioned to be their first houseguest, whom they fetched in a rattling ox cart at the railway station in Weligama. Guggenheim, who stayed a week, loved everything about the island, and could not understand why Jane was not "crazy about it, too."[13]

Despite the daily distractions, Bowles was determined to progress at a faster rate on this novel, now tentatively titled *The Spider's House*, than he had on the two novels that preceded it. In a letter to his editor, David McDowell, he explained that the title was derived from the sacred text of Islamic law, the Koran, and that its reference was to the frailty of lives based on considerations other than the laws of Allah. "The likeness of those who choose other patrons than Allah is as the likeness of the spider when she taketh unto herself a house, and lo! the frailest of all houses is the spider's house, if they but know." Bowles cautioned McDowell not to allow on the book jacket or anywhere else a drawing or picture of a spider or web since an actual spider had nothing to do with the story line.[14]

In early February 1955, Bowles wrote McDowell what had become a monthly or semimonthly progress report. At this point, he had typed 367 pages and estimated that he had another 60 pages to go. Surprisingly accurate in his forecasts, Bowles wanted to assure McDowell that he had not taken on other literary projects such as those he allowed to interrupt his work on *Let It Come Down*. "Obviously it was not a good idea to bring Jane out here, but I thought she needed the change and would be able to work better. Unfortunately she couldn't work at all and left with Temsamany, who had accompanied us, after being here only two months."

By mid-March of 1955, Bowles had finished the manuscript, but worried that it lacked certain melodramatic flourishes to which his readers had become accustomed. Although he anticipated what McDowell's criticism might be, he chose to head it off by setting out on a new adventure by sea, having learned that the SS *Chusan* would leave Colombo on April 4 on a round-trip cruise to the Far East and return in time for him to proceed to Gibraltar on May 20, as scheduled. Bowles knew that on the return trip he would have ample time to make whatever changes McDowell might insist upon, or to convince McDowell that certain suggested changes were inappropriate.

Bowles was convinced that fate stepped in once more on his behalf. Never having been to the Far East and intrigued by the idea of visiting Penang, Singapore, Hong Kong, and Kobe, Japan, in scheduled stops along the way, he began calculating how he could afford first-class accommodations for both him and Yacoubi and know that his island would be properly maintained in his absence. Again he was struck by the efficacy of *Mektoub*. Of course he could afford it. He needed only to discharge his temporary help—the cook, his assistant, and the "lavatory coolie"—and retain his gardener and maid. *"It is written,"* he concluded.

In letters to Jane and his mother, Bowles commented upon almost every aspect of the journey as they proceeded from port to port. Penang was "surprisingly beautiful" and Singapore simply "a large Chinese city with a few Malays wandering around like displaced persons."[15] In Hong Kong, at Bowles's urging, Yacoubi left twenty pictures in a gallery with the understanding that he would pick up what had not sold on their return. "Most were gone by the time we got back, and of course Yacoubi attributed his good fortune to Allah."[16]

Back in Colombo on May 11, 1955, Bowles was not surprised to find a letter from McDowell awaiting him. After dispensing with the amenities, Bowles wrote a detailed response: "Ever since *Let It Come Down* appeared, I've felt it would be fatal for me to write another melodramatic novel at this juncture, or one into which had been injected any element of sensationalism extraneous to the normal development of the story. Three shockers in a row would have sufficed to stamp me as a not-entirely-serious writer. I went out of my way to choose material that would not demand doses of violence, sex, drugs, insanity or crime. So I don't feel eager to pep it up with unmotivated, decorative elements."[17]

On the return leg of his journey to Gibraltar, Bowles incorporated a number of McDowell's suggestions, but allowed that he had no intention of "sexing up" the book to help it sell. To Jane, he wrote of his concern that since its subject matter was set against the present-day struggle in Morocco, the whole thing might be out of date by the time he returned. He also worried that Morocco's internal troubles would reach Tangier before he did, and he did not want to miss out on that either.[18]

Contrary to his apprehensions, Bowles noted that little appeared to have changed in Tangier during his absence except that Muslim shops were closed on Fridays based on an order of the political party demanding independence. "In some ways the place looks like a ghost town, but the rest of the time it seems perfectly normal. In the French Zone all Muslim and Jewish shops are closed all the time, which means that the merchants are ruined."[19]

Bowles was astonished to learn that his parents might still wish to come to Tangier now that he had finished his novel, but when his mother sought assurance that the political situation would pose no threat to them, he could not promise anything of the sort since the entire country was on the verge of civil war. "I don't think there will be much trouble here in Tangier this year, but one's activities are seriously curtailed. It is now impossible to go to French Morocco and drive around, so we have only the Spanish Zone to visit if you come now. Everything is prohibited since the Sultan was exiled," he replied.[20]

Bowles's follow-up letter did little to assuage his parents' fears, and his naïveté over the years, no matter what the subject or circumstances, continued to amaze his friends. Finally, after learning that his parents had no intention of visiting Tangier until the political situation settled down, Bowles took a year's lease on two newly completed penthouse flats with adjoining terraces on the top floor of the Edificio San Francisco, a nine-story apartment building not far from the center of town. In the meantime, Jane had returned to New York. The flat was still cluttered with painters, plasterers, and debris when an advance copy of *The Spider's House* arrived on October 1, 1955. He complained that a close reading of the novel and his usual punctuality in answering letters had to be sandwiched in between answering the door, finding cans of paint and hammers for the workmen, and giving instructions to the maid.

McDowell assured Bowles that most of the reviews he had seen were good, especially those in the *Saturday Review*, *Newsweek*, and the *New York Herald Tribune*.[21] It was still too early to expect much in the way of reviews, but by month's end Bowles had begun to hear from friends who had read the new novel, and most wrote enthusiastically about it. A few, however, had reservations. John Lehmann wrote: "I thought the way you create the atmosphere and turmoil is wonderful;

the psychological understanding of the Arab scene, the tensions and undercurrents, the richness and subtlety and the writing–there's scarcely another American of your generation, or younger, who can do all that," wrote John Lehmann. Then he expressed his disappointment in the book as a whole: "I think there is some flaw in *The Spider's House* that prevents its reaching the same class as *The Sheltering Sky*. It is, I find, very slow moving, a problem I attribute in part to the central character's being an Arab boy who is neither interesting nor active enough to bear the weight that is put on him. Perhaps you were too close to immediate events to distance yourself arbitrarily. It was a little sentimental and unconvincing. What all this adds up to, if you can bear with me, Paul, is that I feel the book has unresolved problems, whereas it could have been an absolute top-class Bowles achievement."[22]

Virgil Thomson, having received an advance copy, declared perfunctorily that the book was a beauty, and that he was already lending it out to friends. "I find it a very fine book, an unusually fine book, and absolutely absorbing," he added.[23] Bowles was not impressed by Thomson's platitudes and concluded that he had simply shrugged it off or not read it at all. In reply, Bowles refrained from commenting upon Thomson's take on the novel and noted instead the effects of the current political situation in Tangier, where things obviously were getting worse. "We still come and go in the streets, and no one molests us. But the possibility of being attacked is uppermost in every non-Moslem's mind."[24]

The first print run of *The Spider's House* on November 4, 1955, totaled ten thousand copies. "For my father," the dedication read. Years later, when asked his rationale for dedicating *The Spider's House* to his father, given the fact that he hated him most of his life, Bowles declared that at the time it seemed the thing to do: "I dedicated my first book, *The Sheltering Sky*, to Jane; my second book, *The Delicate Prey*, to my mother; my third book, *Let It Come Down*, to no one; and my fourth book, *The Spider's House*, to my father." Later he admitted that he had asked the dedication to read: "For my father and for all the fathers in Morocco." Yet at some point–he was not sure just when–Bowles scratched through the second line of the dedication so that it read simply "FOR MY FATHER."[25]

It was not until after the publication of *The Spider's House* that his father agreed to accompany his mother to Tangier. Jane inferred that the dedication had something to do with Claude's willingness to come, or that it was Bowles's subtle attempt to bury the hatchet. But as Bowles saw it, he had no hatchet to bury so long as he kept his distance from his father, and that it remained to be seen how all three would fare if his parents came.

For a preface to a new edition of *The Spider's House*, written more than a quarter of a century after the book's original appearance, Bowles wrote that he had intended to write a novel "using as backdrop the traditional daily life of Fez [since] it was a medieval city functioning in the twentieth century," and that it would have been quite a different book if he had started it a year sooner. "I intended to describe Fez as it existed at the moment of writing about it, but even as I started to write, events that could not be ignored had begun to occur there. I soon saw that I was going to have to write, not about the traditional pattern of life in Fez, but about its dissolution."[26] Despite his avowed intentions, Bowles concluded that he had written a political book deploring the attitudes of both the French and the Moroccans, and that the tale was neither autobiographical nor factual, but a roman à clef.

Bowles had finished still another piece for *Holiday* after publication of *The Spider's House* and was now mulling over new potential subjects. Not wanting to start another novel immediately, he thought first of writing several short pieces that might produce some immediate cash. *Holiday* still had three of his pieces unpublished–one on parrots, another on the character of the North African Arab or Muslim, and a third, on Taprobane, which he had finished aboard ship en route home. Writing a piece on Portugal or the Canary Islands appealed to him, but until he made a scouting trip to Portugal to see if events there were as they had been reported, he was still in doubt.[27]

Bowles found it ironic that having just submitted an article for *Holiday* titled "Parrots I Have Known," he was presented with a new parrot, a young African gray brought to him by an American friend who had hand-carried it back from Africa. Bowles loved the fact that the parrot was an African gray since the breed was considered the best talker, but his parrot, whom he named Seth, did not talk at all. Perhaps he was too young to talk, Bowles speculated. For months Bowles carried on many one-sided conversations with him, but it was Jane who got him to repeat the name of her cat, Dubz, then his own name, too, which Seth called out repeatedly. Until the new parrot joined the household, Cotorrito, his Amazon parrot, had ruled the roost and was always talking, but he apparently became so enraged by Seth's intrusion that he refused to talk at all.[28]

Meanwhile, despite having avoided throughout his life sending any message to his father that could have been taken for cordiality or affection, Bowles was annoyed that four months after sending his parents a copy of *The Spider's House*, neither had mentioned its dedication. His mother had merely acknowledged the book's arrival and noted that it was on the best-seller list. "I don't know why I kept urging them to come to Tangier or to Taprobane or to Lisbon, or to any of a half dozen other places I had suggested over the years," he carped. Finally, without preamble, almost a year later, his mother wired Bowles that they had just booked passage to depart New York on May 5, 1956, and would arrive in Gibraltar ten to twelve days later on the SS *Independence*. Surprised that his parents actually were coming, Bowles had no idea, given the turmoil in Tangier, what they might possibly be able to do together. He apologized that his and Jane's adjoining apartments were not well furnished in the European sense and suggested that they think of their visit as "a kind of camping out." Since both apartments had their separate bathrooms and sleeping areas, they were at least assured of privacy.[29]

Since his mother was a worrier, Bowles minimized in his letters the tension in Tangier at present and suggested that whatever trouble she may have heard about in America was mostly the result of different opinions among the Moroccans themselves. Then he explained the situation as he saw it: "What you have now is a wave of banditry all over the country, roving groups of plain highwaymen who have no political convictions at all. If one did not understand Arabic, one could live here without ever suspecting that there was trouble anywhere in Morocco."[30] Bowles chose not to mention that his Canadian friend, Christopher Wanklyn, had been knocked down from behind and stabbed while walking with a companion at 4:00 a.m. in the Casbah.[31]

He had not anticipated his parents staying with them nine weeks, which was "far too long," he said, but they did. Although they preferred whiskey, both smoked kif when it was offered them and made a point of enjoying the Moroccan details of life that many American visitors overlooked or criticized. They joined the American Club and spent considerable time sitting by the swimming pool and eating lunches there. It was in the village of Xauen with its steep streets and smooth slippery stones where they had gone for several days that Bowles first noticed his father's difficulty in walking. "After a few painful sorties, we kept close to the hotel, but it was Mother who had the fall. Toward the end of the summer she stumbled in the darkness into a ditch, broke her ankle, and returned to New York on crutches. Had it not been for her fall, they probably would have stayed longer," Bowles concluded.[32]

For more than a year Bowles had thought of selling Taprobane, a transaction more easily conceived than executed, he realized upon returning to Ceylon with Yacoubi shortly after his parents left. The voyage back to Ceylon was more satisfying to him personally than any previous trip had been because of a short story triggered by his father's visit. "Being in motion always excited me, and I began scribbling. This time the detonating scene was something which I didn't put into the tale itself. I was lying awake in a cold room at the Happy Hollow Farm very early in the morning, before dawn, and heard a fox howling outside. On shipboard I remembered it [and] went to the captain and asked if I could have a room to work in, and he gave me an empty cabin. I had my typewriter and paper in there, and I went every afternoon after lunch and wrote." By the time the ship reached Colombo, Bowles had finished his tale, now titled "The Frozen Fields," and sent it off to *Harper's Bazaar*, where it was published in the July 1957 issue. When queried later about its content and the fact that his parents had just visited him in Tangier, thus sharpening, perhaps, his memories of resentment and hostility toward his father, Bowles denied any direct connection. "Although the father figure in the tale is definitely the main character and bears certain resemblances to my own father, and the fact that the setting is clearly one that I knew firsthand, I am certain that their visit did not trigger my writing the story. In hindsight, of course, I agree that 'The Frozen Fields' is my most autobiographical tale, and that it would not have been written had I experienced a different childhood."[33]

During a stopover in Cape Town, South Africa, Bowles learned firsthand about apartheid. He had met aboard ship a young Asian woman who sat with him at dinner their first night at sea and asked him if he was the author of *The Sheltering Sky*. She said she had recognized him by his picture on the book jacket, and she, in turn, was astonished when he asked if she was Kamala Markandara, a South African. He said he had just read her novel *Nectar in a Sieve*. In Cape Town they were unable to have tea together in a restaurant since she was classified a nonwhite.

When Bowles insisted that they be allowed to sit somewhere, a sympathetic waiter prepared a table for them in the basement, but it was not a happy occasion for either of them. Yacoubi, too, stayed out of sight until Ronald Segal, who edited an antigovernment magazine, *Africa South*, escorted both Bowles and Yacoubi discreetly around the city and invited them to attend several clandestine meetings and benefit parties given in the houses of liberals for the relief of local political martyrs.

Later, Segal wrote: "I do remember Paul Bowles and his visit to Cape Town in 1956, and I found his sympathetic identification with our cause encouraging. Ahmed Yacoubi showed me some of his pictures, exquisite paintings of little luminous fish, which I liked very much. I saw Bowles and Yacoubi on their way to Ceylon, then again on their return. By then, a few things had changed, but nothing startling."[34]

Bowles had been grossly disappointed during his last visit to Ceylon. "I made a stab at living on my island, but found everything against me. So I spent the winter living in hotels and eating their miserable pseudo-European menus which gave me dysentery." Ceylon had grown much more expensive during the year that he was away, and he was now determined to sell Taprobane for whatever he could get out of it. Yacoubi, too, was unhappy. When an Englishman wanted to come down from Bombay to see his paintings and put on an exhibition of his work, Yacoubi declined.[35]

"As usual, it is proving extremely difficult to get out of Ceylon, and I am about to get tickets for a ship called the *Isipingo*, which sails for Mombasa, an eight-day voyage. There I can change to another ship which will take me directly to Las Palmas, in the Canary Islands," he wrote Jane. Never before had Bowles felt quite so defeated in trying to accomplish what seemed a reasonable goal. *"Mektoub,"* he concluded when he set sail for East Africa, ill and disgusted.[36] In the heat of Mombasa, Bowles felt even worse, his condition relieved only upon his return to Cape Town. "I rather liked it there, notwithstanding its latent horror. Friends gave us a very good time; it was rather like being back in San Francisco, being shown the coast to the north and to the south."

It was in Las Palmas in early April that Bowles learned from Gordon Sager that Jane, now barely forty, had suffered a "slight stroke." In his innocence, as Bowles put it later, he failed to recognize Sager's message as the "first statement of a theme which would become the principal leitmotiv of our lives. I did not know it, but the good years were over."[37]

Upon hearing of Jane's illness before Bowles himself could get home to her, Libby Holman, who also had been notified by Sager, discussed Jane's condition with her doctor and showed him the medical reports. Instead of a stroke, she had suffered a subarachnoid hemorrhage, which was not in itself "too serious," and by no means a surprise when he saw that she had suffered from high blood pressure for five years. "Since there is no paralysis," Holman continued, "he feels this may be the only thing that has happened to her, which means that an artery around the outside of the brain has hemorrhaged a little," a diagnosis borne out by a temporary loss of vision and practically intolerable headaches. Since the "best neurologists in the world are in London," the doctor told her, "Jane should be taken there at once."

At the end of August, Bowles confessed in a letter to Virgil Thomson that Jane was on the brink of a mental breakdown. "She is convinced that no one can diagnose her illness and that suicide is the only solution. Her main obsession at the moment is to return to London immediately and see either the neurologist who just released her or some other doctor. At the moment she has a general practitioner and a psychiatrist working on her every day, and that plus massive sedation is keeping her going." In a postscript to Thomson, Bowles added that taking care of Jane was a "totally absorbing chore, night and day, and gives no leisure for letter-writing or even for living, one might say. The last forty-eight hours were pretty awful for everyone, for as the time drew near Jane became much worse. She was convinced she was being sent to be tortured and that she would never come back again; her ability to describe and discuss her own state lucidly, at the same time being imprisoned in it, is perhaps the worst part."[38]

On September 5, 1957, Jane returned to England, where she was treated at the Radcliffe Infirmary in Oxford, then moved to Saint Andrew's, a psychiatric hospital in Northampton, where the doctors asked to try electroplexy. To Virgil Thomson, he wrote: "Naturally she wants very much to go back with me, but that is out of the question. Both the neurologists and psychiatrists involved in her case insist that electroplexy will produce a beneficial result in the shortest possible time. The most painful moment comes each time when I say good-bye to return to London; she is convinced that I'll never come back."[39]

In London, Bowles came down with Asian flu and spent nine days in bed with a high fever. "To my surprise, I was able to write a short story, which I called 'Tapiama.' It was about the effects of an imaginary South American drink, the *cumbiamba*, and was something of an experiment for me, being the only fever-directed piece I had written. On the tenth day, when the story was finished and typed in duplicate, my thermometer registered 98.6; so I got up, dressed, mailed my story to John Lehmann, and went to Harrod's to shop."[40] Bowles did not mention to Lehmann his own hallucinatory voyage from which the story evolved, or that he had suffered a relapse after mailing it. "A few hours later I was delirious. The next morning they plumped me onto a stretcher and removed me to a hospital. Pleurisy set in, and I spent a bad two weeks in a ward with fifty other pneumonia cases, too sick to notice the oxygen tanks being wheeled in, or to watch those who had not been saved by them being wheeled out."

Bowles was still in the hospital when he was informed that Jane had agreed on her own to a series of seven electric shock treatments, and that they had already commenced. On November 11, she was discharged and both were deemed "well enough to travel." Upon their return to Tangier, Bowles learned that Yacoubi had been jailed on charges of having seduced a German youth of fourteen. "It was all a mistake," insisted Yacoubi, who declared that he and the boy were "merely friends." The situation seemed like déjà vu to Bowles, having heard Yacoubi claim that it, too, was "all a mistake, a misunderstanding" when Holman's son Timmy told her that Yacoubi had fondled him. This time, upon Bowles's intervention, which required his paying two hundred thousand francs (the equivalent of five hundred dollars) for Yacoubi's release on bail, Bowles was now less concerned over Yacoubi's guilt or innocence than he was about his and Jane's fates at the hands of the new authorities. While they were in England, hundreds of arrests had been made of Europeans in Tangier who were now being deported or jailed. To add to their distress, Jane suffered a convulsive attack on the ship their first day out of London, and Bowles feared that her health would be further imperiled if she witnessed the latest series of accusations and arrests.

Finally, on May 14, 1958, some five months after his initial imprisonment, Yacoubi was taken to court and acquitted. To Jane, Temsamany reported that Ahmed was out of jail and living quietly. "But he may have more trouble later on because they say that the father of the German youth is furious that nothing more was done to Ahmed. Ahmed wants to get his things from the apartment, and is now waiting for Paul's permission. He looks well, and he may go down to Fez. Maybe he should leave Morocco altogether, but he does not want to do this." Although Temsamany had hoped to visit the United States under the sponsorship of Libby Holman or Tennessee Williams, nothing came of either petition and he left abruptly for Germany, Bowles having given him his Jaguar before leaving for Portugal. Reluctant, however, to drive Bowles's car for fear that he might be accused of having committed a sexual impropriety with his former employer, Temsamany sold the car and used the cash to establish himself in Germany.

As a result of the myriad complications and accusations, Bowles and Jane flew to Lisbon, then boarded a ship bound for Buenos Aires, Argentina. In Funchal, Madeira (Portugal), they disembarked and spent a month. They would have stayed longer, but discovered that Jane's passport had expired and that they would have to return to the American Embassy in Lisbon for its renewal. There they were informed that a new passport could be issued only with the approval of the Federal Bureau of Investigation. Once again they attributed the delay to their memberships in the Communist Party in 1938 and 1939. Finally, after three weeks, Jane's application was turned down, her old passport was confiscated, and she was ordered to leave immediately for the United States. As a document she had only the paper the embassy gave her in exchange for her passport.[41]

Williams was shocked by Jane's appearance when he met her plane. "She looked about ten years older than when I last saw her, very shaky, pitifully nervous, thin, exhausted. I guess 'ravaged' is the word for it. I delivered her to Katharine Hamill and Natasha von Hoershelman, who live near me in the East Sixties, and when I saw her the next day she had made a remarkable recovery and was beginning to look like herself again."[42]

Bowles was alone in Portugal when Libby Holman reached him by telephone to summon him for a production of *Yerma* to be mounted at the University of Denver. On September 7, 1958, the opera now a fait accompli, Bowles reported that "*Yerma* was pretty miserable. After six performances in Denver and nine more in Ithaca, Libby closed it down and planned a new production with a new director, designer, and cast." A reviewer from the *New York World-Telegram and Sun* wrote of the Denver performances: "García Lorca has written a brooding, passionate drama of a Spanish peasant woman whose unfulfilled yearning for a child becomes a consuming obsession. The flame that gnaws within her is as hot and dry as the Andalusian country where the action is set. Paul Bowles, who translated the drama from the original Spanish, has created an outstanding musical score. His music is haunting, weird, mystical. Miss Holman appears to advantage when singing, but displays uncertainty in her acting. She got off to a slow start in Act One, but warmed to the job as the show went on. Her portrayal of Yerma is a sincere one and there were moments in the play when she reached across the footlights with the strong emotion of a peasant woman." Bowles regretted that circumstances that seemed at times to be beyond his control had so delayed the production that "Libby's voice was not up to par. She never blamed me, but I blamed myself."[43]

Except for the production of *Yerma*, Bowles had composed no theater music since his score for Jane's play. Then he was asked by José Ferrer to return to Hollywood in the fall to write a score for *Edwin Booth*. "I had to fly, but at least on the plane I was given a real bed with sheets and blankets." When Bowles was not working on the score or attending rehearsals, he accepted a number of invitations including dinner with the family of his uncle Shirley's son, Dwight Bowles, who lived in Van Nuys with his wife, Elizabeth, and their daughter, Shirley. "I had not seen Dwight or his sister, Barbara, since we were children. Another evening, I had dinner in Hollywood with Christopher Isherwood and Don Bachardy. Don asked if he might sketch me. I hadn't seen either of them since they visited me in Tangier, when

Yacoubi introduced them to *majoun*. Neither mentioned it and I had every reason not to bring it up," said Bowles.[44]

On October 24, 1958, Isherwood recorded in his diary: "We like Paul Bowles. He came last evening to dinner. He was so funny about John Goodwin's taking mescaline. The solemn cult of it." Bachardy said later that he did not remember Bowles's telling about his own mescaline experience, but that he and Isherwood had read in Rorem's *New York Diary* of both Bowles and Rorem being driven from New York City to Goodwin's home in Cresco, Pennsylvania, where they took mescaline with their host and another guest. As Rorem recalled the incident, Bowles took his mescaline pill as though he were "submitting to the experience as to a necessary operation. For an hour, no effect. Paul and I strolled through the forest to a little river while the others weeded the garden. Then began an agreeable withdrawal as with an overdose of codeine. Neither of us had expected physical effects, but they grew worse. Our host and his friend now reappeared with prehistoric grins, and henceforth all came thick and fast. My own physical state became at that point atrocious and I had no sense of touch, my body was glass and fear, and both Paul and I were taken with jitters, chills. Observing the faces of these friends, I saw only varicosed monsters of arteries and teeth." At some point, Rorem sketched his companions and included several of the sketches in his *New York Diary*.[45] Later, Bowles declared: "I recognized one of them as definitely me, and I recalled instantly my horror of the entire event. It was one of the worst, if not *the* worst, experience of my entire life. Fortunately, the passing of time dims memory."[46]

Bowles invited his California cousins to attend a tryout production of *Edwin Booth* during its run at the Huntington Hartford Theatre, but told them he was not optimistic that the play would succeed on Broadway, where it opened at the Forty-sixth Street Theatre on November 24, 1958. "I was right. The reviews were lukewarm, and the play had a very short run." As soon as the final curtain fell, Bowles went immediately to get Jane out of New York Hospital, having already booked passage for their return to Morocco.

Before leaving, Bowles had expected to return to New York shortly, having been invited by Tennessee Williams to write the music for *Sweet Bird of Youth*, but Elia Kazan had someone else in mind. To Williams, Bowles wrote: "I am now somewhat staggered by the sudden shift of plans. If *Sweet Bird* turns out to be unfeasible for me, I'll leave Tangier anyway. . . . We can't live forever in this small apartment, Jane, Cherifa, and I and two maids. At present, however, it's endurable, and I'm merely awaiting some sort of definite news."[47]

To his surprise, in mid-January of 1959, producer Cheryl Crawford wired Bowles in Tangier that Kazan definitely wanted him to do the score for *Sweet Bird of Youth*, and Bowles agreed to have the score completed and to be in New York within six weeks. This time he found a small apartment on the roof of a building in the middle of the European quarter, not far from his own flat, in which he installed "a shrill Erard from the local piano store and set to work." Although Bowles did not finish the score before leaving Tangier, he completed it at the piano in the ship's ballroom after everyone had gone to sleep.

When he arrived in New York, *Sweet Bird of Youth* was already in rehearsal in Philadelphia. To Jane on February 15, 1959, Bowles wrote: "All I'm doing now is going to each performance to hang around watching it from the back. . . . The music is extremely soft, so much so that anyone sitting beyond the tenth row can't tell whether there is any or not."[48] When Brooks Atkinson reviewed the play on March 11, 1959, he said that he was charmed by Bowles's music on opening night at the Martin Beck Theatre, and that he had "contributed spidery and tinkling music of exquisite texture."

The play was still running when Bowles asked Jane if Yacoubi had left for Brazil. A few days later, Yacoubi himself wrote. "He is in Rio and sounds as though he likes it there," he informed Jane. "He refers to the American girl with whom he left Morocco as 'my wife,' so maybe they really are married." Bowles received still another letter from Yacoubi in which he enclosed a catalog of an exhibit of his work in Rio. "It has been running a week, and he has lots of publicity and seems to be having a success. He says he dreams he is going to make much money!"

Although Bowles put considerable stock in dreams, especially if they were his own, he told Jane that he had reservations about Yacoubi's dreams. "I continued to be curious about Ahmed and what he was up to; he was talented in convincing those who claimed to know him well that he could do no wrong. As I once observed, we were never 'in love,' although we were intimates for a number of years in Fez, Tangier, Ceylon, and elsewhere. We had traveled together huge distances many times and had a great deal invested in each other. There was never a time when I was not interested in his welfare."[49]

CHAPTER THIRTEEN

Bowles Records Indigenous Music, Translates, and Survives as Best He Can

(1959–1966)

"There are people in high places in Rabat who imagine that the diffusion of such music abroad will hamper their efforts to persuade the world at large that Morocco is a modern 'civilized' country, and might thus indirectly reduce foreign investment."[1]

—Paul Bowles to Harold Spivacke,
Music Division, Library of Congress,
December 23, 1959

While in New York for the opening of Tennessee Williams's *Sweet Bird of Youth* in the spring of 1959, Bowles was notified that he had been awarded a Rockefeller research grant in the amount of $6,800 to fund a project that he had pursued relentlessly for months: the recording of Morocco's indigenous music before it was irretrievably lost. The Music Division of the Library of Congress, in collaboration with the granting agency, agreed to furnish a reel-to-reel Ampex tape recorder and insisted that he come to Washington, D.C., to learn how to operate it. Bowles went alone to Washington for a week, then as soon as he could book passage was back in Tangier by late May and ready to commence the project. By the time the Moroccan Ministry of Foreign Affairs finished conferring on whether or not to allow the venture, Bowles already had jerry-rigged his own credentials with the help of the American consulate in Tangier and spent three months in the field doing precisely what he had requested in the first place.

In his proposal, he had laid out four geographic itineraries of roughly five weeks duration each that would allow him to record the music of southwest Morocco, northern Morocco, the High Atlas, and the pre-Sahara. In theory, the plan was excellent and much of the project developed accordingly. His assistants were Christopher Wanklyn, who spoke excellent Moghrebi and transported Bowles and his equipment throughout the country in his Volkswagen, and Mohammed Larbi Jilali, a Muslim who had recently escorted a British expedition across the Sahara to Nigeria and could be counted on to negotiate with the natives.

Bowles conceded later that he should have foreseen some of the problems, such as the wide discrepancy between the agreed-upon payment due the performers in each area before the recordings could begin, and the actual sums they insisted upon before performing. In Tafraout they began recording at 10:00 p.m., but even the midnight temperature of 108 degrees caused some of the singers and dancers, accustomed to sleeping through the soaring temperatures of the day, to collapse from heat stroke. On the trail between Taroudant and Tafraout, the engine of Wanklyn's vehicle became clogged in a sandstorm during which temperatures reached 135 degrees in the shade. "Although our Moslem escort muttered repeatedly '*Mektoub,*' Christopher and I held our tongues and waited to be rescued," said Bowles, who conceded that he should have anticipated the difficulties in operating his recording equipment, which had no battery pack and required 110 voltage. In remote areas the generators usually gave off only 220 volts of direct current. In one instance they traveled seventy kilometers into the wilds south of Essaouira and slept on the floor of a military barracks to await the performers, only to discover that there was no usable current in the region. "In Tamanar the only generator supplying what we needed belonged to an irascible Frenchman who would not even discuss allowing us to use it. We had to return to

Essaouira and arrange for the Caïd to transport thirty musicians from Tamanar to where we did have the proper current. It took three days to accomplish what should have been done in one, and we ended up having to pay far more than we had anticipated. Of course the Caïd had to be paid, too. Sometimes we encountered such disapproval from the officials when we presented our papers that the best course was simply to leave the province."[2]

In an essay, "The Rif, to Music," published two years after the expedition ended, Bowles described the music of Morocco's indigenous people, the Berbers, as a "highly percussive art with complicated juxtapositions of rhythms, limited scalar range, and a unique manner of vocalizing."[3] Their music of mass participation was considered most successful when it resulted in mass hypnosis. Only in the regions generally inaccessible to non-Berbers was their music left intact.

Bowles had returned periodically to Tangier to pick up the next installment of his grant; to spend a few days with Jane, who appeared much improved; and to catch up on his correspondence.[4] Finally, the project was finished and Bowles left the recording equipment and sixty tapes of Moroccan folk and art music—more than 250 separate selections—at the American Embassy in Rabat to be shipped to the Archive of Folk Song at the Library of Congress.[5] On their way back to Tangier, Wanklyn's Volkswagen was stopped four times by soldiers searching for hidden guns. "I can't help feeling even more lucky than I did last week that my project just happened to fall during the one calm year Morocco has known this decade."[6]

Bowles had always maintained that whatever happened depended upon who, or in some cases, *what* came along; moreover, his calm acceptance of the status quo had served him well in the past, even when a distasteful event may have affected him directly. Bowles admitted later to having overreacted when he feared that Richard Rumbold, whom he had met with Jane and Yacoubi aboard ship en route to Ceylon, may have gotten him into trouble with the law in Morocco. In November 1960, Bowles had just returned to bed one afternoon to look over his mail when a magazine caught his eye from the growing stack of unopened letters on the floor. He recognized at once by the magazine's unique markings that it was the *London Magazine*, now edited by John Lehmann, but he had no idea as he flipped through the pages that he would find an essay in which he himself was the subject.

With considerable interest he began reading. "'An Evening with Paul Bowles' by Richard Rumbold," the piece began. Having written his own essay on Taprobane, and assuming now that his several evenings with Rumbold on his island in 1954–55 had been condensed into one, Bowles was curious to see Rumbold's treatment of the event. "I know of no one who could initiate me better into the mysteries of hashish than Paul Bowles, nor could I imagine anyone whose company I should have preferred to his on such an adventure," Rumbold began.

Astonished, Bowles discovered that the setting of Rumbold's tale was Morocco, not Taprobane, and that the evening in question involved the commission of a now illegal act. The piece continued: "Bowles had often spoken to me of the drug with approval, extolling it variously as a quiet, relaxed, meditative and companionable ritual, comparable to the tea-ceremony in Japan; as a liberating therapy and catharsis as valid as the psycho-analyst's couch–a means of acquiring insight and self-knowledge, or, as he had once expressed it, of recapturing inspiration and releasing the flow of words."[7]

Ordinarily Bowles might have thought appreciatively of the preciseness of Rumbold's use of language or recalled his eloquence in writing of his new environment and the joy it brought him, but he viewed now "An Evening with Paul Bowles" as a betrayal by a friend. It had never occurred to Bowles that his introduction of kif to Rumbold would have been presented so blatantly in an important magazine read both in America and the United Kingdom, a magazine in which Bowles, too, had been published. He could not imagine that Rumbold would not have heard of the anti-kif law passed in Morocco in 1959 that made it a crime either to buy or to be found with kif in one's possession.

To William Burroughs, living then in Paris, Bowles had written on November 15, 1959, of the new anti-kif law in Morocco. "I wonder why they bothered to pass it without having ruled off at least a third of Moroccan territory for concentration camps. How otherwise can they accommodate the seven or eight million who will have to be incarcerated? As Cherifa says: 'Just wind.'"[8]

To Bowles, Morocco's anti-kif law was only a straw in the wind compared with the country's other problems, both natural and man-made, such as the horrendous earthquake in Agadir in 1960 when the town was reduced to rubble and some fifteen thousand residents and countless tourists were killed instantly. Bowles assured his mother that he was in Tangier at the time, and that no one he knew was injured. She was even more alarmed in 1963 upon hearing that an unseasonably cold and drenching rain had inundated most of the country, leaving hundreds of Moroccans drowned or buried beneath the ruins of their villages. In a telegram his mother demanded that he confirm immediately that he and Jane were not among the injured or deceased.

"Nothing much has happened in Tangier save that scores of big trees toppled into the streets and killed a few people," he replied.[9]

To Bowles, it was one thing for him to have mentioned in a piece of private correspondence to Burroughs the new anti-kif law and to have observed glibly that "a third of Moroccan territory would have to be ruled off for concentration camps if the law were enforced," but it had never occurred to him to caution anyone not to talk about being introduced to kif or *majoun* by an otherwise law-abiding American expatriate who had made his home in Morocco for more than a dozen years. Bowles feared that if the authorities were to come across Rumbold's article, the alleged incriminating evidence could be viewed as possible grounds for his own arrest, incarceration, seizure of property, and deportation. Burroughs said later that he had never known an adult as naïve as Bowles. "Of course Paul would not have stopped smoking kif simply because it was illegal; he just did not want someone else to write an article–and to be paid for it–based on something he had done."[10]

Although Rumbold had second thoughts about his essay and apologized to Bowles for having written so blatantly of their shared kif experience, he recognized, too, that his breach involved more than etiquette. Four months after Rumbold's "Evening with Paul Bowles" article appeared in the *London Magazine*, its author stepped from a hotel window in Palermo, Sicily, and plunged many floors to his death. Hearing of it later, Bowles recalled Rumbold's telling him in Ceylon that suicide ran in his family. He was only a boy when his mother threw herself into the Seine, and his sister Rosemary also had committed suicide.[11]

Bowles considered fleeing the country in 1961, as did many others in violation of the law as anti-kif propaganda continued its spread across Morocco, but concluded that he and Jane would only draw attention to themselves if they went anywhere. More to the point, Bowles had no intention of changing his habits where kif was concerned. To Allen Ginsberg he wrote on December 12, 1961: "Kif-weeks fly by, seasons change, the sun shines, one works and writes letters, people come and go, and one remains in just the same position that one was in a good while ago."[12]

Now that his own use of kif was a matter of public record, Bowles sent three stories united by kif to Lawrence Ferlinghetti, who had solicited them at the urging of Ginsberg, whose *Howl* had just been published by City Lights Books. Bowles had a fourth tale almost ready, which he quickly finished, made a few changes to the other three, and added a detailed glossary.[13] His concern now was what to call the collection as a whole. "The difficulty with finding a word that has some reference, even obliquely, to kif, is that the word will necessarily be a Moghrebi word, and thus will have no reference at all, save to the few who know the region. Moghrebi itself could be used. *Four Moghrebi Tales*, for instance. But of course no kif is suggested there," he observed.[14] Then he remembered the Moghrebi proverb "A pipe of kif before breakfast gives a man the strength of a hundred camels in the courtyard." The title *A Hundred Camels in the Courtyard* practically leaped from the page. "Since the theme of all the stories is specifically the power of kif, rather than the subjective effects of it," Bowles thought it perfect for his tome.[15] Ferlinghetti assured him that the title was, indeed, perfect, and that City Lights would be delighted to publish it.

Bowles was convinced that smoking kif was essential to his own creative process and an integral part of the composition technique, as well as to the Muslim society in general. In his preface to *A Hundred Camels in the Courtyard*, Bowles described the role of kif as a passageway to enlightenment to the dedicated smoker. His own technique was "to experiment with the idea of constructing stories in which the subject matter would consist of disparate elements and unrelated character taken directly from life and fitted together as a mosaic." The challenge was to create a story line that would make each arbitrarily chosen episode compatible with the others, to make each one lead to the next with a semblance of naturalness. To Bowles, it was through the intermediary of kif that the "barriers separating the unrelated elements might be destroyed, and the disconnected episodes forced into symbiotic relationships."[16]

For some time Tangier had been on the verge of losing its charter, which meant that money could no longer move freely in and out of the city. As a result, the French and Spanish residents departed in droves, whereas most of the Americans and English stayed on, afraid of losing their homes if they left for any period of time. Every two or three months, Bowles took a boat to Gibraltar to get money since by then bank accounts in Morocco were practically nonexistent. Each person in Morocco, including foreigners, was allowed annually the equivalent of sixty dollars to spend outside the country.

"It's almost impossible to buy canned goods any more," Bowles wrote his mother. "Janie found two cans of corn the other day in a shop, and it was like finding a treasure. We're saving them for a feast! Even British goods are on the forbidden list." From time to time they did find such things from Iron Curtain countries as Bulgarian jam, Czechoslovakian beans, and Hungarian spices, which they hoarded like thieves.[17]

It was Gordon Sager who put Jane up to applying to the Ingram Merrill Foundation for a three-thousand-dollar writing grant. Sager had just received such a grant himself and assured her that it was "no big deal in terms of accountability." Jane knew that she was not single-minded enough to sustain work on a novel, but reasoned that she just might manage to write a play. Bowles was skeptical of her ability to do either in 1960–61 since her health was still precarious. "Although her one salvation lay in her belief in herself and her ability to write, Jane dreaded to account for what she might accomplish," said Bowles.

For a time Jane worked well despite the residue of her stroke, and their lives appeared to be more normal at this juncture than they had been in two years. They talked and laughed, and at lunchtime sometimes took a picnic basket to the roof of their building, only a flight above Bowles's flat on the fourth floor, spread a blanket, and feasted on sandwiches and root beer. Yet both recognized that reversals were bound to come. A severe case of shingles followed by hernia repair and a second operation to correct the effects of the first kept Jane in pain for months. She also suffered from insomnia and lost weight that she could ill afford. "Our combined conversations orbited around the subject of her poor health," said Bowles. Whereas the act of living had been enjoyable, "at some point when I was not paying attention it had turned into a different sort of experience, to whose grimness I had grown so accustomed that I now took it for granted."[18]

Corresponding with friends and continuing to write and publish during the 1960s was Bowles's personal means of survival. As usual, his fiction evolved from his personal experience or from the reportage of others. For example, the death of Jane's cat, Dubz, after falling from a friend's balcony upon the pavement below, provided him with the impetus for "A Friend of the World." "The tale seemed just right for my kif volume, and I think that Jane and I both considered it a resurrection of sorts of Dubz," said Bowles.[19] The title character of his tale was Salam, a Muslim who had moved recently into a Jewish sector of the city. Soon after, he found his much-loved kitten, Mimí, dead. She had swallowed a pellet of bread with a needle inside. Salam was certain that the mother of a neighbor's child, also named Mimí, was responsible since she resented his moving into the Jewish sector and believed that he was making fun of her child by giving his cat the same name. But until the woman accosted him, Salam was unaware of the child's name. He avenged Mimí's death through black magic, and "no one else was the wiser," the tale concluded.

Bowles continued to straddle the realms of his imaginative environment and the reality surrounding him. Like many of his fictional characters and the Moroccans themselves, he was convinced that black magic accounted for the otherwise unaccountable. When Bowles's Amazon parrot died unaccountably in 1961, he was convinced that Cherifa was somehow involved. Jane told him, too, of discovering under her pillow and mattress small packets of *tseuheur* customarily used for black magic. When she ripped the bags open, she found bits of pubic hair, nail clippings, dried blood, and other gross ingredients that she flushed immediately down the toilet. Although Jane made Bowles promise not to try to get rid of Cherifa, whom she was sure he would blame, he admitted later telling Yacoubi of her mischief since he was well versed in magic and portents and might have some ideas of his own to counteract anything Cherifa might decide to do in the future. "Jane resented anyone's interference, especially mine, and she denounced Yacoubi to me repeatedly," said Bowles. Of Cherifa, Yacoubi's identifying phrase was usually "Watch out, she's a witch!" Over the years there were a number of inexplicable events that Bowles attributed to Cherifa's black magic, and he was determined to find some means of expelling her from the household.

As he saw it, the only way Jane could make a strong comeback physically was to stop drinking and get back to her writing. "Since giving up cocktails was out of the question for Jane, I did keep after her to continue writing and to be more single-minded in her daily affairs. We were free, obviously, to do anything we wished. Our 'open marriage' always meant far more than a choice of bed partners, friends, servants, and freedom to travel as we saw fit. Jane never hesitated to take me into her confidence and readily told me of her various crushes on women. I don't think she minded that I was never as open as she."[20]

To his parents Bowles wrote of the invasion of the Beats, whose use of kif was well known in Tangier. "Everyday one sees more beards and filthy blue jeans, and the girls look like escapees from lunatic asylums, with white lipstick and black smeared around their eyes, and matted hair hanging around the shoulders. The leaders of the 'movement' have moved their headquarters here."[21] Bowles named Allen Ginsberg, Gregory Corso, and William Burroughs as leaders of the group, but it was not long before they, too, had scattered: Burroughs to Harvard at the invitation of Timothy Leary, who needed him for a series of experiments; Allen Ginsberg to Greece, Peter Orlovsky to Istanbul, and Gregory Corso to London. To Ginsberg and Orlovsky, Bowles wrote in mid-summer of 1962: "Tangier is full of people because the King [Mohammed V had died in February 1961 and was succeeded by his son Hassan II] is living on the mountain in his palace. Large American cars rush through the streets and there are police at every corner. Members of the Royal Guard walk hand in hand along the boulevard, and a group of Reguibat now wanders about, looking lost, trailing their long blue garments behind them. They have been imported by Miss Hutton, whose guests they will entertain day after tomorrow at [her] annual ball." He said that Jane was going too.[22]

For several months in 1962, at Bowles's urging, Jane began to entertain the possibility of their returning together to the United States to see their parents and to visit friends, but Bowles did not want to get their hopes up. "You know how hard it is for Jane to make up her mind about anything; as soon as she does, she feels she has made a mistake and ought to have decided in some other way," Bowles reminded his parents. Had Tennessee Williams not arrived unexpectedly, they would have been on their way already. "Jane as usual feels responsible for his welfare and has been helping him get settled. He's got to go to Italy for a production of one of his plays [*The Milk Train Doesn't Stop Here Anymore*], but he'll be back."[23]

After Williams's departure, Bowles and Jane flew together to New

York, then went their separate ways. To Ginsberg, Bowles wrote: "I've been moving fast in various directions, with scarcely ever more than three nights in the same bed. . . . Finally down here [in Gulfport, Florida] to visit my parents who live facing a 'yacht-basin' where scores of boats are moored in neat rows, and pelicans swoop above the palms on their way to dive for fish, and the beach herons and cranes wade in proprietary fashion, eating as they go. It's better here than in New York, for a while, at least."[24]

Bowles had already booked passage to Tangier on the SS *Constitution* for him and Jane to leave in mid-November 1962, but upon Williams's urging that he do the score for *The Milk Train Doesn't Stop Here Anymore*, scheduled to open on Broadway in December, he canceled his ticket and suggested that Jane return home by herself. Since she had found little to entertain her in either New York or Miami, where she had visited her mother and stepfather, she needed no further prompting.

In mid-December, Bowles wrote Jane that enthusiastic reviews of *The Milk Train Doesn't Stop Here Anymore* were in all the papers, and that the play was already sold out for its scheduled two-week run. "Maybe it will be a hit. I can't wait to get out of New York and onto the ship. Let me know if there's anything you want, while I'm still here. I don't dare ask if you're working. But for God's sake, do."[25]

Although Jane had promised to show Bowles the first act of her new play upon his return to Tangier, he was dubious about how much she actually had accomplished. When left to her own devices, Jane dreaded writing anything at all. "I was sorry to hear that as you put it, everything has got to be a mess in Tangier and therefore you have not worked. That was the very thing we were making great resolves about while you were still here, that you wouldn't *allow* the mess-tendency to take over, because that has always been the pattern. The mess is just the decor in which we live, but we can't let decor take over," he told her.[26] Jane took such chastising in her stride, but knew that she would continue to do precisely as she chose.

Bowles had several projects awaiting him in Tangier, including the recording and transcribing of a number of tales by a young illiterate Moroccan, Larbi Layachi, whom he had discovered working as a watchman of a boarded-up café on Merkala Beach. He had seen Layachi from time to time during occasional twilight walks along the usually deserted strip of boulders and beach. One day Layachi called out to him, "thus beginning an acquaintanceship which ultimately added a whole new dimension to my writing experience."[27]

In his introduction to *A Life Full of Holes*, the book that eventually evolved from his recording and translating Layachi's tales, Bowles acknowledged that "the man who invented this book, and along with it the name of Driss ben Hamed Charhadi, is a singularly quiet and ungregarious North African Moslem. His forebears are from a remote mountainous region where Moghrebi Arabic rather than a Berber tongue is spoken. He is totally illiterate. His speech in Moghrebi is clear and correct. Like a peasant's it is studded with rustic locutions and proverbs. The fact that translating and compiling the novel was a comparatively simple process is due mainly to the sureness with which he proceeds in telling a story. It was as if he had memorized the entire text and rehearsed the speaking of it for weeks."

In 1964 Layachi's book was published in New York by Grove Press. To editor Richard Seaver, Bowles described the process by which he had translated the young Moroccan: "I encouraged him to think about each episode at length before coming to record it. Once the words are on tape they remain exactly as they were spoken, and I translate them literally. Since story-telling here is an oral art, a certain amount of emotional effect is inevitably lost in transferring it to the silent, written word."[28] Soon after publication of *A Life Full of Holes*, Bowles reported to Seaver a more personal tale: "Charhadi does things fast: he divorced his wife a fortnight ago, and is already remarried, once again to a country girl whom he has never seen, save swathed in *litham* and *haik* at the actual ceremony before his stepfather, her father, and the *qadi*. . . . This one, it seems, is a virgin."[29] Two weeks later, the saga having continued, Bowles reported that when he asked Charhadi how his new wife was, he replied. "Oh, I've divorced her. I'm remarried to the first one. How can you know whether you can live with a woman or not until you've married her?"

By the end of 1964, Bowles's agent had negotiated contracts for Dutch, French, Spanish, British, and Italian editions of Charhadi's book, and more were pending. Although Bowles and Charhadi shared evenly in all of the proceeds derived from *A Life Full of Holes*, Charhadi later accused Bowles of cheating him, but pressed no formal charges. "Of course I didn't cheat him," said Bowles. Twenty years later, Black Sparrow Press published a new book by Charhadi, titled *Yesterday and Today*, under his true name, Larbi Layachi. "Naturally I was interested in what he might have said in a preface. 'When people are good, you never forget them,' he began. Then he named about fifty people to whom he expressed gratitude, but I was not one of them," said Bowles.[30]

Meanwhile, Yacoubi had returned to Tangier and resumed his own storytelling. To Ginsberg, Bowles characterized Yacoubi at this point in his life as *meshugah*, a slang word derived from the Yiddish *meshuge*, which in American English means "crazy" or "insane." "He's now got a German girl on the string, intends to go with her to Berlin and live with her family for four years until she is of age and can marry him. Few people alive could have less sense of reality. . . . I never tried to guess what Ahmed might do next."[31]

Although several of Bowles's friends suggested that he spend more time writing his own books instead of recording and translating the words of others, he insisted that he was doing what he wanted, and that he especially enjoyed translating from the Moghrebi. "When I began recording and translating [Mohammed] Mrabet's tales, I had no idea where it would take me, but I've never regretted the time I have spent on the translations. The best translator I've ever had of my own work is Madame Claude-Nathalie Thomas."[32]

One of Bowles's visitors in 1963 was Lawrence Stewart, a scholar who had studied his writings intensely, then interviewed Bowles at length in Morocco, which resulted in the first important book on his work: *Paul Bowles: The Illumination of North Africa*. Stewart concluded that "translation [had] perceptibly affected Bowles's fiction, particularly the length of his sentences," and acknowledged that Bowles himself believed that such pre-translation stories as "The Hyena" and "The Garden" did not read as well aloud as those written later. "In their brevity and subject matter these stories have the strongest affinities to the translations," said Stewart, to whom Bowles explained his method of working as a translator: "If there's a word or a phrase that seems to have any kind of equivocal meaning or ramifications of meaning, I stop the machine and we get to the bottom of it. Then, if it seems that it's not clear to the average reader, it's not clear to people who have never been to Morocco, I say 'You're going to have to record a few more sentences explaining this.'"[33]

To escape from Tangier with its great many tourists during the summer of 1963, Bowles took a house by the sea in the small village of Asilah. The waves came up to the windows and either splashed against them or pounded, depending on the wind. Once a week, Jane came by bus with Cherifa or Tetum, journeys that prompted her to write Ruth Fainlight that summer: "My life has turned into a veritable farce, schlepping between Arcila [Asilah] and Tangier as I do, and if I did not find it humorous I would weep. My mind is full of food that has to be taken to Arcila because there is nothing to eat except some tomatoes, giant-sized string beans, and sometimes fish. Otherwise everything must be taken there in great baskets and burlap bags."[34]

Coincidental with one of Jane's visits to Asilah was the arrival, on motorcycle, of John Hopkins and Joseph A. McPhillips III, who had just concluded their first year of teaching at the American School of Tangier. In their early twenties, Hopkins and McPhillips had been classmates at Princeton, and upon graduating, traveled extensively through Peru, Europe, North Africa, and, finally, to Tangier, where McPhillips had a friend whose father was one of the founders of the school. Hopkins was writing a novel, and in his diary made meticulous entries from which he expected to draw in the future. On April 1, 1963, he wrote: "Dinner with the Bowleses in Jane's apartment. The spontaneous affection and sense of fun they share make them seem more like brother and sister than man and wife. Their intimacy is more fraternal than sexual. They live in separate apartments, one above the other, and communicate by a squeaking mauve toy telephone. Jane likes to cook. Tonight it was jugged hare in a red wine sauce. It was like being in New York except for Cherifa, who rattled on in Arabic in her gruff mannish voice and laughed uproariously at her own jokes. A rough alien presence who acted as though she owned the place. Jane, a fragile figure like a priceless vase that has been knocked to the floor. The pieces have been glued back together, but crudely and the cracks show. Cherifa stood there, arms crossed, hammer in hand. We took Jane for a swim in the ocean, but the seaweed frightened her. In the evening we ate with our fingers, listened to music, and took in the stars–kiffed-up stars that revolved, changed colours, and winked on and off."[35]

Bowles relished both the anticipation and the actuality of visitors. Upon meeting Alfred Chester at a party in New York in 1968, he encouraged Chester to come to Morocco. Chester had traveled widely, lived in Paris, published a novel, and had a second in progress. After an exchange of several letters, Chester wrote Bowles: "Your new place sounds delicious, and I am grateful for invitation to stay, but since I will be coming with dogs, maybe better find me a place nearby."[36] His travel plans firm at last, Chester wrote Edward Field, a friend from New York abroad on a Fulbright Fellowship: "I'm sailing on the 21st of June [1963]. Paul is expecting me in Tangier, or rather, Asilah (he even offered me the passage money but I declined, told him I didn't need it)."[37]

Later, Bowles explained: "As soon as Alfred Chester wrote me he was definitely coming to Morocco, I began to coach Dris [a Moroccan fisherman] on how to behave with him. We would meet for tea every afternoon in the public garden, when I'd tell him all I knew, and what I surmised, about Alfred. . . . I was curious to see what would happen."[38]

Long after Chester's death and the events themselves, Edward Field prepared a manuscript of Chester's letters written from Morocco and submitted them to John Martin, editor of Black Sparrow Press, who was publishing Bowles's work as well. Upon reading the letters, Martin informed Field that he could publish the book only if Bowles did not object. Upon reading Chester's letters, Bowles replied: "Compared to his short stories and his critical essays, Alfred's letters are a bit hit-or-miss. The public should be given a chance to see how beautifully he could think and write before it's bombarded with his epistles. I can see that you're intending exactly that, to start with his stories and essays. I've read through the letters again, searching for statements I consider false. There's one report that I continually 'come on to Dris,' which I suppose means 'to proposition him.' It's hard to believe that Alfred never became aware that it was I who provided Dris for him."[39]

Bowles's admission to Field of having choreographed Chester's meeting with Dris confirmed Bowles's tendency to play Poe's "Imp of the Perverse" by setting certain wheels into motion in order to observe what the characters in question made of them. Bowles took no small pleasure in manipulating two or more players upon a platform of his own construction, then watching the ensuing action. Later he insisted that he had never considered himself a catalyst for other peoples' actions, "although some people concluded that I sometimes tinkered with chance. People behave as they wish, and things often turn out quite differently from what they anticipate. The main thing is that they avoid getting their hopes up, thus do not risk disappointment."[40]

Over the years Bowles and Virgil Thomson had stayed in touch, and Thomson, who was especially devoted to Jane, wrote Bowles that Knopf had approached him with a proposal and contract for a book of memoirs. "Why wait and have somebody else writing about me after I'm gone?" Thomson asked, and Bowles agreed. "At least it would be Virgil's version of the truth. I think he wanted to exclude those who might be inclined to say too much or to be outrageous in their comments."[41] When Thomson informed him that he already had accepted an advance of fifteen thousand dollars from Knopf, Bowles was staggered by the figure and decided that he, too, should think seriously about preparing his own memoir; yet without a contract he had no intention of writing one any more than he would consider writing music at this juncture without a commission and money in the bank.

It had been almost seven years since *The Spider's House* was published, followed four years later by a collection of short stories, *The Hours After Noon.* Short fiction came easy for Bowles, and with his growing reputation, he had no trouble getting his stories published. His latest was "The Garden," which he sent to *Art and Literature,* a magazine being published in Lausanne, Switzerland. "My story was only three pages long, and I wasn't completely happy with it, so I did something I don't usually do. I changed the ending because it lacked appropriate closure, and added two sentences: 'Little by little the trees died, and very soon the garden was gone. Only the desert was there.' My editor had not suggested it, but the new ending seemed just right."[42] Perhaps it *was* time to begin another novel, he mused.[43]

Bowles told John Bainbridge, a staff writer for the *New Yorker* who came to Tangier in 1965 to interview him and others for a book, *Another Way of Living: A Gallery of Americans Who Choose to Live in Europe*: "If you live here, you either go crazy very quickly or become more or less philosophical. You learn how to arrange your life so it isn't always catching on these particular nails. You don't want to move in rhythm with the outside world. You want to move only in your own rhythm, so that what began as a drawback eventually becomes your desire."[44]

Friends of Bowles who read his extended interview in Bainbridge's book were not surprised that little of a personal nature came to light. "Of course Paul told things obliquely. No doubt his sense of obligation, guilt, perhaps, and the inevitable resentment of certain actions by both parents lay just beneath the surface of his always polite and guarded language," surmised John Hopkins. "Paul never mistook what he was doing when he held back so much of himself in interviews and in his autobiography, unlike Jane, who could transform into her writing the flesh and blood actuality of life around her if she got bogged down and couldn't work. Jane said anything she wanted."[45]

A few months before being interviewed by Bainbridge, Bowles talked with Oliver Evans, a poet and university professor with whom he had formerly corresponded about Carson McCullers, whose biography Evans was writing. In a foreword to the interview published in the *Mediterranean Review*, Evans presented the setting as though a play was in progress. "The scene of the interview was the eastern end of a 60' room at the edge of a cliff on the Old Mountain. The sea was audible, breaking against the rocks 300 feet below. It was autumn and the wind roared in the trees. A Moroccan servant brought us tea. I sat with my machine at one end of the divan, and Mr. Bowles sat at the end near the fireplace, sometimes moving to the floor."[46] Before the interview was published, Bowles inquired: "I'm curious to know what you've been able to do with what little we discussed in the house on the mountain, and I hope I shall have plenty of time to reflect and add to my sparse and uninteresting remarks."[47] When a copy of the interview arrived, Bowles could not resist editing it. "As you can see, I've changed a good many words, but not such a great deal of the gist. It's much closer now to what I meant to say originally and never managed. How you gave it any semblance of form and coherence I'll never know."[48] After the interview was rejected by the *Paris Review* and *Playboy*, Bowles concluded that "interviews were not *in* just then" or that he was not a fit subject. He was pleased when Evans adjusted his sights and sent it to the *Mediterranean Review*.

Several years later, a more extensive interview, conducted by Jeffrey Bailey, was published in the *Paris Review*. "I thought Mr. Bailey's a good interview and I guess the timing was right. At any rate, it pleased me when it finally came out," said Bowles, whose door he opened to almost every petitioner, strangers for the most part who desired merely an hour or so of his time and sometimes requested an inscription on a volume they had just purchased from the Librairie des Colonnes, the local bookstore. "Sometimes they had no place to sit because of guests already there, but they seemed not to mind and rushed off shortly to their cruise ship in port for only a half day."[49]

John Hopkins noted that in the early 1960s he was probably the only person who visited Bowles consistently late at night. "I could usually count on having him to myself at such an hour, and it was a marvelous way both to start and end an evening."[50] In a diary entry dated December 1, 1964, Hopkins wrote:

> When I go to Paul's I knock on his door about midnight and stay until two or three. We go up on the roof to look at the stars, listen to music, talk. Paul is an attentive host during these late night sessions and deftly anticipates the effects of the weed he loves to smoke. When you get the munchies, he produces a box of cookies or a bowl of fruit. When the pipe makes you so thirsty your throat begins to feel like the inside of a tin cup, he serves Lapsang Souchong with lemon and sugar. When there's a gap, something missing–and you're too spaced out to know what it is–he lights a joss stick dipped in some magic ointment brought back from the Orient. (He has a cupboard full of exotic scents.) When the room lapses into silence you are aroused by the sound of bells, tiny bells that tinkle delicately from a Thai temple, which he has just put on the machine."[51]

After Bowles wrote *Up Above the World*, his next novel, Stephen Davis asked if it was easier for the kif smoker to write short stories, rather than novels. Bowles replied that he had no trouble writing *Up Above the World*, despite his having imbibed a considerable amount of cannabis at the time. "This was the first book for which I really used kif for the purpose of writing. The difficulty for me with novels isn't kif, but finding a novelistic theme worth doing." Davis also asked Bowles how he formulated his own stories in contrast to his work as a translator of the various tales he had been recording by illiterate Moroccans. "With a story like 'Allal,'" he began, "I thought about it for a long time before I started to write, then I wrote it out very quickly. It has to be fast for me or it doesn't come out right. I always think of it as laying an egg: you lay it quickly and painlessly and that's that. A short story, anyway. That's why I like them better than novels."[52]

Two other newcomers who presented themselves at Bowles's door in 1965 were Robert Hines and Jack Fricks, a gay couple who lived then in New Orleans and knew Tennessee Williams. "You'll adore Janie, and I've no doubt Paul's New England reserve will relax before your mannerly Southern charm," the playwright had advised them. "You can put up with the inhabitants. Things are cheap there. Bootleg liquor is $2.50 for a quart of the best Scotch. A piece of ass is two bucks and the swimming is great in the summer. You must go see them."[53]

Still another visitor to Tangier that summer was Andreas Brown, future owner of Gotham Book Mart in New York City, who was preparing a bibliography of Bowles's work, including his music, fiction, and translations. He also hoped to arrange for the possible sale and transfer of some of Bowles's and Jane's archival materials to the University of Texas in Austin. "I have been looking through correspondence since receiving your letter," said Bowles, who told Brown that he had many letters from Williams, Ginsberg, Burroughs, and others whose names he would recognize. "As you suggest, I'll hold off on all that has to do with papers and manuscripts and letters until I see you some time next month, *incha'Allah*."[54]

Brown stayed a fortnight in Tangier, and he, too, commenced a correspondence of some regularity with Bowles, who liked what he thought of as "holding up his end of the correspondence." When he replied to a letter, even from someone he had never met, he expected a timely acknowledgment. "It's only common courtesy," he insisted. Usually Bowles wrote far more than his correspondent could possibly have anticipated, unaware that Bowles usually did not stop writing until he had filled a page. He could count on entertaining his correspondents by citing some of Cherifa's "endless dire monologues" and reporting on her ever-present switch-blade knife that she kept handy to castrate "any male who may say good evening to her. Never knew a woman who hated men so violently. I'm told she makes a speciality of stealing brides on the eve of their weddings."[55]

When informed that a first printing of thirty-four thousand copies of *Up Above the World* would be published the following spring, Bowles was amazed. "It was the shortest of my novels, 223 pages, and had the largest first printing of any of my books that preceded it."[56] To his mother Bowles described his new novel as "a murder mystery about beatniks, decidedly light," then added with characteristic pessimism: "It probably will get awful notices." Bowles said later that he thought of *Up Above the World* as a "light novel, an entertainment" in the manner of Graham Greene, or "as a *sortie*, after Gide."[57] To John Goodwin, upon seeing a number of reviews of *Up Above the World* in distinguished newspapers and magazines, Bowles declared: "It seemed the emperor had on very fine garments for once. I thought *Life*'s piece the most intelligent. Financially it did very well, because of the film sale and paperback rights."[58] Earlier, he had written Libby Holman to thank her for sending the review from the *New York Times* and added: "The only reviewer who seemed completely to understand it was the one who covered it for *Life* [Wilfred Sheed]: He was withering about it, but he at least gave proof of having understood what he had read. It's better to communicate hostility than not to communicate anything."[59]

Another review of *Up Above the World* on which Bowles commented was W. G. Rogers's observation in the *Saturday Review*, Rogers having concluded that "the author has let us down, or lets himself down. It is as if, finally fed up with his inspired subtleties, he deliberately decides to cap the extraordinary with the ordinary. For the mystery so tantalizingly, even poetically evoked, comes to a solution as banal as, say, a gangland murder. Yet until within hailing distance of the very end, reading it was wonderful going."[60]

He was pleased to inform his mother, also, that Jane had a contract with Farrar, Straus and Giroux, who wished to publish an omnibus of her work. "She of course has qualms: 'But my work isn't good enough to be done that way.' Jane had balked at the thought of having her short stories included and declared that all of the copies had been lost, but this presented no insurmountable problem. I was able to come up with tear-sheets of everything at hand, including the travel article 'East Side: North Africa' that she had written for *Mademoiselle*. I saw that in ten minutes it could be transformed into a story. As I expected, she refused to consider it. So I did it myself, called it 'Everything Is Nice,' and included it with the manuscripts to be sent to London. When I showed her the result, she said angrily: 'Do whatever you like.' "[61]

In hindsight, Bowles observed with some embarrassment that in his enthusiasm to help get Jane's work back into print, he may have done more than he should have in making changes to her travel article and converting it into the short story "Everything Is Nice." "I suppose I believed that because we had collaborated before when she was having difficulties getting something down on paper that she desperately wanted to say and asked me to look at it and make suggestions, it would be fitting for me to tinker with this one. I was wrong, of course."[62]

In the spring of 1966, Joseph McPhillips asked Bowles if he would be willing to write theater music for the chorus for his school's forthcoming production of Yeats's translation of Sophocles' *Oedipus the King*. Bowles agreed, saying that he had no desire to return to the vagaries of Broadway productions. "When Joe asked me I may have demurred at first, but I very much enjoyed doing it. He involved several of us from the community: Marguerite McBey did the poster for the production, and Brion Gysin, the make-up."[63]

To his mother, Bowles wrote on May 24, 1966, that he was busy going to rehearsals of the chorus for *Oedipus* and trying to book passage to Bangkok, but that he and Jane looked forward to spending a few days in Florida with their respective parents.[64] Although his father had not been well for several months, Bowles had no idea that it was his mother he should have worried about. The day after he posted his letter to her, he received a wire saying that she had died. "I had no idea that she was even sick, and I never knew her cause of death, but three days later, my father died, also. It was he who had been the sick one. Perhaps he did not want to live if my mother were not at his elbow waiting on him," said Bowles.

"Joe's production of *Oedipus* had just gone on the road when I received word of my father's death. Since Jane and I were already booked to leave July 1 on the SS *Independence*, her plan being to go on to Miami to see her mother, and mine to go to Florida to see my parents, there was no need for us to change our departure plans for New York. For some reason the death of my parents diminished my unwillingness to leave Tangier. Very likely the shock itself left me in a state of indifference. I can only deduce that I felt profoundly guilty for having excised them from my life. My Uncle Paul was my mother's only surviving sibling, Uncle Fred having died two years earlier, and he and his wife, Dorothy, who was devoted to my mother, took charge of the arrangements. There was no question of my ever returning to Gulfport. My lawyer told me that the business involving the property and other matters could be handled by mail, and I was relieved not to have to go."[65]

Jane was still in Florida with her mother and stepfather when Bowles boarded a Norwegian freighter for Bangkok. "I felt considerable ambivalence," he admitted. Bowles was skeptical that he could stay long enough to write a book on Bangkok and its culture upon discovering that the visa he had been granted was good for only two weeks and that an extension appeared to be next to impossible. He wondered if his FBI file had surfaced and feared that he would be sent home.

Oliver Evans was already in Bangkok, having accepted a Fulbright appointment at Chulalongkorn University, and sought out Bowles as soon as he arrived. "It was Oliver who had suggested that I do a book or piece for *Holiday* on Bangkok." The next day, after seeking out the appropriate officials regarding his visa extension or a different kind of visa, Bowles was told that the only way to extend his visa was to take salaried employment, or at least to get a potential employer to declare that he was hiring him. "In other countries one has to agree

NOT to take a paid job. The whole thing is perverse, but the people are charming, which is a blessing."[66]

Confronted daily by confirmation that it would take years to learn enough about Bangkok to write a book on it, Bowles turned his attention to things that did interest him, such as kickboxing. "The boxers come into the ring and pray for five minutes; then they dance a while; then the music changes and the fight rhythm begins (oboes, drums and cymbals that sound more like triangles) and they go to it, kicking and punching every part of each other's anatomy, all in strict rhythm. When they finish, the winner often prostrates himself before the loser, if he's conscious."[67]

To Frances Bishop, a classically trained musician who lived in New York City, whom Bowles met aboard ship when they boarded in San Francisco, he wrote fairly often during his several months in Thailand. Bishop played the cello and violin and had a passion for Oriental music. She had left the ship in Hong Kong to travel to Taipei and Japan, and Bowles encouraged her to join him in Bangkok, or failing that, in Chiangmai, to which he traveled next to escape the heat and humidity of the capital. They corresponded often about Thai music.[68]

Bowles's only other correspondent to whom he wrote in great detail about Thai music and his attempt to tape it was Ira Cohen, a New Yorker whom he had known in Morocco. Meanwhile, fearing the worst after not hearing from Jane for a number of weeks, he implored her to write. Finally, he heard from Jane's doctor in Tangier saying that she was "not at all well, either physically or psychically," and urged him to return as soon as possible. After Bowles left for Bangkok, Jane had traveled alone by train to New York to promote her book through several interviews arranged by her editor. "I was not surprised to hear later that she had said little in the interviews and considered them an embarrassment for the interviewer as well as for herself. For a week she stayed at the Hotel Chelsea, then spent a weekend with Libby Holman at Treetops, but her special friends were nowhere to be seen," he said. Bowles insisted that he did not recognize when he left for Bangkok that Jane's health, both emotionally and physically, was dire, or that she was headed on a downward spiral so severe that she was unable to recover. "For Jane, and for me as well, the next six years were pure hell. There was a seventh year, too–part of one–but of it she was barely aware."[69]

CHAPTER FOURTEEN

Six Years of Abject Sadness

(1967–1973)

"You may be sure that for a good many years I've reflected on the possibility of being left alone by Jane, and now that it has happened . . . my degree of interest in everything has been diminished almost to the point of non-existence."[1]

—Paul Bowles to Virgil Thomson,
Tangier, June 1973

A week before Bowles returned home from Bangkok on March 2, 1967, having been summoned by both Gordon Sager and Libby Holman, Holman flew immediately to Tangier with her husband, Louis Schanker, to see what they could do to help. "As soon as I walked in the door Libby came to me in tears, crying, 'I can't take another hour of Jane,'" said Bowles. Her condition was far worse than he had feared. She could walk only if someone held her, and if she tried to get out of bed by herself, she often fell and had to be lifted from the floor and carried to the bathroom or back to her bed.[2]

On the eve of Jane's fiftieth birthday, her mother wrote that she had drunk a midnight toast to her good health and happiness and asked how she was celebrating the event. Jane was only vaguely aware that it was her birthday, and that some of her best friends had gathered for a dinner party organized by David Herbert. She may not have noticed, even, that her husband was not among them. Her mother had closed her letter with its usual refrain: "Paul loves you so much, but no one can love you as much as I do."[3] When Jane felt well enough to write even a few lines to her mother, she seldom addressed her dire predictions or commands. Bowles, too, had written Jane's mother over the years in an attempt to mollify her concerns, but upon his return home this time, he was ready to throw up his hands. "Claire Fuhs was a thorn in our sides for far too many years. As I saw it, we owed her nothing."[4]

Jane hated that the aphasia accompanying her original attack interfered with her recollection of even the simplest words and her ability to spell. Carla Grissman, a friend of both Bowles and Jane who taught English at the American School of Tangier and who lived for a time in the Inmeuble Itesa, did what she could to help, including the typing of countless letters dictated by Jane. Grissman sometimes added a few lines of her own to give a context to Jane's disconnected and repetitive messages.

Wakeful through much of the night while the rest of the household tried to sleep and insistent that Cherifa and the servants remain awake, too, Jane slept most of the day, binged on food then fasted, and telephoned incessantly to her once devoted friends. Smoking a great many cigarettes, a habit she had given up for years, and quaffing a fifth or more of liquor daily, with which she washed down an indeterminate number and variety of pills, all worked alternately as tranquilizer and stimulant. She also took the pills her mother's doctor in Miami had prescribed for her hypertension, high blood pressure, depression, and epilepsy, and had no inkling what might prove dangerous in combination with the drugs prescribed by Yvonne Marillier-Roux, her doctor in Tangier.[5] It was Dr. Roux who insisted that Bowles commit his wife for another indefinite stay in a psychiatric hospital or clinic, and he agreed. The closest and most accessible was in Málaga, to which visitors could travel in three hours.

To Virgil Thomson, Bowles reported that he had been in Málaga again and taken Jane out to lunch and tea. "Probably there will have to be electricity again. The general health risk isn't so great in spite of the arteriosclerosis, but my feeling is that it blots out whole departments of memory permanently."[6] In June 1967, Jane's doctors recommended shock treatment, and Bowles consented. When he saw her a month later, she had lost considerable weight and appeared to be much weaker than she had been in the spring, yet overall she seemed better. To Ned Rorem, Bowles wrote that he would have to establish her in a nearby hotel so that the doctor in Málaga could continue to observe her after she left the hospital, which he thought would be soon.[7] Jane had begged so insistently to be allowed to return to Tangier after three and a half months in the Sanatorio del Sagrado Corazón and a month in a nearby resident hotel that Bowles agreed, finally, to her being at home with supervised care. Jane also had been diagnosed as a manic-depressive, a condition that Bowles concluded was brought on by her stroke.

She had been out of the hospital and at home for a week when a team from *Life* magazine, Jane Howard and Terrence Spencer, arrived from New York to interview her and take photographs. "Her *Collected Works* had just been published by Farrar, Straus and Giroux, and Peter Owen had published her *Two Serious Ladies* in 1965 and *Plain Pleasures* in 1966, so it was a celebratory time for all of us," said Bowles. "The two people from *Life* were here for five days scribbling and snapping lenses, and Peter Owen and his wife were here, too. It was far too much activity for Jane just then, but I certainly could not tell her that."[8] Peter Owen said later that he remembered being served Jane's jugged hare and a chicken tajine with lemon and olives, and that it was the best meal he had ever had in Tangier."[9]

Bowles recalled, too, how pleased Jane was to be back in her own kitchen and cooking again. "When she felt well, she loved giving small dinner parties. The Jilala party to which we were all invited was to celebrate her return from Málaga and to show the visitors from *Life* an aspect of life in North Africa that they might otherwise miss."[10]

In his own detailed account of the Jilala party and the visitors from *Life*, Bowles wrote: "For a week and a half they stayed with us like our shadows–in the house, in the street, at the beach, and at whatever social engagements we had made. At a party given by John Hopkins, there was a group of Jilala musicians to entertain the guests. To Europeans, the music of the Jilala is Moroccan folk music being played on long, low-pitched transversal flutes and large flat hand drums. To a member of the cult, however, it is a sequence of explicit choreographic instructions, designed to bring about a state of trance, or possession." Mohammed Mrabet, a Jilali, began dancing, too, but his casual participation quickly became compulsive and, before anyone seemed to be aware of what was happening, he fell into a deep trance, followed shortly by a crash and an "explosion of burning embers" that showered the dancers. To the horror of the unsuspecting spectators from *Life* magazine and others unacquainted with such a dance, Mrabet produced a long curved knife and prepared to slash his arms and legs in a "ceremony of self-laceration." He was tackled by their host and three of the guests, but the "psychic shock of being interrupted in his ritual" was relieved only by the musicians, who played the necessary repetitive music to bring him out of his trance, which took almost an hour.[11]

After the trio from *Life* departed, Jane collapsed and spent a week in the hospital, then on her own decided to throw out all of the medicines she had been on for almost a decade. "She had two abdominal surgeries, the stitches having ripped out of the first, and nearly died of the pain," said Bowles. "Dr. Roux was horrified to see what had happened."[12]

To Ned Rorem, who had written of his concern for Jane's health, Bowles replied that he was leaving shortly on a brief motor trip into the Rif since it would be easier on Jane and her caregivers if he was not underfoot. "I should have stayed because on my return six days later I found Jane in even worse shape than before I left. She lies screaming all night, and no injection calms the pain. This preoccupation has kept me from doing much of anything, as I'm always on the alert for poundings on the ceiling by one of the maids summoning me."[13] At this point, Bowles returned the advance for his aborted book on Bangkok and recommended Alec Waugh in his stead. "Alex's book proved to be a far better book than mine would have been," he told Oliver Evans.[14]

From time to time during the past decade, an American college or university had invited Bowles to be a visiting professor, but he was never pressed for a decision after officials learned of his former membership in the American Communist Party. It was Evans, teaching now in the department of English at San Fernando State College in Northridge, California, who encouraged Bowles to accept a one-semester visiting professorship at a salary of eighteen thousand dollars. "Your only responsibility will be to conduct two three-hour classes a week and to be available to the students," Evans assured him.

Pessimistic as usual, Bowles doubted that he would receive clearance even if he wanted to accept. "It's happened five times to me before, this sort of offer, and it's always from a state-controlled institution, which means no ex-members."[15] He was still mulling over the possible scenarios when Jane astonished almost everyone who knew her by moving with Cherifa into the Hotel Atlas, situated in the heart of town. "None of us anticipated the commotion that followed. Naturally I went to see her, but for a month she refused to come home and insisted upon doing only what she chose."[16] When John Hopkins stopped by to say that he would be in New York for several weeks and to ask if there was anything he could do for them there, Bowles informed him that Jane was spending most of her time at the Parade Bar and "handing out money and drinks to every lush in Tangier." She also had gone through his bank account in a matter of days.

"'Talk to her,'" he pleaded.

Instead of the basket case Hopkins expected, he found Jane "dolled up" as if she was going to a party. "Completely manic, she was pacing the floor sipping a highball and cracking jokes in English, Spanish and Arabic. Her entourage of women were rolling on the floor bellowing with laughter. The odd thing was that she seemed completely sane–drunk, yes, but bursting with life and humor, whereas Paul appeared to be the neurotic one."[17]

To Frances Bishop, Bowles summarized Jane's present condition: "She began to deteriorate about two months ago, and the process went on and on, with terrible results, inasmuch as she went on a spending spree without my knowledge, emptied two bank accounts, and began to issue checks without provision. In this country that is considered a crime. The account in Tangier was a joint one, thus all blame fell on me. I've been paying off the debts a thousand dollars at a time, am on my third thousand now. I got her back to the hospital in Málaga ten days ago. One uninterrupted nightmare until then."[18] Bishop was surprised, given Bowles's insistence upon privacy, at how intimately he wrote her about Jane and their various problems concerning money.[19]

Again Bowles reconsidered the visiting appointment he had been offered. Although Jane's mother had urged him to take Jane with him to California, or to accompany her to Miami and put her in a psychiatric facility there, he saw no reason to do either. "Jane knows everyone at the sanatorium where she is, and the cost there is nearer $500 monthly instead of the insane cost at New York Hospital, where I had her in 1958. Naturally I am inclined to leave her in Spain," he replied.[20]

Finally, Bowles committed himself to "trying his hand at teaching" since his projected salary was considerably more than his royalties had earned him in any year as a writer. When he was asked to select the books he wished to use "in considering creative writing and a course in existentialism," Bowles was stymied. "I had no idea what goes on in a college classroom, how classes are conducted, who does the talking, and what the teaching process is."[21] Evans tried to reassure him and offered to send him books in advance so that he would feel better prepared. After cogitating in a manner not unlike Jane herself, Bowles asked for three books by Albert Camus (*The Stranger*, *The Plague*, and *Exile and the Kingdom*); two by Jean-Paul Sartre (*Intimacy* and *Nausea*); and one by Simone de Beauvoir (*The Blood of Others*). "I'm wondering if it wouldn't be useful to include, also, one expositional book on existentialism," he added. As the date drew nearer for his departure for California, Bowles became increasing nervous and worried that he might have to return home emergently, just as he had when he was summoned from Thailand.[22]

Finally, upon the recommendation of Dr. Roux, Bowles moved Jane to the Clínica de Reposo de los Angeles, a facility for women in

Málaga operated by a medical doctor, a mother superior, and a group of nuns. "Our friends assured me that they would visit Jane often and that I should take the teaching job and try not to worry," said Bowles. "Naturally, I did worry, but it seemed the best course of action for us both." In a letter to Jane before leaving, Bowles chided: "I've got letters from the doctor and from the Madre Superiora, but none from you."

Bowles was still in Tangier when John Hopkins visited Jane in Málaga on July 27, 1968. In his journal entry, Hopkins wrote: "A nun led me up the path through the garden to the sanatorium. It was nearing lunchtime and the ladies were sitting on the front porch, chattering to each other. My eyes went among them and picked out Jane sitting silent and alone on a bench in the back. The nun helped her to her feet. I kissed her, and she said: 'What are you doing here?' Two hours later I went away from that place. The life had been crushed out of her by drugs and by disease. There was no spirit left. She was ashamed of her shaggy appearance and told me not to ask other friends in Tangier to visit."[23]

Tamara Kamalakar Dragadze, whose mother was also a patient of Dr. Roux, declared: "Madame Roux told me that Jane would die and that I would have to accept it. So I went to see her in Málaga. At one point she became absolutely lucid when we were sitting in a café drinking tea and hot chocolate. When I suggested that I take her to the hairdresser, she asked me, instead, to take her away. 'We should run away together,' she said. I reacted in a rational way, all proper, and said no. We got into a taxi and I took her back to the nuns. I never saw her again."[24]

On September 7, 1967, Bowles left from Algeciras for New York, where at Andreas Brown's request, he gave a private reading at the Gotham Book Mart. "It was the least I could do for Andreas since he had been generous to me. I suppose I thought that my reading at the Gotham might help get me ready to face my students, about which I was still apprehensive, but it mattered little." Upon his arrival in Los Angeles, Bowles was met by Oliver Evans, who announced that they were having dinner that evening with Christopher Isherwood and

Don Bachardy, whom Bowles had not seen since Yacoubi served them *majoun* in Morocco without warning. Later, he wrote: "We were to have dinner a few nights later with Tennessee Williams, who was in Los Angeles for a revival of *Camino Real.* It was obvious that Tennessee was drinking heavily and strung out on drugs. It was not long afterwards that he ended up in the psychiatric wing of a hospital in Saint Louis and claimed to have almost died. I did not mention then Jane's dire condition since it resembled too closely his own problems at the time."[25]

To Bowles, Williams declared a few weeks later: "If it is true that Janie has been hospitalized, I hope it is under much better circumstances than those that my brother subjected me to, and which I barely survived. I had two heart attacks and three convulsions in one day. . . . I believe two things are responsible for Janie's condition: that witch Cherifa and the premature edition of her 'collected' works. Her stay with the 'sisters' in the 'casa de reposa' will give her new materials that will demand expression. We must have faith."[26]

Jane herself had no such hope, and Bowles had very little. Although he wanted desperately to believe that she would get better, he knew that she would not. "I had passed the stage of being devastated, and despite Tennessee's assurances, faith in her recuperative powers and her doctors would have been, in Jane's words, 'a lark.'"[27]

When David Herbert visited Jane in Málaga, he brought with him some reviews of the collected edition of her works, hoping that they would cheer her up. "Janie made me read them to her. For a little while, she said nothing, then, hopelessly, she said: 'I know you meant this kindly, darling, but you couldn't have done anything more cruel! It all makes me realize what I was and what I have become.'"

"Seeing that I was terribly upset, Janie looked at me with a ghost of a smile. 'Give me the book,' she said. I handed her *The Collected Works*. With trembling hand she picked up a pencil and added '*of Dead Jane Bowles*.' She had not quite lost her touch for mingling the absurd with the tragic."[28]

Bowles was still in California when William Targ, a senior editor at

G. P. Putnam's Sons, expressed an interest in publishing his autobiography, but wished to see a detailed proposal first. In response, Bowles devised a list of events and people in an effort to recapture the material year by year. His intention was to begin the memoir with a section dealing with happenings "before memory begins," then to relive, in a sense, and recapture his evolvement from early to late childhood while stressing "the opposing pressures of the paternal and maternal family groups and the resulting need for developing secrecy."[29] Bowles's five-page proposal concluded with his visiting professorship and his return to Tangier.

Just as he had once observed while writing *The Sheltering Sky* that he did not know what would happen next until he had experienced its counterpart in his own life, so too did Bowles prepare his memoir with a similar trajectory. "It's no wonder that I called it *Without Stopping*, just as I had written its predecessor by the same name at my desk on that bookstore balcony on Fifth Avenue. I knew I could not stop writing my memoir until I had lived that very moment on the page itself."[30]

Although he had not yet signed a contract, Bowles admitted that the proposed fifteen-thousand-dollar advance would ease his financial demands considerably since he was, in effect, maintaining Jane's residence in Málaga and their adjoining flats in Tangier.[31] On June 7, 1969, having brought Jane home for a few days, Bowles wrote Oliver Evans that she talked with great difficulty, and understood with equal difficulty; moreover, she had become deaf and seemed barely aware of her environment. "She is nothing but bones with skin stretched over them, and she refuses to eat unless the food is put into her mouth." At month's end, Bowles escorted Jane back to the clinic.

Three months later, the Moroccan police confiscated his passport and refused to let him out of the country unless it was to be a permanent departure. To Andreas Brown, Bowles wrote: "We are now prisoners in the country, in the sense that if an American leaves Morocco he can't get back in, as it has been declared off-limits [by the State Department] for U.S. citizens. As long as Americans stay where they are everything is all right."[32] The ban prohibiting American citizens from returning to Morocco after they exited the country applied also to Jane, despite her having a documented medical record supporting her departure. The ban, also, stopped Bowles's visits to Málaga to see Jane. After six weeks the ruling was rescinded, and Jane, in a rare moment of lucidity in August 1971, begged him to take her back with him to Tangier, but the doctors and nuns urged him not to. With Bowles's consent a few weeks later, Jane converted to Roman Catholicism upon the assurance that she could be buried in the Catholic cemetery near the hospital.

Scarcely six weeks before Jane's death Bowles wrote Carol Ardman, a writer from New York who spent considerable time in Tangier during the early 1970s and had just returned home. "Victor Kraft was here, saying he had been to see Jane and had communicated with her by putting his finger between her teeth, and having her bite once for yes and twice for no."[33]

Meanwhile, after working on *Without Stopping* for almost three years, Bowles decided that he had written enough. "It is clear that telling what happened does not necessarily make a good story. In my tale, for instance, there are no dramatic victories because there was no struggle." He braced himself for his editor's suggestions for revision, but was skeptical that he could revise to suit him. "Yet I reasoned that since I had accepted a nice advance, I was obliged to give my editor and the marketing people a saleable product, but not a salacious one. I've never been able to be single-minded about any project to the exclusion of all others, although I think I have met my obligations. My work, my life, was layered, and I was careful to allow only a few friends to see beneath the surface."[34]

By mid-February 1972, Bowles had finished his autobiography, read the galleys, and made more than a thousand corrections. "Yes, I counted each one," he added.[35] After reading the corrected copy, his editor urged him to "flesh out" the people in his life who had been most important to him, to which Bowles replied: "For years critics have objected to the facelessness of my fictional people, although that is deliberate on my part. I did not have reactions to people as people, but only as faces to propel me, as a glider uses air-currents. I have been very careful to keep hazy recall and invention out of the chronicle."[36] He said that he also wanted to avoid writing anything that might offend those with whom he had interacted over the years, whether they were living or dead. "Besides, places have always been more important to me than people. . . . My dreams are seldom of people; they are almost always of places, directions, relative positions of objects around me. The human beings in them are faceless. . . . If the mention of people whom I have glimpsed on my way past them lacks precision in describing them, it is only because I never really *saw* them or thought about them, since for me they were manipulatable objects to be used or somehow got around, in order to continue my trajectory. It's a bit late now to try to give them personalities."[37]

On March 25, 1972, G. P. Putnam's Sons published seven thousand copies of *Without Stopping: An Autobiography*, and Bowles waited skeptically for the reviews. The earliest was Anatole Broyard's in the *New York Times*, its headline proclaiming "A Talent for Traveling." The review was largely a summary of the events of Bowles's life, and withheld judgment on the book as a whole. Broyard did note that the ambiguous nature of Bowles's relationship to his wife was "never clarified, owing to Bowles's belief that, in an autobiography, one ought to 'reserve judgment and give a minimum importance to personal attitudes.'" The "cool and detached tone" of *Without Stopping* he mentioned only in passing.[38]

A review of greater substance was Virgil Thomson's "Untold Tales" in the *New York Review of Books*: "I would not have expected out of him either 'confessions' or true-story gossip, anything indiscreet or scabrous. But Paul has always been so delicious in talk, games, laughter and companionship, so unfailingly gifted for both music and letters, so assiduous in meeting his deadlines with good work, so relentless in his pursuit of authenticity among his own ethnic associates, that it is a bit surprising to find oneself in the same flat pattern of casual acquaintance that includes everybody else he ever knew. His life, as told, unrolls like a travelogue."[39]

Ned Rorem's review of *Without Stopping* in the *New Republic* did not set well with Bowles either. "Scores of names are dropped with no further identification than their spelling, while close acquaintances vanish and die without so much as an editorial sign from their friend. He displays no envy of competitors, no sign of carnal or intellectual passion. His one obsession would seem to be for investigation–not of the heart, which even his fiction avoids–but of the body as affected by foreign cultures, by the implacability of nature, exotic cuisine, ill health, hard drugs, but never, never by sex."[40]

For over a year and a half, Bowles refrained from commenting upon the reviews by either Thomson or Rorem since he could neither agree with nor refute what each had written. "Obviously, if the reviews had been favorable, I shouldn't have taken umbrage. What I want is not tranquility, as you put it, and not happiness–merely survival. Life needn't be pleasurable or amusing; it need only continue playing its program."[41]

Bowles considered the most insightful essay on his memoir to be Marilyn Moss's "The Child in the Text: Autobiography, Fiction, and the Aesthetics of Deception in *Without Stopping*," written while Moss was a doctoral student at the University of California, Berkeley. As she saw it, Bowles was able to recall or construct events microscopically, but chose to aim vision "outward, not interiorly to investigate himself in the text. . . . He does, indeed, move rapidly and 'without stopping,' his sequential narratives now perpetuating themselves of their own volition as if stopping to reflect would pose a clear and present danger, and as if the catalogue of those names to postulate his life and text were, for the most part, not integral to these narratives."[42] It seemed to Moss that in her subject's attempt to conceal himself, he had "paradoxically created an exquisitely intimate representation of his own psychology. If deception leads to fiction, as it did for Bowles the child, then *Without Stopping* is his greatest fiction to date, and his greatest fiction of himself."[43]

Later, Bowles remarked: "I may not have liked everything Miss Moss said, but I like the way she said it."[44]

CHAPTER FIFTEEN

Without Jane

(1973–1999)

"There is nothing to keep me here now, save habit, but I shall probably stay on until outer circumstances force me to leave."[1]

—Paul Bowles to Audrey Wood,
Tangier, May 11, 1973

After Jane's death on May 4, 1973, there were no significant outer circumstances to provoke Bowles's departure from Morocco. "My irritants were much closer to home, and I dealt with them, or ignored them, on a day-to-day basis," he said.[2] To Howard Griffin, who had recently visited and mailed him a parcel upon his return to the United States, Bowles wrote that his driver was certain it was a letter bomb and would not let him open it in the car. "Instead, he took it into the courtyard of the market and slit open its backside very carefully with a wire. I think he was annoyed to discover that it wasn't what he thought."[3]

Jane's obituary appeared in the *New York Times* on May 31, 1973. In addition to the facts of her life and career, it included a passage from John Ashbery's review of Jane's *Collected Stories* in the *New York Times Book Review*, in which he declared: "Jane Bowles is a writer's writer. Few literary reputations are as glamorous as the underground one she has enjoyed since her novel, *Two Serious Ladies*, was published in 1943. The extreme rarity of the book, once it went out of print, has augmented its legend. When a London publisher [Peter Owen] wanted to reprint it three years ago, even Mrs. Bowles was unable to supply him with a copy. Jane Bowles has at last surfaced. It is to be hoped that she will be recognized for what she is: one of the finest modern writers of fiction in any language. At the same time it should be pointed out that she is not quite the sort of writer that her imposing list of Establishment admirers seem to suggest. Her work is unrelated to theirs, and in fact stands alone in contemporary literature."

To Virgil Thomson, Bowles observed: "No one's personal life can be satisfactory in Morocco, as we all know. Perhaps the best thing about the place is the feeling it gives one of being in a pocket of suspended time and animation." To Bowles, the months went past without enough happening to make landmarks along the way. "Unless one wants to talk about his soul-state, there is little to write about to your friends," he added.[4]

Bowles's first literary project after Jane's death was putting together a volume of posthumous writings. Virgil Thomson sent him a packet of what few letters he had kept, for which Bowles thanked him, then added: "I didn't find any of them outstanding, which is too bad. I have a feeling that Jane's best letters were sent to people who didn't save them, like me."[5]

Tennessee Williams acknowledged that in recent years he never kept letters once he had answered them, if he answered them at all. Since he had none of Jane's to contribute, he proposed writing a foreword to the volume.[6] "I was deeply touched by Tennessee's 'Foreword,'" said Bowles, who insisted that for him, "Jane still lives."[7]

In the spring of 1977, Bowles and Jane's newly declared biographer, Millicent Dillon, were luncheon guests of Alec and Virginia Waugh when the subject of Jane's unmarked grave came up. After corresponding with Bowles before making her initial trip to Tangier, Dillon settled in for six weeks of conversations, interviews, and assorted engagements with a number of people who knew Jane well, most especially with Bowles himself. It was Virginia Waugh who had first mentioned Jane's fiction to Dillon while both were guests at the MacDowell Colony in Peterborough, New Hampshire. Waugh told Dillon that Jane was her friend, and that she was very ill in a convent hospital in Málaga, Spain. Until then, Dillon, who had published both a novel and a book of short fiction, had never come across Jane's work, and she was interested in learning more about her. Several weeks later, Dillon read Jane's obituary in the *New York Times* and learned that she had died only a few days before Waugh brought Jane to her attention.[8]

On April 7, 1975, twenty-three months after Jane's death, John Hopkins recorded in his *Tangier Diaries* that he and Joseph McPhillips had made a pilgrimage to Jane's grave, but had difficulty locating it in the San Miguel Cemetery, a Catholic graveyard on a hill overlooking Málaga. "In the end, one of the gardeners led us to it," wrote Hopkins. "It was lower than the others because there were no tiles; there wasn't even a cross. Only a stick with a number on it: 453-F. We stood around and stared at it for a while, clutching our flowers. The brief moment of satisfaction at having found it was quickly swept away by the realization [that] we were looking at Jane Bowles's unmarked grave. It had become the refuse dump of broken flower pots and bottles and dead stalks cast aside by the assiduous ladies in black." Hopkins was reminded that the last time he had seen Jane was in the summer of 1968 at the Clínica. "The nun had led her out, and we sat for an hour on the terrace. She had seemed numb or drugged, her speech disjointed and halting but coherent. She looked terrible and knew it. Her life was already over. . . . She must have welcomed death and even prayed for it."[9]

Bowles recalled later that while Jane was still able to communicate she had asked him to give her love to Tennessee. "Naturally I wanted him to know at once that she had died, but had no idea where to find him." From Positano, Italy, Williams wrote Bowles six weeks after her death: "The news about Jane was delivered to me in the most shocking fashion. Audrey Wood handed a sealed legal-size envelope to Bill Barnes, my new agent, with no remark except 'This will interest Tennessee.' He [Barnes] had no idea of its contents when he gave it to me, and the opening line of your letter went through me like a knife and for one of the rare occasions in my life I burst into a torrent of tears. Perhaps I should have been prepared but I certainly wasn't. Recently Bill Inge killed himself [at the age of sixty in 1973]. I have done an homage to him which will appear in the *New York Times*. I hope they don't cut out the final paragraph which concerns the loss of Jane, of whom I said: 'I am not alone in regarding Jane as the finest writer of the century in English prose-fiction.' I had also written an homage entirely for Jane, but it was just before my departure for Italy and I didn't feel it was given sufficient time. It's strange: the playwright Harold Pinter and I had planned to visit Jane together in Málaga this month. He had precisely the same opinion of her work as mine."[10]

To Daniel Halpern, whose journal *Antaeus* Bowles had helped found, he wrote: "If I haven't written, it's because I've been in Spain. Jane died last Friday. You could do me a favor if you'd tell some of her friends. Eventually I can write them all, but at the moment I have neither the energy nor the time to write a series of letters. The burial was completely private, in the chapel of the Sagrado Corazón cemetery in Málaga. I'll write again when I'm a bit more tranquil."[11]

Bowles continued writing to both his and Jane's friends, making each letter personal. To Carol Ardman, who came often to Tangier, he wrote on May 11, 1973: "A week ago yesterday I received a telegram from the doctor in Málaga asking me to go there as quickly as possible because Jane was gravely ill. At the clinic I found Jane unconscious. She had had another stroke on Monday night." At nine, now back at the hotel, Bowles received a call from the Mother Superior. "So at last, after sixteen years of anguish, it is over."[12]

To Jane's publisher, Peter Owen, Bowles wrote: "Jane died last week. I thought you as both friend and publisher ought to be informed. It was a long trial for her, these past sixteen years, and I'm thankful she doesn't have to undergo any more suffering."[13] Upon receiving Bowles's letter, Owen immediately wrote an obituary for the London *Times*:

> Jane Bowles, the American writer, has died in Málaga, aged 55, after a long illness. She is best known for her novel, *Two Serious Ladies*,

which was first published in the USA in 1943, where it soon acquired a reputation as a book of unusual wit and originality and subsequently became known as a contemporary classic. It remained out of print for many years, despite a spiraling "underground" demand, until the English publisher Peter Owen acquired the world rights and published a British edition in 1965, henceforth acting as Jane Bowles's international agent, and arranging for many foreign translations and the American republication of her *Collected Works* with an introduction by Truman Capote, who referred to her as "that modern legend, one of the original pure stylists." She was revered as a stylist by many contemporary writers, among them Tennessee Williams, who commented on *Two Serious Ladies*: "My favorite book. I can't think of a modern novel that seems more likely to become an imperishable work, which I suppose means a classic."

In the spring of 1977 when Virginia Waugh told Bowles that a "movement had been initiated by some expatriates in Tangier to take up a collection for a stone for Jane's grave," he stiffened, then declared in a quiet but resolute voice, "I don't want a cross on Jane's grave. As far as I'm concerned, she has no grave. The marker would be a symbol that someone is there. But she was never there. Only a body is there. I don't believe in cemeteries."[14]

By this time, Bowles had resumed his collaboration with Mohammed Mrabet, but was impatient to begin a new work of his own. Ostensibly its impetus was a request by Ira Cohen for a poem he wished to publish for his Starstreams Poetry Series that he had established in Kathmandu, Nepal. Cohen did not want "just any poem"; he wanted a long poem of ten to twelve pages in the form of a dream that would "stand alone as a book."

In February 1975, Cohen received the manuscript he had requested, now titled *Next to Nothing*. "It's unlike what I'd imagined it would be like," Bowles told him in an accompanying note. "You may not consider it even remotely dreamlike, but then, one man's dream is another man's reality." Bowles knew that having written the poem, he would send it elsewhere at once if it did not suit Cohen's purpose.

"It was certainly the most extraordinary looking book of all of my writings with its handmade Nepalese papers between brown tissue leaves, each copy unique. I was very impressed, more so by its production than the poem itself," Bowles wrote Cohen. A few days later he noted that the *Soho News* had listed *Next to Nothing* as one of its alternative best-sellers. "Charles Henri Ford writes that there's a pile next to the cash-register, and that 'it *sells*!' Naturally I'm very glad, even though it makes everything seem very mysterious. I can't help asking myself who buys it. And why, apart from its exotic packaging, would anyone lay out $6.95 for a 'poem' which is not even by a poet?" A year later he was astonished to find that a rare book dealer had listed *Next to Nothing* in his catalog for $150.

In the spring of 1994, Bowles read with interest a discussion of *Next to Nothing* in Gena Dagel Caponi's *Paul Bowles: Romantic Savage*, but the book's subtitle gave him pause. "Romantic, indeed!" he snorted. "In Professor Caponi's dissertation she identified me as a 'manufactured savage,' which Gertrude Stein once called me; and now I see that I am a 'romantic savage.'"[15] Bowles inspected the book, looked over its table of contents and notes, scrutinized the pictures, flipped through the index, then turned to the pages pertaining to *Next to Nothing* from which she had quoted. These he read closely.[16]

"*Next to Nothing* turns out to be the most eloquent and final expression of ideas that had obsessed Bowles for years," she declared. "Qualitatively, *Next to Nothing* stands apart from the rest of Bowles's poetry. For a reader familiar with his life story, it holds great emotional power." Then she noted a section that "could refer with equal strength to the Bowleses' marriage or to their life in Tangier":

On our way out we used the path that goes around the swamp.
When we started back the tide had risen.

. . .

There were many things I wanted to say to you
before you left, and now I shall never say them.
Though the light spills onto the balcony
making the same shadows in the same places,
only I can see it, only I can hear the wind
and it is much too loud.
The world seethes with words. Forgive me.[17]

Bowles smiled as he read the excerpts Caponi had singled out and her comments accompanying them. "Yes, that's true. . . . She's right. . . . I like what she says here," he said, his voice barely audible.

The next afternoon, Bowles announced that he wanted to read Caponi's book again, this time from start to finish. Then, with pen in hand, he offered to make a few corrections marginally in the text "for the record, in case there's a second printing." Again, Bowles paused at Caponi's observations regarding *Next to Nothing*. "Very perceptive," he declared. Then he closed the book, tucked it under his arm, and headed down the hall to the guest bedroom of his biographer, Virginia Spencer Carr. "I think I'm going to lie down for a while," he said, patting Caponi's book.[18]

In the autumn of 1974, while still working on his poem for Ira Cohen, Bowles began corresponding with Alec France, a doctoral student in the South who wrote of his keen interest in Bowles's writings. Intrigued by what lay beneath the surface of certain stories, France posed a number of questions, to which Bowles replied carefully:

> I follow you in your concern with exactly what purpose I put language to, but not in your assumption that one necessarily uses words in only one of two possible ways. . . . My own design has been to re-create reality in such a way that it becomes unreal. There is no way of doing that unless unreality can be made to seem as real as the original reality. Then it isn't fantasy, but still a recognizable kind of reality.[19]

In another letter to Alec France, Bowles declared that their writing to each other had helped solidify his own thoughts while composing his poem for Ira Cohen:

> *Without Stopping*, of course, has no revelation. On the contrary, everything is covered, but there are clues everywhere. I have several which I thought showed the presence of excessive compulsiveness and overriding anguish. . . . One might have thought that the angst would diminish as time went on, but instead, it increased to the point of being well-nigh unbearable. The writing of music . . . was useless for helping to reduce the tension. But then I discovered that fiction-writing, by fanning the angst until it was at "white-heat," produced a sort of immunity from the abiding worry. . . . My problem was continuing to live from one day to the next without exploding. . . . Then I discovered that kif was a brake on the reaching of the white-heat. As soon as I realized that, all the compulsiveness, all the angst and nightmares, vanished."[20]

On March 27, 1975, Bowles responded to a final round of questions from Alec France, to which he had no reply.

Surprised when his correspondence with Alec France ended abruptly without closure, Bowles attributed the silence to ill health and wrote again. "Then I received a note from Alec's widow, saying that he had committed suicide. I never heard the particulars and I did not pry, but the knowledge of his death made me very sad."[21]

Meanwhile, Bowles's collaboration with Mohammed Mrabet slowed significantly after Jane's death, Mrabet having been diagnosed with hepatitis and complications from a variety of ailments.

Bowles wrote John Martin, whose Black Sparrow Press had published two of Mrabet's books in 1976: "It's not the rendering of the oral Arabic texts into written English that makes collaborating with Mrabet difficult, but trying to help him maintain some sort of diplomatic relationship with the outside world. Long ago I learned that when he dictates a letter he uses me purely as a machine. 'I asked you to write a letter, not to make suggestions,' he admonished. He knows enough English to be aware of any alteration in the text, as I've discovered when he has crumpled a slightly changed missive and tossed it into the fireplace."[22]

At this point, Bowles was more concerned with how far his fixed income could carry him if he, too, became sick, than he was with Mrabet's argumentative nature. "If one has to live on the identical income one had in 1965, as I do, one's activities are forcibly reduced. Even one's diet!"[23] To numerous correspondents Bowles complained that in addition to the rising cost of living and the unavailability of all manner of desired commodities, the legality of his residency was being challenged. He was told that since he had not received permission to be in Morocco from 1975 to 1976, he was there illegally, thus could have neither a renewal of his visa nor permission to travel to Ceuta or Gibraltar. If he left the country for any reason he would be disqualified from applying for a reentry visa. "The only explanation the police can give me is that I've been here too long, but Abdelouahaid says it's all a question of a big enough bribe."[24]

To Peter Garland, who lived in Santa Fe, New Mexico, and wrote Bowles that he was compiling a volume of his songs, he replied: "What a rattlesnake den you uncovered when you decided to collect my songs. I have lived in the same very small flat for twenty-seven years and have accumulated far more books and papers than I have room for or can keep up with—all lie together in piles in suitcases, cupboards, on brass trays, more or less everywhere."[25]

For several years Bowles had listened politely to well-meaning friends who suggested that he move into a larger flat or build a house of his own in the country and wall out the intrusions to which he objected. If pressed, he scoffed at the idea, declaring that since he lived on a fixed income, such action was out of the question. Yet he found himself entertaining the idea, and with Abdelouahaid Boulaich went often into the hills and countryside along the strait east of Tangier to consider the view and imagine what it might be like to have such a home as a summer place remote from visitors.

Frances Bishop was one of the few outsiders to whom he wrote of the possibility of building a house. In one letter, he wrote that the construction had actually begun, and that he had put the house in Boulaich's name since foreigners were no longer allowed to buy or own agricultural land in the country. On October 3, 1979, he declared: "The little house I've been constructing out in the country, perhaps thirty-five miles east along the Strait, is still growing; at the moment a well is being dug. . . . Next, there has to be a fireplace, and I suppose some day a pump to get the water out of the well." Bowles wondered if he would ever spend a night in it, or if he would drop dead before it was done.[26]

In 1986 Cherie Nutting wrote of her first visit to Abdelouahaid's "country house":

> Today, Paul, Abdelouahaid, his son Mohammed, and I drove toward Ksar el Seghir on the Mediterranean coast. We took the coastal route, passing an old fortress on our way, toward Djebel Moussa, which is the Moroccan counterpart to the Rock of Gibraltar. Abdelouahaid's house sat on a hill at the end of a dusty trail in Farsioua. It was surmounted by turrets and surrounded by fig trees. Kaftans hung from the whitewashed adobe walls and opaque white curtains waved gently in the breeze. . . . On the terrace overlooking the sea, we smoked kif.

Nutting observed later that she "had no idea that the house was actually Pablo's [Paul's]. Surely by then he must have considered it Abdelouahaid's house, which it was, of course, since it was in his name."[27]

Although it was Jane who observed originally that they "lived on people passing by," Bowles recognized that very little had changed in that regard either, although people he was not expecting often had difficulty finding him. To Peter Garland, Bowles observed: "I work and entertain visitors to Tangier, of whom there always seem to be a good many. They come and ring the doorbell, saying they've read this or that, or that Whoozits has told them to look me up."[28]

In 1980 Bowles was prevailed upon to conduct a summer seminar in fiction writing at the invitation of the New York School of Visual Arts in collaboration with the American School of Tangier, and he agreed "to try it for a summer." Joseph McPhillips, headmaster of the school since 1973, saw the collaboration with the New York School of Visual Arts as a means of helping finance the school's operation during its academic year. "Even my teaching in California in 1968 cost me more than I earned, and I decided that I simply did not want to relocate again. Having students come to me at the American School and sometimes to my own flat, *did* appeal to me, especially as a means of coping with the outrageous inflation rampant then. I accepted eleven students in my first workshop."[29]

Bowles was impressed by one student who stood out that summer, a young Guatemalan named Rodrigo Rey Rosa. "He spoke very little English, and like most of the other students, had never submitted anything for publication. I don't know how he thought he could profit from that class. No one else spoke Spanish, but he knew intuitively that I did, so we communicated that way, and everything he wrote was in Spanish. He had a great imagination and knew how to create atmosphere quickly. One of the stories he was working on then was published the following year by the Red Ozier Press in a signed, limited, and numbered edition. He asked me if I would like to translate it, and of course I did. . . . He was a natural writer. Before long he had some twenty-five stories ready, and I began translating those, too. In 1985, they were published by City Lights Books as *The Beggar's Knife*."[30]

Bowles had no idea how the workshop was originally announced and promoted, but when he agreed to conduct it a second year, the New York School of Visual Arts published an advertisement in the *New York Review of Books* announcing a "Paul Bowles Writing Workshop in Morocco." It was promoted as "an intensive writing workshop for serious students on the thirty-one-acre campus of the American School of Tangier with class size limited to allow ample time for personalized instruction and criticism. You will be encouraged to pursue your own individual projects, either novels or short stories. Students will be accepted on the basis of submitted manuscripts." This time the workshop was scheduled for two three-week sessions and met twice a week. Most students stayed for both sessions.

To Peter Garland, Bowles wrote on August 24, 1981, that his classes were over until next year, and that his students were better. "They seemed to understand more about the construction of sentences; whereas I had spent considerable time trying to teach my students at San Fernando Valley State College to write proper English, and hours at a stretch marking mechanical errors and inappropriate word choice before commenting upon what appeared to make their stories work, or not work. The new group already knew how to write, but the trick was getting them to write something that others found compelling."[31]

There was still a third summer session of fiction writing conducted by Bowles the following year. On August 21, 1982, he reported to Virginia Waugh that his classes had finally ended last week. "Not that I didn't enjoy them, but the work involved such a great deal of reading of manuscripts that I had no time for anything else. . . . At the moment I have a list of twenty-nine unanswered missives. Your letter came this afternoon, so it wasn't necessary to add it to the list." To another correspondent, Bowles wrote: "A letter which I haven't answered is like a time-bomb. The only way to defuse it is to reply."[32]

It seemed to Bowles that the political situation in Morocco was uneven at best during the early 1990s. "I remember being fined upon claiming a package sent to me that contained only a jar of jam, but the postal authority declared that it was an insult to Morocco since there was 'perfectly good jam made here.' It made no difference that I had not ordered it, and that it was not my fault someone had seen fit to send it to me, but they were inflexible. Their response was that I should not have been consorting with people who believed Morocco to be an under-developed country. They've been burning the American flag publicly, and the streets are empty of tourists."[33]

To Peter Garland, who found himself spending far more time collecting Bowles's songs than he had envisioned, Bowles ventured that he sometimes regretted having spent so many years writing music. "No one's fault but mine, of course, but I can still regret the wasted time. But I imagine that on one's deathbed all time must seem to have been wasted. So, wasted or used to 'advantage,' it all comes to the same thing."[34]

Meanwhile, Jeffrey Miller, a scholar and bibliographer who lived in the Bay Area of California, completed in 1983 with Bowles's cooperation a meticulously researched book titled *Paul Bowles: A Descriptive Bibliography*, published by John Martin, founder of Black Sparrow Press, which had published Bowles's first book of poetry, *Scenes*, in 1968, and a second collection of poems titled *Thicket of Spring* in 1972. Miller decided that his next project would be a collection of Bowles's extant letters for publication. Upon proposing the book, he declared that he would do the actual work if Bowles would write a brief letter that Miller would send out to Bowles's several hundred correspondents, along with Miller's own letter of intent. Although amenable to the proposal, Bowles cautioned Miller that some people might not find his letters "all that interesting." Miller also asked Bowles to collaborate with him in the selection and final editing of the letters, and suggested that if he agreed, they would split the royalties. Bowles replied: "I doubt that there will be any." He also declared that despite his wanting no introduction to his collected stories, to be published by Black Sparrow Press in 1979, John Martin was adamant that there be one. "But who?" Bowles asked. "So having respect for Vidal's critical mind I chose him rather than taking a chance on someone the publisher might find."[35]

Many of Bowles's friends sent copies of reviews of his collected stories as soon as they were discovered, and the volume as a whole was considered highly successful. Richard Dyer informed readers of the *Boston Globe* that "most of the stories tackle cross-cultural themes that have often been the traffic of novelists," but that Bowles presented them with the "resonant condensation of incident and the vivid specificity of imagery characteristic of poetry; all of them are 'composed' both in the sense of 'carefully fashioned' and in the sense of 'keeping on an even keel,' no matter how violent and terrifying the incidents might be. In all of them Bowles writes out of a sensibility that is foreign, or at least remote from the American ordinary."

"He writes as if *Moby Dick* had never been written," noted Gore Vidal in his introduction to the collection.

Joyce Carol Oates wrote for the *New York Times* that "this handsomely bound collection, a companion to *The Thicket of Spring* which brought together four decades of Bowles's poetry, should strengthen the author's somewhat amorphous position in our literature. Like Bowles's novels, the best of these stories are beautifully fashioned and as bleakly unconsolable as the immense deserts about which he writes with such power. They have a way of lingering in the memory for decades–disturbing, vexing, like a partly-recalled dream. The reader is advised to approach them with caution, however, limiting himself to one or two at a sitting, beginning perhaps with the wonderful 'Pastor Dowe at Tacaté.'"[36]

In the fall of 1980, Bowles was invited into membership of the American Academy and Institute of Arts and Letters and informed that he had been nominated by Joyce Carol Oates and seconded by Ned Rorem and Susan Sontag. Upon being notified by Rorem of his nomination, Bowles thanked him, adding, "I take it that to be elected is purely honorary, and would involve no responsibilities on my part. (I don't really know what the institution is, or what it does, or what it means. You might be able to tell me in one sentence.)"[37] Since membership did not require his appearing for the induction ceremony in New York, Bowles accepted.

When Michael Lee interviewed Bowles for *Trafika*, a journal published in Prague, he asked if Bowles ever consciously tried to construct an image of himself for others. "No, my God! I probably repel some people, attract others, interest some, leave others cold. But to imagine that one has a fixed image which doesn't change? . . . One is whatever one is at the moment, but it doesn't mean anything. One has a name, but the name really has nothing to do with oneself. It's exterior. Is it important to be conscious of one's identity? I don't think it matters. . . . As soon as one gets the concept that one has an image, then one is hooked with the idea, which I don't think is very healthy."[38]

A spate of critical articles and unexpected appearances of countless journalists and other writers seeking interviews at Bowles's door increased significantly in the 1980s and 1990s. Many petitioners were interested in meeting Mrabet and were pleased if it was he who let them in. "Such visitors seemed both curse and blessing, yet I suppose at the time I was flattered by the attention, and certainly Mrabet was. It was something to do, and although we met some interesting people, I don't think the various interviews added anything to our pocketbooks. Of course, it may have contributed something to their own. Abdelouahaid urged me to start charging for interviews, but that did not seem right either."[39]

In the fall of 1984, Bowles flew to Bern, Switzerland, for treatment for cancer of the prostate gland, which required surgery and hospitalization for a month. On September 2, he wrote Millicent Dillon that he was more ill now than when he was in Switzerland, an infection having set in that "masses of sulpha drugs" and "two intramusculars" each day did little to assuage. If it were not for Mrabet's cooking him three meals a day and serving him in bed, Bowles was skeptical that his weight could be "pushed up above one hundred pounds."[40]

Although Bowles eventually regained enough strength to walk with care, his eyesight remained poor and he chafed at the thought of perhaps having to live out his remaining years in perpetual ill health. Two years later, Bowles developed what the doctors identified as an aneurysm in his right knee, which interfered with the circulation in his lower leg and foot. "I felt an increasing numbness below the knee of my right leg, and my right foot had become almost unbearably cold. In mid-September I was operated on in Rabat to sever my sympathetic nerve, after which it was painful either to walk or to remain seated."

To Peter Garland, Bowles declared that in order to save his leg from gangrene he must have the sympathetic nerve severed in his torso. "So anyway, at this point I'm still alive, which occasionally surprises me when I think about it."[41] Bowles also told Garland that he had just finished correcting the translations into French of two of his books ("neither the work of Claude Thomas"), and was "appalled that one had 290 errors and the other 184."

Bowles's friends were amused by his precise count in noting such errors. In his memoir, *Second Son: An Autobiography*, David Herbert attributed Bowles's compulsion to count things to his being meticulous. "I once had a headache and asked Janie if she had any aspirin. 'No, but look in Paul's medicine cabinet,' she said. I did, and took two. The following day Paul said; 'Janie, did you take two aspirins out of the bottle?' 'No, but David did.' 'Oh, that's all right. I just wondered because the last time I took one there were seventy-three left in the bottle, and now there are only seventy-one."[42] Herbert's memoir was in press when his publisher asked Bowles if he would be willing to write a foreword to it. Bowles accepted, but noted that Tennessee Williams had written his own foreword to his memoirs, about which he declared later: "Tennessee's *Memoirs* gave me an epidermal affliction. My skin crawled for the entire time it took me to get through it. Simple embarrassment at the strip-tease of the soul. And then the added discomfort of the writing. Or was it written? Dictated, recorded, transcribed, perhaps, and never reread? Nothing else could account for the sloppiness of the writing. Agony."[43] Upon reading Williams's obituary in 1983, Bowles declared: "One accepts car accidents, bathtub accidents, falling from a ladder while painting the kitchen, and those more common causes of death. But swallowing the top of a bottle of eye-drops seems very far-fetched of fate."[44]

In 1987 journalist Michelle Green wrote Bowles that she had decided to write a "sort of 'Peyton Place Goes to Tangier'" book that would feature him and a number of his expatriate literary friends and acquaintances who had lived for a time in Tangier, or had stayed and were still there. Green said that when she failed to hear from Bowles, she decided to go anyway. "I showed up in the afternoon, at tea time, and he claimed never to have got the letter. But he let me in. He is the most accessible eccentric in the world." Green stayed three weeks, then returned twice the following year.

"I'll give her this–she did her homework well," said Bowles. "She talked to a lot of other people in Tangier whom she thought of as old-timers, as well as with people like Christopher Wanklyn in Marrakesh; she also dug though old newspapers in the library of the American Legation. I thought her casual and breezy manner a welcome contrast to what I later considered Christopher Sawyer-Lauçanno's plodding style in his biography. Fortunately there was a very good one a few months later, in French, by Robert Briatte."[45]

To Briatte, Bowles wrote on October 25, 1989: *"J'ai lu la biographie et je la trouve excellente. Merci d'avoir écrit un livre dans lequel le lecteur peut avoir confiance."* ["I have read the biography and find it excellent. Thank you for writing a book the reader can trust."]

"I was very pleased, and deeply touched, by Millicent Dillon's perceptive biography of Jane," Bowles told Virginia Spencer Carr upon her first visit to Tangier in September 1989. "I read it and reread it and dreamed about Jane all over again. Although Miss Dillon dwelled considerably upon Jane's death, and dying, I know it was fitting. It did make me very sad, though, for I did not want readers to lose sight of Jane's wonderfully wry sense of humor, and those wildly funny turns of phrase no matter how sick she was."[46]

To that, Carr replied: "As an appreciative reader of your wife's work, and also of Miss Dillon's biography, I could never lose sight of that."

"Good!" Bowles answered. "I will assist you, for whatever it's worth, but I hope you will not drag out my own dying."[47]

"I won't," she promised.

"Or better yet, that your tale is finished before I am–"

In the spring of 1994 Carr arranged for Bowles to travel to Atlanta, Georgia, for what was deemed "essential 'fem-to-fem' bypass surgery" performed by Dr. Thomas F. Dodson of Emory University Hospital. Dr. Dodson donated his services, followed by a weeklong residency in a private room as a guest of the hospital. Since Emory University Hospital was a teaching hospital, Bowles said that he did not mind at all being gawked at and probed a bit by countless interns who stopped in to observe and chat, having discovered that their patient was an acclaimed writer. He was amazed that he was charged nothing for his food, medicines, or other services, and that even the plane tickets for him and Abdelouahaid were donated by a friend of his biographer's. "Both before and after my hospital stay I was the guest of Mary Robbins, whom I had known previously during her several visits to Tangier with Virginia. I returned a second time to Atlanta in the fall of 1994 for more surgery, this time to remove a cancer that had spread like wildfire from my nose to my mouth and cheek after being 'nipped' earlier in Paris. Dr. Mundy Papadopoulos performed that surgery gratis, also. I was declared free of all cancerous growth and about ten days later Emory's Dr. Gerald Gussik performed delicate repair surgery on my nose, cheek, and mouth."[48]

Before leaving Atlanta in June 1994, Bowles knew that he would return for the cancer surgery, but chose to wait until autumn. "This time Abdelouahaid and I were Virginia's houseguests for three months."

Still another operation on Bowles's leg was essential in November 1996. This time the surgery was performed in Mobile, Alabama, by Joseph McPhillips's brother Frank. To avoid publicity and a new influx of visitors, Bowles's doctor registered him under the name Palmer. "I don't know how they came up with that name, but I had no say in the matter. I wouldn't have minded being simply Paul Bowles and having a few friends drop in."

Despite Bowles's declaration to Millicent Dillon upon her first visit to Tangier that he believed himself to be "no longer connected with anything," and that he had lived his life "vicariously and didn't know it," he was by no means unmindful that he had lived in such a manner for most of his life. His awareness of living vicariously did not commence with his marriage to Jane, nor did it end with her death and his present sense of disconnectedness. A raconteur as well as a superb listener all his life, Bowles thrived on the gossip of friends and passersby about people he knew or might be introduced to shortly, and in that regard Jane had been an ideal companion. The solitary and immensely pleasurable mind games he had played as a child, games by which he hoisted himself from his physical world, he continued to play throughout his life.

In his autobiography, the details still as fresh in his mind as when he lived them, Bowles told of the planet he had invented with its great landmasses, seas, mountain ranges, rivers, cities, railways, junctions, and houses with street addresses, lawns, flowers, and smoke curling out of chimneys; yet in his imaginary world he lived in none of them. The whole point of Bowles's creativity in childhood was *not* to put himself into any picture, but to survey the scene as an uninvolved spectator, or better yet, to be only the eyes of T. S. Eliot's Prufrock or a "pair of ragged claws / Scuttling across the floors of silent seas."

Bowles, too, had lolled in dreams and learned from his mother to empty his mind and enter into his own blank state. He traveled on a carpet of his own weaving, and it did not stop with childhood. As a composer he derived immense pleasure from his music and songs; he collected the folktales and indigenous music of other lands, which culminated in his collaborations with illiterates who had never imagined their utterances reaching beyond earshot of their immediate listeners. Through his fiction and travel writing Bowles both entertained and informed readers who had never heard of a camel udder box, traveled into the Rif Mountains, or sipped mint tea outside the Caves of Hercules. As a child he had pored over his own made-up timetables of ship sailings and maps. He was intrigued by the palm of his hand and noted that his lifeline was long and well defined, crisscrossed by sallies and tributaries begging to be navigated. He avoided professional palm readers lest they tell him something he preferred to discover on his own. Bowles was his own man; yet he also was an opener of doors and admitted almost all petitioners who peered into his darkened hallway on the fourth floor of the Inmeuble Itesa. "It was my own fault, not having a telephone then; I felt obliged to receive anyone who knocked. Late at night, having napped earlier yet ready now to retire, I saw my last visitor out the door and bolted it, locked the door to my bedroom, and brooked no interruption until I chose to emerge at mid-morning the next day."[49]

CHAPTER SIXTEEN

Coda

"Was Hart Crane aware of the incredible deviousness of his language? He must have been, since he did not hesitate to use it here and there throughout his oeuvre."[1]

—Paul Bowles

Bowles was much too modest to have imagined that a reader might view the words he had chiseled in his foreword to a new collection of Hart Crane's letters, *O My Land, My Friends*, to be applicable to his own wordsmithing. Yet one could easily substitute the name Paul Bowles for Hart Crane and the meaning would be just as applicable to Bowles as to Crane. Bowles had mentioned in his preface that after Crane threw himself over the rail of the SS *Orizaba* into the sea, an eyewitness to the event had seen him surface and begin swimming. Bowles's wry observation was that "this was surely not because he had changed his mind and no longer wished to die. He probably hoped to attract the attention of a passing shark." Bowles's foreword to the letters of Hart Crane was written shortly after his eighty-sixth birthday, and it put him in mind once again of the possible disparity between what *he* wanted regarding the disposition of his remains and the actuality that might ensue despite the good intentions of those charged with the task.

Since Bowles had approved Carr's writing his biography, she asked him, eventually, if he wished to be cremated, rather than being buried full body, to which he replied:

> It's a difficult question to answer. Cremation is the preferable reply, but in Morocco it is forbidden. (The Spanish also look at cremation with a jaundiced eye, considering it un-Christian.) If I have to be buried in the ground, I'd like it to be in the animal cemetery here in Tangier, along with the dogs and cats that belonged to the European residents. I feel certain, however, that the authorities would object to that, if only because the cemetery was founded by David Herbert, and the Moroccans always considered it vaguely obscene to erect tombstones in the memory of dogs. Abdelouahaid is very much in favor of my being buried in the pet graveyard. His idea is that it should be done surreptitiously, which to me puts it completely in the realm of the fantastic. He insists that I write a document giving permission for him to bury me along with all the Rexes and Fidos. I shall do it, but I feel certain that Joseph McPhillips, my executor, will have something to say about it.
>
> I already have written my authorization for Abdelouahaid to claim my body upon my death and bury me there. Naturally, since I would be an interloper, my interment in the pet graveyard would have to be carried out surreptitiously, presumably late at night before anyone realized what was happening. Officially, no person can be interred there. As you know, I wouldn't want a marker of any kind, just as I did not want one for Jane. I do rather relish the thought of lying anonymously amidst the Fidos and Rexes and aged eucalyptus trees that shade their graves, where hundreds of unsuspecting people pass each day as they go up and down the mountain.[2]

Bowles laughed as he envisioned the scenario. Abdelouahaid Boulaich stood nodding in agreement at Bowles's bedroom door, having just served tea, then cookies from a tin on the bedside table, and he lingered to hear what else Bowles might say about the matter. "Of course someone might happen along and alert the police while Abdelouahaid was still digging the hole and throw him in jail. Then what?" Boulaich nodded and uttered something in Spanish to indicate that he was willing to risk the clandestine send-off, with perhaps only his son Mohammed as witness and shovel bearer.

Bowles said that the conversation about the disposition of his body with its surreal trappings reminded him of something he himself had written in *Without Stopping*, a passage of which he was particularly fond: "I relish the idea that in the night, all around me in my sleep, sorcery is burrowing its invisible tunnels in every direction, from thousands of senders to thousands of unsuspecting recipients. Spells are being cast, poison is running its course; souls are being dispossessed of parasitic pseudo-consciousnesses that lurk in the unguarded recess of the mind."[3]

Late one evening in the spring of 1998, Phillip Ramey asked Bowles if he might turn on the tape player and couch a few questions in the form of an interview, just as he had a few weeks earlier when they had talked largely about Choukri and Mrabet and the hazards and immense satisfaction derived from translating Moroccan storytellers. This time Ramey wanted to focus upon Bowles's dual career as writer and composer:

RAMEY: Until fairly recently, your concert music has been pretty much forgotten. But there has been a spate of new records, there was a three-day festival of your musical works in New York in 1995, and now there is a film about your career as a composer. Is this important to you?

BOWLES: It's flattering—ego massage. But I see my music as part of the past. I'm curious to know how it holds up, but in the context of the 1930s, not the 1990s.

RAMEY: Do you still have the desire to write music?

BOWLES: Perhaps more than fiction.

RAMEY: You once noted that you thought music and prose involved different parts of the brain.

BOWLES: Who knows how the mind is divided? I always found it a great relief to write if I had been composing, and if I had been writing it was wonderful to sit down and compose.

RAMEY: Do you still have ideas for stories?

BOWLES: It's the writing itself that gives me ideas. Since I can no longer write, there are none.

RAMEY: What was your procedure in starting a story? Would you write just any sentence?

BOWLES: Yes, the old Surrealist method.

RAMEY: Invent a sentence now.

BOWLES: "In those days he always walked by the pool, because he was not worried about what might be in it. But now he felt different."

RAMEY: Your fiction is notable for its nihilism and fascination with violence, while your music tends to be light and charming.

BOWLES: Perhaps I just didn't know how to compose dark music. Lenny Bernstein always said that my music sounded postcoital.

"I think the foregoing excerpt is typical of the way Paul and I have always talked together," said Ramey. "I would nudge him, and he would reply, usually tongue-in-cheek unless it was about music. I don't think anyone would guess that Paul was eighty-seven years old when we had this conversation. His mind was as clear as a bell, and his humor as sharp and quick as I've ever seen it."[4]

When Philip Weiss, a journalist who wrote for the *New York Observer*, visited Bowles with his wife in February 1999, they were admitted by a man whose "disapproving gaze" despite their appointment made them conclude that they had presented themselves at the wrong door. Bowles apologized for their discomfort, saying: "I'm afraid I really can't see you. I have glaucoma in both eyes."

Weiss declared later that he did not know what to say next, but that his wife "behaved as though she were visiting her grandmother in the hospital and sat down on Bowles's bed."

"'Hello, Mr. Bowles. My husband faxed you. We're here because of the fiftieth anniversary of *The Sheltering Sky*,' she began.

"'The poor book,' he said. 'It's getting on. Of course, it's not nearly so old as I am.'

"'But you're still so handsome,' she told him.

"He tilted his head. 'If only I were alive.'"

The Weisses talked amiably with Bowles, and he engaged them as though their visit was the most important event of his day. When Mrs. Weiss asked if he missed anything about New York, he replied: "Yes, the chocolate malts. You can't get them in Morocco." He said that when he lived in New York, he was "busy with plays, busy at rehearsals. That's how I made my living. I was not the beneficiary of someone's will."

"'No family trust?' my wife asked.

"'My family didn't trust me at all.'"

When asked about the countless visitors who trekked to his door, Bowles replied, "I don't understand what drives people to come. Last week there were people from Chile, and at the same time, people from Scotland and someone from Japan."

"'Do you ever send them away?' she asked."

He pulled his knees up under the blanket, and replied: "My manservant does that. Sometimes he says to people, 'You know how much it costs to see Mr. Bowles?' Occasionally he names a fantastic figure, and they say, 'That's all right.' Once he shook down a Dutch journalist for a hundred dollars."[5]

Bowles said later that he was unaware that Abdelouahaid had gone to the hotel room of the Dutch journalist that evening to collect the hundred-dollar fee he had set, "since he had gotten away without paying it," he explained. "Had it transpired in front of me, naturally I would have been embarrassed. On one hand, it seems reprehensible, but he is the one who sends my replies to their faxes requesting interviews, keeps track of appointments, lets people in (with their cameras, lights, notepads, and sometimes heavy equipment), brings out chairs, rearranges the furniture, plugs in their electrical devices, serves tea, empties their ash trays, and cleans up the mess after they leave. He also keeps an eye on things, always wary that some stranger is going to walk off with a book or trinket he fancies. Many of my visitors arrived with stacks of books for me to sign. I could barely see the page."[6]

Ramey recalled that many people brought Bowles tapes and compact discs over the years, along with cereals from America and his favorite sweets. "But the thing he loved best was 'talking music' and having someone at hand with whom he could listen to it. Such moments illuminated Paul's last few years. I suppose I was his only close friend during the 1990s with whom he 'talked music.'

"One evening shortly before I left Tangier to return to New York–in the autumn of 1999–Paul and I were sitting in his bedroom (as we usually did since his tape player, tapes, VCR, and television were there, and he held court, no matter who his visitors were, in bed). I got up to say goodnight and to go down to my own flat (just beneath his), when he said suddenly, 'Wait, I have something for you.' Other than his telling me that he wanted his ashes interred in New York, I was never surprised by what he said. Usually I was simply entertained. This particular night he handed me his hand-painted Persian silver cigarette case, which I knew he cherished; he had once promised to leave it to me when he died. 'You'd better have this now because if I die before you come back in the spring, it could disappear. In fact, it could easily disappear anyway, even if I don't die in the meantime.'

"Paul was always very matter-of-fact in talking about his mortality, as though we were discussing a garment hanging in his closet in the next room. Then he reached over and handed me the cigarette case, but held on to it for an instant and sniffed it. He said he was simply checking to make sure it had no lingering residue of kif. I nodded and smiled. 'It's just that I would worry about your going through customs with this, but it seems to be okay,' he concluded.

"Then he said, reaching again for the cigarette case, 'Give it back for a moment,' which I did, and he held it up to his face and kissed it.

"What's that for?" I asked.

"'I'm saying good-bye to an old friend.'"

Ramey said that a few nights earlier, he had asked Bowles if he wanted to see a pornographic film. "We watched them occasionally, and Paul thoroughly enjoyed them. That evening we viewed one I had labeled *The Edward R. Murrow Story*, in case Moroccan customs gave me trouble when I brought it in. It was Paul's favorite. (Unlike what some writers have surmised, he never lost interest in sex.) At a certain point I became bored and fast-forwarded the videotape. Paul was indignant. 'You're ruining the plot!' he cried. I was amused to realize that he even looked at 'blue' movies through his novelist's eye."[7]

Bowles was convinced that Jane had become a Roman Catholic so that she could be buried in the Catholic cemetery in Málaga. "I am sure her thinking was that it would make her death less burdensome on me. I certainly don't want the disposal of my body to be more difficult than necessary on my executor. Joe McPhillips has always been a taskmaster of the first order. I suppose that's why he's been highly effective as headmaster of the American School of Tangier. Without his insistence I certainly wouldn't have returned to composing theater music, which I did for several of his productions at the American School. Of course he wasn't headmaster when he got me to compose my first score there in 1966, for Sophocles' *Oedipus*. Actually, Joe is an excellent director, and he could choreograph anything he put his mind to. He's also been my friend for thirty-five years. These two factors alone make him a perfect choice to be my executor, and he has agreed."[8]

Despite his love of the fantastic and the heady appeal of being buried anonymously in the pet cemetery, by the time Bowles died he already had made other plans for the disposition of his body. According to Ramey, "Paul's plan for a New York burial was a posthumous surprise to all of his intimates in Tangier except Joe McPhillips. Just before I left Tangier in October 1999, Paul told me that he had added a codicil to his will directing that he be buried alongside his parents. I'm sure he meant beside his *mother*, for I knew that he hated his father and had spent much of his life avoiding America (none of us knew then, including Paul, that his parents had been cremated and their ashes mingled in the same urn). I found the very idea of his being buried in New York incredible and asked Paul why he would choose to do such a thing.

"'It's the logical choice,' he replied.

"I certainly wasn't one to argue with Paul's logic."[9]

Some of Bowles's intimates had speculated that he would manage somehow to be cremated in Spain and his ashes scattered into the Atlantic above the Caves of Hercules at Cap Spartel, in the presence of a few friends perhaps, as had Brion Gysin, in whose simple ceremony Bowles had participated more than a decade earlier. "Brion died in Paris, so bringing his ashes here was not a problem. I intend to die in Tangier, preferably here in this bed," said Bowles, fingering his blanket. "But since cremation is not an option in Morocco, my body would have to be transported elsewhere, maybe to Spain, then the ashes brought back here, which sounds like a lot of trouble for my executor."[10]

Bowles's sense of humor seldom failed him. A few days before he died, Bowles was visited by Philip Krone, a friend from Chicago who had brought him on earlier visits such things as popcorn and a microwave oven in which to cook it. Krone stepped into the room, took one look at him, and declared: "If you feel half as bad as you look, Paul, you're probably already dead."

Bowles's eyes widened. "Oh, no–I don't feel that bad."[11]

The last thing Bowles wrote for publication was a foreword to a book called *Literary Trips: Following in the Footsteps of Fame* for a Canadian editor, Victoria Brooks. Bowles wrote it out in longhand, and when he had finished, he signed and dated it in his usual fashion, "Tangier–2/vii/1999," then handed it to Ramey to read. "I had volunteered to type it, and after Paul read it again he said that he thought it was all right. Later he told me that the editor had written him to request that he make it longer and more explicit," said Ramey.

"'Absolutely not! They've asked for a foreword, and I've given it to them.'[12]

"I thought the foreword quite extraordinary for a person of any age, let alone for Paul at the age of eighty-eight," said Ramey.

Vicki Vorreiter, a filmmaker and musician who taught violin at

DePaul University, had visited Bowles in the fall of 1998, then twice again in 1999. She was documenting some of the indigenous Berber tribes and taping the music that accompanied the centuries-old ceremonies for a film, *Tea in the Sahara: Photographic Scenes of Morocco*. Vorreiter asked Paul to say a few words that might serve to introduce her film, and when she returned he handed her a sheet of paper with a paragraph of some 130 words.

"Will this do?" he asked her. "It's something I wrote earlier, but it seems appropriate now."

A month before Bowles died, Vorreiter returned to Bowles's bedside, this time with twenty-seven audiotapes, and gave him a progress report. She knew that he was not well enough to listen to any of them then, but they talked for a while. "I learned that he had just been released from the Malabata clinic and had gone home, but it was obvious that he was too ill to stay there. He wanted to die in his own bed. Later that same day he was taken to the Italian Hospital, where I visited him. He was alert and in good spirits, and his color looked practically normal. He had been moved from the small room in which he was first installed, to room five, since it had a private bathroom and two wide windows with shutters on the outside to keep out the light. . . . I didn't stay long because I didn't want to tire him, and I had a plane to catch. He kissed my hand and thanked me for coming. I knew it was the last time we would see each other. I had brought him a recent picture of his old friend Bruce Morrissette, whom he had not seen for over fifty years, and of Bruce's son and his wife, who lived now in Chicago. They were my friends, too. Paul looked at the picture a long time, then nodded his approval."[13]

Bowles was not alone when he died in Tangier at 11:10 a.m. on November 18, 1999. Abdelouahaid Boulaich had kept an almost round-the-clock vigil, and Souad, his cook and housekeeper, brought him food treats daily to stimulate his appetite. "These are the friends of my home," declared Bowles, smiling, as he introduced Abdelouahaid and Souad to the doctors and visitors whom they had not already met.

"From all reports by those at his bedside during Paul's final week, I am sure that his was a peaceful death, a good death," said Joseph McPhillips, who had to be in New York on school business the week Bowles died. "Naturally I regretted not being able to be with him at the very end. But the evening before I left, Paul and I talked at length in his room at the hospital. We talked about the great influences on his life and career, and he mentioned Gertrude Stein, Aaron Copland ('of course,' he added), Gore Vidal, and Tennessee Williams. When I asked him if Ned Rorem were an influence, he smiled, and replied, 'No, I was an influence on him.'

"He had already told me that he wanted to be cremated and his ashes interred in Lakemont Cemetery, in Glenora, New York, where he had happy memories as a child. He also showed me a drawing of the double headstone he had designed on which he wanted both his and Jane's names carved with only the years of their births and deaths. He said he already had made arrangements with the American Embassy for his body to be flown to the United States, cremated, and the ashes housed somewhere until such time that I could pick them up and see that they were properly interred. Paul was very much himself as he talked objectively about his last wishes. There was nothing sentimental or weepy-eyed about him during that last conversation. Of course I was feeling weepy, but refused to show it. We embraced, and I left.

"It was my assistant from the school, Karim Bensakour, who called me with the news of Paul's death. The American consul came from Casablanca to seal his flat. Then the United States Embassy in Rabat released the official death notice, which was upsetting because it was wrong. We knew that Paul had not been in a coma before his death, nor did he have a heart attack, as the wire services reported. His heart simply stopped beating. Paul had all of his faculties except clear vision, yet with the aid of a magnifying glass he was able to read, and even to write, until shortly before his death."[14]

On Monday, November 22, 1999, the *New York Times* published four lines submitted by Daniel Halpern on behalf of Bowles's publishers,

Ecco Press and HarperCollins, and also four lines of Bowles's own words:

In memory
of our
Dear Friend and Author
PAUL BOWLES

"If I knew I were going to die tomorrow,
I'd think, so soon? Still, if a man has spent
his life doing what he wanted to do,
he ought to be able to say goodbye without regrets."
Paul Bowles
1910–1999

There were two memorial services to honor him, one in Tangier on February 14, 2000, organized by McPhillips, and the other, on October 30, 2000, at the Unterberg Poetry Center of the 92nd Street Y in New York City. Here, Russell Banks, Daniel Halpern, Joyce Carol Oates, Ned Rorem, Debra Winger, and Virginia Spencer Carr presented reminiscences. Two days earlier, Carr was the guest speaker at a celebratory "biographer's brunch" at the Unterberg Poetry Center, followed by a chamber concert of Bowles's music performed by the Eos Ensemble and conducted by Jonathan Sheffer, whose newly formed EOS Orchestra had performed his music in an inaugural concert in the autumn of 1995.

At twelve noon on November 1, 2000, Bowles's ashes were interred in Lakemont Cemetery overlooking Seneca Lake and the little town of Glenora, New York. Here, the bodies or ashes of Bowles's parents; his paternal grandparents; Adelaide Bowles, his father's sister; his great-aunt Mary Elizabeth Robbins Mead and her brother Charles Franklin Robbins; his cousin Elizabeth Robbins Kenny and her husband George Kenny–all had been interred in Lakemont Cemetery, and the ashes of Shirley West Bowles, his father's brother, had been sprinkled in Seneca Lake some fifty years earlier.

Witness to the interment and participants in the simple service were a handful of local residents including Polly Marks Smith and Tom Chadwick, president of the cemetery association, for whom the name Bowles had historical significance. In addition, a few intimates had come considerable distances to say their farewells.[15]

As Bowles had anticipated when asking Joseph McPhillips to serve as the executor of his estate, McPhillips had already dealt efficiently with the thorny problems associated with the administering of his friend's will, and as a choreographer with a dramatic flair, he handled well the memorable events of the day. He invited those who gathered around the grave site to say a few words of farewell, or to drop an autumn leaf, a rose (Philip Krone had brought long-stemmed roses), a coin, or other token of farewell into the mahogany box McPhillips had carried from Tangier. Krone produced a Gideon Bible appropriated from the motel in which he had stayed the night before, and read a few verses from Psalms ("Paul would have hated that," whispered Ramey as they gathered around the open grave).

Bowles's favorite poem, "Nights," read by Carr, concluded the informal graveside service. It also was "Nights" that he had selected to conclude a new edition of his poetry, *Air to the Sea: Collected Poems of Paul Bowles, 1918–1977*.[16] As a foreword to the volume, Bowles wrote: "I'm not a poet–Gertrude Stein told me that, and for a time I believed her. Yet there occurred a period when I allowed myself to imagine that perhaps Gertrude Stein had been mistaken. At this point there was no place for nonsense or hermeticism. These last efforts are probably the most shameful of all. I was a mature adult willing to sign my name to what I hoped were poems, and to publish them. If, as a good American, I am born again and find myself in the company of someone called Gertrude Stein, I shall listen carefully to whatever she tells me, and arrange my life accordingly."

McPhillips had planned to read something too, but remembered only after leaving the cemetery. "Ah, here's the passage," he announced to friends accompanying him to the airport. "It's the scene from *The Sheltering Sky* in which Port dies." McPhillips read the passage aloud in his sonorous voice:

"A black star appears, a point of darkness in the night sky's clarity. Point of darkness and gateway to repose. Reach out, pierce the fine fabric of the sheltering sky, take repose."

ADDITIONAL ACKNOWLEDGMENTS

It is my pleasure to acknowledge and to thank once again the librarians and their assistants in countless research centers throughout the United States, all vital confederates to my mission.

In Alabama, I received considerable assistance from the Alabama Department of Archives and History, Montgomery; from the Tutwiler Collection of the Birmingham Public Library; from Cindy Reed and Madine Evans in the Harrison Regional Library of Columbiana; from Renee Palmer in the Parnell Memorial Library; from the Harrison Regional Library staff in Columbiana; from Rachel Polhill in the Carmichael Library of Montevallo University; from Rose and Henry Emfinger in the Museum of Aldrich, Alabama (also known as the Museum Company Store); and from the Shelby County Historical Society.

In California, I was helped by Sara S. Hodson and the Department of Manuscripts of the Henry E. Huntington Library, Art Collections and Botanical Gardens; by Patricia White in the Department of Special Collections and Manuscripts Division of the Stanford University Libraries; and by Anne Caiger and Flora Ito in the University Library and the Department of Special Collections of the University of California, Los Angeles.

In Connecticut, Kendall L. Crilly and Harold E. Samuel assisted me in the John Herrick Jackson Music Library; as did Donald Gallup and Patricia C. Willis in the Beinecke Rare Book and Manuscript Library of Yale University, and several members of the staff of the Sterling Memorial Library of Yale University. Candace Bothwell and Leith G. Johnson walked me through the Cinema Archives of Wesleyan University; and Mary Palomba and the staff of the Department of

Libraries of the Town of Enfield, Connecticut, where Bowles's maternal grandparents grew up, were also exceedingly helpful.

In Delaware, I learned much from Marjorie G. McNich in the Hagley Museum and Library; in Georgia, Stephen Enniss, David Estes, and Linda Matthews guided me through much useful material housed in the Robert W. Woodruff Library at Emory University. Similarly, Mary Ellen Brooks, Melissa Bush, Thomas E. Camden, and J. Larry Gulley in the Hargrett Rare Book and Manuscript Library of the University of Georgia were essential to my research, as were Carolyn Blumenthal, Rebecca Drummond, Jane Hobson, Anne Page Mosby, Brian Patterson, Carolyn Robison, and Ralph Russell in the Pullen Library of Georgia State University.

In Chicago, Illinois, I learned a great deal about the career of Bowles's father in the archives of the American Dental Association. Similarly, the reference department of the Chicago Public Library was a trove of helpful information.

At the University of Iowa, I was ably assisted by Richard M. Kalbert in the extensive Special Collections of the University Libraries; and in Kansas, Ann Hyde guided me through the Kenneth Spencer Research Library and the Department of Special Collections of the University of Kansas in Lawrence.

In Massachusetts, the reference department of the Boston Public Library was vital to my research, as was the City Clerk's Office of the Bureau of Vital Statistics in Northampton. Margaret R. Goostray assisted me in the Mugar Memorial Library of Special Collections of Boston University; Peter Carini produced vital statistics regarding Emma Winnewisser from the College Archives of Simmons College; Joan L. Gearin and Chris Hannon assisted me in the William Allan Neilson Library of Smith College, and the staffs of the Springfield Historical Society, the Springfield Library and Museum, and the public library in Provincetown were similarly helpful.

In New Hampshire, I was assisted by Laurie Burt in the Archives of the Cheshire Superior Court; by Ann Campbell in the Alumni Records Office and by Ed Durocher in the Communications Department of Phillips Exeter Academy; and by the staff of the public library of Walpole.

In the state of New Jersey, Charley Martay assisted me in the Jersey City Public Library, as did several staff members of the Jersey City Historical Society and others in the New Jersey Room of the New Jersey Public Library. The Bureau of Vital Statistics in Trenton also provided important information.

In New York, I was helped on several occasions by Virginia Dajani, Nancy Johnson, Kathleen Kienholz, and Larry Landon of the American Academy and Institute of Arts and Letters; by Frances Bishop and Staci Johnston, who provided vital information concerning Bowles's career as a composer housed in the American Music Center Library of the American Music Center; and by Patricia Cahill, Bernard R. Crystal, and Kenneth A. Lohf in the Butler Rare Book and Manuscript Library of Columbia University. Brian Fitzgerald and Craig Hutchings assisted me regarding Claude Bowles's schooling at the Elmira Free Academy, and I was helped similarly by the staff of the Chemung County Historical Society. Robert Colasacco and Sharon Laist assisted me in the Archives of the Ford Foundation; Robert Friedrich and Charles Young were vital to my research in the Queens Borough Public Library of Jamaica, Long Island; librarian Dennis F. Jensen was especially helpful in the Research Library of Jamaica High School, from which Bowles graduated; similarly, several of the administrative staff of the Mary Immaculate Hospital of Jamaica, the hospital in which Bowles was born, were very helpful; Dorothy Swerdlove and Bob Taylor were vital sources in leading me through the Performing Arts Research Center of the New York Public Library, as was Francis Matson in the Berg Collection of English and American Literature of the New York Public Library. Rodney Phillips and Rob Rucker assisted me in the Research Libraries of the New York Public Library, and Frank Waller helped similarly in the Fales Library of New York University. The staffs of the Schuyler County Historical Society in Montour Falls, New York; of the Springfield Historical Society of New York and the Springfield Library and Museum; and of the Steel Memorial

Library of Elmira were also helpful. Kathleen Manwaring guided me through the George Arents Research Library and the E. S. Bird Library of Syracuse University; Susan Brynteson, the summer librarian, and other staff members of the artists' colony Yaddo in Saratoga Springs helped me acquire important materials regarding Bowles's brief residency there.

In North Carolina, Robert Byrd and Linda McCurdy assisted me in the Special Collections Department of the William R. Perkins Library of Duke University, as did Libby Chenault in the Rare Book Collection of the Wilson Library of the University of North Carolina in Chapel Hill.

In Pennsylvania, Kenneth Riegel provided valuable records housed in the Railroad Museum of Pennsylvania in Strasburg, as did Thomas M. Whitehead in the Special Collections Department of the University Archives of Temple University. Also helpful were Carol Ann Harris in the Temple University Central Library System; Curtis Ayers in the University Archives and Records Center of the University of Pennsylvania; the staff of the Historical Society of Pennsylvania; and the staff of the Charles Patterson Van Pelt Library of the University of Pennsylvania.

In Rhode Island, Meredith Sorozan provided helpful information housed in the Rhode Island Historical Society; and in Vermont, Patty Mark in the Rockingham Free Public Library and the staff of the Rockingham Chamber of Commerce were exceedingly helpful, as were the staffs of the Town Clerk's Office of Bellows Falls and of the Great Falls Regional Chamber of Commerce.

In Virginia, the staffs of the Fenwick Library Special Collections and Archives of the George Mason University Library; Ruth Kerns and Robert Vay in the Research Center for the Federal Theatre Project; Patricia A. DeMasters in the Office of the University Registrar of the University of Virginia; Lorraine Johnson in the Records Department of the Alumni Association of the University of Virginia; and Joan St. Clair Crane, Sharon Definbaugh, Margaret Hrabe, Gregory Johnson, Kathryn Morgan, and Michael Plunkett in the Clifton Waller Barrett

Library and the Special Collections/Manuscripts Division of the Alderman Library of the University of Virginia—all proved vital to my research.

In Wisconsin, Harold L. Miller and Maxine Fleckner Ducey of the State Historical Society of Wisconsin and the Wisconsin Center for Film and Theater Research, Madison, were helpful, also, as were the staffs of the Department of Vital Statistics and the Reference Department of the Waukesha Public Library.

In the District of Columbia, Peter J. Fay and the Reference Department of the Music Division and the Archive of Folk Song of the Library of Congress were important to my research, as was the director of archives maintained by the Federal Bureau of Investigation, under the Freedom of Information–Privacy Branch.

In Tangier, Morocco, I was assisted by Mr. and Mrs. Thor A. Kuniholm in the American Legation Library and Museum, and by several members of the Moroccan American Commission for Educational and Cultural Exchange.

Many others, both in the United States and abroad, have helped in the development of this biography in a variety of ways, and for their favors, advice, and encouragement, I thank Daniel Aaron, Jadir Abdelaziz, Karim Achouate, Mindy Adams, Lauren Adamson, Elaine Alacón-Totten, René Alexandre-Blachot, Elizabeth Alvarez, Amber Amari, Elizabeth and Raffaello Amati, Ray Anderson, Alan Ansen, David Applefield, Juanita Arbour, Rachel Archer, Carol Ardman, Akemi Asai, Bridget Aschenberg, Ann and Robert Ashcroft, John Atteberry, Betty Ann Austin, John Austin, Don Bachardy, Jennifer Baichwal, Deirdre Bair, Joanne Balingit, Clement Barclay, Herbert Bard, Ann Basart, Sandy Bederman, Ari Behn, Hercules Bellville, Guy Bemis, Diana and Peter Benet, Farida Benlyazid, Karim Benzakour, William Berger, Bernardo Bertolucci, Brian and Amy Bischoff, Simon Bischoff, Frances Blackburn Bishop, Roy Bishop, Reine Bismarck, Karl Bissinger, Jon Blair, Christopher Blake, Kenny P. Boas, Pociao Bonn, Abdelouahaid Boulaich, Souah Boulaich, John Bradshaw, Bonnie Braendlin, Melvin Bragg, Bruce Brandt, William Brantley,

Bruno Braunrot, Claudio Bravo, Juan Bravo, Sonsoles Bravo, Robert Bray, Robert Briatte, David and Sally Brown, Owsley Brown III, Matthew J. Bruccoli, Barry Brukoff, Patricia Bryan, Jackson Bryer, Edward Joseph Burke, Robin Burke, Bradden Burns, John A. Burrison, Carol Cannon, Gena Dagel Caponi, Michael Carlisle, Jon Carlson, Michael A. Carpenter, Karen Carter, Lyn and Tom Chadwick, Mohamed Choukri, Frank Cibulka, Jeffrey Clemmons, Michelle Cloonan, Ira Cohen, Tammy Cole, Rae Carlton Colley, Jack Collins, Gary Conklin, Joan Covero, Edgardo Cozarinsky, April Lee Craig, Vincent Crapanzano, Mary Cross, Janice Crotch, Juan Cruz, Jack Culbertson, Martin Dain, Edgar Daniels, Paul Danquah, Douglas Barker Danser Jr., Duane Bradford Danser, Harold Wesley Danser II, Barbara Thompson Davis, Lawrence Davis, Ned Davis, Karim Debbagh, David Deiss, Nancy Bowles Delmotte, George E. Nolthenius de Mann III, Peggy and Robert Dennis, Neil Derrick, Lisa and David Desmond, Albert Devlin, David Diamond, Steven Diamond, Salvador Díaz-Versón, John Disney, Maggie Dodd, Thomas F. Dodson, Jennifer Dorr, Mitch Douglass, James Thomas Dowell, Tamara Dragadze, Judy Drury, Sally and James Dry, Steve DuPouy, Vicki Duval, Rebecca Earnshaw, Geoffrey Elborn, Marilyn Elkins, Kenward Elmslie, Robert Emerson, Molly Epstein, Tom Erhardt, Wayne Erickson, Beth Erling, David Espey, Jerry Etheridge, Lillian Faderman, Ruth Fainlight, John Farquharson, Leon Fassler, Richard Ferda, Lawrence Ferlinghetti, Elizabeth Fernea, Neal Ferris, Edward Field, Nigel Finch, Stephen Jay Fisher, Sister Annelle Fitzpatrick, Joseph Flora, Horton Foote, Shelby Foote, Aimee Ford, Ruth Ford, Kathleen Franzen, Todd Freeman, Jack Fricks, Norman Friedman, Janet Gabler-Hover, Karen Carr Gale, Peter Garland, Jellel Gasteli, Adrian Gearse, Carol Gelderman, Kathy Gentile, Isabelle Gilbert, Matthew Gilson, Gabrielle Giordano, John Giorno, John A. Glusman, Lynda Goldfarb, Milton Goldman, John Goodwin, Cliff Graubert, James Grauerholz, Patricia Graves, Michelle Green, Katherine Grimes, Carla Grissman, J. Larry Gulley, Mel Gussow, John Haberlen, Carol Haggerty, Peter Hale, Wade Hall, Mohammed Hamri, Lyu Hanabusa, Peter

Hancock, George Harper, Roger Harris, Tammy Harvey, Jeff Haydon, Erik Herdon, James Leo Herlihy, José Hernández, Marta Hess, Robert Hines, Jon Holden, Kenneth Holditch, Pociao and Roberto de Hollanda, Scott Hollingsworth, Edith Lynn Hornik-Beer, G. Johnson Hubert, John Hudson, Walter Hunt, Jacqueline Hurtley, Andrea Inselmann, Phyllis Irwin, Joanne F. Jacobson, Abdelaziz Jadir, Mick Jagger, Gregory Johnson, Peter Johnson, Stacie Johnston, John Jopling, Franklin Julie, Fred Kaplan, Mohamed El Karch, Mary Rose Kasraie, David and Lynn Kaufelt, Don Lee Keith, Shirley Bowles Kendall, Mona Khazindar, Doreen Kilbane, Arthur Kinney, Gloria Kirby, Karl Kirchway, Yvonne Kleefield, Phillip Kolin, Charles Knox, John Kolomvakis, Kenneth Krayeske, Jill Krementz, Brooke W. Kroeger, Philip and Joan Krone, Edmond and Mandy Nash Kudarowskas, John Kuehl, Joseph Kuhl, Marion Leathers Kuntz, Ricardo Labougle, Kevin Lacy, Gavin Lambert, Jack Larson, Owen Laster, Bill Laswell, Hugh Latta, Richard Layman, Anthony Wallace Lee, Catherine Carr Lee, Michael Lee, Bennett Lerner, Alain Lesage, Wendy Lesser, Nicholas Lezard, Sheryl Lockhart, Richard Long, Grant Luckhardt, Farida Lyazid, Louis J. Lyell, Randy Malamud, Phillip Malebranche, Irving Malin, David Marcus, Mary Ellen Mark, Sylvia Marlowe, Andrew Marshall, John Marshall, John Martin, Ron Martin, Earl L. Masters Jr., George Mattingly, Hubert McAlexander, Erin McAlister, Kim McCloud, John McClure, James McCrary, Hetti McGee, Pearl Amelia McHaney, Thomas H. McHaney, Joan and Norman McMillan, Frank McPhillips, John McWilliams, Nicolette Meeres, John R. Meir, Samuel Menashe, Valerie Miles, Valerie Miller, John Monroe, Nancy M. Moore, Bill Morgan, Ted Morgan, Anna Morris, Kimberly Carr Morris, James Morrissette, Michelle Morrison, Emil P. Moschella, Noel Mostert, Mohammed Mrabet, Bernard E. Mullen, James Murray, Rachel Muyal, Lawrence Mynott, Michael Neal, Levio Negri, Stuart Noel, Jdaoudi Med. Nourredene, Bill Nowlin, Barbara Grant Nutting, Joyce Carol Oates, Don O'Briant, Patrick O'Connor, Gail O'Donnell, Julie Owen, Peter Owen, Diamondis J. Papadopoulos, Anthony Paris, Peter Parker, Neil Parsley,

Carl Patton, Julia Payne, Nick De Pencier, Irving Penn, Robert Phillips, Frances Picci, Danuta Piestrzynska, Michael Pinker, Donald Pizer, Scott Pluckhahn, Charles Plymell, Nora Poling, Howard Pollack, Peter Pollack, James Poulakas, Phil Poulos, Erik Powell, Coen Pranger, Elena Prentice, Patrick Procktor, Gary Pulsifer, James Purdy, Michelle Pzyak, Mostafa Quaffi, Hassan Quakrim, Temsemani Rachid, Catherine Rainwater, Dorothy Ramsey, Richard Rayner, Sherrill Redman, Rex Reed, George Reeves, Hannelore Rezzonico, Noah Richler, Janet Rienstra, Charles Franklin Robbins, Ron Roizen, Lisa Roney, Rodrigo Rey Rosa, Edward Rothchild, Matthew Roudané, Charles Ruas, John Ryle, Ahmed Saber, Susan Gail Sackett, Vittorio Santoro, Sherry Satterwhite, Beth Sawyer, Larry Sawyer, Christopher Sawyer-Lauçanno, William Scheick, Frieder Schlaich, Philip D. Schuyler, Megan Sexton, Michelle Shamasneh, Jonathan Sheffer, Stephen A. Shepard, Chad J. Shonk, David Simmons, Kim Sisson, Jennie Skerl, Erin Sledd, John Simon, Sharon Smith, Sylvia Smith, William Jay Smith, Reiner Smolinski, Paul Sperry, Elizabeth Stafford, Clyde Stallings, John Stallworthy, Fred Standley, David Starkey, Lawrence Stewart, Robert S. Stewart, John Stone, Jane Kielty Stott, William Stott, John Supko, Claudia Swan, Gregg Swemm, Edward Swift, Eve Sylvester, Donald Taebel, Indra B. Tamang, Elizabeth Henderson Taylor, Leonard and Katy Teel, Touria Haji Temsamani, Paul Thiel, Barbara Thomas, Edward M. Thomas, Lynne Tillman, Nancy Tischler, Jacques Tournier, Cy Twombly, Florian Vetsch, Ed Victor, Carlos J. Morales Villanueva, Kurt Vonnegut, Vicki Vorreiter, Alison Voth, Aaron Walker, Ann Wallach, Mark Watson, Colin Weber, Frederick J. Weber, Gary Webster, Mark Weimer, Regina Weinreich, Philip Weiss, Jan Wenner, John Ross West, Charles Whaley, Tessa Codrington Wheeler, George Whitman, Dakin and Joyce Williams, Kirsten Williams, Donald Windham, Debra Winger, Kirk Winslow, Michael Wolfe, Paula Wolfert, Sandra Wong, Charles K. Wright, Ina Jane Wundram, Andrew Wylie, Warren Wyss, Benjamin and Rachel Yarmolinsky, Ira Yeager, Lamar York, Deborah Zeringue, Michel Zink, and Samuel Ziskind.

I wish to acknowledge, too, those deceased friends and acquaintances who contributed significantly to the making of this book: Elena Díaz-Versón Amos, Ardis Blackburn, John Malcolm Brinnin, Rudy Burckhardt, William S. Burroughs, Paul Cadmus, Xenia K. Cage, Hannetta Clark, Walter Clemmons, Harold Clurman, Gregory Corso, Harold Wesley Danser Jr., Oliver Evans, Harry Finestone, Robert Fizdale, Charles Henri Ford, Larry Fruwirth, Mercedes Guitta, Allen Ginsberg, Morris Golde, Richard Goldstone, Gerald Gussick, David Herbert, Ted Joans, Elia Kazan, Richard Kennedy, James Laughlin, Richard Freeman Leavitt, Lyle Leverich, Robert Lewis, Jerre Mangione, Marty Mann, Marguerite McBey, David McDowell, Jordan Massee, Leonard Melfi, James Merrill, Bruce Morrissette, Edouard Roditi, Ramon Salvatore, David Seidner, Christopher Wanklyn, Hall Winslow, Gavin Young, and Mohammed Zaïn.

To others who helped in the making of this book, yet have been inadvertently omitted from my acknowledgments, I sincerely apologize.

Virginia Spencer Carr
Atlanta, Georgia
May 1, 2004

CHRONOLOGY OF THE LIFE OF PAUL FREDERIC BOWLES

1910 Born December 30 to Rena and Claude Bowles in Jamaica, New York; teaches himself to read at age two and at three writes "The Fox and the Wolf" and other stories about animals; writes first poem at four and begins keeping a diary.

1917 At six enters the Model School in Jamaica and is assigned to second grade; at seven hears music for the first time, discovers jazz, and composes "Le Carré, an Opera in Nine Chapters," which he played on a zither; spends summers in western Massachusetts and upper New York. Bowles's future wife, Jane Auer, is born on February 22, the daughter of Sidney and Claire Auer.

1919 At eight begins piano lessons; studies theory, solfeggio, and ear training, and learns musical notation on his own.

1924 At thirteen graduates from eighth grade at the Model School; attends Flushing High School for three semesters, then transfers to Jamaica High School, where he discovers leftist magazine the *Masses*; is named humor editor and poetry editor of his school's literary magazine, the *Oracle*, and president of the poetry society; at sixteen publishes two poems, "Spire Song" and "Entity," both products of automatic writing, in *transition*, a surrealist magazine published in Paris.

1928 Graduates from Jamaica High School in January; enters four-month program at School of Design and Liberal Arts in New York City, wins two awards; in April performs with amateur theatrical group the Phylo Players; works briefly at Bank of Manhattan; in September enters University of Virginia.

1929 In March aborts his university studies and flees to Paris (passport dated April 27, 1929, declares "for Paris for study purposes"); gets job at *International Herald-Tribune*, then at Bankers Trust, both in Paris; hikes in Alps and on French Riviera; publishes dozens of poems in avant-garde reviews in Europe and America; returns reluctantly to New York in July and takes job at Dutton's Bookshop, where he begins writing a novel, and moves to Greenwich Village.

1930 In March returns to University of Virginia for a second semester; studies composition and harmony informally with Aaron Copland, whom he meets through Henry Cowell; arranges piano recital at UVA for Copland, who is snubbed by music faculty, which prompts Bowles to leave the university and vow never to return; in September joins Copland at Yaddo, an artists' colony in Saratoga Springs, New York; begins correspondence with Gertrude Stein upon being asked by a friend at the University of Richmond to guest-edit an issue of the *Messenger*, a literary quarterly published by the university, and invites Stein and other literary figures to contribute; returns home to save money, but in fit of anger throws steak knife at his father and again leaves for Paris.

1931 In April meets Stein, Pound, Gide, and Cocteau in literary world of Paris, where he continues writing poetry and composing music; accompanies Copland to Berlin, where they meet Christopher Isherwood and Stephen Spender; in August, Stein tells Bowles he is "no poet" and urges him to "stick to composing"; to that end, he travels with Copland to Tangier, which Copland hates and Bowles loves; Copland leaves, Bowles stays. In December, Copland introduces Bowles's Sonata for Oboe and Clarinet at a concert of new

American music in London's Aeolian Hall. In Morocco he is diagnosed with typhoid A and recuperates at the American Hospital of Paris in Neuilly-sur-Seine.

1932–33 Ada MacLeish sings Bowles's "Six Songs," accompanied by Copland, in concert at Yaddo, but Bowles does not attend; in December returns to North Africa and composes *Cantata: Par le Détroit* (*By the Strait*) and other music; in June 1933 returns to New York after traveling through the Algerian Sahara and Tunisia with George Turner, who becomes Tunner in Bowles's novel *The Sheltering Sky*.

1934–35 Bowles's piano sonatina is performed by John Kirkpatrick at League of Composers concert; scores film for Harry Dunham's *Bride of Samoa*; in June returns to North Africa, having wangled job in Fez with the American Fondouk, "dedicated to the relief of mistreatment of pack animals in Morocco"; returns to New York by way of South America, Los Angeles, and San Francisco, where he meets Henry Cowell, who publishes five of Bowles's compositions in *New Music: A Quarterly of Modern Compositions*; completes a six-song cycle, *Memnon*, based on Cocteau text, and two songs, "Scenes from the Door," adapted from Stein's book *Useful Knowledge*, and publishes them under his own label, Éditions de la Vipère. For next fifteen years, Bowles is based in New York, where he supports himself largely as a composer for the theater; also writes music reviews and music columns for the *New York Herald Tribune*.

1936 Federal Music Project presents on April 2 in New York City an all-Bowles concert; in July, helps form Committee on Republican Spain and writes score for *Who Fights This Battle?* to raise money for Madrid government; writes scores for Orson Welles's *Horse Eats Hat* and *Doctor Faustus*, and film score for *America's Disinherited*, produced by Southern Tenant Farmers' Union.

1937 Meets Jane Auer, his future wife, through John Latouche and travels with her and two friends, Kristians Tonny and his wife, Marie-Claire, by bus to Mexico City, a harrowing trip. Frightened and ill, Jane leaves Mexico City upon arrival without telling Bowles, who remains for four months, organizes a May Day parade, and distributes fifteen thousand stickers calling for death of Trotsky; returns to New York to orchestrate ballet for Lincoln Kirstein's *Yankee Clipper*, performed June 19 by the American Ballet Caravan and the Philadelphia Symphony Orchestra; during summer, works on *Denmark Vesey*, an opera based on libretto by Charles Henri Ford.

1938 Participates on February 6 in a *New Masses* concert, at which excerpts from *Denmark Vesey* are played; on February 21 marries Jane Auer in small Dutch Reformed church in Manhattan, leaves for honeymoon in Central America and France; is in Eze, a village above the Riviera, when Orson Welles summons him to New York to write music for William Gillette's *Too Much Johnson*; Bowles vows never again to compose for theater without commission in advance; refashions score of *Too Much Johnson* as a suite, titled *Music for a Farce*; with Jane, joins the Communist Party USA, and reads regularly the *Daily Worker*; feels sorely the lack of money.

1939 As a composer, goes on WPA relief rolls and receives $23.86 weekly; writes scores for Group Theatre's production of *Twelfth Night*, a Broadway success, William Saroyan's *My Heart's in the Highlands*, directed by Robert Lewis, and *Love's Old Sweet Song* (in collaboration with Saroyan), produced by the Theatre Guild; leaves for New Mexico with Jane and Robert (Boo) Faulkner, a drinking companion of Jane's, to compose music for *Roots in the Soil*, a Soil Erosion Service film on the Rio Grande Valley; writes "Tea on the Mountain," his first short story as an adult.

1940 In Acapulco meets Tennessee Williams and then settles in Taxco. Is summoned to New York to compose music for

Twelfth Night and Philip Barry's *Liberty Jones*; is dropped from relief rolls after investigator visits his parents' home in Jamaica; writes a number of "On the Film Front" columns in 1940 and 1941 for *Modern Music*; at urging of Katharine Hepburn writes score for play *Love Like Wildfire*, by Hepburn's brother Richard (never produced); then, accompanied by Jane and Faulkner, goes to Acapulco, where they meet Tennessee Williams. Jane takes house in Taxco and begins affair with Helvetia Perkins, an American divorcée. In New York, composes music for *Twelfth Night* and *Liberty Jones*, directed by John Houseman, and spends winter writing music for Lillian Hellman's *Watch on the Rhine*; with Jane moves into brownstone at 7 Middagh Street in Brooklyn Heights, at invitation of George Davis and W. H. Auden; others in the eclectic household include Carson McCullers, Gypsy Rose Lee, Benjamin Britten, Peter Pears, Chester Kallman, Oliver Smith, Lincoln Kirstein, Golo Mann, and Richard Wright.

1941 In March is awarded a Guggenheim Fellowship to write an opera ballet with libretto by Saroyan, but loses interest in the project and writes, instead, a zarzuela based on last act of play by García Lorca, *Así Que Pasen Cinco Años*, which Bowles translates and adapts as *The Wind Remains* (performed in spring of 1943 at the Museum of Modern Art, conducted by Leonard Bernstein, staged by Merce Cunningham); commissioned by Kirstein, Bowles writes *Pastorela* in Mexico City for the American Ballet Caravan; in April returns with Jane to Taxco, where they meet Ned Rorem, who becomes a lifelong friend, and Jane finishes a novel, *Two Serious Ladies*, published April 19, 1943, by Knopf; contracts jaundice and is hospitalized in Mexico City and Cuernavaca.

1942–43 Returns to New York in July and moves into Hotel Chelsea, then to a house on Staten Island; spends summer in

Watkins Glen, New York (in home of his recently deceased aunt, Mary Robbins Mead), with Jane, Helvetia Perkins, and Antonio Álvarez, a Mexican painter whose work he wants to launch in New York; when examined by the Selective Service Board for possible active duty in the U.S. Army, is rejected on grounds of being "psychologically unfit." In November begins writing music criticism for the *New York Herald Tribune* at invitation of Virgil Thomson, and in 1943, a column on jazz for *View*; incidental music for *'Tis Pity She's a Whore*; and a score for Dorothy Heyward's premusical, *South Pacific*; also in 1943, Peggy Guggenheim inaugurates her Art of this Century recordings with Bowles's *Flute Sonata*; travels by train with Jane to Canada.

1944 Publishes translation of de Chirico's *Hebdomeros*; is commissioned by the Belgian government in exile to write score for *Congo*, a film by John Latouche; in collaboration with Salvador Dalí, composes music for *Colloque Sentimentale*, a ballet, then leaves with Jane for Mexico; returns to rehearse score and considers production a travesty. Translates Jean-Paul Sartre's *Huis Clos* (*No Exit*); writes score for *Jacobowsky and the Colonel*, and for José Ferrer's *Cyrano de Bergerac*. In a single weekend writes music for Tennessee Williams's *The Glass Menagerie* and flies to Chicago for its opening tryouts.

1945 *The Glass Menagerie* opens on Broadway March 31 to rave reviews; guest-edits issue of *View* on "Tropical America" (devoted to his own translations, photographs, and texts from Central and South America), and translates, for *View*, such other writers as Jorge Luis Borges; also publishes in *View* (issue 5) his own short story "The Scorpion." Travels with Oliver Smith to the Caribbean and Central America, returns to write score for *Ondine*, and moves into 28 West Tenth Street with Smith, Jane, and Helvetia Perkins, with whom Jane has fallen in love; writes music for Jane's puppet play, *A Quarreling Pair*, performed in September at Spivy's Roof; begins work on short story "A Distant Episode."

1946 "The Echo" is published in *Harper's Bazaar*; "By the Water," in *View*; Sartre's *No Exit*, translated by Bowles and directed by John Huston, opens in November and wins Drama Critics' Circle Award for "best foreign play of the year"; composes Concerto for Two Pianos, Winds and Percussion, commissioned by Arthur Gold and Robert Fizdale; completes scores for *Twilight Bar*, *The Dancer*, *Cyrano De Bergerac*, and *Land's End*. Jane's short story "Plain Pleasures" is published in *Harper's Bazaar*.

1947 Completes score for *On Whitman Avenue*; upon publication of "A Distant Episode" in *Partisan Review*, is convinced that he has achieved sufficient literary success to devote himself to a career as a writer; in spring he meets Helen Strauss, an agent with William Morris, who secures him a contract with Doubleday for a novel on the strength of his short stories; begins dreaming of Tangier and leaves for Morocco on July 1 on the SS *Ferncape*; aboard ship, writes "Pages from Cold Point," a short story; in Tangier, writes "How Many Midnights" and "Call at Corazón"; moves to Fez in December to begin *The Sheltering Sky*. Jane, whose first act of *In the Summer House* was published in *Harper's Bazaar* in the spring, remains in New York; torch singer Libby Holman goes to Morocco to ask Bowles to make an opera for her from Lorca's *Yerma*; Bowles agrees, but insists upon translating it himself.

1948 In Fez becomes enamored of a sixteen-year-old, Ahmed Yacoubi, a *cherif*, who becomes a major character in his later novel *The Spider's House*; in Tangier, Jane joins Bowles and is enamored of a young Moroccan woman to whom he introduces her; known only as Cherifa, she is the reported daughter of the patron saint of Tangier. Bowles publishes "You Are Not I" and "At Paso Rojo" in *Mademoiselle*, "Under the Sky" in *Partisan Review*, and "Call at Corazón" in *Harper's Bazaar*; returns to New York to write score for Tennessee Williams's *Summer and Smoke*, which opens on Broadway on October 6 after lengthy tour in Cleveland, Buffalo, and Detroit; it is not a success. His Concerto for Two Pianos, Winds and Percussion, conducted by Lukas Foss, is premiered in November at Town Hall; in December, Bowles returns to Tangier, this time accompanied by Williams and his companion, Frank Merlo.

1949 Publishes "Pastor Dowe at Tacaté" in February issue of *Mademoiselle*; *The Sheltering Sky* is rejected by Doubleday on basis that it is "not a novel," but is published in September in London by John Lehmann, Ltd., then in New York by New Directions; in January it is named to bestseller list of the *New York Times*, where it remains for ten weeks. With Oliver Smith, Bowles purchases a house in the Casbah at Plac Amrah in Tangier; "The Delicate Prey" is published in Tangier in the summer issue of *Zero*. To promote his novel, he goes to London in November, then leaves on a freighter for Ceylon and India to spend the winter. While passing Tangier, he begins writing his second novel, *Let It Come Down*; during his absence, Jane stays in Paris with girlfriend Jody McLean, then falls in love with Marty Mann.

1950 In November, Bowles's first short story collection, *A Little Stone*, is published by John Lehmann, Ltd.; and an expanded edition, titled *The Delicate Prey and Other Stories*, is published by Random House.

1951 Returns in the spring from Ceylon, but does not finish *Let It Come Down* for almost a year. It is published by Random House in March 1952. Meanwhile, Bowles translates a French novel by R. Frison-Roche, *The Lost Trail of the Sahara*, at request of Prentice-Hall.

1952–53 Jane takes Yacoubi's paintings to New York for an exhibition at the Betty Parsons Gallery; Bowles takes Yacoubi to India and Ceylon, then to Venice to visit Peggy Guggenheim. In July 1953, they go to Rome, where he joins Tennessee Williams in cowriting a film, *Senso* (produced by Luchino Visconti), and begins writing travel pieces for *Holiday*; before returning to New York, Bowles pays six thousand dollars for Taprobane, a small island with a house on it off the coast of Ceylon. In New York, accompanied by Yacoubi, writes incidental music for a production of Jane's play, *In the Summer House*, then returns alone to Tangier, Yacoubi having fallen in love with Libby Holman.

1954–55 Meets William Burroughs, who asks him for advice regarding the publication of *Naked Lunch*. In Fez begins a new novel, *The Spider's House*; in December travels to Ceylon and Taprobane with Yacoubi, Jane, and Temsamany, his aide and chauffeur; whereas Jane had hoped to write a play there, she finds she cannot work in the primitive environment and heat, misses her friends, drinks heavily, and in the spring returns to Morocco, accompanied by Temsamany; after Jane's departure, Bowles finishes *The Spider's House*, and with Yacoubi boards a ship in Colombo for a monthlong round-trip to Japan and China, then returns to Tangier. In November *The Spider's House*, dedicated to Bowles's father, is published by Random House; Jane's *In the Summer House* is published in *Best Plays of 1953–1954*, edited by Louis Kronenberger.

1956 In February, Bowles's mother and father, with whom he has an uneasy truce, visit him and Jane in Tangier for nine weeks; after they leave, Bowles begins recording and transcribing Moghrebi tales by Yacoubi; publishes travel essays in *Holiday* and the *Nation*, then returns to Taprobane, accompanied by Yacoubi, determined to sell his island; writes "A Frozen Field," a short story that explores his troubled relationship with his father.

1957 In January, Jane's short story "A Stick of Green Candy," is published by *Vogue*. In April, Bowles is en route home from Ceylon when Jane, now forty, suffers a stroke; upon his return to Tangier, Bowles arranges for Jane to be hospitalized in England, where she undergoes shock treatment; doctors allow her to return home, accompanied by Bowles; in September, Jane returns to England and is hospitalized again, first at Radcliffe Infirmary in Oxford, then in a psychiatric hospital, Saint Andrew's, in Northampton. In July, Bowles's "A Frozen Field" is published in *Harper's Bazaar* and included in *Best Short Stories of 1958*; *Yallah*, a book of his photographs of North Africa and accompanying text, is published by McDowell, Obolensky.

1958 Bowles's opera *Yerma*, written for Libby Holman, opens in September in Denver, but is not a success; in Hollywood, he visits Christopher Isherwood and Don Bachardy, and writes score for José Ferrer's production of *Edwin Booth*, which opens on Broadway in November; in April, Jane returns to New York and is admitted to psychiatric hospital in White Plains, New York. A British edition of *The Spider's House* is published by Peter Owen. In May, "Tapiama" is published by John Lehmann in the *London Magazine*. By year's end, Jane, her health somewhat improved, returns with Bowles to Tangier.

1959–64 At Tennessee Williams's urging, Bowles returns to New York to write score for *Sweet Bird of Youth*, which opens on Broadway in March 1960; Bowles receives Rockefeller research grant to travel throughout Morocco recording its indigenous music for the Library of Congress. In 1959 *The Hours After Noon*, a collection of short stories, is published. Upon the arrival of the Beats in 1961, Bowles develops friendships with William S. Burroughs, Allen Ginsberg, Peter Orlovsky, Gregory Corso, and Alan Ansen; in December, Jane is awarded a three-thousand-dollar Ingram Merrill

Foundation grant to write a new play; in 1962, Bowles publishes *A Hundred Camels in the Courtyard*, four tales whose themes involve kif. In 1963, in New York, Bowles writes incidental music for Williams's *The Milk Train Doesn't Stop Here Anymore*; in August a book of travel pieces, *Their Heads Are Green and Their Hands Are Blue*, is published in London and New York. In November he begins his fourth novel, *Up Above the World*, in which he uses his own considerable experience with drugs and Jane's mental collapse for material; contributes recipe for *majoun* to *The Artists' and Writers' Cookbook*; spends summer in Moroccan village of Asilah and begins translating Driss ben Hamed Charhadi's *A Life Full of Holes*, published in 1964; in November finishes *Up Above the World*.

1965–67 Returns to the United States to visit his parents, now living in Gulfport, Florida. In November *Up Above the World* is published. At invitation of Joseph A. McPhillips III, headmaster of the American School of Tangier, writes music for the school's production of *Electra*; in 1966 writes music for the American School's production of *Oedipus the King*; in 1967 writes music for the American School's production of *The Garden*, based on a short story by Bowles, who adapts it as a play while in Bangkok, to which he travels in January to write a book; stays seven weeks, but Jane's mental and physical collapse forces his return to Tangier, where he abandons the project. In April 1967 Bowles takes Jane to a rest home in Málaga, Spain. His first collaboration as Mohammed Mrabet's translator, *Love with a Few Hairs*, and his own collection of short stories *The Time of Friendship* are published this year.

1968–73 In 1968 Bowles teaches a semester at San Fernando Valley State College in Northridge, California; also published is his collection *Pages from Cold Point and Other Stories*; in 1969 translates Mrabet's *The Lemon* and *M'Hashish*; in 1970 founds *Antaeus*, a literary review, with Daniel Halpern, whom he met in California, and helps edit it; in 1972 publishes *The Thicket of Spring*, a book of poems, and *Without Stopping*, an autobiography. On May 4, 1973, Jane dies.

1974 For the next seventeen years, Bowles engages primarily in translating the tales of Moroccans: in 1974 Mrabet's *The Boy Who Set the Fire*; Mohamed Choukri's *For Bread Alone* and *Jean Genet in Tangier*; in 1975 Mrabet's *Harmless Poisons, Blameless Sins* and *Look and Move On*; in 1975 Isabelle Eberhardt's *The Oblivion Seekers*; in 1977 Mrabet's *The Big Mirror*; in 1979 Choukri's *Tennessee Williams in Tangier*; in 1980 Mrabet's *The Beach Café & the Voice*; in 1983 Mrabet's *The Chest*; in 1986 Mrabet's *Marriage with Papers*; in 1992 Mrabet's *Chocolate Creams and Dollars*. In 1982 Bowles translates Guatemalan writer Rodrigo Rey Rosa's *The Path Doubles Back*; in 1985 Rey Rosa's *The Beggar's Knife*; in 1989 Rey Rosa's *Dust on Her Tongue*; and in 1991 Rey Rosa's *The Pelcari Project*. In 1979 publishes *Collected Stories, 1939–1976*; in 1981 *Midnight Mass*; in 1988 *Unwelcome Words* and *Call at Corazón and Other Stories*. In 1981 publishes his second book of poems, *Next to Nothing: Collected Poems, 1926–1977*; in 1982 his collection of historical tales, *Points in Time*, is published; in 1990 travels to Paris for premiere of Bernardo Bertolucci's film *The Sheltering Sky*; in 1991 his *Days, Tangier Journal: 1987–1989* (a reprint of 1989's *Two Years Before the Strait*) is published; in 1992 *Too Far from Home, Selected Writings* is published, edited by Daniel Halpern, introduction by Joyce Carol Oates.

1985 *Out in the World: Selected Letters of Jane Bowles, 1935–1970*, edited by Millicent Dillon (Santa Barbara: Black Sparrow Press, 1985), is published.

1999 On November 18, Bowles dies in Tangier at the age of eighty-eight after a brief illness; at his request, his body is brought to Casablanca for shipment to New York, where he is cremated and his ashes interred beside his mother and other family members on November 1, 2000, at Lakemont Cemetery in Glenora.

2001 A definitive collection, *The Stories of Paul Bowles*, edited by Dan Halpern, with an introduction by Robert Stone, is published by Ecco Press.

2003 *Paul Bowles on Music*, edited by Timothy Mangan and Irene Herrmann, is published by the University of California Press, Berkeley and Los Angeles.

2004 *Paul Bowles: A Life* by Virginia Spencer Carr is published.

NOTES

Chapter One

1. *In Touch: The Letters of Paul Bowles*, Jeffrey Miller, ed. (New York: Farrar, Straus and Giroux, 1994), p. 30, hereafter cited as *In Touch*; also Paul Bowles to Virginia Spencer Carr (hereafter cited as PB to VSC), Atlanta, Georgia, May 15, 1994.
2. PB to Bruce Morrissette, January 14, 1930, *In Touch*, pp. 29–30; also PB to VSC, February 14, 1995. The Mary Immaculate Hospital, later a division of the Catholic Medical Center, is still in its original location at 152–11 89th Street, Jamaica, New York.
3. Paul Bowles, *Without Stopping: An Autobiography* (New York: G. P. Putnam's Sons, 1972), pp. 42–43; hereafter cited as *Without Stopping*.
4. From the Winnewisser family archives of Bowles's cousin Harold Wesley Danser III.
5. *In Touch*, p. 30; also PB to VSC, Atlanta, May 16, 1994.
6. "Autobiography," *Antaeus*, April 15, 1985, p. 7; also PB to VSC, Tangier, October 9, 1996.
7. *Without Stopping*, p. 12.
8. PB to VSC, Atlanta, May 16, 1994.
9. *Without Stopping*, pp. 56–57.
10. PB to VSC, Atlanta, May 16, 1994.
11. Millicent Dillon, *A Little Original Sin: The Life and Work of Jane Bowles* (New York: Holt Rinehart and Winston, 1981), pp. 44–45; hereafter cited as *A Little Original Sin*.
12. PB to VSC, September 10, 1989.
13. From the Winnewisser family archives of Bowles's cousin Harold Wesley Danser III.
14. *Without Stopping*, pp. 10–11.
15. Ibid., p. 11.
16. Ibid., p. 13; also PB to VSC, Atlanta, May 25, 1994.
17. PB to VSC, Atlanta, May 26, 1994.
18. Ibid., Tangier, October 9, 1996.
19. Ibid., October 10, 1996.
20. *Without Stopping*, p. 14.
21. PB to VSC, Atlanta, May 26, 1994.
22. *Without Stopping*, p. 18.
23. Ibid., p. 32.

24. Ibid., pp. 22–23.
25. PB to VSC, Atlanta, May 26, 1994.
26. The Harry Ransom Humanities Research Center at the University of Texas, Austin (hereafter cited as HRHRC), has ten of Bowles's early notebooks. Several are leather-bound, their dimensions 3 x 5½ inches; some have numbered pages, and some are unnumbered. The earliest notebook, numbered on both sides of each leaf, has 175 pages and is secured by a flap that snaps. Most of the early notebooks are in pencil, in block printing. The earliest, bound in red morocco leather, is titled "THE ALWAYS BOOKS FOR YOUNG AND OLD." Bowles was four when he began his first diary, dated July 11, Sunday (1915). Many pages bear consecutive letters, rather than numbers. The first begins with the letter *F*. Each page is lettered alphabetically and consecutively, from *F* to *Z*. After the letter *Z* are consecutive numbers beginning with *1*. On the back flyleaf, Bowles wrote twice the phrase *The End* and underlined it. In a box of this page, he wrote: "CONTINUED IN THE NEWS OF ALL WORLDS, p. 102."
27. PB to VSC, Atlanta, June 22, 1994.
28. Ibid.

Chapter Two

1. PB to VSC, February 15, 1995. His father's office, known later as the Colonial Arms, was at 76 Herriman Avenue, on the corner of Herriman and North Shelton in Jamaica, New York.
2. PB to VSC, February 23, 1995.
3. Horace Fletcher (1849–1919) was an American nutritionist who conceived and popularized the method of Fletcherization. He was convinced that if children were taught his method and practiced it faithfully, they would maintain such habits as adults and teach them to their children; *Without Stopping*, p. 24; also PB to VSC, Atlanta, June 8, 1994.
4. PB to VSC, Atlanta, June 9, 1994; also *Without Stopping*, p. 43.
5. PB to VSC, Atlanta, May 17, 1994; also *Without Stopping*, p. 28.
6. PB to VSC, Atlanta, May 17, 1994.
7. Ibid., May 10, 1994; also *Without Stopping*, p. 29.
8. PB to VSC, Atlanta, May 10, 1994; also PB to Bruce Morrissette, January 14, 1930, *In Touch*, pp. 30–31.
9. PB to Bruce Morrissette, January 14, 1930, *In Touch*, p. 30; also PB to VSC, Atlanta, May 17, 1994.
10. PB to VSC, Atlanta, May 31, 1994; also *Without Stopping*, p. 28. According to *Early Histories of the New York Philharmonic*, part 3, "The Philharmonic-Symphony Society of New York: Its First Hundred Years," Leopold Stokowski conducted the Philadelphia Orchestra in a performance of Tchaikovsky's Fourth Symphony, opus 36, in Carnegie Hall on November 19, 1918. Bowles was certain that his parents had attended the concert and thus were motivated to buy the gramophone.

11. *Without Stopping*, p. 36.
12. According to Bowles, "Give Me Wine" was the first poem he wrote; it was published for the first time in *Blades*, edited by Francis Poole and JoAnn Balingit, published in *Portugal* 17 (Summer 1983), p. 21; reprinted by permission of Poole and Balingit; also PB to VSC, Tangier, October 16, 1997.
13. *Without Stopping*, p. 38.
14. PB to VSC, Atlanta, May 10, 1994; also *Without Stopping*, pp. 50–51.
15. PB to VSC, March 2, 1997; also *Without Stopping*, pp. 29–30.
16. PB to VSC, March 2, 1997; also *Without Stopping*, p. 34.
17. PB to VSC, Tangier, September 9, 1996.
18. PB to VSC, March 2, 1997; also *Without Stopping*, p. 65.
19. Ibid.
20. *Without Stopping*, p. 31.
21. Ibid., p. 40.
22. PB to VSC, March 2, 1997; also *Without Stopping*, p. 41.
23. PB to VSC, Tangier, September 9, 1996; also *Without Stopping*, p. 42.
24. PB to VSC, Tangier, September 9, 1996; also *Without Stopping*, pp. 49–50.
25. PB to VSC, Atlanta, May 21, 1994; also *Without Stopping*, pp. 49–50.
26. PB to VSC, Atlanta, October 1, 1994.
27. Ibid., October 2, 1994.
28. PB to VSC, March 2, 1997; also *Without Stopping*, pp. 47–48.
29. PB to VSC, Tangier, September 9, 1996; also *Without Stopping*, p. 54.
30. *Without Stopping*, p. 58.
31. PB to Phillip Ramey, interview, November 20 and 24, 1997, published as "A Talk with Paul Bowles" in *Contemporary Review*, May 1997, pp. 41–47; also PB to VSC, Tangier, March 18, 1995, and *Without Stopping*, p. 58.
32. PB to VSC, Tangier, September 9, 1996; also *Without Stopping*, pp. 66–67.
33. PB to VSC, October 16, 1997; also *Without Stopping*, pp. 60–61.
34. *Without Stopping*, pp. 32–33.
35. In *Without Stopping*, p. 58, Bowles spoke of mice, rather than frogs, being dissected in his tenth-grade biology class at Flushing High School. "I was mistaken; they were definitely frogs," Bowles told Carr.
36. *Without Stopping*, pp. 66–67.
37. Ibid., pp. 69–70.
38. PB to VSC, Atlanta, October 1, 1994; also *Without Stopping*, pp. 69–70.
39. Patricia A. DeMasters, Office of the Registrar, University of Virginia, Charlottesville, to VSC, February 16, 1996.

Chapter Three

1. PB to VSC, Atlanta, May 25, 1994.
2. Ibid., May 15, 1994; see also *Program*, The Phylo Players, Studio Playhouse, Whitestone Landing, April 10 and 12, 1928.
3. PB to VSC, Atlanta, May 9, 1994; also PB to Daniel Burns, summer 1928, *In Touch*, p. 3.

4. PB to Daniel Burns, undated letter (1928), Paul Bowles Collection, HRHRC.
5. PB to VSC, Atlanta, May 15, 1994; also *Without Stopping*, p. 72.
6. "Elegy" was the second poem in Bowles's first published collection of poetry: *Thicket of Spring: 1926–1969* (Los Angeles: Black Sparrow Press, 1972).
7. PB to VSC, Atlanta, May 25, 1994.
8. Ibid., May 26, 1994.
9. Ibid.
10. PB to Daniel Burns, undated letter (1928), Paul Bowles Collection, HRHRC.
11. PB to VSC, Atlanta, May 26, 1994; also *Without Stopping*, p. 75.
12. PB to Daniel Burns, November 1928, *In Touch*, p. 6.
13. PB to VSC, Atlanta, October 14, 1994; also *Without Stopping*, pp. 77–78.
14. PB to VSC, Atlanta, October 13, 1994.
15. *Without Stopping*, p. 79.
16. Ibid., p. 82.
17. PB to VSC, Atlanta, October 13, 1994; also *Without Stopping*, p. 83.
18. PB to VSC, Atlanta, October 13, 1994.
19. Ibid.; also *Without Stopping*, p. 86.
20. PB to VSC, Atlanta, October 14, 1994.
21. *Without Stopping*, p. 89.
22. Ibid., p. 91.
23. Ibid.
24. PB to VSC, Tangier, October 16, 1997.
25. *Without Stopping*, p. 93.
26. Ibid., p. 95; also PB to VSC, October 16, 1997. For a version of Bowles's meeting with Hardy and their subsequent travels together, see *Without Stopping*, pp. 92–95. Years later, upon reading Gena Dagel Caponi's biography, *Paul Bowles: Romantic Savage*, Bowles noted that Caponi had alleged that his homosexual relationship with Uncle Hubert was an extended one. Bowles circled the word *extended*, and in the margin, wrote "Out. By no means was it an extended relationship–it wasn't a relationship at all."
27. *Without Stopping*, p. 96.
28. Ibid., p. 86.
29. Ibid., p. 98.
30. Ibid., p. 99.
31. Aaron Copland to Gena Dagel Caponi, quoted in Caponi's book *Paul Bowles: Romantic Savage* (Carbondale: Southern Illinois University Press, 1994), p. 42.
32. *Without Stopping*, pp. 90–91.
33. Bowles's poems in *Tambour* included "Blessed Be the Meek," "Poem" (which began "I will have my spy hunt you out"), "Hymn," "America," "Dream," and "Slow Song."
34. *Without Stopping*, p. 97; also PB to VSC, Tangier, October 17, 1997.
35. PB to Bruce Morrissette, December 30, 1929, *In Touch*, p. 20.
36. PB to Daniel Burns, unpublished letter (1928), Paul Bowles Collection, HRHRC.
37. PB to Bruce Morrissette, October 23, 1929, *In Touch*, p. 12. Bowles said later that he had no idea what eventually happened to it; "I don't remember giving it

away. I only know that I never made another sculpture." PB to VSC, Tangier, October 16, 1998.

38. PB to VSC, December 29, 1997; also Patricia A. DeMasters, Office of the Registrar, University of Virginia, Charlottesville, to VSC, October 17, 1997.
39. *Without Stopping*, p. 100.
40. Ibid., pp. 99–100.
41. PB to VSC, Tangier, December 29, 1997.
42. Ibid.
43. William Carlos Williams to PB, unpublished letter (1928), Paul Bowles Collection, HRHRC.
44. PB to VSC, Tangier, October 21, 1997.
45. *Without Stopping*, pp. 104–5.

Chapter Four

1. PB to Edouard Roditi, March 4, 1931, Edouard Roditi Collection, Department of Special Collections, UCLA Library, University of California, Los Angeles.
2. PB to VSC, Tangier, December 29, 1997.
3. Ibid.
4. *Without Stopping*, p. 106; see also Paul Bowles/Florian Vetsch, *Desultory Correspondence: An Interview with Paul Bowles on Gertrude Stein* (Zurich: Memory/Cage Editions, 1997), pp. 8–10.
5. PB to Ira Cohen, 1965, in *Conversations with Paul Bowles*, ed. Gena Dagel Caponi (Jackson: University Press of Mississippi, 1993), p. 10.
6. Anthony Tommasini, *Virgil Thomson: Composer on the Aisle* (New York: W. W. Norton, 1997), p. 216; for details of what led up to Stein's dismissal of Thomson, see pp. 209–17.
7. PB to VSC, Tangier, October 15, 1997; also *Without Stopping*, p. 108.
8. PB to Charles Henri Ford, December 10, 1931, *In Touch*, p. 93.
9. Ibid.; also Bowles quoted in Jeffrey Bailey, "The Art of Fiction LXVII: Paul Bowles," in *Paris Review* 23, no. 81 (Fall 1981), p. 75.
10. PB to Regina Weinreich, interview, *The Complete Outsider* (film documentary), 1985.
11. PB to VSC, Tangier, December 29, 1997.
12. Ibid.
13. Ibid., October 16, 1997.
14. Ibid.
15. PB to VSC, Tangier, October 17, 1997.
16. PB to Jeffrey Bailey, in Caponi, ed., *Conversations with Paul Bowles*, pp. 118–19; also PB to Elizabeth Updike, Tangier, May 20, 1998.
17. PB to Edouard Roditi, June 13, 1931, Edouard Roditi Collection, Department of Special Collections, UCLA Library.
18. Hugh Ford, *Published in Paris: American and British Writers, Printers, and Publishers in Paris, 1920–1939* (New York: Macmillan, 1975), p. 310.
19. PB to VSC, Tangier, October 17, 1997; also *Without Stopping*, p. 115.

20. PB to VSC, Tangier, December 28, 1997; also PB to Edouard Roditi, undated letter (1931), Edouard Roditi Collection, Department of Special Collections, UCLA Library.
21. Hugh Ford, *Published in Paris*, pp. 309–10.
22. Ibid., p. 310.
23. *In Touch*, pp. 79–80.
24. PB to VSC, January 5, 1998.
25. Ibid.
26. PB to Rena Bowles, August 4, 1931, *In Touch*, pp. 80–82.
27. Ibid.
28. PB to Rena Bowles, undated letter (August 1931), Paul Bowles Collection, HRHRC.
29. PB to VSC, Tangier, December 9, 1997; also Phillip Ramey to VSC, New York, May 20, 1997. "Paul told me that it was Aaron who seduced him," said Ramey, who was a friend of both Copland and Bowles for over thirty years. "Paul's comments in his letter to Aaron in 1932 would have been veiled, but they both told me, separately, that it was true. Paul was very embarrassed. It was not syphilis but clap [gonorrhea] that he caught, and both he and Copland were treated for it in Tangier. He said that Aaron had gotten it in Berlin and inflicted it upon him. Aaron was Paul's mentor and at the time Paul did not want sex to be a part of their relationship." In Tangier on January 7, 1998, Bowles told Carr that his relationship with Copland had been a sexual one, both in the 1930s and later, in the 1940s.
30. *Without Stopping*, p. 126.
31. Ibid., p. 127.
32. PB to Bruce Morrissette, Tangier, August 13, 1931, *In Touch*, pp. 82–83.
33. PB to Rena Bowles, undated letter (August 1931), Paul Bowles Collection, HRHRC.
34. *Without Stopping*, pp. 130–31.
35. PB to VSC, Tangier, December 9, 1997; also *Without Stopping*, p. 131.
36. PB to Aaron Copland, undated letter, *In Touch*, p. 89.
37. *Without Stopping*, p. 133.
38. PB to "Dear Mother," unpublished letter, September 16, 1931, Paul Bowles Collection, HRHRC.
39. *Without Stopping*, p. 140.
40. Ibid., p. 141.
41. Henry Boys, "America in London," *Modern Music* 9, no. 2 (January–February 1932), pp. 92–93.
42. *Without Stopping*, p. 142.
43. *In Touch*, p. 97.
44. Bowles was not being secretive about who was providing him shelter. He simply saw no reason to mention the specifics to Roditi. PB to VSC, Tangier, December 21, 1998.
45. PB to VSC, Tangier, December 21, 1998.
46. *Without Stopping*, p. 145.
47. Ibid.

48. PB to VSC, Tangier, October 21, 1997; also *Without Stopping*, p. 153.
49. "In 1933, Aaron became a member of the board of the League of Composers, and by the mid-1930s, he was generally recognized as the most influential composer in the shaping of twentieth-century American music. It was in this capacity that he was named to the board of directors of Yaddo." PB to VSC, Tangier, December 21, 1998.
50. Anthony Tommasini, *Virgil Thomson: Composer on the Aisle*, pp. 298–301; also Minna Lederman, *The Life and Death of a Small Magazine: Modern Music, 1924–1946* (Brooklyn, N.Y.: Institute for Studies in American Music, 1983), p. 22.
51. PB to Aaron Copland, Tangier (May 1932), *In Touch*, p. 101.
52. PB to VSC, Tangier, December 27, 1998.
53. Charles Henri Ford to VSC, New York City, May 15, 1997.
54. PB to VSC, Tangier, December 27, 1998.
55. *Without Stopping*, pp. 152–53; also PB to VSC, Tangier, December 27, 1998.
56. *Without Stopping*, p. 154.
57. Ibid.
58. PB to Virgil Thomson, undated letter (October 7, 1932), Virgil Thomson Collection, Irving S. Gilmore Music Library, Yale University.
59. Anthony Tommasini, *Virgil Thomson: Composer on the Aisle*, pp. 298–301; also Minna Lederman, *The Life and Death of a Small Magazine: Modern Music, 1924–1926*, pp. 9, 22.
60. PB to Virgil Thomson, undated letter (October 7, 1932), Virgil Thomson Collection, Irving S. Gilmore Music Library, Yale University.

Chapter Five

1. PB to Aaron Copland, *In Touch*, p. 110.
2. PB to Rena Bowles, Laghouat, Algeria, January 13, 1933; unpublished letter, Paul Bowles Collection, HRHRC.
3. PB to Charles Henri Ford, undated letter (1933), Afric Hôtel, Algiers, Paul Bowles Collection, HRHRC.
4. PB to Charles Henri Ford, March 1933, *In Touch*, p. 113.
5. *Without Stopping*, pp. 157–58.
6. Virgil Thomson to Aaron Copland, in Aaron Copland and Vivian Perlis, *Copland: 1900 Through 1942* (New York: St. Martin's Press), p. 195. "A *poule de luxe* is a woman who is supported by a man in a very luxurious fashion; she may, or may not, be a prostitute." PB to VSC, Tangier, May 25, 1995.
7. *Without Stopping*, p. 158; also PB to Rena Bowles, January 1, 1933, Paul Bowles Collection, HRHRC.
8. PB to VSC, Tangier, December 19, 1998. Bowles's letter to his mother dated March 17, 1933, was mailed from Algiers; also PB to VSC, May 26, 1995.
9. PB to VSC, Tangier, December 20, 1998; also *Without Stopping*, pp. 158, 165–66.
10. PB to Aaron Copland, January 1933, *In Touch*, pp. 109–10.
11. PB to VSC, May 26, 1995.
12. *Without Stopping*, p. 161.

13. The banks reopened on March 12, 1933, following the President's announcement in his first "fireside chat" to the American people, but Bowles had no idea while in Tunisia when the banks would reopen.
14. *Without Stopping*, p. 162; also PB to VSC, Tangier, December 31, 1998, Paul Bowles Collection, HRHRC.
15. Christopher Sawyer-Lauçanno, *An Invisible Spectator: A Biography of Paul Bowles* (New York: Ecco Press, 1990), p. 148. Saint-Jean Perse was the adopted name used by Alexis Saint-Léger Léger as poet, diplomat, and statesman. The poem was translated by T. S. Eliot in 1930.
16. Charles Henri Ford to VSC, New York City, May 20, 1997.
17. Ibid.
18. PB to VSC, Atlanta, September 17, 1994; also PB to Ira Cohen, 1965, *Conversations with Paul Bowles*, ed. Gena Dagel Caponi (Jackson: University Press of Mississippi, 1993), p. 11.
19. PB to Aaron Copland, undated letter (May 1933), *In Touch*, pp. 114–15.
20. PB to Virgil Thomson, undated letter (June 1933), Virgil Thomson Collection, Irving S. Gilmore Music Library, Yale University; also PB to Gertrude Stein, undated letter, Stein Collection, Beinecke Rare Book and Manuscript Library, Yale University.
21. "It was *Tamanar* that later disappeared." PB to VSC, Tangier, October 18, 1996.
22. Ibid.
23. PB to Virgil Thomson, undated letter (summer 1933), Westhampton, Massachusetts, *In Touch*, p. 116. Although Bowles was unaware of it at the time, a short story of his own, "Massachusetts 1932," was brewing during his stay in Westhampton. PB to VSC, Tangier, October 19, 1996.
24. PB to VSC, Tangier, October 19, 1996; also PB to Aaron Copland, undated letter (summer 1933), Westhampton, *In Touch*, pp. 116–17.
25. PB to Virgil Thomson, undated letter (summer 1933), *In Touch*, p. 122.
26. PB to Phillip Ramey, interview, "You Didn't Want to Meet Prokofiev?" in Claudia Swann, ed., *Paul Bowles: Music* (New York: Eos Music, 1995), pp. 25–26.
27. PB to Phillip Ramey, interview, "You Didn't Want Even to Meet Prokofiev?" in *Paul Bowles: Music*, p. 27; also Phillip Ramey to VSC, Tangier, October 20, 1997.
28. PB to VSC, Tangier, October 18, 1996.
29. Ibid., January 2, 1999; also Aaron Copland, *Copland on Music*, p. 162.
30. According to Christopher Sawyer-Lauçanno, the apartment belonged to Harold and Stella Clurman, who passed it on to Copland, who gave it to Bowles and split the rent with him. See *An Invisible Spectator*, p. 151.
31. PB to VSC, Tangier, January 1, 1999.
32. Ibid., January 2, 1999; also *Without Stopping*, p. 172.
33. PB to VSC, Tangier, October 19, 1996.
34. Ibid., January 1, 1999.
35. Ibid., January 2, 1999; also *Without Stopping*, p. 170.
36. PB to VSC, Tangier, January 1, 1999; also *Without Stopping*, pp. 170–71.
37. PB to VSC, Atlanta, June 3, 1994.
38. PB to VSC, Tangier, January 1, 1999.
39. *In Touch*, p. 156.

40. PB to VSC, Tangier, January 1, 1999; also *Without Stopping*, pp. 182–83.
41. PB to Gertrude Stein, no date (March 1935), Beinecke Rare Book and Manuscript Library, Yale University.
42. PB to Bruce Morrissette, undated letter (December 1934), Hollywood, California, *In Touch*, pp. 153–54.
43. PB to Rena Bowles, January 13, 1933, Laghouat, Algeria; unpublished letter, Paul Bowles Collection, HRHRC.
44. PB to VSC, Tangier, January 1, 1999.
45. Christopher Sawyer-Lauçanno, *An Invisible Spectator*, p. 152.
46. *Without Stopping*, p. 185; also PB to VSC, Tangier, January 2, 1999.
47. *Memnon*, written as a cycle of six songs for voice and solo piano, included "Les Statues," "Athena," "La Grèce," "Recette," "Le Sourire" (The Smile), and the title piece, "Memnon," in which Bowles used handclappings executed by the singer between strophes.
48. A number of Bowles's early songs that had not been published previously appeared as part 2 of Peter Garland's edited collection of Bowles's *Selected Songs*, published in 1984: "In the Platinum Forest," composed in Paris in February 1932; "Voici la Feuille," originally known as "Valse," composed in Laghouat, Algeria, in December 1932; "April Fool Baby" (text by Gertrude Stein), composed in New York in March 1944; "This Place of Fire" (text by D. H. Lawrence), composition undated; "Down in Yonder Meadow" (1944, anonymous); two songs by Charles Henri Ford, "Song for My Sister" (Ruth Ford) and "Night Without Sleep," composed in New York in December 1943; "My Sister's Hand in Mine" (originally titled "Bluebell Mountain"), text by Jane Auer Bowles, composed in New York in 1945; "Cancioncilla," "Media Luna," "Balada Amarilla," and "Murió al Amanecer" (texts by Federico García Lorca), composed in New York in 1944; "The Feathers of the Willow" (text by Canon Dixon), composed in New York in 1944; "The Piper" (text by Seamus O'Sullivan), composed in New York in 1944; "They Cannot Stop Death" (text by Joe Massey), composed in New York in February 1944; "Mes de Mayo" (anonymous), composed in New York in February 1944; "The Heart Grows Old" (text by David Villiers), composed in Tangier in August 1949; texts of five songs by Tennessee Williams: "Testa dell'Efebo," "San Sebastiano di Sodoma," "The Goths," "Faint as Leaf Shadow," "Death Is High," composed in Tangier in August 1960; and Bowles's "Her Head on the Pillow," composed in Tangier in 1961.
49. PB to Katherine Cowen, August 21, 1935, from Watkins Glen, New York, *In Touch*, p. 159–60.
50. *Without Stopping*, p. 186.
51. PB to Gertrude Stein, undated letter (spring 1936), Jamaica, New York, *In Touch*, p. 160.
52. *Without Stopping*, p. 190.
53. Ibid., p. 190.
54. PB to Bruce Morrissette, April 12, 1935, *In Touch*, p. 157.
55. PB to VSC, Tangier, January 2, 1999.
56. Ibid.
57. PB to William Treat Upton (spring 1935), *In Touch*, pp. 158–59.

58. *Without Stopping*, p. 188.
59. PB to Alec France, undated letter, Virgil Thomson Collection, Irving S. Gilmore Music Library, Yale University.
60. *Without Stopping*, p. 192.
61. Ibid., p. 195. *Doctor Faustus* opened January 8, 1937, at the Maxine Elliott Theatre and ran four months.
62. *Without Stopping*, p. 194.
63. Bowles's articles on film music appeared in the *New York Herald Tribune* on January 17, 1943; January 31, 1943; June 29, 1943; and November 21, 1943. See also *Paul Bowles on Music*, ed. Timothy Mangan and Irene Herrmann (Berkeley: University of California Press, 2003), pp. 79–82, 84–86, 116–18, 127–30.
64. *Without Stopping*, p. 194.
65. Ibid., p. 195.
66. Ned Rorem, *Setting the Tone: Essays and a Diary* (New York: Coward-McCann, 1983), pp. 355–56.
67. PB to VSC, Tangier, December 23, 1998.
68. PB to Katherine Cowen de Baillou, undated letter (1936), Katherine Cowen de Baillou Archives, Hargrett Library Special Collections, University of Georgia Libraries, Athens.

Chapter Six

1. *A Little Original Sin*, p. 37.
2. PB to VSC, Tangier, September 9, 1989; also *Without Stopping*, p. 196.
3. When Bowles knew Tonny in Paris, then later, in Tangier, they always spoke in French. Bowles gave no thought to the fact that Tonny spoke no English; also *Without Stopping*, pp. 195–96.
4. PB to VSC, January 1, 1999; also *Without Stopping*, p. 196.
5. PB to VSC, Tangier, December 23, 1998.
6. *A Little Original Sin*, p. 42; also PB to VSC, Tangier, December 24, 1998.
7. "Jane Bowles," in *World Authors, 1950–1970*, ed. John Wakeman (New York: H. W. Wilson, 1975), p. 203.
8. PB to VSC, Tangier, September 4, 1989; also *A Little Original Sin*, pp. 37–38.
9. PB to VSC, Tangier, September 9, 1989; also Tangier, December 24, 1998.
10. PB to VSC, Tangier, September 9, 1989.
11. Ibid.
12. *Without Stopping*, p. 186.
13. *A Little Original Sin*, p. 45.
14. PB to VSC, Tangier, September 4, 1989.
15. Ibid., September 9, 1989.
16. *Without Stopping*, pp. 198–99.
17. PB to VSC, Tangier, January 1, 1999; also *Without Stopping*, p. 204.
18. PB to VSC, Tangier, January 1, 1999.
19. *A Little Original Sin*, p. 49.
20. PB to VSC, Tangier, January 1, 1999; also *Without Stopping*, p. 205.

21. "The Composers Organize. A Proclamation," *Modern Music* 15, no. 2 (January–February 1938), pp. 92–95; see also *ACA Bulletin* 9, nos. 2–4 (December 1963), Twenty-fifth Anniversary Issue. Copland served as president of the American Composers' Alliance from its founding until 1945, when he was succeeded by Otto Luening.
22. PB to VSC, Tangier, January 2, 1999.
23. Ibid.; also *Without Stopping*, pp. 205–6.
24. PB to VSC, Tangier, January 1, 1999.
25. Ibid., January 2, 1999.
26. Ibid., September 10, 1989.
27. Charles Henri Ford to VSC, New York, May 15, 1997.
28. PB to VSC, Tangier, January 2, 1999; also *Without Stopping*, p. 206.
29. PB to VSC, Tangier, January 2, 1999.
30. Ibid., September 9, 1996.
31. Ibid., January 2, 1999.
32. *A Little Original Sin*, pp. 54–55; also PB to VSC, Tangier, January 2, 1999.
33. PB to VSC, Tangier, January 2, 1999; also *A Little Original Sin*, p. 55.
34. "All Parrots Speak," *Their Heads Are Green and Their Hands Are Blue* (New York: Random House, 1984), pp. 146–49; see also *Their Heads Are Green* (London: Peter Owen, 1963), pp. 23–33.
35. PB to VSC, Tangier, September 9, 1996; also PB to Levio Nigri, taped interview/drama documentary, Happy Valley Films, May 1990, Tangier (tape 3, side A; transcription courtesy of Warwick Hembry and Levio Nigri); also Warwick Hembry to VSC, London, September 10, 1994; and *A Little Original Sin*, p. 54.
36. *Without Stopping*, pp. 209–10; also PB to VSC, Tangier, January 2, 1999.
37. PB to VSC, Tangier, October 19, 1998.
38. Hall Winslow to VSC, Atlanta, February 2, 1995.
39. PB to VSC, Atlanta, September 21–22, 1994; also Tangier, January 2, 1999.
40. Bowles's essay "Calypso—Music of the Antilles" appeared in the March–April 1940 issue of *Modern Music*; see also *Paul Bowles on Music*, ed. Timothy Mangan and Irene Herrman (Berkeley: University of California Press, 2003), pp. 15–22.
41. PB to VSC, Tangier, December 27, 1998.
42. Ibid.; also *Without Stopping*, pp. 210–11.
43. PB to VSC, Tangier, January 2, 1999.
44. Ibid.; also *Without Stopping*, p. 211.
45. PB to VSC, Tangier, January 2, 1999.
46. Ibid.; also *Without Stopping*, pp. 210–11; and *A Little Original Sin*, pp. 56–57.
47. PB to VSC, Tangier, January 23, 1997.
48. Ibid., January 2, 1999.
49. Ibid.; also *A Little Original Sin*, pp. 56–57.
50. PB to VSC, Tangier, January 2, 1999.
51. Ibid.
52. Ibid.
53. Ibid.
54. "His name was Hans Namuth, a friend of Samuel Barlow's, whom I met in

New York." PB to VSC, Tangier, January 2, 1999; also "undated letter," Paul Bowles Collection, HRHRC.

55. Katherine Cowen to her mother, August 11, 1938, Katherine Cowen de Baillou Archives, Hargrett Library Special Collections, University of Georgia Libraries, Athens.
56. PB to Charles Henri Ford, undated letter (September 1938), Charles Henri Ford Archives, HRHRC.
57. PB to VSC, Tangier, January 2, 1999.
58. Ibid., January 3, 1999.
59. Ibid., January 2, 1999.
60. Charles Hingham, *Orson Welles: The Rise and Fall of an American Genius* (New York: St. Martin's Press, 1985), pp. 116–19.
61. "Paul Bowles," interview and photos by David Seidner, *Bomb* no. 4 (New York: Center for New Art Activities, 1982), pp. 11–12.
62. PB to VSC, Tangier, January 2, 1999; also John Houseman, *Run-Through: A Memoir* (New York: Simon & Schuster, 1972), p. 377.
63. PB to VSC, Tangier, January 2, 1999; also *Without Stopping*, pp. 212–13. In 1939, the League of Composers gave *Music for a Farce* its first performance.
64. PB to VSC, Tangier, December 29, 1998.
65. Ibid.; also fax, PB to VSC, April 14, 1999; and *Without Stopping*, p. 213.
66. PB to VSC, Tangier, December 29, 1998; also *Without Stopping*, pp. 214–15, 222.
67. "I do not remember the precise date we joined the Party, but I know it was in December of 1938." PB to VSC, April 14, 1999.
68. PB to VSC, Tangier, October 7, 1997.
69. *Without Stopping*, p. 215. On November 11, 1938, Bowles wrote Katherine Cowen that he and Jane were attending a "magnificent series of old Russian films at the Roosevelt Theatre." Katherine Cowen de Baillou Archives, Hargrett Library Special Collections, University of Georgia Libraries, Athens.
70. Bowles's FBI file, #100–329281, and Jane's file, #100–428983, were released to VSC on February 25, 1996, through the Freedom of Information–Privacy Acts Section.
71. In the biographical sketch in the *Playbill* of *My Heart's in the Highlands*, the editor of the *Playbill* declared: "He wrote his first musical composition at the age of six; it was called *Opera in Nine Chapters*, and he played it on the zither, which he kept tuned with a roller skate key. Although he has had no formal training in music, he has studied with Aaron Copland for the past few seasons and was responsible for the scores in the Federal Theatre's productions of *Dr. Faustus* and *Horse Eats Hat*. He also composed *Ballet Caravan*, which was produced recently, and is the creator of an impressive amount of chamber music."
72. PB to VSC, January 3, 1999; also miscellaneous clippings from the William Saroyan Archive, Special Collections, Stanford University Libraries; and Robert Lewis, *Slings and Arrows: Theatre in My Life* (New York: Stein and Day, 1984), pp. 108–13.
73. Ruth Chatterton's chief film credits were *Madame X* (1929); *Once a Lady* (1931); *Female* (1933); and *Dodsworth* (1936); see *Without Stopping*, p. 217. Chatterton had borrowed fifty thousand dollars from Mary Oliver and could not repay it.

74. Bowles declared that after he moved to Brooklyn, Jane forwarded him a telephone bill for $180 and a copy of Oliver's long distance calls. "I wrote to the telephone company saying that I was on relief and could not pay the bill." *Without Stopping*, p. 218.
75. PB to VSC, Tangier, January 3, 1999.
76. Ibid.
77. Ibid.
78. PB to Bruce Morrissette, January 3, 1940, *In Touch*, p. 171.
79. PB to Katherine Cowen, August 3, 1939, Katherine Cowen de Baillou Archives, Hargrett Library Special Collections, University of Georgia Libraries, Athens.
80. *Without Stopping*, p. 222.
81. PB to Katherine Cowen, August 3, 1939, Katherine Cowen de Baillou Archives, Hargrett Library Special Collections, University of Georgia Libraries, Athens.
82. Ribbentrop's rise to power had been swift. Having joined the Nazi party in 1932, he soon became Hitler's chief adviser on foreign affairs. He was Germany's ambassador to Great Britain from 1936 to 1938, and foreign minister from 1938 to 1945, during which time he negotiated the Non-Aggression Pact signed in Moscow between Germany and the Soviet Union. In 1946, Ribbentrop was tried at Nuremberg as a war criminal and executed, one of the eleven sentenced to death by hanging.
83. PB to VSC, Tangier, January 3, 1939; also *Without Stopping*, p. 216.
84. PB to VSC, Tangier, October 8, 1997.
85. *A Little Original Sin*, p. 80.
86. PB to VSC, Tangier, October 8, 1997.
87. Ibid.
88. Ibid., January 3, 1999; also *A Little Original Sin*, p. 83; and *Without Stopping*, p. 226.

Chapter Seven

1. Tennessee Williams's letter to Bennett Cerf, dated "12 or 13 September 1940," is housed in the Rare Book and Manuscript Library, Butler Library, Columbia University, New York.
2. Tennessee Williams, *Memoirs* (New York: Doubleday, 1975), p. 59; also *Without Stopping*, p. 229; and PB to VSC, December 29, 1998.
3. PB to VSC, Tangier, December 29, 1998.
4. Ibid.
5. *Without Stopping*, p. 226; also PB to VSC, December 29, 1998.
6. *Without Stopping*, p. 228.
7. PB to VSC, December 29, 1998.
8. Morris Golde to VSC, New York City, September 9, 1992.
9. PB to VSC, Tangier, December 29, 1998. According to Bowles, their mailing address was Lista de Correos, Taxco, Guerrero, Mexico.
10. "Scene I," "Scene II," and "Scene III" were written several years earlier, but remained unpublished, as did Scenes IV through IX, until 1972 when they were

published in *The Thicket of Spring: Poems 1926–1969*, ed. John Martin (Los Angeles: Black Sparrow Press, 1972).

11. PB to VSC, Tangier, December 29, 1998.
12. PB to VSC, October 19, 1997; also Ned Rorem, *Knowing When to Stop: A Memoir* (New York: Simon & Schuster, 1994), p. 193.
13. PB to VSC, Tangier, October 19, 1997; also Lyle Leverich, *Tom: The Unknown Tennessee Williams* (New York: Crown Publishers, 1995), p. 398.
14. Virgil Thomson, *New York Herald Tribune*, November 19, 1940.
15. PB to VSC, Tangier, October 19, 1997.
16. Ibid., October 18, 1997.
17. *Without Stopping*, p. 232–33; also Humphrey Burton, *Leonard Bernstein* (New York: Doubleday, 1994), p. 88.
18. PB to VSC, Tangier, October 19, 1997.
19. Ibid.; also Sawyer-Lauçanno, *An Invisible Spectator: A Biography of Paul Bowles* (New York: Ecco Press, 1990), p. 224.
20. PB to VSC, Tangier, October 19, 1997. Thomson's archives at Yale University house three letters pertinent to the issue, herein paraphrased: an undated letter from Bowles pointing out the chief usage of his music in the film; Thomson's letter of November 16, 1943, to Bowles's lawyer, Maurice J. Speiser; and Speiser's reply to Thomson on November 22, 1943, acknowledging Thomson's letter and declaring that he would "be glad to incorporate it in the case of Mr. Paul Bowles."
21. PB to VSC, Tangier, October 18, 1997; also *Without Stopping*, p. 233.
22. Michael Meyer to Donald Mitchell and Philip Reed, June 22, 1988, *Letters from a Life: The Selected Letters and Diaries of Benjamin Britten, 1913–1976*, vol. 2 (London: Faber and Faber, 1991), p. 900.
23. Louis MacNeice, *The Strings Are False: An Unfinished Autobiography* (London: Faber and Faber, 1965), p. 35; also John Stallworthy, *Louis MacNeice: A Biography* (London: Faber and Faber, 1995).
24. PB to VSC, Tangier, October 18, 1987; also Susan Edmiston and Linda D. Cirino, *Literary New York: A History and Guide* (Boston: Houghton Mifflin, 1976), pp. 348–53; and *A Little Original Sin*, p. 94.
25. PB to VSC, Tangier, October 22, 1997.
26. Ibid.
27. Ibid.
28. Bowles's first "On the Film Front" column was published in the October–November 1935 issue of *Modern Music*.
29. PB to VSC, Tangier, October 20, 1997.
30. Ibid., September 17, 1997.
31. In his second "On the Film Front" column, in the January–February 1940 issue of *Modern Music*, Bowles incorrectly identified Hindustani as the native language of Ceylon, an error most likely rendered in the film itself; rather, it was Sinhalese and Tamil, as Bowles discovered upon going there himself in 1950.
32. Ibid.; also *Without Stopping*, p. 235
33. PB to VSC, Tangier, September 17, 1997.
34. Tamara Schee was the widow of choreographer Joel Schee, whom Bowles

knew in New York. She was among the first wave of Americans to settle in Taxco before the war; also *Without Stopping*, p. 236.

35. *Without Stopping*, pp. 235–36.
36. PB to VSC, Tangier, January 3, 1999; also *Without Stopping*, p. 236.
37. PB to VSC, Tangier, September 17, 1997; also *Without Stopping*, p. 237.
38. PB to VSC, Tangier, December 18, 1992.
39. Ibid.
40. *Knowing When to Stop*, pp. 148–49.
41. PB to VSC, Tangier, December 18, 1992.
42. *Without Stopping*, pp. 238–39.
43. PB to VSC, Tangier, December 18, 1992.
44. *Without Stopping*, p. 240.
45. Undated letter, Jane Bowles to Virgil Thomson, from Calle Sinaloa 43, Apt. 4, Mexico City; Virgil Thomson Collection, Irving S. Gilmore Music Library, Yale University.
46. Ibid.
47. Bowles confirmed that the doctor in whose clinic/sanitarium in Cuernavaca he was treated was Dr. Wurzburger, but every name in Bowles's FBI file (#100–329281) other than his own was blacked out before its release under the Freedom of Information Act.
48. Miscellaneous FBI documents in Bowles's file, #100–329281.
49. PB to VSC, Tangier, October 13, 1997.
50. *Without Stopping*, pp. 242–44. Bowles identified the "miracle-working doctor" as Dr. Max Jacobson, who was often referred to by his patients as "Dr. Feel-good." Jacobson, reportedly a psychiatrist, became notorious in the 1960s for his overmedication of Tennessee Williams through shots and pills. Maureen Stapleton declared: "The pill situation was so bad that we'd enter a restaurant and before Tenn had had even one drink, he'd fall down. After a while he was always falling down, and it wasn't alcohol–it was the pills and the shots. To my knowledge, I was the only one who tried to convince Tennessee that Jacobson was an exploitive quack, but he always defended him"; also Donald Spoto, *The Kindness of Strangers: The Life of Tennessee Williams* (Boston: Little, Brown, 1985), p. 264; and Dakin Williams and Shepherd Mead, *Tennessee Williams, An Intimate Biography* (New York: Arbor House, 1983), pp. 253–54, 260.
51. *Without Stopping*, p. 241.
52. Ibid., pp. 243–44.
53. Ibid., p. 244.
54. Ibid., pp. 244–45; also "Autobiography" in *Antaeus* 55 (Autumn 1985), pp. 16–17.
55. *Without Stopping*, p. 245.
56. Ibid., pp. 245–46.
57. PB to VSC, Tangier, December 28, 1997.
58. Ibid., December 29, 1997.
59. PB to VSC, Tangier, October 13, 1997; also PB to Peter Garland, October 19, 1983, from Paul Bowles's personal archives housed in his apartment in Tangier, Morocco, acquired in the spring of 1999 by Tim Murray for the Special Collections Library of the University of Delaware, Newark.

60. PB to VSC, Tangier, October 13, 1997.
61. Ibid., December 29, 1997.
62. In addition to the marquise de Casa Fuerte, other committee members for the Serenade series were Prince George Chavchavadze, Aaron Copland, René Le Roy, Virgil Thomson, and Carl Van Vechten. The final item on the program was the following statement: "The entire proceeds from the sale of tickets for the SERENADES, which have been made possible by the gracious assistance of the executant artists and by the generosity of the Marquis and Marquise de Cuevas, will be contributed to the Armed Services Program of the Museum of Modern Art and to the American Theater Wing."
63. PB to VSC, Tangier, October 18, 1997.
64. Ibid.
65. Harold Matson to Paul Bowles at the Hotel Chelsea, 222 West Twenty-third Street, New York, Paul Bowles Collection, HRHRC. Bowles's last statement from Matson & Duggan reported that his 1942 income was $2,816 before commission. It was this letter that prompted Bowles's request to be released from the contract.
66. PB to VSC, Tangier, October 19, 1998. On March 8, 1944, during the second royalty period after publication of *Two Serious Ladies*, Harold Ober sent Jane a royalty statement and check from Knopf for $53; for the period ending October 31, 1943, she received $139.42 ("at ten per cent commission, less purchases and unearned balance from previous statement").
67. *New York Times Book Review*, May 9, 1943.
68. PB to VSC, Tangier, October 19, 1998.
69. Ibid.

Chapter Eight

1. PB to VSC, Tangier, September 9, 1989.
2. Ibid.
3. PB to VSC, Tangier, October 8, 1997.
4. Foreword by Paul Bowles in Charles Henri Ford, *View: Parade of the Avant-Garde: An Anthology of View Magazine (1940–1947)*, comp. Catrina Neiman and Paul Nathan; introduction by Catrina Neiman (New York: Thunder's Mouth Press, 1992), pp. ix–x.
5. "Bluey: Passages from an Imaginary Diary," *View* (October 1943), pp. 81–82.
6. Charles Henri Ford to VSC, New York, June 28, 1997.
7. PB to VSC, Tangier, January 7, 1999.
8. Ibid., January 5, 1999.
9. A collection of a number of Bowles's translations that appeared originally in *View* was published in *She Woke Me Up So I Killed Her*, ed. Jean Ferry (San Francisco: Cadmus Editions, 1985). In addition to the *View* pieces, the volume included four pieces that appeared originally in the journal *Antaeus*, edited by Daniel Halpern and cofounded with Bowles.

10. *Without Stopping*, pp. 261–62; also Jeffrey Miller, *Paul Bowles: A Descriptive Bibliography* (Santa Barbara, Calif.: Black Sparrow Press, 1986), C530, p. 159.
11. PB to Peggy Glanville-Hicks, *In Touch* (Fez, December 1947), p. 183.
12. "Pages from Cold Point," *Wake* (Autumn 1949), pp. 60–70.
13. PB to VSC, Tangier, January 4, 1999; also Howard Pollack, *Aaron Copland: The Life and Work of an Uncommon Man* (New York: Henry Holt, 1999), pp. 182–85. Copland died on December 2, 1990, in North Tarrytown, New York.
14. *Without Stopping*, pp. 259–60; also PB to VSC, Tangier, January 5, 1999.
15. PB to VSC, Tangier, October 13, 1997.
16. Ibid., October 14, 1997.
17. *Without Stopping*, pp. 252–53.
18. Ibid., p. 255.
19. Quoted in Fleur Cowles, *The Case of Salvador Dali* (London: Heinemann, 1959), pp. 80–81; also Jeffrey Miller, *Paul Bowles: A Descriptive Bibliography*, p. 244; and *Without Stopping*, pp. 255–56.
20. PB to Phillip Ramey, Tangier (date unknown); Ramey to VSC, May 20, 2001. According to Ramey, Jonathan Sheffer searched in vain for the score for the 1995 Festival of Paul Bowles's music in New York.
21. *Without Stopping*, p. 265.
22. "'Exit Singing': 'What's Left of Jazz' Is Presented at Town Hall," *New York Herald Tribune* (Monday, February 11, 1946), p. 14, col. 5, late city ed.
23. PB to VSC, Tangier, October 18, 1997.
24. Other reviewers included John Chapman for the New York *Daily News*; Burton Rascoe for the *New York World-Telegram*; Robert Garland for the *New York Journal-American*; and Ward Morehouse for the *New York Sun*; see, especially, pp. 184–86 of the *New York Theatre Critics' Review, 1943*.
25. PB to VSC, Tangier, October 18, 1987.
26. Elia Kazan, *Elia Kazan: A Life* (New York: Knopf, 1988), p. 242.
27. PB to VSC, Tangier, October 18, 1997.
28. *Without Stopping*, p. 256.
29. PB to VSC, Tangier, October 18, 1997; also Lyle Leverich, *Tom: The Unknown Tennessee Williams* (New York: Crown, 1995), pp. 557–58.
30. PB to VSC, Tangier, September 9, 1989; also Mike Steen, *A Look at Tennessee Williams* (New York: Hawthorn Books, 1969), p. 145.
31. At this point in his acting career, Canada Lee had played an angry Bigger Thomas in Orson Welles's production of Richard Wright's novel *Native Son* (1941), and a convincing Caliban in Margaret Webster's production of *The Tempest* (1946); he also played a role in "whiteface" in *The Duchess of Malfi* (1946).
32. Upon the death of President Roosevelt on April 12, 1945, in Warm Springs, Georgia, Eleanor Roosevelt commenced a column titled "My Day" in which she wrote supportively of *On Whitman Avenue*.
33. Lewis Nichols, "Canada Lee in *On Whitman Avenue*," *New York Times*, May 9, 1946, p. 28, col. 2; also "*On Whitman Avenue* Will Close Oct. 5," *New York Times*, August 24, 1946, p. 7, col. 1.
34. PB to VSC, Tangier, October 18, 1997; also, *Without Stopping*, p. 266.

35. On April 7, 1947, Ferrer was one of five actors to receive an Antoinette Perry (Tony) Award for his "outstanding contribution to the American theater during the 1946–1947 season." Other recipients were Ingrid Bergman for *Joan of Lorraine*, Helen Hayes for *Happy Birthday*, Patricia Neal for *Another Part of the Forest*, and Fredric March for *Years Ago*.
36. PB to VSC, Tangier, October 18, 1997.
37. *Without Stopping*, p. 265.
38. Ibid.
39. PB to VSC, Tangier, October 18, 1997; also *Without Stopping*, pp. 256–57.
40. PB to VSC, Tangier, October 18, 1997.
41. *Without Stopping*, p. 267.
42. Paul Bowles to Richard Seaver, editor, Grove Press, February 25, 1963, *In Touch*, p. 349.
43. "Interview by Daniel Halpern with Paul Bowles" (1975), in *Conversations with Paul Bowles*, ed. Gena Dagel Caponi (Jackson: University Press of Mississippi, 1993), pp. 99–100.
44. Brooks Atkinson, *New York Times*, November 27, 1946, p. 21, col. 1.
45. PB to VSC, Tangier, October 18, 1997; also *Without Stopping*, p. 272.
46. PB to VSC, Tangier, January 5, 1999.
47. *Without Stopping*, p. 274.
48. Ibid., p. 276; also PB to VSC, Tangier, January 5, 1999.
49. PB to VSC, Tangier, January 5, 1999.
50. Daniel Halpern, "Interview with Paul Bowles," *TriQuarterly* (Spring 1975), pp. 160–61; also Caponi, ed., *Conversations with Paul Bowles*, p. 88.
51. PB to Lawrence D. Stewart, in *Paul Bowles: The Illumination of North Africa* (Carbondale: Southern Illinois University Press, 1974), p. 37.
52. *Without Stopping*, p. 276.

Chapter Nine

1. Sager told Bowles that he would stay only briefly in Marrakech, then proceed to Sicily and Venice, sites he had selected for the settings of *Run Sheep Run* and *The Invisible Worm* (both published in 1950). Two years later, he published *The Formula*, set in Venice, and *The Rape of Europa*.
2. Jane Bowles to PB, in *Out in the World: Selected Letters of Jane Bowles, 1935–1970*, ed. Millicent Dillon (Santa Barbara, Calif.: Black Sparrow Press, 1985), p. 38.
3. *Without Stopping*, p. 277.
4. Ibid., p. 278.
5. PB to Peggy Glanville-Hicks, July 8, 1947, Paul Bowles Collection, HRHRC; also *In Touch*, pp. 174–76; and PB to VSC, Tangier, January 6, 1998.
6. After a lengthy legal battle, Holman was awarded $750,000; upon her son's coming of age, he inherited $6.25 million (after taxes). Other heirs were his first wife, who received $9.7 million; each of Reynolds's brothers, whose portions ($9.7 million) were "to go to charity"; and Ab Walker, who was left $50,000. For an in-depth account of Reynolds's death and its aftermath, see Holman's

biography: Jon Bradshaw, *Dreams That Money Can Buy: The Tragic Life of Libby Holman* (New York: William Morrow, 1985), pp. 112–52.
7. Jane Bowles to PB, *Out in the World*, p. 35.
8. PB to VSC, Tangier, January 6, 1998.
9. *A Little Original Sin*, p. 147.
10. *Out in the World*, pp. 93, 140.
11. PB to VSC, Tangier, December 20, 1992.
12. Jane Bowles to "Dearest Bupple," *Out in the World*, p. 34.
13. Bowles had informed Jane in a recent letter that "The Echo," published originally in *Harper's Bazaar* (September 1946), was being reprinted in *O. Henry Memorial Award Stories of 1947*; also Jane Bowles to "My dear Bubble," *Out in the World* (September 1947), p. 46.
14. *Without Stopping*, p. 278.
15. PB to Peggy Glanville-Hicks, Tangier, November 8, 1947, *In Touch*, p. 177.
16. *Without Stopping*, pp. 278–79.
17. Ibid., p. 279.
18. PB to VSC, Tangier, December 5, 1998.
19. *Out in the World*, pp. 62–64.
20. *In Touch*, p. 183.
21. PB to Peggy Glanville-Hicks (December 1947), *In Touch*, p. 181.
22. PB to Kay Cowen, Fez, December 17, 1947, Katherine Cowen de Bailou Archives, Hargrett Library Special Collections, University of Georgia Libraries, Athens.
23. PB to VSC, Tangier, December 22, 1992.
24. PB to Charles Henri Ford, December 17, 1947, Charles Henri Ford Archives, HRHRC.
25. PB to VSC, Tangier, December 22, 1992.
26. Ibid.
27. Ibid.
28. PB to Peggy Glanville-Hicks, January 16, 1948, *In Touch*, pp. 187, 190.
29. Ibid., p. 186.
30. PB to Charles Henri Ford, January 25, 1948, *In Touch*, p. 192.
31. PB to VSC, Tangier, December 22, 1992.
32. Ibid., January 2, 1999.
33. *Without Stopping*, p. 287.
34. PB to VSC, Tangier, December 2, 1999; also *Without Stopping*, p. 287.
35. PB to Peggy Glanville-Hicks, Hôtel Belvedere, Fez, May 10, 1948, *In Touch*, p. 197.
36. Jane Bowles to Libby Holman, *Out in the World*, p. 77.
37. Paul Bowles, gallery announcement for Ahmed Yacoubi exhibit, Amici Gallery, New York, 1964, p. 4.
38. PB to VSC, Tangier, December 3, 1998; also Peter Mayne to PB, in Mayne's book *The Alleys of Marrakech* (London: John Murray, 1953); and interview, PB to Simon Bischoff, in *Paul Bowles: Photographs: "How Could I Send a Picture into the Desert?"* ed. Simon Bischoff, in collaboration with the Swiss Foundation for Photography (Zurich: Scalo Publishers, 1994), p. 224.

39. PB to Simon Bischoff, in *Paul Bowles: Photographs*, p. 224.
40. *In Touch*, p. 199.
41. *Without Stopping*, p. 286.
42. Ibid., p. 280.
43. Ibid., pp. 287–88.
44. PB to VSC, Tangier, September 14, 1997.
45. Jon Bradshaw, *Dreams That Money Can Buy*, pp. 329–30; also *Without Stopping*, p. 288.
46. Tennessee Williams to Paul Bigelow, February 18, 1948, Tennessee Williams Papers, HRHRC.
47. PB to VSC, Tangier, September 14, 1997.
48. *Out in the World*, p. 123.
49. *A Little Original Sin*, p. 209; also PB to VSC, Tangier, September 13, 1997.
50. *Out in the World*, p. 81.
51. It was published a few weeks later in *Zero*, a new magazine being edited in Tangier; "I thought no one would ever see it there except possibly a few hundred readers who regularly read the magazine. I was mistaken, of course. The story caused a considerable stir." PB to VSC, Tangier, September 13, 1997.
52. Tennessee Williams to VSC, New York, December 14, 1973.
53. Jordan Massee to VSC, New York, July 25, 1971; and *In Touch*, p. 200.
54. PB to James Laughlin, *In Touch*, p. 200.
55. PB to VSC, Tangier, September 1, 1997.

Chapter Ten

1. Jane Bowles to Katherine Hamill and Natasha von Hoershelman, March 17, 1949, Taghit, Algeria, in *A Little Original Sin*, pp. 180–81.
2. *A Little Original Sin*, p. 183. "A Stick of Green Candy" was published in the January 1957 issue of *Vogue*.
3. Cecil Beaton, "Tangier Holiday," *The Strenuous Years: Diaries, 1948–1955* (London: Weidenfeld and Nicolson, 1956), p. 51.
4. PB to VSC, Tangier, January 6, 1998.
5. Fred Kaplan, *Gore Vidal: A Biography* (New York: Doubleday, 1999), p. 312.
6. Jack Dunphy, *"Dear Genius . . .": A Memoir of My Life with Truman Capote* (New York: McGraw-Hill, 1987), pp. 110–11.
7. PB to VSC, Tangier, January 6, 1998.
8. John Lehmann, *The Ample Proposition: Autobiography III* (London: Eyre and Spottiswoode, 1966), pp. 111–13.
9. *Without Stopping*, pp. 294–95.
10. *Time* (review), December 5, 1949, p. 112.
11. *Evening Standard* (review): "*The Sheltering Sky*, not a pretty book, but a powerful one for adults," September 27, 1949.
12. Tennessee Williams, "An Allegory of Man and His Sahara," *New York Times Book Review*, December 4, 1949, p. 38.

13. *Without Stopping*, p. 296; also *Let It Come Down*, with a preface by the author (Santa Rosa, Calif.: Black Sparrow Press, 1994), pp. 7–8.
14. PB to VSC, Tangier, December 17, 1998.
15. *Without Stopping*, p. 297.
16. PB to Gore Vidal, February 22, 1950, *In Touch*, pp. 212–13; also Fred Kaplan, *Gore Vidal: A Biography*, p. 323.
17. PB to James Laughlin, January 25, 1950, *In Touch*, pp. 211.
18. PB to David McDowell, March 25, 1950, from Mount Lavinia, Ceylon, Random House Archives, Rare Book and Manuscript Library, Columbia University, New York.
19. Ibid.
20. *Without Stopping*, p. 303.
21. Ibid., p. 300.
22. PB to David McDowell, February 26, 1950, Random House Archives, Rare Book and Manuscript Library, Columbia University, New York.
23. PB to Gore Vidal, April 24, 1950, *In Touch*, p. 218.
24. PB to David McDowell, 1950.
25. PB to VSC, Tangier, September 16, 1997.
26. John Lehmann, *The Ample Proposition: Autobiography III*, pp. 112–13.
27. PB to VSC, Tangier, September 17, 1997.
28. Jane Bowles to PB, Paris, January 17, 1950, *Out in the World*, p. 145.
29. *Without Stopping*, p. 304; also PB to VSC, Tangier, September 9, 1997.
30. Sally Brown and David Brown, *A Biography of Mrs. Marty Mann: The First Lady of Alcoholics Anonymous* (Center City, Minn.: Hazelden Publishing and Educational Services, 2001), pp. 222–27.
31. *Out in the World*, pp. 167–69.
32. PB to David McDowell, Paris, August 13, 1950, Random House Archives, Rare Book and Manuscript Library, Columbia University, New York.
33. PB to David McDowell, September 6, 1950; David McDowell to PB, October 17, 1950, Random House Archives, Rare Book and Manuscript Library, Columbia University, New York.
34. PB to David McDowell, Fez, October 17, 1950, Random House Archives, Rare Book and Manuscript Library, Columbia University, New York.
35. PB to David McDowell, September 6, 1950, Random House Archives, Rare Book and Manuscript Library, Columbia University, New York.
36. David McDowell to PB, November 15, 1950, *In Touch*, pp. 226–27.
37. PB to David McDowell, November 15, 1950, *In Touch*, p. 227.
38. PB to Rena Bowles, unpublished letter, December 19, 1950, Paul Bowles Collection, HRHRC.
39. Twenty years later, Bowles used the same quotation in the closing paragraph of *Without Stopping*. In this instance, he updated it with a note of his own: "When I quoted Valéry's epigram in *The Sheltering Sky*, it seemed a poignant bit of fantasy. Now, because I no longer imagine myself as an onlooker at the scene, but instead as the principal protagonist, it strikes me as repugnant. To make it right, the dying man would have to add two words to his farewell. 'Thank God!'"

40. *In Touch*, p. 226; also PB to VSC, September 11, 1997.
41. PB to David McDowell, December 15, 1950, Random House Archives, Rare Book and Manuscript Library, Columbia University, New York; also *In Touch*, p. 227.
42. Tennessee Williams, "The Human Psyche–Alone," *Saturday Review of Literature*, December 23, 1950, pp. 19–20.
43. PB to David McDowell, Tangier, December 20, 1950, Random House Archives, Rare Book and Manuscript Library, Columbia University, New York.

Chapter Eleven

1. *Without Stopping*, p. 305.
2. PB to VSC, Atlanta, October 2, 1994; also *Without Stopping*, pp. 305–6; and "Paul Bowles, 'The Secret Sahara'" in *Ten Years of Holiday: An Anniversary Collection of 40 Memorable Pieces* (New York: Simon & Schuster, 1956), pp. 223–35.
3. PB to VSC, Tangier, September 7, 1993.
4. Ibid.
5. *Let It Come Down* (New York: Random House, 1952), p. 311.
6. *In Touch*, pp. 238–39.
7. PB to Oliver Evans, "An Interview with Paul Bowles," from *Mediterranean Review* (Winter 1971), in *Conversations with Paul Bowles*, ed. Gena Dagel Caponi (Jackson: University Press of Mississippi, 1993), p. 52.
8. John Raymond, *New Statesman and Nation*, April 26, 1952; also PB to VSC, September 7, 1993.
9. According to Muslim demonology, a *djinn* belongs to a class of spirits that inhabit the earth in various forms and exercise supernatural control over humans.
10. PB to Peggy Glanville-Hicks, November 5, 1951, *In Touch*, pp. 242–43.
11. Bowles's "No More *Djinns*" was the subtitle of an article, "Foreign Intelligence," published in *American Mercury* (June 1951), pp. 650–58; also PB to Ira Cohen, "Interview, 1965," Columbia University Archives, published in *Conversations with Paul Bowles*, pp. 16–18.
12. PB to James Laughlin, *In Touch*, December 22, 1950, p. 228.
13. "Talk with Paul Bowles" by Harvey Breit, *New York Times*, March 9, 1952.
14. PB to Peggy Glanville-Hicks, December 15, 1951, *In Touch*, p. 245.
15. The press run was 244,000 for the twenty-five-cent reprint edition published in January 1952 by the New American Library.
16. Bowles was shocked, also, upon reading his agent's payment voucher for royalties earned from John Lehmann, Ltd., for the six months ending December 31, 1951. "I could hardly believe my eyes: for *The Sheltering Sky* in pounds, it amounted to £4.4; in dollars, $11.76. For *A Little Stone*, in pounds, £2.16.; in dollars, $7.91 (less commissions and taxes)." According to the records, Strauss deposited a total of $9.12 to the Park Avenue Branch of Corn Exchange Bank

for "all monies due then from John Lehmann, Ltd." Also PB to VSC, Atlanta, October 4, 1994.

17. PB to VSC, Atlanta, October 4, 1994.
18. Paul Bowles, "How to Live on a Part-time Island," *Holiday*, March 1957, pp. 41, 43, 45–46, 49, 143, 145.
19. *Without Stopping*, pp. 318–19; also PB to VSC, Atlanta, October 4, 1994.
20. PB to VSC, Atlanta, October 4, 1994.
21. Helen Strauss to PB, May 27, 1952; access to Paul Bowles files courtesy of Michael Carlisle and William Morris Agency, New York.
22. PB to VSC, Atlanta, September 28, 1994. As best he could remember, Bowles received a thousand dollars a day for four days of work.
23. Ibid., September 29, 1994.
24. Ibid.
25. PB to VSC, Atlanta, May 30, 1994.
26. David McDowell to PB, December 4, 1952, Paul Bowles Collection, HRHRC.
27. PB to VSC, Atlanta, May 30, 1994.
28. Ibid., May 31, 1994; also PB to Mr. Hollyman, May 2, 1953, *In Touch*, pp. 250–51.
29. *Without Stopping*, p. 320.
30. PB to VSC, Atlanta, May 31, 1994; also *Without Stopping*, p. 320.
31. PB to VSC, Atlanta, May 31, 1994.
32. PB to Phillip Ramey, Tangier, undated letter; and Ramey to VSC, November 21, 1999. Ramey declared: "Now that Paul is dead, there are certain things that I feel comfortable telling you, as his biographer, which I think you ought to know."
33. Jon Bradshaw, *Dreams That Money Can Buy: The Tragic Life of Libby Holman* (New York: William Morrow, 1985), p. 262; also PB to VSC, Atlanta, September 28, 1994. Note: Holman had adopted two sons, Timmy and Tony, in 1945 and 1947, both younger than Topper, who was born in 1933.
34. Tennessee Williams to PB, Rome, June 22, 1953, Tennessee Williams Archives, HRHRC.
35. PB to VSC, Atlanta, May 31, 1994.
36. *Tennessee Williams' Letters to Donald Windham, 1940–1965* (New York: Henry Holt and Company, 1977), p. 284.
37. *Without Stopping*, p. 321; also PB to VSC, Atlanta, May 23, 1994.
38. Telegram from Tennessee Williams to the Lydia Mendelssohn Theater of the University of Michigan at Ann Arbor, "to be used for publicity purposes"; from the Michigan Historical Collection, Bentley Historical Library, University of Michigan, Ann Arbor; cited, also, in *A Little Original Sin*, p. 227.
39. PB to VSC, Atlanta, May 23, 1994; also *Without Stopping*, p. 320.
40. PB to VSC, Atlanta, May 23, 1994.
41. Ibid.
42. Jane Bowles quoted in Walter Kerr's "Confessions of an Honest Playwright," *Vogue*, May 1, 1954; also *A Little Original Sin*, p. 235.
43. PB to VSC, Atlanta, May 31, 1994.

Chapter Twelve

1. William S. Burroughs to Allen Ginsberg, *The Letters of William S. Burroughs, 1945–1959*, edited and with an introduction by Oliver Harris (New York: Viking, 1994), February 9, 1954, p. 197.
2. Ansen had been a classics student at Harvard, where he wrote a bachelor's thesis on Milton and graduated *summa cum laude*, then attended lectures on Shakespeare with Wysten Auden at the New School for Social Research, and became his secretary for a time (Ansen's other best friend was Chester Kallman, Auden's longtime companion and lover).
3. *The Letters of William S. Burroughs, 1945–1959*, March 1, 1954, p. 199.
4. Ibid., January 26, 1954, p. 195.
5. According to Ted Morgan in *Literary Outlaw: The Life and Times of William S. Burroughs* (New York: Henry Holt and Company, 1988), p. 251, Burroughs was given a monthly allowance of two hundred dollars by his parents, who made it clear that he was no longer welcome as a houseguest in their Palm Beach home.
6. *The Letters of William S. Burroughs, 1945–1959*, July 15, 1954, p. 223.
7. Ibid., August 18, 1954, p. 224.
8. *Without Stopping*, p. 323; also *The Letters of William S. Burroughs, 1945–1959*, September 21, 1955, pp. 280–81.
9. William S. Burroughs to VSC, Lawrence, Kansas, November 3, 1993.
10. Richard Rumbold, *A Message in Code: The Diary of Richard Rumbold, 1932–1960*, ed. William Plomer (London: Weidenfeld and Nicolson, 1964), December 15, 1954, p. 157; also December 22, 1954, p. 158. One of Rumbold's books was *The Winged Life: A Portrait of Antoine de Saint-Exupéry, Poet and Airman*, cowritten with Lady Margaret Stewart (London: Weidenfeld and Nicolson, 1953).
11. *A Message in Code: The Diary of Richard Rumbold, 1932–1960*, p. 160.
12. PB to VSC, Atlanta, May 31, 1994; also *Without Stopping*, pp. 325–26.
13. PB to David McDowell, October 15, 1955, Random House Archives, Rare Book and Manuscript Library, Columbia University, New York.
14. PB to David McDowell, November 11, 1955, Random House Archives, Rare Book and Manuscript Library, Columbia University, New York.
15. *Without Stopping*, p. 325.
16. PB to David McDowell, October 15, 1955, Random House Archives, Rare Book and Manuscript Library, Columbia University, New York.
17. PB to David McDowell, May 11, 1955, Random House Archives, Rare Book and Manuscript Library, Columbia University, New York.
18. PB to Virgil Thomson, November 8, 1955.
19. PB to Rena and Claude Bowles, June 10, 1955, unpublished letter, Paul Bowles Collection, HRHRC.
20. Ibid., June 17, 1955.
21. David McDowell to PB, October 15, 1955, Random House Archives, Rare Book and Manuscript Library, Columbia University, New York.
22. John Lehmann to PB, October 21, 1955, Paul Bowles Collection, HRHRC.

23. Virgil Thomson to PB, November 8, 1955, Virgil Thomson Collection, Irving S. Gilmore Music Library, Yale University.
24. PB to Virgil Thomson, November 22, 1955, Virgil Thomson Collection, Irving S. Gilmore Music Library, Yale University.
25. PB to David McDowell, June 28, 1955, Random House Archives, Rare Book and Manuscript Library, Columbia University, New York.
26. "Preface," *The Spider's House* (Santa Rosa, Calif.: Black Sparrow Press, 1982).
27. PB to "Dear Mother and Dad," April 3, 1956, Paul Bowles Collection, HRHRC.
28. PB to Jane Bowles, May 5, 1956, Paul Bowles Collection, HRHRC.
29. PB to Rena Bowles, April 19, 1956, Paul Bowles Collection, HRHRC.
30. PB to "Dear Mother and Dad," April 19, 1956, Paul Bowles Collection, HRHRC.
31. Allen Ginsberg to Allen Ansen, February 17, 1956, in *The Letters of William S. Burroughs, 1945–1959*, p. 307.
32. *Without Stopping*, p. 332; also PB to Peggy Glanville-Hicks, July 22, 1956, *In Touch*, pp. 367–69; and PB to VSC, Atlanta, May 30, 1994.
33. PB to VSC, Tangier, September 7, 1993. "The Frozen Fields" was published in the July 1957 issue of *Harper's Bazaar*, with a biographical note and photograph of Bowles in "The Editor's Guest Book," p. 37. The story was also included in the *Best Short Stories of 1958*.
34. Ronald Segal to VSC, August 25, 2000.
35. PB to VSC, Tangier, January 2, 1994.
36. PB to Jane Bowles, January 24, 1957, Paul Bowles Collection, HRHRC.
37. *Without Stopping*, p. 336. Upon hearing of Jane's stroke from Gordon Sager, Bowles arrived in Tangier on May 11, 1957.
38. *In Touch*, pp. 274–75.
39. PB to Virgil Thomson, undated letter, Virgil Thomson Archives, Irving S. Gilmore Music Library, Yale University.
40. *Without Stopping*, p. 338.
41. Jane's FBI File (#100–428983) declared that "on April 11, 1958, the American Embassy, Lisbon, advised the Department of State, that subject would arrive in New York City on April 16, 1958, via Pan American Airways."
42. Tennessee Williams to PB, undated letter, Tennessee Williams Collection, University of Delaware Library, Newark; also PB to VSC, Tangier, January 2, 1994.
43. PB to VSC, Tangier, January 2, 1994.
44. Ibid.
45. Ned Rorem, *The New York Diary* (New York: George Braziller, 1967), pp. 162–63.
46. PB to VSC, Tangier, January 2, 1994.
47. PB to Tennessee Williams, May 28, 1958, Tennessee Williams Collection, University of Delaware Library, Newark.
48. PB to Jane Bowles, February 15, 1959, Jane Bowles Collection, HRHRC.
49. PB to VSC, Tangier, January 2, 1994.

Chapter Thirteen

1. *In Touch*, pp. 305–6.
2. PB to VSC, Tangier, January 5, 1994; also Christopher Wanklyn to VSC, Marrakech, December 28, 1993.
3. Paul Bowles, *Their Heads Are Green and Their Hands Are Blue* (London: Peter Owen, 1963), p. 84.
4. *Without Stopping*, pp. 344–45; also "The Rif to Music," *Their Heads Are Green*, pp. 83–118.
5. PB to VSC, Tangier, January 5, 1994. Many of these tapes were reproduced in 1972 by the Library of Congress recording laboratory for the Archive of Folk Culture on two twelve-inch phonodiscs and released in a double-sleeve slipcase titled *Music of Morocco* (LCM 2057 and 2058, AFS L63–L64) and (LCM 2059 and 2060 AFS L-64A and AFS L-64B).
6. *In Touch*, pp. 304–5.
7. "An Evening with Paul Bowles," *London Magazine* (November 1960), p. 66.
8. *In Touch*, pp. 300–301.
9. PB to Rena Bowles, March 2, 1963, Paul Bowles Collection, HRHRC.
10. William S. Burroughs to VSC, Lawrence, Kansas, December 4, 1993.
11. According to Rumbold's cousin William Plomer, Rumbold died on March 13, 1961. It was Plomer who later edited Rumbold's *A Message in Code*, a collection of letters.
12. *In Touch*, p. 333.
13. Bowles's four tales published in *A Hundred Camels in the Courtyard* (San Francisco: City Lights Books, 1962) were "A Friend of the World," "The Story of Lahcen and Idir" (formerly "Merkala Beach"), "He of the Assembly," and "The Wind at Beni Midar."
14. *In Touch*, p. 335.
15. PB to Lawrence Ferlinghetti, January 12, 1962, *In Touch*, pp. 334–35.
16. Preface to *A Hundred Camels in the Courtyard* (San Francisco: City Lights Books, 2nd edition, 1986), p. ix; also PB to VSC, Atlanta, May 2, 1994. See Bowles's note on "mode of composition" in the inside cover of record sleeve in which he reads *A Hundred Camels in the Courtyard* (Santa Barbara, Calif.: Cadmus Editions, 1981).
17. PB to Rena Bowles, October 18, 1961, *In Touch*, p. 327.
18. *Without Stopping*, p. 351.
19. PB to VSC, Tangier, December 12, 1993.
20. PB to VSC, Atlanta, June 6, 1994.
21. PB to Rena and Claude Bowles, December 6, 1961, Paul Bowles Collection, HRHRC.
22. PB to Allen Ginsberg and Peter Orlovsky, August 2, 1962, *In Touch*, pp. 339–40.
23. PB to "Dear Mother and Dad," March 3, 1962, Paul Bowles Collection, HRHRC.
24. PB to Allen Ginsberg, October 30, 1962, *In Touch*, pp. 341–42.
25. PB to Jane Bowles, December 11, 1962, *In Touch*, pp. 346.
26. Ibid..

27. *Without Stopping*, p. 350.
28. PB to Richard Seaver, February 26, 1963, the E. S. Bird Library, Syracuse University, New York; also Grove Press Archives, Syracuse University, New York; and *Evergreen Review* and Grove Press Archives, the George Arents Research Library, Syracuse University, New York.
29. Ibid.
30. PB to VSC, Atlanta, June 10, 1994.
31. PB to Allen Ginsberg, November 1, 1961, *In Touch*, pp. 328–29. The stories to which Bowles referred were Yacoubi's "The Man and the Woman," published in *Zero Anthology* 8 (1956), pp. 149–52; and "The Man Who Dreamed of Fish Eating Fish," published in *Zero* (Spring 1956), pp. 56–61, both transcribed and translated by Bowles. Two other tales of Yacoubi's, published in 1961, were "The Game," published in *Contact* 8 (May 1961), pp. 65–67; and "The Night Before Thinking," published in *Evergreen Review*, with Bowles's introduction and Burroughs's commentary in the September–October 1961 issue, pp. 18–30.
32. PB to VSC, Atlanta, May 31, 1994. Claude-Nathalie Thomas's French translations of Bowles's work include *The Spider's House*; *Up Above the World*; *Too Far from Home*; most of the stories in *Midnight Mass* and *Things Gone and Things Still Here*; several nonfiction pieces, including *17 Quai Voltaire* (reminiscences of Bowles's early travels to Europe); captions and prefaces to several books of photographs of Morocco; a piece on Isabel Eberhardt ("legendary figure of French North Africa"); and "The Sky," published in a book of photographs by Vittorio Santoro. "These projects have spanned a quarter of a century," said Bowles. See also Claude-Nathalie Thomas, "On Translating Paul (and Jane and Mrabet)," *Journal of Modern Literature* (Fall 1999), pp. 35–43.
33. Lawrence D. Stewart, *Paul Bowles: The Illumination of North Africa*, preface by Harry T. Moore (Carbondale: Southern Illinois University Press, 1974), p. 113.
34. Jane Bowles to Ruth Fainlight (summer 1963), *Out in the World*, pp. 235–36. Fainlight and her husband, Alan Sillitoe, had lived in Tangier for two years before returning to their home in England. When their son was eight weeks old, they returned to Tangier for ten months and saw Bowles and Jane often.
35. John Hopkins, *The Tangier Diaries, 1962–1979* (Tiburon-Belvedere, Calif.: Cadmus Editions, 1998), p. 236.
36. PB to Alfred Chester, May 25, 1963; from personal archives of Edward Field, New York, New York; also unpublished manuscript by Field titled "Voyage of Destruction."
37. Alfred Chester to Edward Field, June 10, 1963, from personal archives of Edward Field.
38. PB to VSC, Tangier, December 12, 1993. Dris, a twenty-two-year-old Moroccan fisherman to whom Bowles introduced Chester, had immediately become his lover.
39. PB to Edward Field, November 4, 1989, in a letter that Field included in "Voyage to Destruction"; also Field to VSC, New York, June 3, 1993.
40. PB to VSC, Tangier, December 12, 1993.
41. Anthony Tommasini, *Virgil Thomson: Composer on the Aisle* (New York: W. W. Norton, 1997), p. 472.

42. PB to VSC, Tangier, December 13, 1993. The original typescript is housed in the Paul Bowles Archives, Special Manuscript Collections, Columbia University Libraries, New York.
43. PB to Virgil Thomson, September 8, 1963, Virgil Thomson Collection, Irving S. Gilmore Music Library, Yale University.
44. PB to John Bainbridge, interview, February 1965, in *Another Way of Living: A Gallery of Americans Who Choose to Live in Europe* (New York: Holt, Rinehart and Winston, 1968), p. 243.
45. John Hopkins to VSC, Tangier, February 16, 2002.
46. Oliver Evans, "An Interview with Paul Bowles," *Mediterranean Review* (Winter 1971), pp. 3–14.
47. PB to Oliver Evans, December 22, 1964, Paul Bowles Collection (#9917-A), Barrett Library of American Literature, Special Collections, University of Virginia Library, Charlottesville.
48. Ibid., January 15, 1965.
49. Paul Bowles, interview by Jeffrey Bailey, "The Art of Fiction," *Paris Review* (Fall 1981), pp. 62–98.
50. John Hopkins to VSC, Tangier, February 16, 2002.
51. John Hopkins, *The Tangier Diaries, 1962–1979*, p. 62.
52. PB to Stephen Davis, *Stone Age* (Spring 1979), pp. 38–39.
53. Unpublished manuscript, "The Tangier Summer and the Villa on the Marshan (an homage to Jane and Paul Bowles and Tangier)," Robert Hines to VSC, Atlanta, May 7, 1994; also Robert Hines, *Memoir: I Remember Tennessee Williams and Others* with a foreword by Kenneth Holditch and an afterword by Dakin Williams (Xlibris, 2003).
54. PB to Andreas Brown, August 3, 1965, Paul Bowles Collection, HRHRC.
55. PB to Andreas Brown, October 15, 1965, Paul Bowles Collection (#9917-A), Barrett Library of American Literature, Special Collections, University of Virginia Library, Charlottesville.
56. PB to VSC, Tangier, September 12, 1997. According to Jeffrey Miller's *Paul Bowles: A Descriptive Bibliography* (Santa Barbara: Black Sparrow Press, 1986), pp. 34–35, the publishers, dates, and press runs in English of first printings of Bowles's books were 4,000 copies of *The Sheltering Sky* (London: John Lehmann, September 1949); 6,000 copies of *The Delicate Prey and Other Stories* (New York: Random House, November 1950); 7,000 copies of *Let It Come Down* (London: John Lehmann, February 1952); 15,000 copies of *Let It Come Down* (New York: Random House, February 28, 1952); 10,000 copies of *The Spider's House* (New York: Random House, November 4, 1955); and "an unknown number of copies" of *The Spider's House* (London: MacDonald, January 18, 1957); and 34,000 copies of *Up Above the World* (New York: Simon & Schuster, 1966).
57. Paul Bowles to Christopher Sawyer-Lauçanno, *An Invisible Spectator: A Biography of Paul Bowles* (New York: Weidenfeld and Nicolson, 1989), p. 376.
58. PB to John Goodwin, October 5, 1966, *In Touch*, p. 389.
59. PB to Libby Holman, April 29, 1966, Libby Holman Collection, Boston University Library.
60. PB to VSC, Tangier, December 15, 1993.

61. Ibid.
62. PB to VSC, Atlanta, June 6, 1994.
63. PB to VSC, Tangier, December 16, 1993.
64. *In Touch*, p. 382.
65. PB to VSC, Tangier, September 6, 1996.
66. PB to Andreas Brown, September 27, 1966, Paul Bowles Collection, HRHRC; also PB to VSC, Tangier, September 6, 1996.
67. PB to Herbert Machiz, September 29, 1966, Machiz Archives, Special Manuscript Collections, Columbia University.
68. PB to Frances Bishop, October 24, 1966; also Bishop to VSC, from her personal archives in New York City.
69. PB to VSC, Tangier, January 2, 1994.

Chapter Fourteen

1. PB to Virgil Thomson, June 26, 1973, Virgil Thomson Collection, Irving S. Gilmore Music Library, Yale University.
2. PB to Millicent Dillon, *A Little Original Sin*, pp. 389–90; also PB to VSC, Tangier, April 15, 1990.
3. Claire Auer Fuhs to Jane Bowles, *A Little Original Sin*, p. 389.
4. PB to VSC, Tangier, October 19, 1997.
5. Ibid., Tangier, April 14, 1990.
6. PB to Virgil Thomson, June 1, 1967, Virgil Thomson Collection, Irving S. Gilmore Music Library, Yale University.
7. PB to Ned Rorem, July 11, 1967, *Dear Paul, Dear Ned: The Correspondence of Paul Bowles and Ned Rorem* (North Pomfret, Vt.: Elysium Press, 1997), p. 44.
8. PB to Libby Holman, July 30, 1967, Libby Holman Collection, Boston University Library.
9. Peter Owen to VSC, London, December 5, 1991.
10. PB to VSC, Tangier, September 6, 1997.
11. *Without Stopping*, pp. 363–64.
12. *In Touch*, p. 408.
13. PB to Ned Rorem, November 1, 1967, *Dear Paul, Dear Ned: The Correspondence of Paul Bowles and Ned Rorem*, pp. 50–51; also *In Touch*, p. 409.
14. PB to Oliver Evans, November 13, 1967, *Without Stopping*, p. 411.
15. PB to Frances Bishop, October 3, 1967, from the personal archives of Frances Bishop; also PB to VSC, Tangier, September 6, 1997.
16. PB to VSC, September 6, 1967.
17. John Hopkins, January 8, 1968, *The Tangier Diaries: 1962–1979* (Tiburon-Belvedere, Calif.: Cadmus Editions, 1998), pp. 94–95.
18. PB to Frances Bishop, January 29, 1968; from the personal archives of Frances Bishop.
19. Frances Bishop to VSC, New York, September 6, 1997.
20. PB to Claire Auer Fuhs, July 1968, Jane Bowles Collection, HRHRC.
21. PB to Oliver Evans, March 20, 1968, Paul Bowles Collection (#9917-A), Barrett

Library of American Literature, Special Collections, University of Virginia Library, Charlottesville.

22. PB to Oliver Evans, June 12, 1968, Paul Bowles Collection (#9917-A), Barrett Library of American Literature, Special Collections, University of Virginia Library, Charlottesville.
23. John Hopkins, July 27, 1968, *The Tangier Diaries: 1962–1973*, pp. 103–4.
24. Tamara Dragadze, "Remembering the Good" (unpublished manuscript); also interview, Tamara Dragadze to VSC, London, December 12, 1992.
25. PB to VSC, Atlanta, May 29, 2003.
26. Tennessee Williams to PB, undated letter, Paul Bowles Collection, HRHRC.
27. PB to VSC, Atlanta, May 29, 2003.
28. David Herbert, *Second Son: An Autobiography* (London: Peter Owen, 1972), p. 127.
29. PB to Don Gold, February 23, 1969, *In Touch*, pp. 420–24.
30. PB to VSC, Tangier, May 15, 1998.
31. Ibid.
32. PB to Andreas Brown, May 13, 1968, Paul Bowles Collection, HRHRC.
33. PB to Carol Ardman, March 16, 1973; from the personal archives of Carol Ardman in New York, New York. Bowles and Kraft had not seen each other in several years, but each wrote occasionally. It was Kraft whom Bowles once identified as "Aaron's new pet."
34. PB to VSC, Atlanta, June 10, 1994.
35. PB to Frances Bishop, January 14, 1972, from the personal archives of Frances Bishop.
36. PB to William Targ, February 23, 1971, *In Touch*, p. 439.
37. Ibid., June 13, 1971, *In Touch*, pp. 439–40.
38. *New York Times*, March 21, 1972.
39. Virgil Thomson, "Untold Tales," *New York Review of Books*, May 18, 1972, p. 34.
40. Ned Rorem, "Come Back Paul Bowles," review of *Without Stopping*, *New Republic*, April 22, 1972; also Ned Rorem, *Pure Contraption: A Composer's Essays* (New York: Holt, Rinehart and Winston, 1974), pp. 36–37.
41. PB to Ned Rorem, July 8, 1973, *Dear Paul, Dear Ned*, p. 67; see also Ned Rorem, *Pure Contraption: A Composer's Essays*, pp. 36–37.
42. Marilyn Moss, "The Child in the Text: Autobiography, Fiction, and the Aesthetics of Deception in *Without Stopping*," *Twentieth Century Literature* 32, nos. 3–4 (Fall/Winter 1986), pp. 314–33.
43. Ibid.
44. PB to VSC, Tangier, May 15, 1998.

Chapter Fifteen

1. PB to Audrey Wood, May 11, 1973, *In Touch*, p. 451.
2. PB to VSC, Atlanta, May 30, 1994.
3. PB to Howard Griffin, August 29, 1973, *In Touch*, p. 454.

4. PB to Virgil Thomson, March 29, 1974, Virgil Thomson Collection, Irving S. Gilmore Music Library, Yale University.
5. Ibid., August 27, 1974.
6. Tennessee Williams, foreword, dated November 11, 1974, in Jane Bowles, *Feminine Wiles* (Santa Barbara, Calif.: Black Sparrow Press, 1976), pp. 7–8. *Feminine Wiles* also included a drawing of Jane by Marguerite McBey, dated 1963; Williams's foreword; four stories and sketches ("Andrew," "Emmy Moore's Journal," "Going to Massachusetts, "Curls and a Quiet Country Face"); *At the Jumping Bean* (a play); nine photographs; and six letters (two to Katharine Hamill and Natasha von Hoeschelmann, spring 1949 and 1954; two to "Dearest Bupple" (Bowles), January 17, 1950, and 1955; "Dear Paul," February 1957; and "Dearest Libby" (Holman), circa 1958; and an afterword, "About Jane Bowles" signed P.B. Each of these letters appeared later, with more precise dating, in *Out in the World: Selected Letters of Jane Bowles, 1935–1970*, ed. Millicent Dillon (Santa Barbara, Calif.: Black Sparrow Press, 1985).
7. PB to VSC, Tangier, April 20, 1990.
8. *A Little Original Sin*, pp. 1–2.
9. John Hopkins, *The Tangier Diaries, 1962–1979* (Tiburon-Belvedere, Calif.: Cadmus Editions, 1998), pp. 182–83.
10. Tennessee Williams to PB, June 24, 1973, Paul Bowles Archives, Manuscript Collection, Hugh M. Morris Library, University of Delaware, Newark.
11. PB to Daniel Halpern, May 9, 1973, *In Touch*, p. 449.
12. PB to Carol Ardman, May 11, 1973, *In Touch*, p. 450.
13. PB to Peter Owen, May 14, 1973, Paul Bowles Collection, HRHRC.
14. Millicent Dillon, *You Are Not I: A Portrait of Paul Bowles* (Berkeley: University of California Press, 1998), p. 18.
15. PB to VSC, Atlanta, May 31, 1994.
16. Paul Bowles, "Next to Nothing," in *Next to Nothing: Collected Poems, 1926–1977* (Santa Barbara: Black Sparrow Press, 1981), pp. 65, 70.
17. *Next to Nothing* (Kathmandu, Nepal: Starstreams Poetry Series, 1976), as quoted in Gena Dagel Caponi, *Paul Bowles: Romantic Savage* (Carbondale: University of Southern Illinois Press, 1994), pp. 212–13.
18. PB to VSC, Atlanta, October 1, 1994.
19. PB to Alec France, November 28, 1974, *In Touch*, pp. 461–62.
20. PB to Alec France, March 2, 1975, *In Touch*, pp. 465–67.
21. PB to VSC, Atlanta, May 31, 1994.
22. PB to John Martin, March 24, 1976, *In Touch*, p. 473. In addition to the two hundred numbered and signed copies (by both Mrabet and Bowles) of *Harmless Poisons, Blameless Sins*, are twenty-six lettered, hand-bound copies, also signed by Mrabet and Bowles, and each with an original drawing by Mrabet.
23. PB to Ned Rorem, June 12, 1976, *Dear Paul, Dear Ned: The Correspondence of Paul Bowles and Ned Rorem* (North Pomfret, Vt.: Elysium Press, 1997), p. 78.
24. PB to Frances Bishop, April 9, 1979, from the personal archives of Frances Bishop.
25. PB to Peter Garland, January 5, 1983, February 10, 1983, Paul Bowles Collection

(#9917-A), Barrett Library of American Literature, Special Collections, University of Virginia Library, Charlottesville.

26. PB to Frances Bishop, October 3, 1979, from the personal archives of Frances Bishop.
27. Cherie Nutting with Paul Bowles, *Yesterday's Perfume: An Intimate Memoir of Paul Bowles* (New York: Clarkson Potter/Random House, 2000), p. 84; also Nutting to VSC, December 30, 2001.
28. PB to Peter Garland, Sept. 10, 1977, Paul Bowles Collection (#9917-A), Barrett Library of American Literature, Special Collections, University of Virginia Library, Charlottesville.
29. PB to VSC, Atlanta, June 3, 1994.
30. Ibid.
31. PB to Peter Garland, August 24, 1981, Paul Bowles Collection (#9917-A), Barrett Library of American Literature, Special Collections, University of Virginia Library, Charlottesville.
32. PB to VSC, Atlanta, June 3, 1994.
33. PB to VSC, December 20, 1991; also PB to Carol Ardman, March 4, 1991.
34. *Paul Bowles: Selected Songs*, ed. Peter Garland (Santa Fe, N.M.: Soundings Press, 1984).
35. PB to John Martin, July 12, 1978, *In Touch*, pp. 482–83.
36. Joyce Carol Oates, "Bleak Craft: *Collected Stories of Paul Bowles, 1939–1976*," *New York Times*, September 30, 1979, pp. 9, 29.
37. PB to Ned Rorem, September 29, 1980, *Dear Paul, Dear Ned*, p. 105.
38. PB to Michael Lee, "A Conversation with Paul Bowles," *Trafika: An International Literary Review* (1994), pp. 125–41.
39. PB to VSC, Tangier, September 9, 1989.
40. PB to Millicent Dillon, September 2, 1984, Millicent Dillon Collection, HRHRC.
41. PB to Peter Garland, October 15, 1986, Paul Bowles Collection (#9917-A), Barrett Library of American Literature, Special Collections, University of Virginia Library, Charlottesville. According to Garland, 1,200 copies of Bowles's *Selected Songs* were published on April 20, 1984.
42. David Herbert, *Second Son: An Autobiography* (London: Peter Owen, 1972), p. 124.
43. PB to Alec France, June 3, 1976, *In Touch*, p. 474.
44. PB to Frances Bishop, Ocober 13, 1992, from the personal archives of Frances Bishop.
45. PB to VSC, Tangier, October 2, 1991.
46. Ibid., September 10, 1989.
47. Ibid., December 12, 1993.
48. PB to Frances Bishop, undated letter, from the personal archives of Frances Bishop.
49. PB to VSC, October 19, 1997.

Chapter Sixteen

1. The quotation is an excerpt from Bowles's foreword to *O My Land, My Friends: The Selected Letters of Hart Crane*, ed. Landon Hammer and Brom Weber (New York: Four Walls Eight Windows, 1997).
2. PB to VSC, August 13, 1997.
3. *Without Stopping*, p. 366.
4. A conversation between Paul Bowles and Phillip Ramey, Tangier, undated; Phillip Ramey to VSC, November 21, 1999.
5. Phillip Weiss, "Midnight at the Oasis," *New York Observer*, February 22, 1999, pp. 1, 19.
6. PB to VSC, Tangier, October 15, 1997.
7. Phillip Ramey to VSC, November 21, 1999.
8. PB to VSC, Tangier, October 19, 1997.
9. Phillip Ramey to VSC, November 21, 1999.
10. PB to VSC, Tangier, October 19, 1997.
11. PB to Philip Krone, Tangier, November 12, 1999.
12. Phillip Ramey to VSC, May 18, 2001; *Literary Trips: Following in the Footsteps of Fame*, ed. Victoria Brooks (Vancouver, B.C.: GreatestEscapes.com Publishing, 2000).
13. Vicki Vorreiter to VSC, March 2, 2001.
14. Joseph A. McPhillips III to VSC, November 19, 1999 (by telephone and fax), Tangier, February 13, 2000.
15. For a published version of the events of the day, see Robert Sullivan's "Bowles at Rest," *New Yorker* (December 11, 2000), pp. 43–44.
16. Paul Bowles, *Next to Nothing: Collected Poems, 1926–1977* (Santa Barbara: Black Sparrow Press, 1981), p. 73; also *Air to the Sea: Collected Poems of Paul Bowles, 1918–1977*, ed. Virginia Spencer Carr, with an introduction by Bowles, currently housed in the Special Collections Library of the University of Delaware, Newark.

INDEX

Page numbers beginning with 353 refer to notes.

ABOUT THE AUTHOR

Virginia Spencer Carr is the John B. and Elena Díaz-Versón Amos Distinguished Professor Emerita of English Letters at Georgia State University. Her books include *Understanding Carson McCullers*, *Dos Passos: A Life*, and *The Lonely Hunter: A Biography of Carson McCullers*.